Windows 8.1 Administration: Essentials & Configuration

Pocket Consultant

William R. Stanek
Author and Series Editor

PUBLISHED BY
Microsoft Press
A Division of Microsoft Corporation
One Microsoft Way
Redmond, Washington 98052-6399

Library of Congress Control Number: 2013949893
ISBN: 978-0-7356-8265-8

Printed and bound in the United States of America.

Second Printing: April 2014

Microsoft Press books are available through booksellers and distributors worldwide. If you need support related to this book, email Microsoft Press Book Support at mspinput@ microsoft.com. Please tell us what you think of this book at http://www.microsoft.com/ learning/booksurvey.

Acquisitions Editor: Anne Hamilton
Developmental Editor: Karen Szall
Editorial Production: Online Training Solutions, Inc. (OTSI)
Technical Reviewer: Randall Galloway; Technical Review services provided by Content Master, a member of CM Group, Ltd.
Copyeditor: Denise Bankaitis (OTSI)
Indexer: Krista Wall (OTSI)
Cover: Best & Company Design

Contents

What do you think of this book? We want to hear from you!

Microsoft is interested in hearing your feedback so we can continually improve our books and learning resources for you. To participate in a brief online survey, please visit:

microsoft.com/learning/booksurvey

What do you think of this book? We want to hear from you!

Microsoft is interested in hearing your feedback so we can continually improve our
books and learning resources for you. To participate in a brief online survey, please visit:

microsoft.com/learning/booksurvey

Acknowledgments

To my readers—thank you for being there with me through many books and many years. It has been an honor and a privilege to be your pocket consultant.

To my wife—for many years, through many books, many millions of words, and many thousands of pages she's been there, providing support and encouragement and making every place we've lived a home.

To my kids—for helping me see the world in new ways, for having exceptional patience and boundless love, and for making every day an adventure.

To Anne, Karen, Martin, Lucinda, Juliana, and many others who've helped out in ways both large and small.

Special thanks to my son Will for not only installing and managing my extensive dev lab for all my books since *Windows 8 Pocket Consultant* but also for performing check reads of all those books as well.

—William R. Stanek

Acknowledgements

Introduction

Writing *Windows 8.1 Administration Pocket Consultant: Essentials & Configuration* was a lot of fun—and a lot of work. As I set out to write this book, my initial goals were to determine how Windows 8.1 was different from its predecessors and what new features and options were available. As with any new operating system, I had to do a great deal of research and a lot of digging into the internals of the operating system to determine exactly how things work.

Anyone transitioning to Windows 8.1 from Windows 8 might be surprised at just how much has been updated, because changes both subtle and substantial have been made throughout the operating system. For anyone transitioning from Windows 7 or earlier, the extensive UI changes will be among the most substantial revisions to the operating system. Like Windows 8, Windows 8.1 supports a touch-based UI, as well as the traditional mouse and keyboard. When you are working with touch UI-enabled computers, you can manipulate on-screen elements in ways that weren't possible previously. You can do any of the following:

- **Tap** Tap an item by touching it with your finger. A tap or double-tap of elements on the screen is generally the equivalent of a mouse click or double-click.

- **Press and hold** Press your finger down and leave it there for a few seconds. Pressing and holding elements on the screen is generally the equivalent of a right-click.

- **Swipe to select** Slide an item a short distance in the opposite direction compared to how the page scrolls. This selects the items and also might bring up related commands. If press and hold doesn't display commands and options for an item, try using swipe to select instead.

- **Swipe from edge (slide in from edge)** Starting from the edge of the screen, swipe or slide in. Sliding in from the right edge opens the Charms panel. Sliding in from the left edge shows open apps and allows you to switch between them easily. Sliding in from the top or bottom edge shows commands for the active element.

- **Pinch** Touch an item with two or more fingers, and then move the fingers toward each other. Pinching zooms in or shows less information.

- **Stretch** Touch an item with two or more fingers, and then move the fingers away from each other. Stretching zooms out or shows more information.

You also are able to enter text by using the on-screen keyboard. Although the UI changes are substantial, they aren't the most significant changes to the operating system. The most significant changes are below the surface, affecting the underlying architecture and providing many new features. Some of these features are revolutionary in that they forever change the way we use Windows.

Because Pocket Consultants are meant to be portable and readable—the kind of book you use to solve problems and get the job done wherever you might be —I had to carefully review my research to make sure that I focused on the core essentials and configuration of Windows 8.1. The result is the book you hold in your hands, which I hope you'll agree is one of the best practical, portable guides available.

Because my focus is on giving you maximum value in a pocket-size guide, you don't have to wade through hundreds of pages of extraneous information to find what you're looking for. Instead, you'll find exactly what you need to address a specific issue or perform a particular task. In short, the book is designed to be the one resource that you turn to whenever you have questions regarding Windows 8.1 essentials and configuration. It zeroes in on daily procedures, frequently used tasks, documented examples, and options that are representative, although not necessarily inclusive.

One of the goals for this book is to keep its content concise so that it remains compact and easy to navigate, while at the same time packing it with as much information as possible to make it a valuable resource. Instead of a hefty 1,000-page tome or a lightweight, 100-page quick reference, you get a valuable resource guide that can help you quickly and easily perform common tasks, solve problems, and implement everyday solutions.

Who is this book for?

The focus of *Windows 8.1 Administration Pocket Consultant: Essentials & Configuration* is on the Standard, Professional, and Enterprise editions of Windows 8.1. The book is designed for the following readers:

- Accomplished users who want to configure and maintain Windows 8.1
- Current Windows system administrators and support staff
- Administrators upgrading to Windows 8.1 from earlier releases of Windows
- Administrators transferring from other platforms

To pack in as much information as possible, I had to assume that you have basic networking skills and a basic understanding of Windows operating systems. As a result, I don't devote entire chapters to understanding Windows basics, Windows architecture, or Windows networks. I do, however, cover desktop customization, system optimization, automation, maintenance, and much more. The book also goes into depth on troubleshooting, and I've tried to ensure that each chapter, where appropriate, has troubleshooting guidelines and discussions to accompany the main text. From the start, troubleshooting advice is integrated into the book, instead of being captured in a single, catchall troubleshooting chapter inserted as an afterthought. I hope that after you read these chapters and dig into the details, you'll be able to improve the overall experience of your users and reduce downtime.

How is this book organized?

Rome wasn't built in a day, nor was this book intended to be read in a day, or in a week, or even in a month for that matter. Ideally, you'll read this book at your own pace, a little each day as you work your way through each of the ten chapters. The chapters are arranged in a logical order, taking you from deployment and installation to configuration, optimization, and maintenance.

Ease of reference is an essential part of this hands-on guide. This book has an expanded table of contents and an extensive index for finding answers to problems quickly. Many other quick-reference features have been added to the book as well, including quick step-by-step procedures, lists, tables with fast facts, and extensive cross references.

As with all Pocket Consultants, *Windows 8.1 Administration Pocket Consultant: Essentials & Configuration* is designed to be a concise and easy-to-use resource. This is the readable resource guide that you'll want on your desktop at all times. The book covers everything you need to perform the essential tasks for deployment, installation, configuration, optimization, maintenance, and much more.

Although designed and written to stand on its own, this book can also be used with *Windows 8.1 Administration Pocket Consultant: Storage, Networking, & Security.* The latter book focuses on boot configuration and startup, drive configuration and encryption, advanced storage, file sharing and security, TCP/IP networking and remote accesses, advanced networking solutions, and much more.

Conventions used in this book

I've used a variety of elements to help keep the text clear and easy to follow. You'll find code listings in monospace type, except when I tell you to actually enter a command. In that case, the command appears in **bold** type, as does any text that the user is supposed to enter. When I introduce and define a new term, I put it in *italics*.

Other conventions include the following:

- **Best Practices**   To examine the best technique to use when working with advanced configuration and maintenance concepts
- **Caution**   To warn you about potential problems
- **Important**   To highlight important concepts and issues
- **More Info**   To provide more information on a subject
- **Note**   To provide additional details on a particular point that needs emphasis
- **Real World**   To provide real-world advice when discussing advanced topics
- **Security Alert**   To point out important security issues
- **Tip**   To offer helpful hints or additional information

I truly hope you find that *Windows 8.1 Administration Pocket Consultant: Essentials & Configuration* provides everything that you need to perform essential tasks on Windows 8.1 systems as quickly and efficiently as possible. You are welcome to send your thoughts to me at williamstanek@aol.com. Follow me on Twitter at WilliamStanek and on Facebook at *www.facebook.com/William.Stanek.Author*. Thank you.

Other resources

No single magic bullet for learning everything you'll ever need to know about Windows 8.1 exists. Although some books are offered as all-in-one guides, there's simply no way one book can do it all. With this in mind, I hope you use this book as it is intended to be used—as a concise and easy-to-use resource. It covers everything you need to perform essential tasks, but it is by no means exhaustive.

Your current knowledge will largely determine your success with this or any other Windows resource or book. As you encounter new topics, take the time to practice what you've learned. Seek out further information as necessary to get the practical hands-on know-how and knowledge you need.

For topics this book doesn't cover, you may want to look to *Windows 8.1 Administration Pocket Consultant: Storage, Networking, & Security*. I also recommend that you regularly visit the Microsoft website for Windows (*microsoft.com/windows/*) and *support.microsoft.com* to stay current with the latest changes. To help you get the most out of this book, you can visit my corresponding website at *pocket-consultant.com*. This site contains information about Windows 8.1 and updates to the book.

Errata and book support

Every effort has been made to ensure the accuracy of this book and its companion content. Any errors that have been reported since this book was published are listed at:

http://aka.ms/W81PCv1/errata

If you find an error that is not already listed, you can report it to us through the same page.

If you need additional support, email Microsoft Press Book Support at *mspinput@microsoft.com*.

Please note that product support for Microsoft software is not offered through the addresses above.

We want to hear from you

At Microsoft Press, your satisfaction is our top priority, and your feedback is our most valuable asset. Please tell us what you think of this book at:

http://www.microsoft.com/learning/booksurvey

The survey is short, and we read every one of your comments and ideas. Thanks in advance for your input!

Stay in touch

Let's keep the conversation going! We're on Twitter: *http://twitter.com/MicrosoftPress*.

Introduction to Windows 8.1 administration

W indows 8.1 is designed primarily as an operating system for client devices. This chapter covers getting started with Windows 8.1 and the fundamental tasks you need for Windows 8.1 administration. Throughout this and the other chapters in this book, you'll find detailed discussions of changes that enhance all aspects of computer management and security. Although this book focuses on Windows 8.1 administration, the tips and techniques discussed throughout the text can help anyone who develops for, works with, or supports Windows 8.1.

This book zeroes in on user and system administration tasks. You'll find detailed coverage of the following topics:

- Customizing the operating system
- Optimizing the Windows environment
- Configuring hardware devices
- Installing and maintaining programs
- Managing user access and global settings
- Troubleshooting system problems

Also, it is important to note that just about every configuration option in the Windows operating system can be controlled through Group Policy. Rather than add caveats to every discussion that feature A or B can be configured only if allowed in Group Policy, I'm going to assume that you understand the global impact of Group Policy on system configuration and management. I'm also going to assume that you are familiar with the command line and Windows PowerShell. This will allow me to focus on essential tasks for administration.

Getting started with Windows 8.1: the quick tour

Windows 8.1 is the latest release of the Windows operating system for client computers. Windows 8.1 natively supports image-based installation and deployment. Windows 8.1, Windows 8.1 Pro, and Windows 8.1 Enterprise support 32-bit x86 and 64-bit x64 processors for PCs and tablets. Windows 8.1 RT supports ARM processors. For many advanced features, including BitLocker, Encrypting File System, Domain Join, Group Policy, and the Remote Desktop host, computers will need Windows 8.1 Pro or Windows 8.1 Enterprise.

Windows 8.1 has many enhancements to improve security, including memory randomization and other improvements to prevent malware from inserting itself into startup and running processes. Windows 8.1 uses address space layout randomization (ASLR) to randomly determine how and where important data is stored in memory, which makes it much more difficult for malware to find the specific locations in memory to attack.

Windows 8.1 has enhanced support for devices that use Trusted Platform Module (TPM). Although always-on devices require TPM 2.0, all other devices require at least TPM 1.2. Firmware can use TPM to store hashes, which verify that important operating system files haven't been changed, and keys, which verify that digital signatures are valid.

Windows 8.1 requires a processor that includes hardware-based Data Execution Prevention (DEP) support. DEP uses the Never eXecute (NX) bit to mark blocks of memory as data that should never be run as code. DEP has two specific benefits. It reduces the range of memory that malicious code can use and prevents malware from running any code in memory addresses marked as Never eXecute.

If your organization doesn't use an enterprise malware solution, you'll also be interested to know that Windows Defender for Windows 8.1 has been upgraded to a more fully featured program. Windows Defender now protects against viruses, spyware, rootkit, and other types of malware. Rootkit detection helps to safeguard PCs and tablets from malware that inserts itself into non-Microsoft drivers. If Windows Defender detects that a non-Microsoft driver has been infected, it prevents the driver from starting. It's important to point out that other features, such as Secure Boot, Trusted Boot, and Measured Boot, protect Microsoft drivers and other critical operating system files.

> **REAL WORLD** Firmware runs internal integrity checks to verify the firmware's digital signature as part of initialization. With Secure Boot, firmware also verifies the digital signature on the Windows bootloader as part of initialization. If a rootkit is installed and the firmware or the Windows bootloader has been modified, the computer will be prevented from starting. After the Secure Boot, the bootloader verifies the digital signature of the operating system kernel as part of Trusted Boot. Also as part of Trusted Boot, the kernel in turn verifies all remaining boot components, including boot drivers and startup files. Finally, Measured Boot allows third-party software running on a remove server to verify the security of every startup component as well.

Separate distribution media is provided for 32-bit and 64-bit editions of Windows 8.1. To install the 32-bit edition of Windows 8.1 on an x86-based computer, you need to use the 32-bit distribution media. To install the 64-bit edition of Windows 8.1 on an x64-based computer, you need to use the 64-bit distribution media. Generally, if you are running a 32-bit operating system and want to install a 64-bit operating system (on hardware that supports both), you need to restart the computer and boot from the installation media. The same is generally true if you want to install a 32-bit operating system on a computer running a 64-bit operating system.

NOTE Windows 8.1 RT normally is preinstalled on devices with ARM processors, and it is very different from other editions of Windows 8.1.

Windows 8.1 uses modularization for language independence and disk imaging for hardware independence. Each component of the operating system is designed as an independent module that you can easily add or remove. This functionality provides the basis for the configuration architecture in Windows 8.1. Microsoft distributes Windows 8.1 on media with disk images that use compression and single-instance storage to dramatically reduce the size of image files. The format for disk images is the Windows Imaging (WIM) format.

The Windows Preinstallation Environment (Windows PE) replaces MS-DOS as the preinstallation environment and provides a bootable startup environment for installation, deployment, recovery, and troubleshooting. The Windows Preboot Environment provides a startup environment with a boot manager that lets you choose which boot application to run to load the operating system. On systems with multiple operating systems, you access operating systems prior to Windows 7 in the boot environment by using the legacy operating system entry.

User Account Control (UAC) enhances computer security by ensuring true separation of standard user and administrator user accounts. Through UAC, all applications are run by using either standard user or administrator user privileges, and you get a security prompt by default whenever you run an application that requires administrator privileges. The way the security prompt works depends on Group Policy settings. Additionally, if you log on by using the built-in Administrator account, you typically do not get elevation prompts.

Windows 8.1 has several key UI elements, including the following:

- Start screen
- Charm bar
- Search panel
- Settings panel
- PC Settings screen
- Apps screen (also referred to as All Apps)

The Start screen replaces the traditional Start menu. Start is a window, not a menu. Programs can have tiles on the Start window. Tapping or clicking a tile runs the program. When you press and hold or right-click a tile, an options panel rather than a shortcut menu normally is displayed.

From Start, one way to quickly open a program is by simply typing the file name of the program and then pressing Enter. This shortcut works as long as the Everywhere Search box is in focus (which it typically is by default).

Pressing the Windows key switches between the Start screen and the desktop or the current app you are working with (or, if you are working with PC Settings, between Start and PC Settings). On the Start screen, there's a Desktop tile that you can tap or click to display the desktop. You also can display the desktop by pressing Windows key + D or, to peek at the desktop, press and hold Windows key + , (that's the Windows key plus the comma key).

The Charm bar is an options panel for Start, Desktop, and PC Settings. With touch UI, you can display the Charm bar by sliding in from the right side of the screen. With a mouse and keyboard, you can display the Charm bar by moving the pointer over the hidden button in the upper-right or lower-right corner of the Start, Desktop, or PC Settings screen; or by pressing Windows key + C.

The Charm bar has the following five charms:

- **Search** Tap or click the Search charm to display the Search panel. Any text typed while on the Start screen is entered into the Search box on the Search panel. Areas the Search box can be focused on include Everywhere, Settings, or Files. When it is focused on Everywhere, you can use Search to quickly find installed programs, files, settings, and more. When it is focused on Settings, you can use Search to quickly find settings and options in Control Panel. When it is focused on Files, you can use Search to quickly find files.

- **Share** Tap or click the Share charm to share from a desktop app. For example, when working with the Maps app, you'll typically get options for sharing the map with which you are working.

- **Start** Tap or click the Start charm to switch between Desktop and Start (or, if you are working with PC Settings, between Start and PC Settings).

- **Devices** Tap or click the Devices charm to work quickly with attached devices, such as a second screen.

- **Settings** Tap or click the Settings charm to access the Settings panel, which provides access to important options, including the power options for sleep, shutdown, and restart.

TIP Normally, Everywhere Search is the default. Thus, from Start, you can quickly open a program by typing the program name and pressing Enter.

You also can display the Settings panel by pressing Windows key + I. From the settings panels, you can:

- View connected networks and network status.
- View and change audio output levels.
- Change brightness levels of the display (portable devices only).
- Hide notifications temporarily.

- Access power options.
- Display the touch keyboard (touch UI devices only).
- Access the PC Settings screen (by clicking Change PC Settings).

Start Settings, Desktop Settings, and PC Settings have nearly—but not exactly—identical Settings panels. The Start Settings panel has a Tiles option that you can tap or click to display an option for adding or removing tiles for the administrative tools to the Start screen and an option for clearing personal information from tiles. The Desktop Settings panel has several quick links, including:

- **Control Panel**   For opening Control Panel
- **Personalization**   For opening personalization settings in Control Panel
- **PC Info**   For opening the System page in Control Panel
- **Help**   For opening Windows Help and Support

Thus, when you are working with the desktop, one way to quickly open Control Panel is by pressing Windows key + I, and then clicking Control Panel on the Settings panel.

File Explorer is pinned to the desktop taskbar by default, which means you can also access Control Panel by following these steps:

1. Open File Explorer by tapping or clicking the taskbar icon.
2. Tap or click the leftmost option button in the address list.
3. Tap or click Control Panel.

Another technique you'll want to quickly master is getting to the Apps screen, which lists installed apps alphabetically within app categories. Apps are listed first in the results whenever you perform an Everywhere search. On the Start screen, you'll find a button with an arrow pointing down; tapping or clicking this button displays the Apps screen. On the Apps screen, you'll find lists of all installed programs, organized by category. Apps listed in the Windows System category are ones you'll often use for administration, including Command Prompt, Control Panel, Task Manager, File Explorer, This PC, and Windows PowerShell. Administrative tools are only displayed on the Apps screen if you previously selected the Tiles option on the Start Settings panel and then selected Show Administrative Tools.

NOTE   With Windows 8.1 Pro and Windows 8.1 Enterprise, Windows PowerShell is normally added as a feature. From Start, a quick way to open Windows PowerShell is to type **powershell,** and then press Enter. This shortcut works as long as Windows PowerShell is the first match found for the keyword "powershell." If multiple matches are found, tap or click the one that you want to run rather than pressing Enter.

TIP   If you've opened the Apps screen on your computer, you might want to add pinned items to Start or to the desktop taskbar. To do this, press and hold or right-click the item, and then tap or click Pin To Start or Pin To Taskbar as appropriate. For easier administration, I recommend adding Command Prompt and Windows PowerShell to the taskbar.

With Windows 8.1, you might want to use Windows PowerShell as your go-to prompt for entering both standard Windows commands and Windows PowerShell commands. Although anything you can enter at a command prompt can be entered at the Windows PowerShell prompt, it's important to remember that this is possible because Windows PowerShell looks for external commands and utilities as part of its normal processing. As long as the external command or utility is found in a directory specified by the PATH environment variable, the command or utility is run as appropriate. However, keep in mind that Windows PowerShell execution order could affect whether a command runs as expected. For Windows PowerShell, the execution order is (1) alternate built-in or profile-defined aliases; (2) built-in or profile-defined functions; (3) cmdlets or language keywords; (4) scripts with the .ps1 extension; and (5) external commands, utilities, and files. Thus, if any element in 1 to 4 of the execution order has the same name as a command, that element will run instead of the expected command.

Windows 8.1 ships with Windows PowerShell. When you've configured Windows PowerShell for remote access, you can execute commands on remote computers in a variety of ways. One technique is to establish a remote session with the computers with which you want to work. The following example and partial output shows how you can check the Windows edition on remote computers:

```
$s = new-pssession -computername engpc15, hrpc32, cserpc28 invoke-command
-session $s {dism.exe /online /get-currentedition}
```

The following is the resulting partial output:

```
Deployment Image Servicing and Management tool Version: 6.1.7600.16385

Image Version: 6.1.7600.16385

Current Edition : Ultimate
The operation completed successfully.
```

The internal version number for Windows 7 is 6.1, whereas the internal versions for Windows 8 and Windows 8.1 are 6.2 and 6.3 respectively. Thus, based on this output, you know the computer is running Windows 7 Ultimate edition (and hasn't been upgraded to Windows 8.1 yet).

NOTE With the New-PSSession command, you use the −ComputerName parameter to specify the remote computers to work with by Domain Name System (DNS) name, NetBIOS name, or IP address. When working with multiple remote computers, separate each computer name or IP address with a comma.

Understanding 32-bit and 64-bit computing options

Since it was introduced for Windows operating systems, 64-bit computing has changed substantially. Not only do computers running 64-bit versions of Windows perform better and run faster than their 32-bit counterparts, they are also more scalable because they can process more data per clock cycle, address more memory, and perform numeric calculations faster.

Windows 8.1 PCs and tablets support x64 architecture. This architecture is based on 64-bit extensions to the x86 instruction set, which is implemented in AMD Opteron (AMD64) processors, Intel Xeon processors with 64-bit extension technology, and other processors. This architecture offers native 32-bit processing and 64-bit extension processing, allowing simultaneous 32-bit and 64-bit computing.

In general, 64-bit computing is designed for performing operations that are memory intensive and that require extensive numeric calculations. With 64-bit processing, applications can load large data sets entirely into physical memory (that is, RAM), which reduces the need to page to disk and increases performance substantially.

Currently, the prevalent firmware interfaces are:

- Basic input/output system (BIOS).
- Extensible Firmware Interface (EFI).
- Unified Extensible Firmware Interface (UEFI).

Computers based on x86 use BIOS and the master boot record (MBR) disk type for boot and system volumes. Computers based on x64 use UEFI wrapped around BIOS or EFI. UEFI and EFI support the GUID partition table (GPT) disk type for boot and system volumes. This means that there can be differences in the way you manage computers with these architectures, particularly when it comes to setup and disk configuration. However, with the increasing acceptance and use of UEFI and the ability of Windows 8.1 to use both MBR and GPT disks regardless of firmware type, the underlying chip architecture won't necessarily determine what firmware type and disk type a computer uses. This decision is in the hands of the hardware manufacturer.

NOTE Generally, BIOS-based computers use MBR for booting or for data disks and GPT only for data disks. EFI-based computers can have both GPT and MBR disks, but you must have at least one GPT disk that contains the EFI system partition (ESP) and a primary partition or simple volume that contains the operating system for booting.

In most cases, 64-bit hardware is compatible with 32-bit applications; however, 32-bit applications perform better on 32-bit hardware. Windows 64-bit editions support both 64-bit and 32-bit applications by using the Windows on Windows 64 (WOW64) x86 emulation layer. The WOW64 subsystem isolates 32-bit applications from 64-bit applications. This prevents file system and registry problems. The operating system provides interoperability across the 32-bit/64-bit boundary for the Component Object Model (COM) and for basic operations such as cutting, copying, and pasting using the Clipboard. However, 32-bit processes cannot load 64-bit dynamic-link libraries (DLLs), and 64-bit processes cannot load 32-bit DLLs.

In the shift to 64-bit computing, you might want to track which computers in the enterprise support 64-bit operating systems, which computers are already running 64-bit operating systems, or both.

With Windows PowerShell, you can:

- Determine whether a computer has a 64-bit operating system installed by using the OSArchitecture property of the Win32_OperatingSystem object. An example is

```
get-wmiobject -class win32_operatingsystem | fl osarchitecture
```

And the resulting output is

```
osarchitecture : 32-bit
```

- Determine whether a computer supports a 64-bit operating system by using the Name and Description properties of the Win32_Processor object:

```
get-wmiobject -class win32_processor | fl name, description
```

```
name        : Intel(R) Core(TM)2 Quad CPU        @ 2.66GHz
description : x64 Family 6 Model 15 Stepping 7
```

Here, the first sample output tells you the computer is running a 32-bit version of Windows. The second sample output tells you the computer has an x64 processor. As a result, you know the computer can be upgraded to a 64-bit version of Windows 8.1. Rather than check each computer individually, you could create a script to do the work for you.

Although Windows 8.1 continues to support 16-bit applications, it's important to point out that Windows 8.1 might restrict access to the 16-bit MS-DOS subsystem (ntvdm.exe). If so, the MS-DOS subsystem is prevented from running, and this in turn prevents 16-bit applications from running.

In Group Policy for Active Directory Domain Services or local policy for the computer, the Prevent Access To 16-bit Applications setting under Computer Configuration\Windows Components\Application Compatibility controls whether 16-bit applications can run. As with previous versions of Windows, when this setting is enabled, Windows 8.1 blocks access to 16-bit applications and prevents them from running.

In an important change, if the setting is not configured in policy, Windows 8.1 runs the 16-bit application control panel, which might require elevated administrator privileges to run the 16-bit application. Therefore, if you want to allow 16-bit applications to run without requiring elevated administrator privileges, you must set Prevent Access To 16-bit Applications to Disabled.

Deploying Windows 8.1

With Windows 8.1, you can deploy custom builds to computers through manual and automated processes. To deploy Windows by using manual processes, you need to create the required boot and installation images and optionally create recovery images. To automate the deployment process, you need to install Windows Deployment Services. Whether you use a completely manual process, a completely automated process, or some combination of the two, you'll perform similar administrative tasks. These tasks require you to understand and use the Windows Assessment and Deployment Kit (Windows ADK) for Windows 8.1 and Windows Deployment Services.

The Windows Assessment and Deployment Kit for Windows 8.1 is available from the Microsoft Download Center (*download.microsoft.com*) and contains the tools for deploying Windows images, including the following:

- Application Compatibility Toolkit (ACT)
- The standard deployment and imaging tools
- User State Migration Tool (USMT)
- Volume Activation Management Tool (VAMT)
- Windows Assessment Services
- Windows Assessment Toolkit
- Windows Performance Toolkit (WPT)
- Windows Preinstallation Environment (Windows PE)

You can use Windows Deployment Services to deploy Windows 8.1 over a network. You can add the Windows Deployment Services role to any server running Windows Server 2012 RTM or R2.

Windows 8.1 and Windows Server 2012 RTM or R2 use Windows PE. Windows PE is a bootable startup environment that provides operating system features for the following:

- **Installation**   When you install Windows 8.1, the graphical tools that collect system information during the setup phase are running within Windows PE.

- **Deployment**   When a new computer performs a network boot, the built-in Preboot Execution Environment (PXE) client can connect to a Windows Deployment Services server, download a Windows PE image across the network, and then run deployment scripts within this environment.

- **Recovery**   Windows PE enables you to access and run the Startup Repair tool if Windows 8.1 fails to start because of a corrupted system file.

- **Troubleshooting**   You can manually start Windows PE to perform trouble-shooting or diagnostics testing if Windows 8.1 is experiencing problems that can't otherwise be diagnosed.

Windows PE is modular and extensible, and it provides full access to partitions formatted by using the FAT or NTFS file system. Because Windows PE is built from a subset of Windows components, you can run many Windows applications, work with hardware devices, and communicate across IP networks. Several command-line tools are available in Windows PE, including:

- **BCDBoot**   A tool that initializes the boot configuration data (BCD) store and allows you to copy boot environment files to the system partition.

- **Bootsect**   A tool for creating and working with boot sectors on hard disks and flash drives.

- **Copype**   A tool for creating a directory structure for Windows PE files and then copying the Windows PE media files. Running this tool is a prerequisite for creating bootable Windows PE media.

- **DiskPart**   A tool for creating and working with disks, partitions, and volumes.
- **DISM**   An advanced tool for servicing and maintaining images.
- **Drvload**   A support tool for adding device drivers and dynamically loading a driver after Windows PE has started.
- **ImageX**   A tool for capturing and applying Windows images.
- **Lpksetup**   A tool for adding and removing a language pack.
- **Makewinpemedia**   A tool for creating bootable Windows PE media.
- **Net**   A set of support commands that enables you to manage local users, start and stop services, and connect to shared folders.
- **Netcfg**   A tool that configures network access.
- **Oscdimg**   A tool for creating CD and DVD ISO image files.
- **Wpeinit**   A tool that initializes Windows PE every time it boots.

Copype and Makewinpemedia are new tools that allow you to more easily create bootable Windows PE media. You use Copype to set up the Windows PE build environment. After you optimize the build as necessary, you can use Makewinpemedia to create the bootable media, which can be a CD, DVD, USB flash drive, or external USB hard drive.

Using DISM

Deployment Image Servicing and Management (DISM) is one of the most important deployment tools. DISM is included with Windows 8.1 Pro and Windows 8.1 Enterprise.

By using DISM, you can manage online and offline images of the Windows operating system, including images for deployment and those for virtual machines. Windows Image (.wim) files are used to deploy Windows 8.1. Virtual hard disk (.vhd) files are used with virtual machines. The same commands work on WIM and VHD files.

You can use DISM to:

- Add and remove packages. Packages can include language packs, updates, and utilities.
- Enable and disable Windows features.
- Add and remove third-party device drivers.

You can run DISM at an elevated administrator command prompt by following these steps:

1. On the Apps screen, Command Prompt is listed in the Windows System category. Or, if you are working with Start, enter **cmd**.

2. Press and hold or right-click the Command Prompt shortcut on the Apps screen, and then tap or click Run As Administrator.

3. If the User Account Control prompt appears, proceed as you normally would to allow the application to run with administrator privileges.

4. In the Command Prompt window, enter **dism /?** to view available options for DISM.

5. To view commands available for working with online images, enter **dism /online /?**.

Although DISM is designed to work primarily with offline images and images you've mounted, you can use some DISM commands to get important information about the live operating system running on a computer. Table 1-1 provides an overview of DISM Online subcommands you can use with live operating systems. For example, if you want to display a list of Windows editions to which a computer can be upgraded, you can enter the following command.

```
dism /online /get-targeteditions
```

TABLE 1-1 DISM Online commands for live operating systems

SUBCOMMAND	DESCRIPTION
/Disable-Feature /featurename:FeatureName	Disables a specified feature. Feature names are case sensitive.
/Enable-Feature /featurename:FeatureName	Enables a specified feature. Feature names are case sensitive.
/Get-CurrentEdition	Displays the currently installed edition of Windows.
/Get-DriverInfo /driver:DriverName.inf	Displays information about a specified third-party driver that is installed in the driver store. Driver names are not case sensitive.
/Get-Drivers	Displays information about all third-party drivers that are installed in the driver store.
/Get-FeatureInfo /featurename:FeatureName	Displays information about a specified feature. Feature names are case sensitive.
/Get-Features	Displays the name and state of all features that are available in the online image.
/Get-Intl	Displays information about the default system user interface language, system locale, default time zone, keyboard language, and installed languages.
/Get-PackageInfo /packagename:PackageName	Displays information about a specified package. Package names are case sensitive.
/Get-Packages	Displays information about Windows packages that are installed.
/Get-TargetEditions2	Lists the Windows editions to which the operating system can be upgraded.

DISM Online also is handy when you want to list all available features by their name and status, such as might be needed for PC inventory or to add or remove features. To list available features, enter the following command at an elevated prompt.

```
dism /online /get-features
```

To add a feature, use the /Enable-Feature parameter and then set the name of the feature to enable with the /FeatureName parameter. If a feature has related subfeatures, add the /All parameter to enable all the subfeatures. This example enables Hyper-V and all related features.

```
dism /online /enable-feature /featurename:Microsoft-hyper-v /all
```

Understanding Windows imaging

When you update Windows 8.1 by adding or removing features, applying hotfixes, or installing service packs, you are simply modifying the set of modules available. And because these modules are independent, you can make these changes without affecting the system as a whole. Because language packs are separate modules as well, you can easily implement different language configurations without needing separate installations for each language.

Microsoft distributes Windows 8.1 on media with WIM disk images. Because WIM is hardware independent, Microsoft can ship one binary file for 32-bit architectures and one binary file for 64-bit architectures. A separate binary file is available for Windows 8.1 RT.

Windows 8.1 can be installed through either automated or interactive setup. You can automate the installation of Windows 8.1 in several ways, including the following:

- **Create an unattended installation answer file.** Windows 8.1 uses a standards-based, single-format answer file. This file, called Unattend.xml, is written in XML, making it easier to process by using standard tools. By creating a custom answer file and then running Setup using this answer file, you can perform unattended installations of Windows 8.1. The Setup program can then install the operating system from a distribution share or from media.

- **Use Sysprep image-based installation.** This approach requires running the System Preparation command-line tool (Sysprep.exe) on a computer that you want to use as the master deployment computer, and then creating a disk image of this computer's configuration. Sysprep is stored in the %SystemRoot%\System32\Sysprep folder. The Windows Automated Installation Kit (Windows AIK) includes Windows System Image Manager and ImageX to help you use Sysprep for deployments. You use Windows System Image Manager to create answer files for unattended installations. You use ImageX to create and manage disk images.

By using WIM as its disk-imaging format and taking advantage of the modular design of Windows 8.1, ImageX significantly reduces the number of disk images that must be maintained. You don't need to maintain multiple hardware-dependent disk images or multiple language-dependent disk images. Instead, you typically need only a single disk image for each chip architecture used in your organization. You can then use different installation scripts to customize the operating system installation as necessary.

WIM has other advantages over earlier disk image formats as well. WIM enables you to modify and maintain disk images offline, which means you can add or remove optional components and drivers or perform updates without having to create a new disk image. To do this, you mount the disk image as a folder, and then use File Explorer or other tools to update, manage, or remove files as necessary.

Windows System Image Manager, ImageX, and Sysprep provide several different ways to automate deployment. Here are the basic steps:

1. Set up and configure Windows 8.1 on a computer not being used for normal operations, and then install and configure any necessary components and applications.

2. Run Sysprep to prepare the computer for capture. Sysprep removes unique identifiers from the computer and designates it as a master deployment computer. At the end of this process, the computer no longer has identifying information that allows it to be logged on to and used within a domain or workgroup.

3. Use the ImageX /Capture option to capture the disk image and store this image on media or in a distribution share. The image can be maintained offline by using the ImageX /Mountrw option to mount the image in read/write mode so that you can make any necessary changes. Use the ImageX /Unmount command to unmount the image when you are finished making changes.

   You also can mount images by using DISM /Mount-WIM and unmount images by using DISM /Unmount-WIM. DISM provides functionality for manipulating images. You can set product keys, perform upgrades, add or remove drivers, set language and locale information, add or remove packages and features, and clean up images.

4. Use Windows System Image Manager to create your unattended installation answer files. You can then create deployment scripts that configure the computer, run Setup by using the answer file, and apply the disk image you've previously created.

5. Run your deployment script to configure the computer and install the operating system.

Managing access and prestaging computers

You can manage images by using DISM. To prevent unauthorized users from installing images, you can:

- Prestage computers and allow only known computers to be deployed.
- Modify the security settings of image files so that only appropriate personnel can access them.
- Enable administrator approval for client installation.

Prestaging computers

Prestaging computers involves creating computer accounts in Active Directory Domain Services prior to their use. By prestaging a computer, you control exactly which clients and servers can communicate with each other. Before you prestage computers, you should be sure that Windows Deployment Services is configured to accept requests only from known computers by following these steps:

1. In the Windows Deployment Services console, expand the Servers node. Press and hold or right-click the server with which you want to work, and then select Properties.

2. On the PXE Response Settings tab, tap or click Respond Only To Known Client Computers, and then tap or click OK.

To prestage a computer, you need to know the computer's GUID. A computer's GUID comes from the active network adapter on the computer and must be entered in the format {*dddddddd-dddd-dddd-dddd-dddddddddddd*}, where *d* is a hexadecimal digit, such as {AEFED345-BC13-22CD-ABCD-11BB11342112}.

You can obtain the required identifier in several ways. In some cases, manufacturers print a label with the GUID and attach the label to the computer. However, don't forget that the GUID is valid only for the network adapter that shipped with the computer. If you replace the adapter, the new adapter will have a new GUID.

To obtain the GUID for the installed network adapter, you can check the computer's firmware. If a remote computer is started, you can enter the following command at a Windows PowerShell prompt.

```
get-wmiobject win32_networkadapter | format-list guid
```

Write down or copy the GUID associated with the network adapter connected to the LAN.

To prestage computers, follow these steps:

1. In Active Directory Users And Computers, press and hold or right-click the operating unit (OU) or container in which the computer will be staged, tap or click New, and then tap or click Computer.

2. Enter a name for the computer, and then tap or click Next. Alternatively, tap or click Change to choose the user or group with permission to join this computer to the domain, and then tap or click Next.

3. On the Managed page, choose This Is A Managed Computer, enter the computer's GUID, and then tap or click Next. The GUID can be found in the system firmware or it might be posted on the computer case.

4. On the Host Server page, choose the Windows Deployment Services server that will service this client. Tap or click Next, and then tap or click Finish.

Modifying image file security

To modify the security settings on an image file, open File Explorer. Press and hold or right-click the image file, and then click Properties. In the Properties dialog box, use the options on the Security tab to configure the security settings you want to use. Alternatively, you can configure security settings on the Image Group folder in which the image file is stored. These settings will then be inherited by the images in the Image Group folder.

Requiring administrator approval

Instead of prestaging computers or using image file security, you can require administrator approval before allowing computers to be installed from images. To require administrator approval rather than modify security settings on image files, you can do the following:

1. In the Windows Deployment Services console, expand the Servers node. Press and hold or right-click the server you want to work with, and then tap or click Properties.

2. On the PXE Response Settings tab, select Respond To All (Known And Unknown) Client Computers.

3. Select For Unknown Clients, Notify Administrator And Respond After Approval, and then tap or click OK.

Now computers that are started from the network will enter a pending state. Before the installation can proceed, an administrator can approve or reject the request.

To approve a request, complete the following steps:

1. In the Windows Deployment Services console, select the server with which you want to work. Next, tap or click the server's Pending Devices folder to select it and display a list of computers waiting for approval.

2. Press and hold or right-click the computer, and then tap or click Approve.

To reject a request, complete the following steps:

1. In the Windows Deployment Services console, select the server with which you want to work. Next, tap or click the server's Pending Devices folder to select it and display a list of computers waiting for approval.

2. Press and hold or right-click the computer, and then tap or click Reject.

Customizing Windows images

You can customize a mounted boot or install an image by using the DISM utility. Available options for DISM are summarized in Table 1-2. All components in an image are managed via the component store.

TABLE 1-2 Key options for the DISM utility

COMMAND TYPE/COMMAND	DESCRIPTION
GENERAL COMMANDS	
/Cleanup-Wim	Deletes resources associated with mounted Windows images that are corrupt
/Commit-Wim	Saves changes to a mounted Windows image
/Get-MountedWimInfo	Displays information about mounted Windows images
/Get-WimInfo	Displays information about images in a Windows image file
/Image	Specifies the path to the root directory of an offline Windows image
/Mount-Wim	Mounts an image from a Windows image file
/Online	Targets the running operating system
/Remount-Wim	Recovers an orphaned Windows mount directory
/Unmount-Wim	Unmounts a mounted Windows image
ADDITIONAL OPTIONS	
/English	Displays command-line output in English
/Format	Specifies the report output format
/LogLevel	Specifies the output level shown in the log (1–4)
/LogPath	Specifies the log file path
/NoRestart	Suppresses automatic reboots and reboot prompts
/Quiet	Suppresses all output except for error messages
/ScratchDir	Specifies the path to a scratch directory
/SysDriveDir	Specifies the path to the system loader file named BootMgr
/WinDir	Specifies the path to the Windows directory

After you mount an image, you are able to work with the mounted image by using the Dism /Image subcommands listed in Table 1-3. These subcommands allow you to upgrade the image to a higher edition (such as from Windows 8.1 Pro to

Windows 8.1 Enterprise), add and remove device drivers, specify time zones and language user interface options, display updates and installed message signaled interrupt (MSI) applications, add and remove packages, and more.

TABLE 1-3 Important subcommands for mounted and offline images

SUBCOMMANDS	DESCRIPTION
/Add-Driver	Adds driver packages to an offline image
/Add-Package	Adds packages to the image
/Apply-Unattend	Applies an AnswerFile.xml file to an image
/Check-AppPatch	Displays information if the multiple customization updates (MSP files) are applicable to the mounted image
/Cleanup-Image	Performs cleanup and recovery operations on the image
/Disable-Feature	Disables a specific feature in the image
/Enable-Feature	Enables a specific feature in the image
/Gen-LangIni	Generates a new Lang.ini file
/Get-AppInfo	Displays information about a specific installed MSI application
/Get-AppPatches	Displays information about all applied MSP updates for all installed applications
/Get-AppPatchInfo	Displays information about installed MSP updates
/Get-Apps	Displays information about all installed MSI applications
/Get-CurrentEdition	Displays the edition of the specified image
/Get-DriverInfo	Displays information about a specific driver in an offline image or a running operating system
/Get-Drivers	Displays information about all drivers in an offline image or a running operating system
/Get-FeatureInfo	Displays information about a specific feature
/Get-Features	Displays information about all features in a package
/Get-Intl	Displays information about the international settings and languages
/Get-PackageInfo	Displays information about a specific package
/Get-Packages	Displays information about all packages in the image
/Get-TargetEditions	Displays a list of Windows editions to which an image can be upgraded
/Remove-Driver	Removes driver packages from an offline image
/Remove-Package	Removes packages from the image

SUBCOMMANDS	DESCRIPTION
/Set-AllIntl	Sets all international settings in the mounted offline image
/Set-Edition	Upgrades the Windows image to a higher edition, such as from Windows 8.1 Pro to Windows 8.1 Enterprise
/Set-InputLocale	Sets the input locales and keyboard layouts to use in the mounted offline image
/Set-LayeredDriver	Sets the keyboard layered driver
/Set-ProductKey	Populates the product key into the offline image
/Set-SetupUILang	Defines the default language that will be used by Setup
/Set-SKUIntlDefaults	Sets all international settings to the default values for the specified SKU language in the mounted offline image
/Set-SysLocale	Sets the language for non-Unicode programs (also called system locale) and font settings in the mounted offline image
/Set-TimeZone	Sets the default time zone in the mounted offline image
/Set-UILang	Sets the default system UI language that is used in the mounted offline image
/Set-UILangFallback	Sets the fallback default language for the system UI in the mounted offline image
/Set-UserLocale	Sets the user locale in the mounted offline image

The DISM tool provides commands for working with WIM images. The syntax for mounting images is

```
dism /mount-wim /wimfile:Path /index:Index /mountdir:MountPath
```

where *Path* is the full path to the WIM image, *Index* is the index position of the image number of the image within the .wim file to apply, and *MountPath* is the directory location where you'd like to mount the image, such as

```
dism /mount-wim /wimfile:c:\winpe_x86\iso\sources\boot.wim /index:1 /
mountdir:C:\Win8
```

You can then modify the image as necessary. To commit your changes at any time, you can use Dism /Commit-Wim, as shown in the following example.

```
dism /commit-wim /mountdir:C:\Win8
```

Here, you commit changes to the WIM images mounted in the C:\Win8 directory.

To unmount a WIM file, you can use Dism /Unmount-Wim, as shown in the following example.

```
dism /unmount-wim /mountdir:C:\Win8
```

Here, you unmount the WIM image that was mounted and committed in the C:\Win8 directory. If there are uncommitted changes, you must commit or discard changes when you unmount a WIM image. Add /Commit to commit changes or /Discard to discard changes. This affects only the changes you haven't previously committed.

Installing Windows 8.1

Windows 8.1 Pro and Enterprise are the main editions intended for use in Active Directory domains. When you install Windows 8.1 on a computer with an existing operating system, you can perform a clean installation or an upgrade. The major differences between a clean installation and an upgrade are the following:

- **Clean installation** With a clean installation, the Windows Setup program completely replaces the original operating system on the computer, and all user and application settings are lost. You should use a clean installation when the operating system cannot be upgraded, the system must boot to multiple operating systems, a standardized configuration is required, or when no operating system is currently installed.

- **Upgrade installation** During an upgrade, user accounts, user files, and user settings are retained, existing applications and their settings are kept, and basic system configuration is not required. An upgrade installation should be used when you have computers running the Windows operating system that support upgrading to Windows 8.1 and you want to minimize disruption by maintaining the existing settings, user information, and application configurations.

The way an upgrade works depends on the operating system being upgraded. When you are upgrading from Windows 7, Windows Setup performs an in-place upgrade that ensures the upgrade works as described previously. With Windows Vista and Windows XP, an in-place upgrade works differently. With Windows Vista, you can retain user accounts, user files, and user settings, as well as basic system configuration, but Windows Setup will not retain applications and their settings. With Windows XP, you can retain user accounts, user files, and user settings, but Windows Setup will not retain applications and their settings or basic system configuration.

Preparing for Windows 8.1 installation

To install Windows 8.1, you can start from the Windows distribution media, run Setup from your current Windows operating system, perform a command-line installation, or use one of the automated installation options.

There are two basic approaches to setting up Windows 8.1—interactively or as an automated process. An interactive installation is what many people regard as the regular Windows installation—the kind in which you walk through the setup process and enter a lot of information. It can be performed from distribution media (by starting from the distribution media or running Windows Setup from a command line). The default Windows setup process when starting from the retail Windows 8.1

DVD is interactive, prompting you for configuration information throughout the process.

There are several types of automated setup, which actually have administrator-configurable amounts of user interaction. The most basic form of unattended setup you can perform is an unattended installation using only answer files. An answer file contains all or part of the configuration information usually prompted for during a standard installation process. You can create unattended answer files by using Windows System Image Manager, which is provided in the Windows Assessment and Deployment Kit (ADK). To take unattended setup a step further, you can use Windows Deployment Services.

The standard setup program for Windows 8.1 is Setup.exe. You can run Setup.exe from the currently running Windows operating system to perform an upgrade, or you can start from the distribution media to perform a new installation of Windows 8.1. When you are working with Windows 8.1 on x86-based systems, you should be aware of the special types of drive sections used by the operating system:

- **Active** The active partition or volume is the drive section for system cache and startup. Some removable media devices might be listed as having an active partition.

- **Boot** The boot partition or volume contains the operating system and its support files. The system and boot partition or volume can be the same.

- **System** The system partition or volume contains the hardware-specific files needed to load the operating system. As part of software configuration, the system partition or volume can't be part of a striped or spanned volume.

Partitions and volumes are essentially the same thing; however, two different terms are used at times because you create partitions on basic disks and you create volumes on dynamic disks. On an x86-based computer, you can mark a partition as active by using the Disk Management snap-in.

Although the active, boot, and system volumes or partitions can be the same, each is required nonetheless. When you install Windows 8.1, the Setup program assesses all the hard disk drive resources available. Typically, Windows 8.1 puts boot and system files on the same drive and partition, and then marks this partition as the active partition. The advantage of this configuration is that you don't need multiple drives for the operating system, and you can use an additional drive as a mirror of the operating system partitions.

There are a number of differences when installing to EFI-based hardware. The EFI starts up by loading a firmware-based boot menu. Normally, EFI disks have a partition structure called a GUID partition table (GPT). This partition structure differs substantially from the 32-bit–platform MBR-based partitions.

GPT-based disks have two required partitions and one or more optional (OEM or data) partitions (up to 128 total):

- EFI system partition (ESP)
- Microsoft reserved partition (MSR)
- At least one data partition

The EFI boot menu presents a set of options, one of which is the EFI shell. The EFI shell provides an operating environment supporting the FAT and FAT32 file systems, as well as configuration and file management commands. To view a list of partitions on an EFI-based computer, use the Map command. In the output of the Map command, blk designates partition blocks and fs# designates readable file systems. You can change to a partition by entering the partition block number followed by a colon. Enter **dir** to view files in the partition. EFI has a boot maintenance manager that allows you to configure the boot menu.

When you install Windows 8.1, the Setup program will automatically create a Windows Recovery Environment (Windows RE) partition and install additional components that can be used for recovery and troubleshooting in that partition. As a result, the Windows recovery tools are always available on computers running Windows 8.1. For more information, see the "Recovering from a failed start" section in Chapter 10, "Backing up and recovering a computer."

As an administrator, you can use these tools to recover computers. If a remote user can't start Windows, you can talk the user through the process of starting Windows RE and initiating recovery. You do this by having the user access the Advanced Repair Options menu, as discussed in the "Recovering from a failed start" section in Chapter 10.

Performing a Windows 8.1 installation

Before you install Windows 8.1 on a computer, you should determine whether the underlying hardware meets the requirements for physical memory, processing power, and graphics capabilities. Microsoft provides both minimum requirements and recommended requirements. Requirements for memory and graphics are measured in megabytes (MB) and gigabytes (GB); requirements for processors are measured in gigahertz (GHz).

Windows 8.1 requires:

- A 1-GHz or faster 32-bit (x86) or 64-bit (x64) processor
- At least 1 GB RAM (32-bit) or 2 GB RAM (64-bit)
- A DirectX 9 graphics processor with a Windows Display Drive Model (WDDM) 1.0 or later driver
- Touch UI requires a tablet or a monitor that supports multitouch.

NOTE Microsoft recommends that a computer have available disk space of at least 16 GB (32-bit) or 20 GB (64-bit). Various features in Windows 8.1, such as protection points, which include previous versions of files and folders that have been modified, can quickly increase the size requirements. For optimal performance of the hard disk, you need at least 15 percent free space at all times and adequate space for the paging file, which might be up to twice the size of the system's RAM. Also, if you are doing an in-place upgrade, the Windows.old folder will contain folders and files from the previous installation.

Any computer that meets or exceeds these hardware requirements can run Windows 8.1. You can perform a new installation of Windows 8.1 by completing these steps:

1. Turn on the computer and insert the Windows 8.1 distribution media into the computer's DVD-ROM drive. Press a key to start the Setup program from the DVD when prompted. If you're not prompted to start from DVD, you might need to modify the computer's boot or startup options in firmware.

2. When prompted, choose your language, time, currency format, and keyboard layout, and then tap or click Next. Click Install Now.

3. With retail versions of Windows 8.1, you typically have to provide a product key. If prompted, enter the product key. Tap the onscreen keyboard button if you are working on a device without a keyboard, and then use the onscreen keyboard to enter the product key. Tap or click Next.

   NOTE If Setup determines that the product key is invalid, make sure that you entered each letter and number correctly. You don't need to enter dashes. Sometimes it's easier to reenter the product key than to find the incorrect value in the key sequence.

4. Read the license terms. If you agree, tap or click I Accept The License Terms, and then tap or click Next.

5. The Which Type Of Installation Do You Want? page is displayed to ensure that you really want to perform a new installation rather than an upgrade. To continue with the new installation, select Custom: Install Windows Only (Advanced).

6. When prompted for an installation location, choose the drive partition on which you want to install the operating system, and then tap or click Next.

   TIP During installation, on the Where Do You Want To Install Windows? page, you can access a command prompt by pressing Shift+F10. This puts you in the MinWinPC environment used by Setup to install the operating system, and you have access to many of the same command-line tools that are available in a standard installation of Windows 8.1.

7. If the drive partition you've selected contains a previous Windows installation, you'll get a prompt telling you that existing user and application settings will be moved to a folder named Windows.old and that you must copy these settings to the new installation to use them. Tap or click OK.

8. Setup will then start the installation. During this process, Setup copies the full disk image of Windows 8.1 to the disk you've selected and then expands it. Afterward, Setup installs features based on the computer's configuration and any hardware that Setup detects. When Setup finishes the installation and

restarts the computer, the operating system will be loaded and the system will be set up for first use. After the system is prepared, Setup will restart the computer again.

9. On the Personalize page, pick a background color for the Start page and desktop. Enter a computer name, and then tap or click Next.

10. When prompted, choose your country or region, your time and currency format, and your keyboard layout. Tap or click Next.

11. With wireless connections, you'll need to select the wireless connection to use. When you tap or click Connect, you'll be able to enter the password for the wireless network. Then you'll need to tap or click Connect again. If the computer has a wired connection to the Internet, you shouldn't need to do this.

12. On the Settings page, you can tap or click Use Express Settings to accept the express settings or tap or click Customize to customize the settings. Express settings configure the computer and standard defaults, as follows:

    ▪ Turn on sharing and connect devices, which might be suitable for home and work networks, though not necessarily for domain environments.

    ▪ Automatically install important and recommended updates, as well as updates for devices.

    ▪ Help protect the PC from unsafe content, files, and websites by enabling the SmartScreen Filter for Internet Explorer and Windows.

    ▪ Use Windows Error Reporting to check for solutions to problems.

    ▪ Use Internet Explorer compatibility lists to help resolve website compatibility issues.

    ▪ Let desktop apps use your name and account picture.

    ▪ Enable Windows Location Platform so desktop apps can ask users for their location.

13. If the computer has an Internet connection, the Sign In To Your PC page allows you to set up either a Microsoft Account or a local computer account. Otherwise, only a local computer account can be created. At this point, you'll typically want to use a local account for the computer, so tap or click Sign In Without A Microsoft Account, and then confirm by tapping or clicking Local Account again. Next, enter a user name. Enter and then confirm a password. Enter a password hint. Finally, tap or click Finish.

NOTE Chapter 5, "Managing user access and security," discusses Microsoft accounts and provides details on how they can be created and used. When you connect a local or domain account to a Microsoft account, the account becomes a connected local or connected domain account.

14. Afterward, Windows 8.1 will prepare the computer's desktop.

You can upgrade a computer to Windows 8.1 by completing these steps:

1. Start the computer and log on by using an account with administrator privileges. Insert the Windows 8.1 distribution media into the computer's DVD-ROM drive. The Windows 8.1 Setup program should start automatically. If Setup doesn't start automatically, use File Explorer to access the distribution media, and then double-tap or double-click Setup.exe.

   NOTE Only the current operating system's keyboard layout is available during installation. This also means that if your keyboard language and the language of the edition of Windows 8.1 you are installing are different, you might see unexpected characters as you type.

2. Setup will copy temporary files and then start. If your computer is connected to the Internet, choose whether to get required updates during the installation. Either tap or click Go Online To Install Updates Now or tap or click No, Thanks. Tap or click Next.

   TIP You don't have to get updates during the installation. If you decide not to get required updates, you can update the computer later by using the Windows Update feature. I prefer to install updates as part of the installation to ensure that the computer is ready to go when I finish setting up the operating system.

3. With retail versions of Windows 8.1, you typically have to provide a product key. If prompted, enter the product key. Tap the onscreen keyboard button if you are working on a device without a keyboard, and then use the onscreen keyboard to enter the product key. By default, the computer will automatically activate Windows the next time you connect to the Internet. Tap or click Next.

   NOTE If Setup determines that the product key is invalid, make sure you entered each letter and number correctly. You don't need to enter dashes. Sometimes it's easier to reenter the product key than to find the incorrect value in the key sequence.

4. Read the license terms. If you agree, tap or click I Accept The License Terms, and then tap or click Accept.

5. The options that appear on the Choose What To Keep page depend on the version of Windows currently running on your computer. Upgrade options you might get include the following:

   - **Windows Settings** If this option is available and selected, Setup attempts to keep basic settings, including settings for your desktop background, display, Internet favorites, Internet history, and Ease of Access. Not all settings will be moved and available in Windows 8.1.

   - **Personal Files** If this option is available and selected, Setup saves personal files from the Users folder. This means that the personal files stored in each user's Documents, Music, Pictures, Videos, and other folders are moved and made available in Windows 8.1.

- **Apps** If this option is available and selected, Setup saves settings for desktop apps and makes them available after upgrade. Desktop programs, and some desktop apps, will need to be reinstalled.

- **Nothing** If this option is selected, Setup moves folders and files for the previous installation to a folder named Windows.old, and the previous installation will no longer run.

SECURITY ALERT If you are upgrading and normally log in by using a fingerprint reader or other biometric device, you'll need to write down your password. You'll need to enter the user name and password the first time you sign in to Windows 8.1.

6. Tap or click Next, and then tap or click Install. Continue with steps 8 through 14 of the previous procedure.

You might have trouble installing Windows 8.1 for a variety of reasons. Possible solutions to common problems follow, in problem/solution format.

- **You can't start from the Windows 8.1 installation media.** Although most computers can start from DVD, sometimes this capability is disabled in firmware. Set the boot order in firmware so that the DVD drive appears ahead of hard disk drives and other bootable media.

- **You can't select a hard disk during setup.** Although the Windows 8.1 installation media contains drivers for most disk controllers, you might have a disk controller for which a default driver isn't available. Insert media containing the required drivers, and then tap or click Load Drivers on the Where Do You Want To Install Windows? page. If the driver is on an internal hard drive, press Shift+F10 to access a command prompt, and then use Xcopy to copy the driver files to a USB flash device or other removable media. You can then tap or click Load Drivers to load the drivers from the media.

- **You forgot to modify the hard disk configuration prior to starting the installation.** On the Where Do You Want To Install Windows? page, tap or click Drive Options (Advanced). You can then use the options provided to create, delete, and format partitions as necessary. If you need to shrink or extend a partition (even during an upgrade), press Shift+F10 to access a command prompt, and then use Disk Part to work with the partition. You can extend and shrink partitions without having to delete them. You also can use Disk Part to change the disk type and partition style.

Creating a Windows To Go workspace

Another way to work with Windows 8.1 is to create a Windows To Go workspace. A Windows To Go workspace is a bootable installation of Windows 8.1 that's installed on a 32-GB or larger USB drive. A Windows To Go workspace operates much like a standard installation of Windows 8.1 except in the following respects:

- Hibernate is disabled as a sleep option by default, because this helps ensure that you can easily move the workspace between computers.

- Internal disks are offline by default to ensure that data is stored on the USB drive rather than on the computer into which the Windows To Go drive is inserted.

- Trusted Platform Module (TPM) is not used; however, a pre-operating system boot password can be configured as part of BitLocker Drive Encryption.

- Windows Recovery Environment (Windows RE) is not available, and you cannot refresh or reset a Windows To Go workspace.

Unlike in Windows 8, Windows To Go workspaces for Windows 8.1 are able to use Microsoft accounts and access the Microsoft store. Windows To Go discovers available hardware and installs necessary drivers upon first boot on a host computer. The next time you start Windows To Go on that host computer, Windows To Go identifies the host computer and loads the correct drivers automatically. Applications that you want to run from a Windows To Go workspace must support roaming.

Unlike Windows 8, Windows 8.1 includes a Windows To Go creator tool. You can access this tool and create a Windows To Go workspace by completing the following steps:

1. Insert a 32-GB or larger USB drive into a USB port on your computer.
2. In Control Panel, tap or click Large Icons or Small Icons as the View By option.
3. Tap or click the Windows To Go option.
4. In the Create A Windows To Go Workspace dialog box, tap or click the USB drive on which you want to create the Windows To Go workspace.
5. Tap or click Next, and then follow the prompts.

Running Windows 8.1

When the operating system starts after installation, you can log on and access the desktop. By default, Windows 8.1 stores user profile data under %SystemDrive% \Users\%UserName%. Within the user profile folder, each user who logs on to the system has a personal folder, and that personal folder contains additional folders. These folders are the default locations for storing specific types of data and files:

- **AppData**   User-specific application data (in a hidden folder)
- **Contacts**   Contacts and contact groups
- **Desktop**   The user's desktop
- **Downloads**   Programs and data downloaded from the Internet
- **Favorites**   The user's Internet favorites
- **Links**   The user's Internet links
- **Documents**   The user's document files
- **Music**   The user's music files
- **Pictures**   The user's pictures
- **Videos**   The user's video files
- **Saved Games**   The user's saved game data
- **Searches**   The user's saved searches

NOTE %SystemDrive% and %UserName% refer to the *SystemDrive* and *UserName* environment variables, respectively. The Windows operating system has many environment variables, which are used to refer to user-specific and system-specific values. Often, I'll refer to environment variables by using this syntax: %VariableName%. If you've upgraded to Windows 8.1 from an earlier version of Windows, the user's personal folder might also contain symbolic links (which look like shortcuts) to the folders and settings used by that earlier version. A *symbolic link* is a pointer to a file or folder that often is created for backward compatibility with applications that look for a folder or file in a location that has been moved. You can create symbolic links by using the Mklink command-line utility. At a command prompt, enter **mklink /?** to learn the available options.

Windows 8.1 uses personal folders and personal libraries. Personal folders are listed in the left pane of File Explorer and displayed in the main pane when you select the This PC node. Libraries are displayed in File Explorer only when you select the Libraries node.

Libraries work differently than they do in Windows 8 and earlier versions of Windows. Although libraries are still collections of files and folders that are grouped together and presented through a common view, the data they collect is different.

In earlier versions of Windows, libraries collected a user's personal data and a computer's public data. In Windows 8.1, libraries collect locally stored personal data and cloud-stored personal data. Thus, if a user has a connected local or connected domain account, locally stored data is collected with data stored on SkyDrive. For example, the Documents library collects the data from a user's locally stored Documents folder and a user's cloud-stored Documents folder.

When you are working with the Libraries node in File Explorer, you can create new libraries to act as views to various collections of data by pressing and holding or right-clicking an open area of the main pane, pointing to New, and then selecting Library.

IMPORTANT When you work with libraries, it's important to remember that they are only representations of collected data. Windows 8.1 creates views of files and folders that you add to libraries. The libraries do not contain any actual data, and any action that you take on a file or folder within a library is performed on the source file or folder.

Windows 8.1 provides themes that allow you to easily customize the appearance of menus, windows, and the desktop. In Control Panel, tap or click the Change The Theme link under Appearance And Personalization, and then choose the theme you want to use. Windows Default themes such as Earth or Flowers add improved visual design and enhanced dynamic effects to the interface. If you want to use fewer advanced features, choose the Windows theme. Additional themes are available online as well.

It is important to point out, however, that the interface enhancements that can be used on a computer depend on which Windows 8.1 edition is installed and on the computer's hardware.

Using Action Center and activating Windows

By default, when you log on, the operating system displays an Action Center summary icon in the desktop notification area. This icon has a white flag on it. Action Center is a program that monitors the status of important security and maintenance areas. If the status of a monitored item changes, Action Center updates the notification icon as appropriate for the severity of the alert. If you tap or click this icon, Windows displays a dialog box with a summary listing of each alert or action item that needs your attention. Tap or click an action item link to run the related solution. Tap or click the Open Action Center link to display the Action Center.

If you've disabled Action Center notifications on the taskbar, you can start Action Center by following these steps:

1. In Control Panel, tap or click the System And Security category heading link.

2. Tap or click Action Center.

Action Center, shown in Figure 1-1, provides an overview of the computer's status and lists any issues that need to be resolved. After you have installed Windows 8.1, action alerts in Action Center might let you know that device drivers are available and need to be installed. Simply tap or click the action item to begin the driver installation process. For detailed information on working with Action Center, see the "Using automated help and support" section in Chapter 8, "Managing hardware devices and drivers."

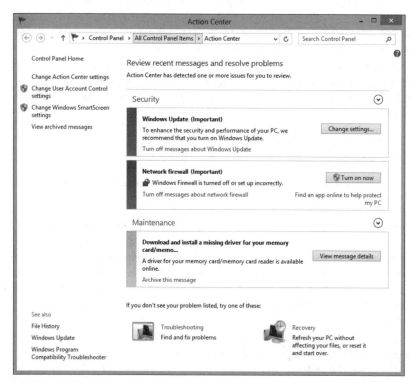

FIGURE 1-1 The Action Center window shows issues that need user attention.

Windows 8.1 Pro and Enterprise editions support volume licensing. Although volume-licensed versions of Windows 8.1 might not require activation or product keys, retail versions of Windows 8.1 require both activation and product keys. You can determine whether Windows 8.1 has been activated in Control Panel by tapping or clicking System And Security, and then tapping or clicking System. On the System page, read the Windows Activation entry. This entry specifies whether you have activated the operating system. If Windows 8.1 has not been activated and you are connected to the Internet, select View Details In Windows Activation, and then tap or click Activate.

Running Windows 8.1 in groups and domains

Computers running Windows 8.1 can be members of a homegroup, a workgroup, a workplace, or a domain. A *homegroup* is a loose association of computers on a home network. Computers in a homegroup share data that can be accessed by using a password common to the users in the homegroup. You set the homegroup password when you set up the homegroup and can modify the password as necessary at any time.

A *workgroup* is a loose association of computers in which each computer is managed separately. A *workplace* is a loose association of computers that grants access to certain internal network resources and business apps. A *domain* is a collection of computers that you can manage collectively by means of domain controllers, which are servers running Windows that manage access to the network, to the directory database, and to shared resources.

REAL WORLD Workplaces are new in Windows 8.1 and so are Work Folders. Don't confuse these two features. Workplaces are a middle ground between traditional workgroups and domains. Computers that are members of a workplace can access internal network resources, such as internal websites and business applications. Work Folders allow users to synchronize their corporate data to their devices and vice versa. Those devices can be joined to the corporate domain or a workplace. To deploy Work Folders, an administrator adds the File And Storage Services > Work Folders role to a server, and then configures Work Folders by using Server Manager. Because Work Folders make use of the IIS hostable web core, the folders are accessed via a remote web gateway running on IIS.

Homegroups are available when a computer running Windows 8.1 is connected to a home network. Workgroups, workplaces, and domains are available when a computer running Windows 8.1 is connected to a work network.

Some aspects of Windows 8.1 vary depending on whether a computer is a member of a homegroup, workgroup, workplace, or domain. The sections that follow discuss these differences as they pertain to UAC, logon, fast user switching, and password management.

Understanding UAC in Windows 8.1

In a homegroup, workgroup, or workplace, a computer running Windows 8.1 has only local machine accounts. In a domain, a computer running Windows 8.1 has both local machine accounts and domain accounts. Windows 8.1 has two primary types of local user accounts:

- **Standard** Standard user accounts can use most software and can change system settings that do not affect other users or the security of the computer.
- **Administrator** Administrator user accounts have complete access to the computer and can make any necessary changes.

Windows 8.1 has a special type of local user account called a Microsoft account. Microsoft accounts can be thought of as synchronized local accounts and are discussed in detail in the "Understanding user and group accounts" section in Chapter 5.

Windows 8.1 includes UAC as a way to enhance computer security by ensuring true separation of standard user and administrator user accounts. Because of the UAC feature in Windows 8.1, all applications run by using either standard user or administrator user privileges. Whether you log on as a standard user or as an administrator user, you get a security prompt by default whenever you run an application that requires administrator privileges. The way the security prompt works depends on Group Policy settings (as discussed in the "Optimizing UAC and Admin Approval Mode" section in Chapter 5) and whether you are logged on with a standard user account or an administrator user account.

When you are logged on with a standard user account, you are asked to provide a password for an administrator account, as shown in Figure 1-2. In a homegroup, workgroup, or workplace, each local computer administrator account is listed by name. To proceed, you must tap or click an account, enter the account's password, and then tap or click Yes.

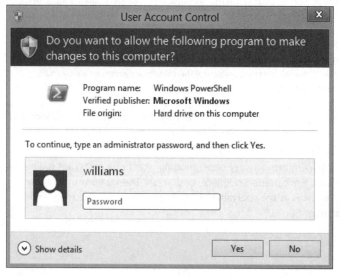

FIGURE 1-2 This User Account Control dialog box prompts for administrator credentials.

In a domain, the User Account Control dialog box does not list any administrator accounts, so you must know the user name and password of an administrator account in the default (logon) domain or a trusted domain to continue. When Windows prompts you, enter the account name and password, and then tap or click Yes. If the account is in the default domain, you don't have to specify the domain name. If the account is in another domain, you must specify the domain and the account name by using the format *domain\username*, such as **cpandl\williams.**

When you are logged on with an administrator user account, you are asked to confirm that you want to continue, as shown in Figure 1-3. You can tap or click Yes to allow the task to be performed, or tap or click No to stop the task from being performed. Tapping or clicking Show Details shows the full path to the program being executed.

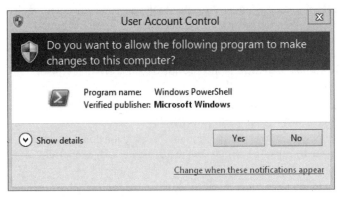

FIGURE 1-3 This User Account Control dialog box prompts for confirmation to continue.

Elevation of privileges allows a standard user application to run with administrator privileges. You can run applications with elevated privileges by following these steps:

1. Press and hold or right-click the application's tile or shortcut, and then tap or click Run As Administrator.

2. When the User Account Control prompt appears, proceed as you normally would to allow the application to run with administrator privileges.

NOTE You must run the command prompt with elevated privileges to perform administration at the command line. If you do not do this, you will get an error when you try to run an administrator utility or perform a task that requires administrator privileges.

Logging on to, shutting down, and restarting Windows 8.1

Windows 8.1 displays a Lock screen at startup. When you click the Lock screen, you get the Welcome screen. The behavior of the Welcome screen depends on Group Policy settings and the computer's homegroup, workgroup, or domain membership.

Keep the following in mind:

- In a homegroup, workgroup, or workplace, the Welcome screen shows a list of accounts on the computer. To log on with one of these accounts, tap or click the account and enter a password if required.

- In a domain, the name of the last user to log on is displayed by default on the Welcome screen. You can log on with this account by entering the required password. You can log on as another user as well by clicking the Switch User button, selecting one of the alternative accounts listed, and then providing the password for that account or clicking Other User to enter the user name and password for the account to use. Note that the Switch User button has a left-pointing arrow in a circle and is to the left of the account picture.

By default, the last account to log on to the computer is listed in *computer \username* or *domain\username* format. To log on to this account, you enter the account password, and then tap or click the Submit button. The Submit button is part of the Password box, and shows a right-pointing arrow. To log on to a different account, tap or click Switch User, press Ctrl+Alt+Del, and then tap or click Other User. The logon information that you must provide depends on what type of account you are using:

- If the account is in the current/default domain, enter the user name and password, and then tap or click the arrow button.

- If the account is in another domain, you must specify the domain and the account name by using the format *domain\username*, such as **cpandl \williams**.

- If you want to log on to the local machine, enter **.*username***, where *username* is the name of the local account, such as **.\williams**.

When you are logged on, you can display the Windows Logon screen by pressing Ctrl+Alt+Del. This screen allows you to lock the computer, switch users, sign out, change a password, or start Task Manager. The Power button is in the lower-right corner of the screen. Tapping or clicking the Power button displays Sleep, Shut Down, and Restart options.

Because Shut down and Restart are options of the Power settings, you also can shut down or restart a computer by following these steps:

1. Slide in from the right side of the screen or press Windows key + C.
2. Tap or click Settings, and then tap or click Power.
3. Tap or click Shut Down or Restart as appropriate.

NOTE Windows 8.1 supports fast user switching in domain, homegroup, and workgroup configurations. When a user is logged on to a computer running Windows 8.1, you can use fast user switching to allow another user to log on without requiring the current user to log off. To switch users, press Ctrl+Alt+Del, and then tap or click Switch User.

Managing user account passwords with Windows 8.1

Windows 8.1 provides fast and easy ways to manage user account passwords. You can easily perform the following tasks:

- Change the current user's password.
- Change the password for another domain or local computer account.
- Create a password reset disk.
- Reset a user's password.

These tasks are discussed in the sections that follow.

CHANGING THE CURRENT USER'S PASSWORD

You can change the current user's password by completing the following steps:

1. Press Ctrl+Alt+Del, and then tap or click the Change A Password option.

   NOTE In a domain, the current user's domain account name is listed in *domain \username* format. In a homegroup, workgroup, or workplace, the current user's local account name is listed.

2. Enter the current password for the account in the Old Password text box.
3. Enter and confirm the new password for the account in the New Password and the Confirm Password text boxes.
4. Tap or click the arrow button to confirm the change.

CHANGING OTHER ACCOUNT PASSWORDS

You can change the password for a domain or a local account other than the current user's account by completing these steps:

1. Press Ctrl+Alt+Del, and then tap or click the Change A Password option.
2. Tap or click in the User Name text box, and then enter the name of the account.

   NOTE For a domain account, specify the domain and the account name by using the format *domain\username*, such as **cpandl\williams**. For a local computer account, enter **.\username**, where *username* is the name of the local account, such as **.\williams**.

3. Enter the current password for the account in the Old Password text box.
4. Enter and confirm the new password for the account in the New Password and the Confirm Password text boxes.
5. Tap or click the arrow button to confirm the change.

CREATING AND USING A PASSWORD RESET DISK

Passwords for domain users and local users are managed in different ways. In domains, passwords for domain user accounts are managed by administrators. Administrators can reset forgotten passwords by using the Active Directory Users And Computers console.

In homegroups and workgroups, passwords for local machine accounts can be stored in a secure, encrypted file on a password reset disk, which is a USB flash drive that contains the information needed to reset your password. You can create a password reset disk for the current user by completing these steps:

1. Press Ctrl+Alt+Del, and then tap or click the Change A Password option.

2. Tap or click Create A Password Reset Disk to start the Forgotten Password Wizard.

3. In the Forgotten Password Wizard, read the introductory message. Insert the USB flash drive you want to use, and then tap or click Next.

4. Select the USB flash drive you want to use in the drive list. Tap or click Next.

5. Enter the current password for the logged on user in the text box provided, and then tap or click Next.

6. After the wizard creates the password reset disk, tap or click Next, remove the disk, and then tap or click Finish.

Be sure to store the password reset disk in a secure location because anyone with access to the disk can use it to gain access to the user's data. If a user is unable to log on because he or she has forgotten the password, you can use the password reset disk to create a new password and log on to the account by using this password.

REAL WORLD You can use BitLocker To Go to protect and encrypt USB flash devices and other removable media drives. When a user is logged on, protected media can be unlocked by using a password or a smart card with a smart card PIN. However, when a user isn't logged on, the protected drive cannot be accessed. Because of this, you shouldn't protect password reset disks with BitLocker To Go.

RESETTING A USER'S PASSWORD

Administrators can reset forgotten passwords by using the Active Directory Users And Computers console. In homegroups and workgroups, you can reset a password by following these steps:

1. On the Log On screen, tap or click the arrow button without entering a password, and then tap or click OK. The Reset Password option should be displayed. If the user has already entered the wrong password, the Reset Password option might already be displayed.

2. Insert the disk or USB flash device containing the password recovery file, and then tap or click Reset Password to start the Reset Password Wizard.

3. In the Reset Password Wizard, read the introductory message, and then tap or click Next.

4. Select the device you want to use in the drive list, and then tap or click Next.

5. On the Reset The User Account Password page, enter and confirm a new password for the user.

6. Enter a password hint, and then tap or click Next. Tap or click Finish.

Power plans, sleep modes, and shutdown

Normally, computers running Windows 8.1 use the Balanced power plan, and this power plan turns off the display and puts the computer in sleep mode automatically after a specified period of time passes with no user activity.

When entering the sleep state, the operating system automatically saves all work, turns off the display, and puts the computer in sleep mode. Sleep mode is a low-power consumption mode in which the state of the computer is maintained in the computer's memory, and the computer's fans and hard disks are turned off.

Windows 8.1 saves the computer state before entering sleep mode, and you don't need to exit programs before you do this. Because the computer uses very little energy in the sleep state, you don't have to worry about wasting energy.

> **TIP** Sleep mode works in slightly different ways depending on the type of computing device. Often you can turn off and turn on mobile computers by closing or opening the lid. When you close the lid, the laptop enters the sleep state. When you open the lid, the laptop wakes up from the sleep state. If the laptop is in the sleep state for an extended amount of time, or the laptop's battery runs low on power, the state of the computer is saved to the hard disk and then the computer shuts down completely. This final state is similar to the hibernate state used in early versions of Windows.

To view or modify the default power options, open Control Panel. In Control Panel, tap or click System And Security, and then, under Power Options, tap or click Change When The Computer Sleeps. The options available depend on the type of computing device. With mobile computers and tablets, as shown in Figure 1-4, you might be able to set On Battery and Plugged In options for turning off the display, putting the computer to sleep, and adjusting the display brightness. With desktop computers, you can only specify when the display is turned off and when the computer goes to sleep. Tap or click Save Changes to save your changes.

You can cause most computers to enter the sleep state by tapping or clicking the Settings charm button, tapping or clicking Power, and then tapping or clicking Sleep. To wake the computer from the sleep state, you can press and hold somewhere on the touch screen, move the mouse, or press any key on the keyboard. Note that some computers have separate power and sleep buttons on their case. The way these buttons work can be set through the power plan options.

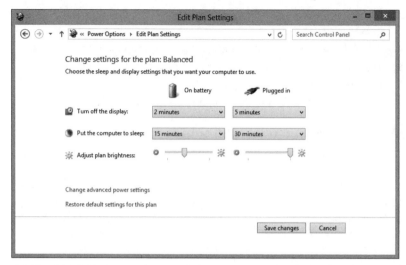

FIGURE 1-4 Configure power options to optimize power management for the computer.

There are instances in which a computer can't use the sleep state. The system hardware, state, and configuration can affect the way the power and sleep buttons work. Some computer hardware doesn't support the sleep state. In this case, the computer can't use the sleep state. This is also the case when the computer has updates installed that require a restart or when you've installed programs that require a restart. Additionally, if an administrator has reconfigured the power options on the computer and set the power button, the sleep button, or both to alternative actions, the computer will use those actions instead of the default shutdown and sleep actions.

> **CAUTION** When working with computers in the sleep state, keep in mind that the computer is still drawing power. You should never install hardware inside the computer when it is in the sleep state. To avoid possible confusion regarding the sleep state and the power off state, be sure to unplug desktop computers running Windows 8.1 before installing internal devices. External devices are exceptions. You can connect USB, FireWire, and eSATA devices without shutting down the computer.

To change the default setting for the power button, open Control Panel. In Control Panel, tap or click System And Security, and then, under Power Options, tap or click Choose What The Power Buttons Do. As before, the options available depend on the type of computing device. With mobile computers, as shown in Figure 1-5, you might be able to set On Battery and Plugged In options that specify what happens when you press the power button, what happens when you press the sleep button, and what happens when you close the lid. Optionally, you can tap or click Change Settings That Are Currently Unavailable, and then do any of the following:

- Choose Require A Password to require a password to log on after waking the computer from sleep.

- Choose Turn On Fast Startup to save system information to a file on the system disk when you shut down the computer. This file is then read during startup to enable faster startup. When you restart a computer, Fast Startup is not used.

- Choose the Power options you want displayed when you click Power.

Save your changes by tapping or clicking Save Changes.

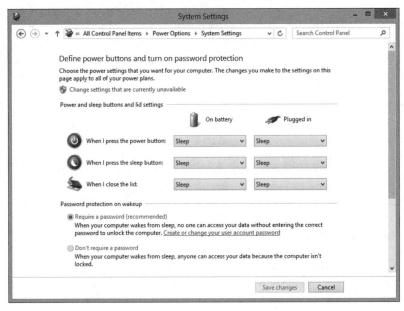

FIGURE 1-5 Configure power button options.

Windows 8.1 architecture

If you want to truly know how Windows 8.1 works and what makes it tick, you need to dig under the hood. Windows 8.1 doesn't start from an initialization file. Instead, the operating system uses the Windows Boot Manager to initialize and start the operating system.

The boot environment dramatically changes the way the operating system starts. The boot environment was created by Microsoft to resolve several prickly problems related to boot integrity, operating system integrity, and firmware abstraction. The boot environment is loaded prior to the operating system, making it a pre–operating system environment. As such, the boot environment can be used to validate the integrity of the startup process and the operating system itself before actually starting the operating system.

The boot environment is an extensible abstraction layer that allows the operating system to work with multiple types of firmware interfaces without requiring the operating system to be specifically written to work with these firmware interfaces. Rather than updating the operating system each time a new firmware interface is developed, firmware interface developers can use the standard programming interfaces of the boot environment to allow the operating system to communicate as necessary through the firmware interfaces.

Firmware interface abstraction is the first secret ingredient that makes it possible for Windows 8.1 to work with BIOS-based and EFI-based computers in exactly the same way, and this is one of the primary reasons Windows 8.1 achieves hardware independence.

The next ingredient for hardware independence is Windows Imaging (WIM) format. Microsoft distributes Windows 8.1 on media by using WIM disk images. WIM uses compression and single-instance storage to dramatically reduce the size of image files. Using compression reduces the size of the image in much the same way that zip compression reduces the size of files. Using single-instance storage reduces the size of the image because only one physical copy of a file is stored for each instance of that file in the disk image.

The final ingredient for hardware independence is modularization. Windows 8.1 uses modular component design so that each component of the operating system is defined as a separate, independent unit or module. Because modules can contain other modules, various major features of the operating system can be grouped together and described independently of other major features. Because modules are independent from each other, modules can be swapped in or out to customize the operating system environment.

Windows 8.1 includes extensive support architecture. At the heart of this architecture is built-in diagnostics and troubleshooting. Microsoft designed built-in diagnostics and troubleshooting to be self-correcting and self-diagnosing or, failing that, to provide guidance while you are diagnosing problems.

Windows 8.1 includes network awareness and network discovery features. Network awareness tracks changes in network configuration and connectivity. Network discovery controls a computer's ability to detect other computers and devices on a network.

Network awareness allows Windows 8.1 to detect the current network configuration and connectivity status, which is important because many networking and security settings depend on the type of network to which a computer running Windows 8.1 is connected. Windows 8.1 has separate network configurations for domain networks, private networks, and public networks and is able to detect the following:

- When you change a network connection
- Whether the computer has a connection to the Internet
- Whether the computer can connect to the corporate network over the Internet

Windows Firewall in Windows 8.1 supports connectivity to multiple networks simultaneously and multiple active firewall profiles. Because of this, the active firewall profile for a connection depends on the type of connection.

If you disconnect a computer from one network switch or hub and plug it into a new network switch or hub, you might inadvertently cause the computer to think it is on a different network, and depending on Group Policy configuration, this could cause the computer to enter a lockdown state in which additional network security settings are applied. As shown in Figure 1-6, you can view the network connection status in the Network And Sharing Center. In Control Panel, under Network And Internet, tap or click View Network Status And Tasks to access this management console.

TIP Through the DirectAccess feature, computers running Windows 8.1 can directly access corporate networks wherever they are as long as they have access to the Internet, and best of all, users don't need to initiate VPN connections. The feature relies on DirectAccess servers being configured on the corporate network and DirectAccess being enabled in Group Policy.

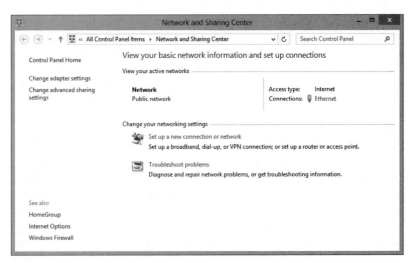

FIGURE 1-6 Determine the network state.

Windows 8.1 tracks the identification status of all networks to which the computer has been connected. When Windows 8.1 is in the process of identifying a network, the Network And Sharing Center shows the Identifying Networks state. This is a temporary state for a network that is being identified. After Windows 8.1 identifies a network, the network becomes an Identified Network and is listed by its network or domain name in the Network And Sharing Center.

If Windows 8.1 is unable to identify the network, the network is listed with the Unidentified Network status in the Network And Sharing Center. In Group Policy, you can set default location types and user permissions for each network state, as well as for all networks, by using the policies for Computer Configuration under Windows Settings\Security Settings\Network List Manager Policies.

When you are working with the Network And Sharing Center, you can attempt to diagnose a warning status by using Windows Network Diagnostics—another key component of the diagnostics and troubleshooting framework. To start diagnostics, tap or click Troubleshoot Problems, tap or click Internet Connections, and then tap or click Next. Windows Network Diagnostics then attempts to identify the network problem and provide a possible solution.

The Windows diagnostics and troubleshooting infrastructure offers improved diagnostics guidance, additional error reporting details, expanded event logging, and extensive recovery policies. Although early versions of Windows include some help and diagnostics features, those features are, for the most part, not self-correcting or self-diagnosing. Windows now can detect many types of hardware, memory, and performance issues and resolve them automatically or help users through the process of resolving them. For more information, see the "Working with the Automated Help and Support system" section in Chapter 8.

Error detection for devices and failure detection for disk drives also are automated. If a device is having problems, hardware diagnostics can detect error conditions and either repair the problem automatically or guide the user through a recovery process. With disk drives, hardware diagnostics can use fault reports provided by disk drives to detect potential failure and alert you before this happens. Hardware diagnostics can also help guide you through the backup process after alerting you that a disk might be failing.

Windows 8.1 can automatically detect performance issues, which include slow application startup, slow boot, slow standby/resume, and slow shutdown. If a computer is experiencing degraded performance, Windows diagnostics can detect the problem and provide possible solutions. For advanced performance issues, you can track related performance and reliability data in the Performance Monitor console, which is an administrative tool.

Windows 8.1 can also detect issues related to memory leaks and failing memory. If you suspect that a computer has a memory problem that is not being automatically detected, you can run Windows Memory Diagnostic manually by completing the following steps:

1. From Start, type **mdsched.exe**, and then press Enter. Normally, text that you type on Start is entered into the Apps Search box by default.

2. Choose whether to restart the computer and run the tool immediately or schedule the tool to run at the next restart, as shown in Figure 1-7.

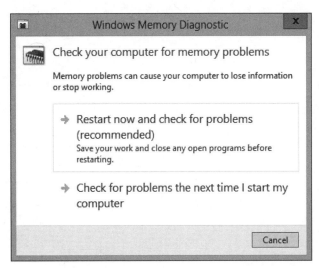

FIGURE 1-7 Test memory for problems.

3. Windows Memory Diagnostic runs automatically after the computer restarts and performs a standard memory test. If you want to perform fewer or more tests, press F1, use the up and down arrow keys to set the Test Mix as Basic, Standard, or Extended, and then press F10 to apply the desired settings and resume testing.

4. When testing is complete, the computer restarts. The test results will be displayed when you log on.

If a computer crashes because of failing memory and Memory Diagnostic detects this, you are prompted to schedule a memory test the next time the computer is started.

CHAPTER 2

Configuring and optimizing Windows 8.1 computers

One of your primary responsibilities as an administrator is to manage the operating system configuration. Windows 8.1 has many unique characteristics, including:

- A modular architecture and binaries distributed by using Windows Imaging (WIM) format disk images. Because of this, you can use the Deployment Image Servicing and Management (DISM) tool to manage packages, drivers, features, and internationalization settings in Windows Image (.wim) files or in virtual hard disk (.vhd/.vhdx) files. Disk Management and DiskPart have both been updated to work with .vhd and .vhdx files.

- A preboot environment in which Windows Boot Manager is used to control startup and load the boot application that you've selected. Because of this, Windows 8.1 doesn't use Ntldr and Boot.ini to load the operating system, as early versions of Windows did, and you have additional boot options. For example, you can start a computer from an operating system on a .vhd or .vhdx file. One way you do this is to create a basic boot image that uses Xcopy to copy the required .vhd or .vhdx file to a specified drive on startup.

- A user privilege and access control handler called User Account Control (UAC) is used to manage which processes can run and how applications interact with the operating system. Because of this, Windows 8.1 handles user privileges and access controls differently than earlier versions of Windows. As you'll learn in Chapter 5, "Managing user access and security," you can optimize or turn off UAC prompting, but this doesn't disable other UAC features, such as application virtualization.

Beyond this, you need to understand the tools and options available to configure Windows 8.1, and that's what I discuss in this chapter. Many of the tools with which you need to work are on the Apps screen. On the Start screen, you'll find a button with an arrow facing down; tapping or clicking this button displays the Apps screen. Because apps are listed first in the results whenever you perform an Everywhere search, one way to quickly search for apps is by pressing the Windows key + Q and then typing the app name in the Search box. If you followed my advice in Chapter 1, "Introduction to Windows 8.1 administration," you might have pinned the key tools you work with every day to Start or to the desktop taskbar for quick access as well.

Supporting computers running Windows 8.1

To successfully manage a computer, diagnose problems, and troubleshoot support issues, you need to know how the computer is configured. Support tools you can use to get information on a computer's configuration include the following:

- **Computer Management**   Provides access to important system, services, and storage-management tools.
- **Performance Monitor**   Allows you to monitor system performance and determine whether any issues are causing performance problems.
- **Resource Monitor**   Allows you to view detailed usage information for system resources, including processors, memory, disks, and networking. Use Resource Monitor when you need more information beyond what Task Manager provides.
- **System**   Allows you to view basic information about a computer and manage system properties.
- **System Information**   Displays detailed system statistics about configuration and resource availability. You can also use System Information to troubleshoot system problems.
- **Task Manager**   Allows you to view usage information for system resources.

In this section, I'll discuss techniques for working with these tools. First, though, you might want to add the Administrative Tools to the Start screen. From Start, you do this by using one of the following techniques:

- With the touch UI, slide in from the right, tap Settings, tap Tiles, and then tap Show Administrative Tools.
- With the mouse and keyboard, point to the hidden button in the lower-right corner of the screen to display the Charms bar. On the Charms bar, click Settings, click Tiles, and then click Show Administrative Tools.

Tapping or clicking the Show Administrative Tools slider switches between Yes and No, meaning either to show the tools or hide the tools. The next time you open Start, the screen is updated to either show or hide the tools as appropriate.

Start and the desktop have a handy menu that you can display by pressing and holding or right-clicking the lower-left corner of the Start screen or the desktop. Alternatively, you can press the Windows key + X to access the shortcut menu, which is helpful for computers with a mouse and keyboard, but a true gift for computers with a touch UI. The shortcut menu has options for Control Panel, Computer Management, Power Options, Search, System, Task Manager, File Explorer, Windows PowerShell, Windows PowerShell (Admin), and more.

MORE INFO On the Start screen, the hidden button in the lower-left corner shows a Windows icon, and tapping or clicking the Windows button opens the desktop. On the desktop, this button is not hidden, and tapping or clicking this button opens Start. Pressing and holding or right-clicking this button is what displays the shortcut menu.

Although you can use the shortcut menu to open both a standard and an elevated, administrator prompt for Windows PowerShell, you cannot use the shortcut menu to open a command prompt. To quickly open a command prompt, press the Windows key + Q, enter **cmd** in the Search box, and then press Enter. One way to quickly open an elevated, administrator command prompt is to follow these steps:

1. Press the Windows key + Q, and then enter **cmd** in the Search box.

2. In the search results, right-click Command Prompt, and then select Run As Administrator.

Working with the Computer Management console

The Computer Management console is designed to handle core system administration tasks on local and remote systems. If you've added Administrative Tools to the Start screen, you can start the Computer Management console by tapping or clicking the related tile. You also can start the Computer Management console by typing **compmgmt.msc** in the Everywhere Search box, and then pressing Enter.

As Figure 2-1 shows, the main window has a multipane view similar to File Explorer. You use the console tree in the left pane for navigation and tool selection. The Actions pane, which can be displayed on the far right, is similar to the shortcut menu that is displayed when you press and hold or right-click an item. To display or close the Actions pane, tap or click the Show/Hide Action Pane button on the console toolbar. Tools are divided into the following three broad categories:

- **System Tools** General-purpose tools for managing systems and viewing system information

- **Storage** Drive management tools

- **Services And Applications** Tools used to view and manage the properties of services and applications installed on a server

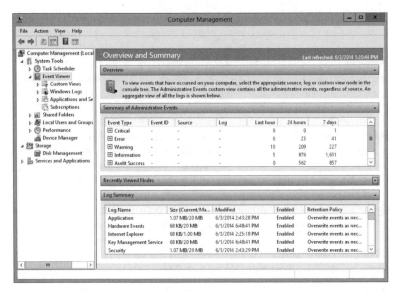

FIGURE 2-1 Use the Computer Management console to manage network computers and resources.

Within these categories are the following tools:

- **Task Scheduler** View and manage scheduled tasks. Scheduled tasks are used to automate processes such as disk cleanup or diagnostics testing. Scheduled tasks and automation are discussed in Chapter 9, "Handling maintenance and support tasks."

- **Event Viewer** View the event logs on the selected computer. Event logs record important events that have taken place on the computer and can be used to determine if a computer has configuration issues or other types of problems. Events and event logs are covered in Chapter 9.

- **Shared Folders** View and manage shared folders, as well as related sessions and open files.

- **Local Users And Groups** Manage local users and local user groups on the selected computer. Each client computer has both local users and local groups, which are separate from domain users and groups. Working with local users and groups is covered in Chapter 5.

- **Performance** Use monitoring and reporting tools to determine a computer's current performance and to track performance over time.

- **Device Manager** Use as a central location for checking the status of any device installed on a computer and for updating the associated device drivers. You can also use it to troubleshoot device problems. Managing devices is covered in Chapter 8, "Managing hardware devices and drivers."

- **Disk Management**   Manage hard disks, disk partitions, and volume sets. Windows 8.1 supports disk spanning, disk striping, disk striping with parity, and disk mirroring . Disk spanning enables you to create a single volume that extends across multiple disks. Disk striping enables you to write data stripes across multiple disks for fast access to data. Neither technique provides failure protection, however, and if any disk in a spanned or striped volume fails, the entire volume fails.

- **Services**   View and manage system services running on a computer. In Windows 8.1, every service has a recovery policy. If a service fails, Windows 8.1 tries to restart it automatically and automatically handles both service and nonservice dependencies as well. Any dependent services and system components are started prior to the attempt to start a failed service. Working with services is discussed in Chapter 8.

- **WMI Control**   View and manage Windows Management Instrumentation (WMI). WMI gathers system information, monitors system health, and manages system components. See the "Working with WMI Control" section later in this chapter for more information.

When working with Computer Management, you can select a remote computer to manage by completing the following steps:

1. Press and hold or right-click the Computer Management entry in the console tree, and then tap or click Connect To Another Computer. This opens the Select Computer dialog box.

2. Select Another Computer, and then enter the fully qualified name of the computer with which you want to work, such as **cspc85.microsoft.com**, where *cspc85* is the computer name and *microsoft.com* is the domain name. Or tap or click Browse to search for the computer with which you want to work.

3. Tap or click OK.

If you want to make it possible to remotely manage a computer running Windows 8.1 by using the WS-Management protocol, enter **winrm quickconfig** at an elevated prompt, and then, each time you're prompted to make configuration changes, enter **Y**. This will start the Windows Remote Management (WinRM) service, configure WinRM to accept WS-Management requests on any IP address, create a Windows Firewall exception for Windows Remote Management, and then configure LocalAccountTokenFilterPolicy to grant appropriate administrative rights for remote management.

Many other types of remote management tasks depend on other exceptions for Windows Firewall. Keep the following in mind:

- Remote Desktop is enabled or disabled separately from remote management. To allow someone to connect to the local server by using Remote Desktop, you must allow related connections to the computer and configure access.

- Remote Event Log Management must be configured as an allowed app in Windows Firewall to remotely manage a computer's event logs. In the advanced firewall, several related rules allow management via Named Pipes (NP) and Remote Procedure Call (RPC).

- Remote Scheduled Task Management must be configured as an allowed app in Windows Firewall to remotely manage a computer's scheduled tasks. In the advanced firewall, several related rules allow management of scheduled tasks via RPC.

- Remote Service Management must be configured as an allowed app in Windows Firewall to remotely manage a computer's services. In the advanced firewall, several related rules allow management via NP and RPC.

- Remote Shutdown must be configured as an allowed app in Windows Firewall to remotely shut down a computer.

- Remote Volume Management must be configured as an allowed app in Windows Firewall to remotely manage a computer's disks. In the advanced firewall, several related rules allow management of the Virtual Disk Service and Virtual Disk Service Loader.

Getting system information

You use the System console to view and manage system properties. In Control Panel, you can access the System console by tapping or clicking System And Security, and then tapping or clicking System. As Figure 2-2 shows, the System console is divided into four basic areas that provide links for performing common tasks and a system overview. These four areas are:

- **Windows Edition**   Shows the operating system edition and version.

- **System**   Lists the processor, memory, and type of operating system installed on the computer. The type of operating system is listed as 32-bit or 64-bit.

- **Computer Name, Domain, And Workgroup Settings**   Provides the computer name and description, as well as the domain, homegroup, or workgroup details. If you want to change any of this information, tap or click Change Settings, and then tap or click the Network ID button in the System Properties dialog box.

- **Windows Activation**   Shows whether you have activated the operating system and the product key. If Windows 8.1 isn't activated yet, tap or click the link provided to start the activation process, and then follow the prompts.

FIGURE 2-2 Use the System console to view and manage system properties.

When you're working in the System console, links in the left pane provide quick access to key support tools, including the following:

- Device Manager
- Remote Settings
- System Protection
- Advanced System Settings

Tapping or clicking Change Settings under Computer Name, Domain, And Workgroup Settings displays the System Properties dialog box. Using System Properties to manage a computer's configuration is discussed later in this chapter in the section "Managing system properties."

When you want to get detailed system information or check computer information on remote systems, use System Information (Msinfo32.exe). You can access system information by tapping or clicking System Information on the Apps screen or by typing **msinfo32** into the Everywhere Search box, and then pressing Enter. As shown in Figure 2-3, you can view system summaries by selecting the System Summary node. All the configuration statistics provided are collected by using the WMI service.

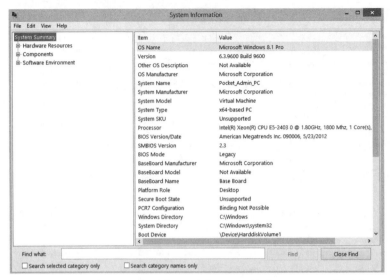

FIGURE 2-3 Advanced system information can help you troubleshoot system configuration problems.

The System Information tool provides detailed information on several major areas of the operating system, including the following:

- **Hardware Resources** Provides detailed information on I/O, interrupt requests (IRQs), memory, direct memory access (DMA), and Plug and Play devices. A key area you'll want to check if a system is having a device problem is the Conflicts/Sharing node, which provides a summary of devices that are sharing resources or causing system conflicts.

- **Components** Provides detailed information on installed components, from audio codecs to input devices to USB ports. A key area you'll want to check if a system is having a component problem is the Problem Devices node. This area provides information on components that have errors.

- **Software Environment** Provides detailed information on the running configuration of the operating system. When you are troubleshooting problems with a remote system, you'll find the Software Environment area to be extremely useful. In addition to drivers, environment variables, print jobs, and network connections, you can check running tasks, services, program groups, and startup programs.

If you want to browse configuration information for a remote computer, follow these steps:

1. Open System Information. Select Remote Computer on the View menu. This displays the Remote Computer dialog box.

2. In the Remote Computer dialog box, select Remote Computer On The Network.

3. Enter the computer name in the text box provided, and then tap or click OK.

The account you use must have appropriate administrator access permissions for the domain or the local machine. If you have other problems obtaining information from a remote system, you might need to check the namespace used by the WMI service, as discussed in the following section. You'll know that you are looking at system information for a remote computer because the System Summary node shows the computer name in parentheses.

Working with WMI Control

Windows Management Instrumentation (WMI) is a key part of the Windows 8.1 operating system. It is used to gather system statistics, monitor system health, and manage system components. To work properly, WMI relies on the WMI service, which must be running and properly configured for the environment.

You control the configuration of the WMI service through WMI Control, which can be accessed on a local or remote system by using the following steps:

1. Open Computer Management from the Apps screen (or by pressing the Windows key + X, and then selecting Computer Management).

2. Press and hold or right-click the Computer Management entry in the console tree, and then select Connect To Another Computer. You can now choose the system that has the services you want to manage.

3. Expand the Services And Applications node by double tapping or double-clicking it. Next, tap or click WMI Control to select it. (This is required for the control to be read in.) Press and hold or right-click WMI Control, and then select Properties. You can now use the WMI Control Properties dialog box to configure WMI, as shown in Figure 2-4.

FIGURE 2-4 WMI Control is used to manage the configuration of the WMI service.

The WMI Control Properties dialog box has the following tabs:

- **General** Items on this tab provide summary information for the system and WMI. WMI uses the credentials of the current user to obtain system information.

- **Backup/Restore** Statistics gathered by WMI are stored in a repository. By default, this repository is located in %SystemRoot%\System32\Wbem \Repository. These statistics are automatically backed up at regular intervals. You can back up or restore the repository manually by using the Back Up Now or Restore Now option on this tab.

- **Security** Security settings determine who has access to different levels of WMI statistics. By default, the Administrators group has full access to WMI, and the Authenticated Users group has permissions to execute methods, enable accounts, and write gathered statistics.

- **Advanced** Advanced settings determine the default namespace for WMI. The default namespace is used in WMI scripting when a full namespace path isn't set for a WMI object. You can change the default setting by tapping or clicking Change, selecting a new default namespace, and then tapping or clicking OK.

NOTE WMI maintains error logs that can be used for troubleshooting problems with the WMI service. These logs are stored by default in %SystemRoot%\System32\Wbem \Logs. WMI maintenance files, logs, and repositories can use a considerable amount of disk space on a system. These files used an average of 65 megabytes (MB) on my test systems—the bulk of this (40–50 MB) to maintain repository backup files.

Information gathered by WMI is stored in a collection of system files called a *repository*. By default, the repository files are stored under %SystemRoot% \System32\Wbem\Repository. The repository is the heart of WMI and the Help And Support services framework. Information is moved through the repository by using a staging file. If repository data or the staging file becomes corrupt, WMI might not function properly. This condition is usually temporary, but you can safeguard against it by backing up the repository file manually.

To back up the WMI repository manually, complete the following steps:

1. Open the WMI Control Properties dialog box, and then tap or click the Backup/Restore tab.

2. Tap or click Back Up Now. Next, use the Specify A Name For Your Backup File dialog box to set the file location and name of the WMI backup file. Tap or click Save.

3. The Backup In Progress dialog box is displayed while the recovery file is being created. The recovery file is saved with a .rec extension, and its size depends on how much information is being stored. Usually this file is between 20–30 MB in size.

If you later need to restore the WMI repository from a backup file, complete these steps:

1. Open the WMI Control Properties dialog box, and then tap or click the Backup/Restore tab.

2. Tap or click Restore Now. Next, use the Specify A Backup File To Restore dialog box to set the location and name of the existing recovery file. Then tap or click Open.

3. The Restore In Progress dialog box is displayed temporarily, and then you'll get a warning prompt. Tap or click OK.

4. Your connection to WMI Control is broken. When the restore operation is complete, you can reconnect to the computer. To do this, close and reopen the WMI Control Properties dialog box, which forces WMI Control to reconnect to the local or remote computer: note that you can do this only if the restore operation is complete.

NOTE If the connection fails, it usually means that WMI Control hasn't finished restoring the repository. Wait for another 30 to 60 seconds, and then try again.

Managing Computer Browser support

Support for Server Message Block (SMB) 1.0 and the Computer Browser service is a holdover from the days of Windows XP and Windows Server 2003. The Computer Browser service periodically performs network broadcasts and collects information about computers on the network. SMB is a client/server technology used for distributing files over networks. Windows desktop operating systems have an SMB client; Windows Server operating systems also have SMB server technology. Current Windows operating systems support SMB 3.0, which supports end-to-end encryption and eliminates the need for IPsec to protect SMB data in transit.

The SMB 1.0/CIFS File Sharing Support feature is installed by default on computers running Windows 8.1. However, if you've removed all computers running Windows XP and Windows Server 2003 from your organization, support for Server Message Block (SMB) 1.0 is no longer needed, nor is the Computer Browser service that was used by SMB 1.0. To remove the SMB 1.0/CIFS File Sharing Support feature, follow these steps:

1. In Control Panel, select Programs. Under Programs And Features, select Turn Windows Features On Or Off.

2. In the Windows Features dialog box, turn off the SMB 1.0/CIFS File Sharing Support feature by clearing its check box.

3. Tap or click OK. When prompted, tap or click Restart Now to restart the computer and apply the changes.

When you remove the SMB 1.0/CIFS File Sharing Support feature, the Computer Browser service also is removed because it's no longer needed. Removing this feature ensures that the Computer Browser service is no longer used to collect information about computers on the network and prevents SMB clients connecting to file shares from using SMB 1.0.

Using system support tools

Windows 8.1 provides a wide range of support tools. Tools that are available include the following:

- **Built-In Diagnostics**   Scans the system, examining hardware components and software configurations for problems. This information can be used to troubleshoot and resolve performance and configuration issues. Working with diagnostics tools is discussed in this chapter and in other chapters throughout this book.

- **DirectX Diagnostic Tool (Dxdiag.exe)**   Runs a diagnostic tool that you can use to troubleshoot problems with Microsoft DirectX, which is used to speed up the performance of applications, provided that the system hardware supports this feature.

- **Disk Cleanup (Cleanmgr.exe)**   Runs the Disk Cleanup utility, which examines disk drives for files that aren't needed. By default, Disk Cleanup examines temporary files, the Recycle Bin, and various types of offline files to check whether there are files that can be deleted.

- **Disk Defragmenter (Dfrgui.exe)**   Runs the Optimize Drives utility, which examines disk drives for fragmentation and can then be used to defragment the drive. A drive with many fragmented files can reduce the system's performance.

- **File Signature Verification Utility (Sigverif.exe)**   Checks operating system files that have been digitally signed. Any critical files that aren't digitally signed are displayed in a results list. The complete list of system files checked is available in a log file stored in %SystemRoot%\Sigverif.txt.

- **Offer Remote Assistance**   Enables you to offer remote assistance to a user. If the user accepts the offer, you can troubleshoot problems on his system as discussed in Chapter 6, "Managing remote access to workstations."

- **Remote Assistance**   Enables you to create a remote assistance invitation that can be used to get remote help from a technician. Remote Assistance is discussed in detail in Chapter 6.

- **System Configuration (Msconfig.exe)**   Enables you to manage system configuration information. You can configure normal, diagnostic, and selective startup as well.

- **System Restore (Rstrui.exe)**   Opens the System Restore utility, which can be used to create restore points or roll back a system to a specific restore point. The System Restore utility is discussed in Chapter 10, "Backing up and recovering a computer."

The tools you might want to take a closer look at now include Disk Cleanup, File Signature Verification, and System Configuration.

Working with Disk Cleanup

Disk Cleanup checks disk drives for files that aren't needed. You can start to work with Disk Cleanup by completing the following steps:

1. Open Disk Cleanup by typing **cleanmgr** in the Everywhere Search box and then pressing Enter, or by tapping or clicking the related option on the Apps screen.

2. If the computer has multiple hard disk drives, the Drive Selection dialog box is displayed. Use the Drives drop-down list to choose the drive you want to clean up, and then tap or click OK.

   Disk Cleanup then examines the selected drive, looking for temporary user files that can be deleted and user files that are candidates for deletion. The more files on the drive, the longer the search process takes.

   When Disk Cleanup finishes its initial run, you can add temporary system files that can be deleted and system files that are candidates for deletion by tapping or clicking Clean Up System Files, selecting a system drive to examine, and then tapping or clicking OK. You will then get a report similar to the one shown in Figure 2-5.

FIGURE 2-5 Use Disk Cleanup to help identify files that can be deleted.

File categories that you might find in the report include the following:

- **Downloaded Program Files**   Contains programs downloaded for use by your browser, such as ActiveX controls and Java applets. These files are temporary and can be deleted.

- **Files Discarded By Windows Upgrade** Contains files from a previous upgrade that were not identified as Windows system files. After you've saved any necessary data from previous Windows installations, including user data, you can use this option to remove the related files and free up space.

- **Hibernation File Cleaner** Contains details about the state of the computer when it enters hibernation. If the computer doesn't use hibernation, you can remove this file to free up space.

- **Microsoft Office Temporary Files** Contains temporary files and logs used by Microsoft Office. These files can be deleted to free up space.

- **Offline Files** Contains local copies of network files that you've designated for offline use. These files are stored to enable offline access and can be deleted.

- **Offline Web Pages** Contains local copies of webpages that you've designated for offline use. These files are stored to facilitate offline access and can be deleted.

- **Previous Windows Installation(s)** Saved under %SystemDrive% \Windows.old, contains files from previous Windows installations. After you've saved any necessary data from previous Windows installations, including user data, you can use this option to remove the related files and free up space.

- **Temporary Offline Files** Contains temporary data and work files for recently used network files. These files are stored to facilitate working offline and can be deleted.

- **Recycle Bin** Contains files that have been deleted from the computer but not yet purged. Emptying the Recycle Bin permanently removes the files.

- **Temporary Files** Contains information stored in the Temp folder. These files are primarily temporary data or work files for applications.

- **Temporary Internet Files** Contains webpages stored to support browser caching of pages. These files are temporary and can be deleted.

- **Thumbnails** Contains thumbnails of pictures, videos, and documents created by Windows 8.1. When you first access a folder, Windows 8.1 creates thumbnails of pictures, videos, and documents. These thumbnails are saved so that they can be quickly displayed the next time you open the folder. If you delete thumbnails, they are re-created the next time you open the folder.

3. Use the check boxes provided in the Files To Delete list to choose files that you want to remove. Then tap or click OK. When prompted to confirm the action, tap or click Yes.

Verifying system files with File Signature Verification

Critical files used by the operating system are digitally signed. Digital signatures help prove the authenticity of these files and ensure that it's easy to track changes that might cause problems on a system. When you are having problems that cannot easily be explained, such as a system becoming unstable after an application is installed, it's a good idea to verify that critical system files haven't been changed. You can do this by using the File Signature Verification utility.

The executable file for the File Signature Verification utility is Sigverif.exe. You can start and work with the File Signature Verification utility by completing the following steps:

1. Enter **sigverif** in the Everywhere Search box, and then press Enter. This starts the File Signature Verification utility, as shown in Figure 2-6.

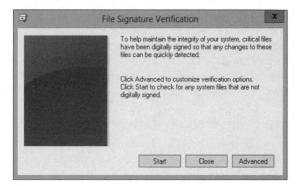

FIGURE 2-6 Use the File Signature Verification utility to help verify system files.

2. By default, the File Signature Verification utility displays a list of system files that aren't digitally signed and writes verification results to %SystemRoot% \System32\Sigverif.txt. Before you verify file signatures, you might want to specify logging options. If so, tap or click Advanced. As Figure 2-7 shows, the verification results are saved to a log file, and by default, any results you generate will overwrite any results that you previously generated. Results are saved to a log file named Sigverif.txt. To help you track changes in files, you might want to append results rather than overwrite. If you append rather than overwrite, you can more easily identify changes. When you are finished working with the logging options, tap or click OK to return to the main window.

FIGURE 2-7 Modify the default logging options as necessary.

3. Tap or click Start to run the File Signature Verification utility. In the results, notice the list of files displayed in the File Signature Verification utility report. These files don't have digital signatures and could have been maliciously replaced by other programs of the same name. Tap or click Close to return to the main window. If you suspect a problem, review event logs and other error reports to check if any of these files show up in the error reports.

4. If you want to review the verification log, tap or click Advanced, and then tap or click View Log. You also can use Notepad to open the verification log, which is located in %SystemRoot%\System32\Sigverif.txt by default. Check the log to find out if there are files that have been altered since they were installed. Files are listed by status, such as Signed and Not Signed. Note the modification date and version of the file. If a computer has been having problems since a certain date, and critical files were changed on this date, this could be the source of the problem. For example, perhaps a program was installed that overwrote a critical file with an older version.

Managing system configuration, startup, and boot

Whether you want to update system configuration files or troubleshoot startup problems, your tool of choice should be the System Configuration utility. System Configuration is an integrated tool for managing system configuration information. Using this utility, you can manage the following elements:

- Operating system startup options
- Startup applications
- Service-startup options

The following sections examine key tasks that you can perform with the System Configuration utility. The executable file for the System Configuration utility is Msconfig.exe. You can run the utility by typing **msconfig** in the Everywhere Search box and then pressing Enter.

> **NOTE** You'll also find the System Configuration utility on the Apps screen. It's under the Administrative Tools heading.

Understanding startup modes and troubleshooting system startup

You can use the System Configuration utility to select the startup mode for a computer. The following three startup modes are available:

- **Normal Startup**   Used for normal system operations. In this mode, the operating system loads all system configuration files and device drivers and runs all startup applications and enabled services.

- **Diagnostic Startup**   Used to troubleshoot system problems. In diagnostic mode, the system loads only basic device drivers and essential services. After you start the system in diagnostic mode, you can modify system settings to resolve configuration problems.

- **Selective Startup**   Used to pinpoint problem areas in the configuration. Here, you can use a modified boot configuration and selectively use system services and startup items. This can help you identify the settings that are causing system problems and correct them as necessary.

Normal is the default startup mode. If you are experiencing problems with a system and want to use a different startup mode, complete the following steps:

1. Open the System Configuration utility by typing **msconfig** in the Everywhere Search box and then pressing Enter, or by tapping or clicking the related option on the Apps screen.

2. On the General tab, shown in Figure 2-8, select either Diagnostic Startup or Selective Startup. If you choose Selective Startup, you can use the following options to specify the items that you want the system to use:

   ■ **Load System Services**   Tells the system to load Windows services on startup. If you select this option, use the settings on the Services tab to specify which services are started.

   ■ **Load Startup Items**   Tells the system to run applications designated for startup at boot time. If you select this option, you can enable and disable startup applications by using the options on the Startup tab.

   ■ **Use Original Boot Configuration**   Tells the system to process the original boot configuration on startup instead of one you've created by modifying the boot settings with the System Configuration utility.

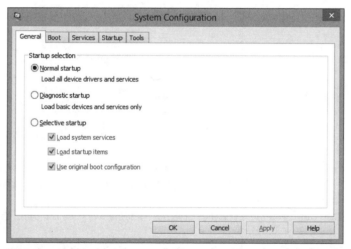

FIGURE 2-8 Use the General tab of the System Configuration utility to control system startup.

NOTE   If you make changes on the Boot, Services, or Startup tab, the Selective Startup option and related suboptions are automatically selected on the General tab.

3. When you are ready to continue, tap or click OK, and then reboot the system. If you have problems rebooting the system, restart the system in Safe mode and then repeat this procedure. Safe mode appears automatically as an option after a failed boot.

Changing boot options

Windows 8.1 uses the Windows Boot Manager and a boot application to start up the operating system. Windows 8.1 doesn't use Boot.ini or other boot files in a standard configuration. When troubleshooting, you can use the options on the Boot tab of the System Configuration utility to control the boot partition, boot method, and boot options used by the operating system.

As shown in Figure 2-9, when you start the System Configuration utility and tap or click the Boot tab, the operating systems that are bootable on the computer are listed. To specify that an operating system other than the current one should be used, simply tap or click the related operating system entry. When working with operating system entries, you can select the following options:

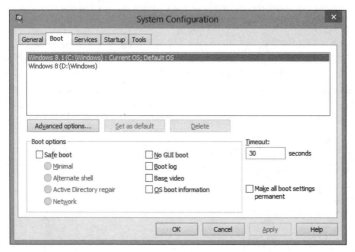

FIGURE 2-9 The Boot tab controls the boot partition, boot method, and boot options used by the operating system.

- **Set As Default**   Sets the currently selected boot partition as the default partition. The default partition is selected automatically if you don't choose an option before the timeout interval.

- **Timeout**   Sets the amount of time the computer waits before using the default boot partition.

- **Delete**   Deletes an operating system entry. The entry cannot be easily re-created, so delete an entry only if absolutely necessary.

NOTE On a computer with a single operating system, the Set As Default and Delete buttons are unavailable because there is no other operating system to switch to or from. Similarly, when you select the default operating system, you can't select Set As Default, and when you select the current operating system, you can't select Delete.

You can also set the following boot options:

- **Safe Boot** Start the computer in Safe mode with additional flags for Minimal, Network, and Alternate Shell minimal boots, as well as the Active Directory Repair state (DsRepair). After you successfully start a system in Safe mode, you can modify system settings to resolve configuration problems.
- **No GUI Boot** Starts the computer to the Windows prompt and doesn't load the graphical components of the operating system. Starting to the prompt is useful when you are having problems with the graphical components of Windows 8.1.
- **Boot Log** Turns on boot logging so that key startup events are written to a log.
- **Base Video** Forces the computer to use VGA display settings. Use this mode when you are trying to resolve display settings, such as when the display mode is set to a size that the monitor cannot display.
- **OS Boot Information** Starts the computer by using verbose output so that you can view the details of startup activities prior to the loading of Windows graphical components.

Any changes you make are stored as modified boot configuration data by the System Configuration utility. After you make changes and tap or click OK, you can restart the computer to apply the temporary changes. To go back to a normal startup after you've made and applied changes, you must select Normal Startup on the General tab and then tap or click OK. You must then reboot the system so that the normal settings are used.

If you tap or click the Advanced Options button on the Boot tab, you can set boot options for processors, maximum memory, PCI locking, and debugging by using the BOOT Advanced Options dialog box, shown in Figure 2-10. Use these options for troubleshooting. For example, if you suspect that a problem is related to multiple processors, you can specify 1 as the number of processors to use. If you suspect that a problem is due to memory beyond the first 4 gigabytes (GB), you can specify the maximum memory to use as 4,096 MB. After you are done troubleshooting, you should remove these options to restore normal operations.

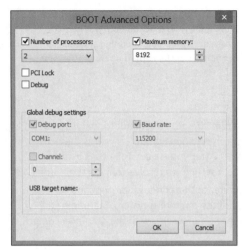

FIGURE 2-10 Set advanced boot options for troubleshooting.

On the Boot tab, to make any of the standard or advanced boot options you select permanent, select the Make All Boot Settings Permanent check box before tapping or clicking OK. In most cases, you won't want troubleshooting or debugging options to be permanent, so be sure to clear these options first.

Enabling and disabling startup applications for troubleshooting

If you suspect that an application loaded at startup is causing problems with the system, you can diagnose this easily. Disable programs from starting automatically, and then reboot the system. If the problem is no longer present, you might have pinpointed the problem and could then try to remedy it by identifying and disabling the automatic startup of the program or programs causing issues.

To disable startup applications temporarily, follow these steps:

1. Open the System Configuration utility by typing **msconfig** in the Everywhere Search box and then pressing Enter, or by tapping or clicking the related option on the Apps screen.

2. On the General tab, ensure that Selective Startup is selected and then clear the Load Startup Items check box.

3. Tap or click OK. You need to reboot the system to check the changes, so restart the computer. If the problem is no longer present, you've isolated the problem to the startup applications.

The Selective Startup check box is cleared automatically, so the next time that you start the computer, the startup applications will load. Next, you need to pinpoint the program causing the system problems by using Task Manager. You can open Task Manager by typing **taskmgr** in the Everywhere Search box or by pressing Ctrl+Alt +Delete. You also can press and hold or right-click in the lower-left corner of the Start screen or the desktop, and then tap or click Task Manager on the shortcut menu that is displayed.

The Startup tab in Task Manager lists each application configured for automatic startup. You can try disabling each application in turn and then restarting the computer to determine if that resolves the problem. To disable an application, tap or click it on the Startup tab, and then tap or click Disable. If you can't identify a single application as the cause of the problem, the trouble might be with a Windows component, service, or device driver.

CAUTION Disable only those programs that you've identified as potential problems, and do so only if you know how they are used by the operating system. If you don't know what a program does, don't disable it. Sometimes you can learn more about a startup program by following its command path and then examining its base installation folder.

Enabling and disabling services for troubleshooting

Just as applications that start automatically can cause problems on a system, so can services that start automatically. To help troubleshoot service problems, you can temporarily disable services by using the System Configuration utility, and then reboot to find out whether the problem goes away. If it does, you might have pinpointed the problem. You can then permanently disable the service or check with the service vendor to find out if an updated executable file is available for the service.

To temporarily disable services, follow these steps:

1. Open the System Configuration utility by typing **msconfig** in the Everywhere Search box and then pressing Enter, or by tapping or clicking the related option on the Apps screen.

2. Tap or click the Services tab. As shown in Figure 2-11, this tab displays a list of all services installed on the computer and includes the state of the service, such as Running or Stopped, and from where the service originated. To more easily find non-Microsoft services, select Hide All Microsoft Services.

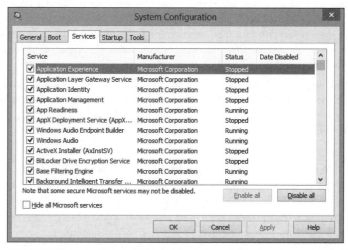

FIGURE 2-11 To troubleshoot problems with Windows services, use the options on the Services tab.

3. Clear the check box next to any service that you do not want to run at startup.

> **CAUTION** Disable only those services that you've identified as potential problems, and only if you know how they are used by the operating system. If you don't know what a service does, don't disable it. The Services tab of the System Configuration utility doesn't provide additional information about services. You can learn the specific purpose of a service by using the Services utility, which is available in Computer Management. In the Services utility, select the service to view its description on the Extended tab, or double-tap or double-click the service to read its description on the General tab of the related properties dialog box.

4. Tap or click OK. You need to reboot the system to check the changes, so if you are prompted to restart the system, tap or click Yes. Otherwise, reboot the system manually.

5. Repeat this procedure as necessary to pinpoint the service causing the system problems. If you can't identify a service as the cause of the problem, the trouble might be caused by a Windows component, a startup application, or a device driver.

Managing system properties

You use the System Properties dialog box to manage system properties. The following sections examine key areas of the operating system that can be configured by using the System Properties dialog box.

The Computer Name tab

The computer's network identification can be displayed and modified on the Computer Name tab of the System Properties dialog box, shown in Figure 2-12. As the figure shows, the Computer Name tab displays the full computer name of the system and the domain or group membership. The full computer name is essentially the Domain Name System (DNS) name of the computer, which also identifies the computer's place within an Active Directory hierarchy.

A quick way to open the System Properties dialog box is to press and hold or right-click the hidden button in the lower-left corner of Start or the desktop, tap or click System, and then tap or click the Change Settings link. Alternatively, you can enter **sysdm.cpl** and then press Enter.

The options on the Computer Name tab enable you to do the following:

- **Join a computer to a domain** Tap or click Network ID to start the Join A Domain Or Workgroup Wizard, which guides you through modifying network access information for the computer.

- **Change a computer's name** Tap or click Change to change the computer's name and the domain or group associated with the computer.

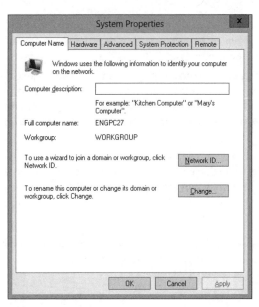

FIGURE 2-12 Use the Computer Name tab to display and configure system identification.

REAL WORLD Before you try to join a computer to a domain, be sure that the IP address configuration, including the DNS settings, are correct for the network to which the computer is connected. For client computers to use the DNS, the computer must have an appropriate computer name and a properly configured primary DNS suffix. Rather than using names that are cute or arbitrary, you should decide on a naming scheme that is meaningful to both users and administrators. In DNS, the computer's name serves as its host name, and the primary DNS suffix determines the domain to which it is assigned for name resolution purposes. Any unqualified host names that are used on a computer are resolved by using the primary DNS suffix. For example, if you are logged on to a computer with a primary DNS suffix of tech.cpandl.com and you ping CorpSvr28 from a command prompt, the computer directs the query to corpsvr28.tech.cpandl.com.

By default, the primary DNS suffix is the domain in which the computer is a member. You can change a computer's primary DNS suffix if necessary. For example, if a computer's primary DNS suffix is seattle.tech.cpandl.com, you might want the computer to use the primary DNS suffix of cpandl.com to simplify name resolution in this large DNS hierarchy. To change a computer's primary DNS suffix, tap or click Change on the Computer Name tab, and then tap or click More. Enter the primary DNS suffix you want to use in the text box provided, and then close all open dialog boxes by tapping or clicking OK three times.

The Hardware tab

The Hardware tab in the System Properties dialog box provides access to Device Manager and Device Installation Settings.

Open the System Properties dialog box by pressing and holding or right-clicking the hidden button in the lower-left corner of the Start screen or the desktop, tapping or clicking System, and then tapping or clicking the Change Settings link. The main options you might want to work with on the Hardware tab are the device installation settings.

When you connect a new device, Windows 8.1 checks for drivers automatically by using Windows Update. If you don't want a computer to check for drivers automatically, tap or click Device Installation Settings, and then select either Yes, Do This Automatically or No, Let Me Choose What To Do, and then tap or click Save Changes.

NOTE The Device Manager button opens Device Manager in a Microsoft Management Console (MMC). Device Manager, also included in the Computer Management console as an MMC snap-in, is discussed in Chapter 8.

The Advanced tab: performance options

The Advanced tab in the System Properties dialog box provides access to controls for many of the key features of the Windows operating system, including application performance, virtual memory usage, user profiles, environment variables, and startup and recovery.

Performance options are a subset of the advanced configuration settings, which are configured by using the Performance Options dialog box. One way to access this dialog box is by completing the following steps:

1. In Control Panel, tap or click System And Security, and then tap or click System.
2. In the System console, tap or click Advanced System Settings in the left pane.
3. To display the Performance Options dialog box, tap or click Settings in the Performance panel.

To open the Performance Options dialog box directly, in the Everywhere Search box, enter **SystemPropertiesPerformance** in the Everywhere Search box, and then press Enter.

Setting Windows performance

The Windows 8.1 interface has many graphics enhancements that can affect the overall performance, including visual effects for menus, toolbars, windows, and the taskbar. By using the Performance Options dialog box, you can fine-tune the way these graphics enhancements are used.

The Visual Effects tab is selected by default in the Performance Options dialog box, and you have the following options for controlling visual effects:

- **Let Windows Choose What's Best For My Computer** Enables the operating system to choose the performance options based on the hardware configuration. For a newer computer, the effect of selecting this option will probably be identical to using the Adjust For Best Appearance option. The key distinction, however, is that this option is chosen by Windows based on the available hardware and its performance capabilities.

- **Adjust For Best Appearance** When you optimize Windows for best appearance, you enable all visual effects for all graphical interfaces. Menus and the taskbar use transitions and shadows. Screen fonts have smooth edges. List boxes have smooth scrolling. Folders use web views, and more.

- **Adjust For Best Performance** When you optimize Windows for best performance, you turn off the resource-intensive visual effects, such as slide transitions and smooth edges for fonts, while maintaining a basic set of visual effects.

- **Custom** You can customize the visual effects by selecting or clearing the visual effects options in the Performance Options dialog box. If you clear all options, Windows does not use visual effects.

When you have finished changing visual effects, tap or click Apply. Tap or click OK twice to close the open dialog boxes.

Setting application performance

Application performance is related to processor-scheduling caching options that you set for the Windows 8.1 system. Processor scheduling determines the responsiveness of applications that are running interactively (as opposed to background applications that might be running on the system as services). You control application performance by using the options on the Advanced tab of the Performance Options dialog box. Type **SystemPropertiesPerformance** in the Everywhere Search box and then press Enter to open this dialog box.

The Processor Scheduling panel on the Advanced tab of the Performance Options dialog box gives you the following options:

- **Programs** To give the active application the best response time and the greatest share of available resources, select Programs. Generally, you'll want to use this option for all Windows 8.1 workstations.

- **Background Services** To give background applications a better response time than the active application, select Background Services. Generally, you'll want to use this option for Windows 8.1 computers running as servers (meaning that they have server-like roles and are not being used as Windows 8.1 workstations). For example, a Windows 8.1 computer might be the print server for a department.

If you change the performance settings, tap or click Apply.

Configuring virtual memory

Virtual memory enables you to use disk space to extend the amount of available RAM on a system by writing RAM to disks through a process called *paging*. With paging, a set amount of RAM, such as 4,096 MB, is written to the disk as a paging file, where it can be accessed from the disk when needed in place of physical RAM.

An initial paging file is created automatically for the drive containing the operating system. By default, other drives don't have paging files, so you must create these paging files if you want them. When you create a paging file, you set an initial size and a maximum size. A paging file is written to the volume as a file named Pagefile.sys.

> **REAL WORLD** Typically, Windows 8.1 allocates virtual memory in an amount at least as large as the total physical memory installed on the computer, to help ensure that paging files don't become fragmented, which can result in poor system performance. If you want to manually manage virtual memory, you can reduce fragmentation by setting an initial page file size that is at least as large as the total physical memory. For computers with 4 GB or less of RAM, you should set the maximum size to at least twice the total physical memory. For computers with more than 4 GB of RAM, you should set the maximum size to at least 1.5 times the total physical memory (or the size recommended by the hardware manufacturer). This can help ensure that the paging file is consistent and can be written to contiguous file blocks (if possible, given the amount of space on the volume).

You can manually configure virtual memory by completing the following steps:

1. Open the Performance Options dialog box. One way to do this is to enter **SystemPropertiesPerformance** in the Everywhere Search box, and then press Enter.

2. On the Advanced tab, tap or click Change to display the Virtual Memory dialog box, shown in Figure 2-13. The following information is provided:

   - **Drive [Volume Label]** and **Paging File Size (MB)**   Shows how virtual memory is currently configured on the system. Each volume is listed with its associated paging file (if any). The paging file range shows the initial and maximum size values set for the paging file, if applicable.

   - **Total Paging File Size For All Drives**   Provides a recommended size for virtual RAM on the system and tells you the amount currently allocated. If this is the first time you're configuring virtual RAM, note that the recommended amount has already been given to the system drive (in most instances) and that this is indicated by the selection of the System Managed Size option.

3. By default, Windows 8.1 manages the paging file size for all drives. If you want to manually configure virtual memory, clear the Automatically Manage Paging File Size For All Drives check box.

4. In the Drive list box, select the volume with which you want to work.

FIGURE 2-13 Virtual memory extends the amount of physical memory (RAM) on a system.

5. Select Custom Size, and then enter an initial size and a maximum size.

6. Tap or click Set to save the changes.

7. Repeat steps 4 through 6 for each volume you want to configure.

8. Tap or click OK, and if prompted to overwrite an existing Pagefile.sys file, tap or click Yes.

9. If you updated the settings for a paging file that is currently in use, you'll get a prompt explaining that you need to restart the system for the changes to take effect. Tap or click OK.

10. Tap or click OK twice to close the open dialog boxes. When you close the System utility, you'll get a prompt stating that the changes will not be applied until you restart your computer.

You can have Windows 8.1 automatically manage virtual memory by following these steps:

1. On the Advanced tab of the Performance Options dialog box, tap or click Change to display the Virtual Memory dialog box.

2. Select the Automatically Manage Paging File Size For All Drives check box.

3. Tap or click OK two times to close the open dialog boxes.

TIP Clearing the page file on shutdown is recommended as a security best practice. You can clear the page file on shutdown by enabling the Shutdown: Clear Virtual Memory Pagefile option. You'll find this Computer Configuration setting under Security Settings\Local Policies\Security Options.

Configuring Data Execution Prevention

Data Execution Prevention (DEP) is a memory protection technology. DEP tells the computer's processor to mark all memory locations in an application as nonexecutable unless the location explicitly contains executable code. If code is executed from a memory page marked as nonexecutable, the processor can raise an exception and prevent the code from executing. This prevents malicious code, such as a virus, from inserting itself into most areas of memory because only specific areas of memory are marked as having executable code.

NOTE The 32-bit versions of Windows support DEP as implemented by Advanced Micro Devices (AMD) processors that provide the No Execute (NX) page-protection processor feature. Such processors support the related instructions and must be running in Physical Address Extension (PAE) mode to support large memory configurations. The 64-bit versions of Windows also support the NX processor feature but do not need to use PAE to support large memory configurations.

To be compatible with DEP, applications must be able to explicitly mark memory with the Execute permission. Applications that cannot do this will not be compatible with the NX processor feature. If you are experiencing memory-related problems running applications, you should determine which applications are having problems and configure them as exceptions rather than completely disabling execution protection. In this way, you still get the benefits of memory protection and can selectively disable memory protection for programs that aren't running properly with the NX processor feature.

Execution protection is applied to both user-mode and kernel-mode programs. A user-mode execution protection exception results in a STATUS_ACCESS_VIOLATION exception. In most processes, this exception will be an unhandled exception and will result in the termination of the process. This is the behavior you want because most programs violating these rules, such as a virus or worm, will be malicious in nature.

Execution protection for kernel-mode device drivers, unlike protection for applications, cannot be selectively disabled or enabled. Furthermore, on compliant 32-bit systems, execution protection is applied by default to the memory stack. On compliant 64-bit systems, execution protection is applied by default to the memory stack, the paged pool, and the session pool. A kernel-mode execution protection access violation for a device driver results in an ATTEMPTED_EXECUTE_OF_NOEXECUTE_MEMORY exception.

You can determine whether a computer supports DEP by using the System utility. If a computer supports DEP, you can also configure it by completing the following steps:

1. Open the Performance Options dialog box. One way to do this is to enter **SystemPropertiesPerformance** in the Everywhere Search box, and then press Enter.

2. The text at the bottom of the Data Execution Prevention tab specifies whether the computer supports execution protection.

3. If a computer supports execution protection and is configured appropriately, you can configure DEP by using the following options:

- **Turn On DEP For Essential Windows Programs And Services Only**   Enables DEP only for operating system services, programs, and components. This is the default setting and is recommended for computers that support execution protection and are configured appropriately.

- **Turn On DEP For All Programs Except Those I Select**   Configures DEP and allows for exceptions. Select this option, and then tap or click Add to specify programs that should run without execution protection. In this way, execution protection will work for all programs except those you have listed.

4. Tap or click OK.

The Advanced tab: environment variables

System and user environment variables are configured by means of the Environment Variables dialog box, as shown in Figure 2-14. One way to access this dialog box is by completing the following steps:

1. In Control Panel, tap or click System And Security, and then tap or click System.

2. In the System console, tap or click Advanced System Settings in the left pane.

3. On the Advanced tab in the System Properties dialog box, tap or click Environment Variables.

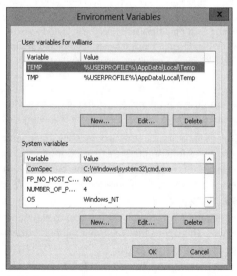

FIGURE 2-14 The Environment Variables dialog box lets you configure system and user environment variables.

Creating an environment variable

When you create or modify system environment variables, the changes take effect when you restart the computer. When you create or modify user environment variables, the changes take effect the next time the user logs on to the system.

You can create an environment variable by completing the following steps:

1. Open the Environment Variables dialog box, as discussed previously.

2. Tap or click New under User Variables or under System Variables, whichever is appropriate. This opens the New User Variable dialog box or the New System Variable dialog box, respectively.

3. In the Variable Name text box, enter the variable name. In the Variable Value text box, enter the variable value. Tap or click OK.

REAL WORLD The command path for executable files is managed through the PATH variable. You can edit this variable to update the command path, as discussed in the section "Managing the command path" in Chapter 7, "Installing and maintaining applications."

MORE INFO User profiles contain global user settings and configuration information. They are created the first time that a user logs on to a local computer or domain and are different for local and domain accounts. A user's profile maintains the desktop environment so that it is the same each time the user logs on. You'll find an extensive discussion on user profiles in Chapter 10, "Managing existing user and group accounts," in *Windows Server 2012 R2 Pocket Consultant: Essentials & Configuration* (Microsoft Press, 2013).

You can access Group Policy and use a preference item to create an environment variable on computers throughout a domain by completing the following steps:

1. Open a Group Policy Object for editing in the Group Policy Management Editor. To configure preferences for computers, expand Computer Configuration\Preferences\Windows Settings, and then select Environment. To configure preferences for users, expand User Configuration\Preferences\Windows Settings, and then select Environment.

2. Press and hold or right-click the Environment node, point to New, and then select Environment Variable. This opens the New Environment Properties dialog box.

3. From the Action list, select Create. Next, select User Variable to create a user variable or System Variable to create a system variable.

4. In the Name text box, enter the variable name. In the Value text box, enter the variable value.

5. Use the options on the Common tab to control how the preference is applied. In most cases, you'll want to create the new variable only once. If so, select Apply Once And Do Not Reapply.

6. Tap or click OK. The next time policy is refreshed, the preference item will be applied as appropriate for the Group Policy object in which you defined the preference item.

Editing an environment variable

You can edit an environment variable by completing the following steps:

1. Open the Environment Variables dialog box, as discussed previously.

2. Select the variable in the User Variables or System Variables list box.

3. Tap or click Edit under User Variables or under System Variables, whichever is appropriate. The Edit User Variable dialog box or the Edit System Variable dialog box opens.

4. Enter a new value in the Variable Value text box, and then tap or click OK.

You can access Group Policy and use a preference item to update an environment variable on computers throughout a domain by completing the following steps:

1. Open a Group Policy Object for editing in the Group Policy Management Editor. To edit preferences for computers, expand Computer Configuration \Preferences\Windows Settings, and then select Environment. To edit preferences for users, expand User Configuration\Preferences\Windows Settings, and then select Environment.

2. Press and hold or right-click the Environment node, point to New, and then select Environment Variable. This opens the New Environment Properties dialog box.

3. From the Action list, select Update to update the variable, or select Replace to delete and then re-create the variable. Next, select User Variable to create a user variable or System Variable to create a system variable.

4. In the Name text box, enter the name of the variable to update. In the Value text box, enter the variable value.

5. Use the options on the Common tab to control how the preference is applied. In most cases, you'll want to create the new variable only once. If so, select Apply Once And Do Not Reapply.

6. Tap or click OK. The next time policy is refreshed, the preference item will be applied as appropriate for the Group Policy Object in which you defined the preference item.

Deleting an environment variable

When you are working with the Environment Variables dialog box, you can delete an environment variable by selecting it and tapping or clicking Delete. To delete an environment variable on computers throughout a domain by using Group Policy, complete the following steps:

1. Open a Group Policy Object for editing in the Group Policy Management Editor. To configure preferences for computers, expand Computer Configuration\Preferences\Windows Settings, and then select Environment. To configure preferences for users, expand User Configuration\Preferences\Windows Settings, and then select Environment.

2. Do one of the following:

   ■ If a preference item already exists for the variable, double-tap or double-click the variable name to open the related Properties dialog box. Select Delete in the Action list. On the Common tab, set the appropriate options, such as Apply Once And Do Not Reapply, and then tap or click OK.

   ■ If a preference item doesn't already exist for a variable that you want to remove from computers, you need to create a preference item by using the techniques discussed earlier in this chapter under "Creating an environment variable." Be sure to select Delete in the Action list and select the appropriate options on the Common tab.

The Advanced tab: startup and recovery options

System startup and recovery properties are configured by means of the Startup And Recovery dialog box, shown in Figure 2-15. One way to access this dialog box is by completing the following steps:

1. In Control Panel, tap or click System And Security, and then tap or click System.

2. In the System console, tap or click Change Settings, or tap or click Advanced System Settings in the left pane.

3. To display the Startup And Recovery dialog box, tap or click the Advanced tab in the System Properties dialog box, and then tap or click Settings in the Startup And Recovery panel.

NOTE If you enter **SystemPropertiesAdvanced** in the Everywhere Search box and then press Enter, you will open the System Properties dialog box to the Advanced tab and can then click Settings in the Startup And Recovery panel.

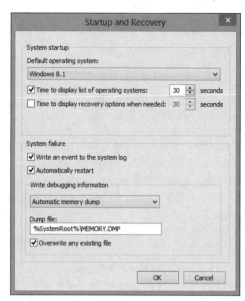

FIGURE 2-15 The Startup And Recovery dialog box lets you configure system startup and recovery procedures.

Setting startup options

The System Startup area of the Startup And Recovery dialog box controls system startup. In a computer with multiple bootable operating systems, to set the default operating system, select one of the operating systems listed under Default Operating System. The startup options change the configuration settings used by the Windows Boot Manager.

At startup of a computer with multiple bootable operating systems, Windows 8.1 displays the startup configuration menu for 30 seconds by default. You can change this by taking either of the following actions:

- Start up immediately to the default operating system by clearing the Time To Display List Of Operating Systems check box.

- Display the available options for a specific amount of time by ensuring that the Time To Display List Of Operating Systems check box is selected, and then setting a time delay in seconds.

Generally, on most systems, you'll want to use a value of 3 to 5 seconds. This period is long enough for a user to make a selection, yet short enough to expedite the system startup process.

When the system is in a recovery mode and booting, a list of recovery options might be displayed. As with the standard startup options, you can configure recovery startup options in one of two ways. You can set the computer to boot immediately using the default recovery option by clearing the Time To Display Recovery

Options When Needed check box, or you can display the available options for a specific amount of time by selecting the Time To Display Recovery Options When Needed check box, and then setting a time delay in seconds.

Setting recovery options

The System Failure and Write Debugging Information areas of the Startup And Recovery dialog box control system recovery. Recovery options enable administrators to control precisely what happens when the system encounters a fatal system error (also known as a Stop error). The available options for the System Failure area are as follows:

- **Write An Event To The System Log**   Select this option to log the error in the system log, which allows administrators to review the error later by using Event Viewer.

- **Automatically Restart**   Select this option to have the system attempt to reboot when a fatal system error occurs.

> *NOTE* Configuring automatic reboots isn't always a good approach. Sometimes you might want the system to halt rather than reboot to ensure that the system gets proper attention. Otherwise, you would know that the system rebooted only when you viewed the system logs or if you happened to be in front of the system's monitor when it rebooted.

The Write Debugging Information list enables you to choose the type of debugging information that you want to write to a dump file. The dump file can in turn be used to diagnose system failures. The options are as follows:

- **None**   Use this option if you don't want to write debugging information.
- **Small Memory Dump**   Use this option to dump the physical memory segment in which the error occurred. This dump is 256 kilobytes (KB) in size.
- **Kernel Memory Dump**   Use this option to dump the physical memory area being used by the Windows kernel. The dump file size depends on the size of the Windows kernel.
- **Complete Memory Dump**   Use this option to dump all physical memory. The dump file size depends on the amount of physical memory being used, up to a maximum file size equal to the total physical RAM on the server.
- **Automatic Memory Dump**   Use this option to let Windows determine which type of memory dump is best and create the dump file accordingly.

If you elect to write a dump file, you must also specify a location for it. The default dump files are %SystemRoot%\Minidump for small memory dumps and %SystemRoot%\Memory.dmp for all other memory dumps. You'll also usually want to select Overwrite Any Existing File to ensure that any existing dump files are overwritten if a new Stop error occurs.

BEST PRACTICES The dump file can be created only if the system is properly configured. The system drive must have a sufficiently large memory-paging file (as set for virtual memory on the Advanced tab), and the drive where the dump file is written must also have sufficient free space. With a kernel-only dump, you must have 35 to 50 percent of the amount of RAM available for the dump file. For example, one of my systems has 16 GB of RAM, so about 6–8 GB of free space must be available to correctly create a kernel-only dump of debugging information.

The System Protection tab

The System Protection tab in the System Properties dialog box, shown in Figure 2-16, provides options for managing the configuration of System Restore. Access this tab by completing the following steps:

1. In Control Panel, tap or click System And Security, and then tap or click System.
2. In the System console, tap or click Change Settings, or tap or click Advanced System Settings in the left pane.
3. In the System Properties dialog box, tap or click the System Protection tab.

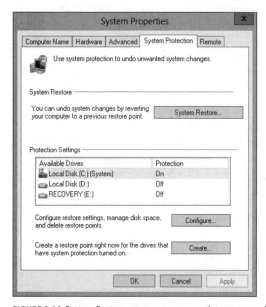

FIGURE 2-16 System Restore manages restore points on a per-drive basis.

You also can access the System Protection tab in the System Properties dialog box by typing **SystemPropertiesProtection** in the Everywhere Search box and then pressing Enter.

Unlike in Windows 7, System Restore no longer includes Previous Versions as a subcomponent. With Windows 8.1, you create previous versions of personal files by using File History backups. The sections that follow discuss techniques for working with and configuring System Restore. Chapter 10 discusses using restore points to recover a computer and file history backups.

REAL WORLD File servers running Windows Server 2012 have a Previous Versions feature. Previous versions come from shadow copies and are created for folders that are shared on the network. In File Explorer, the Properties dialog box for a shared folder that has been mapped as a network drive will have a Previous Versions tab. Use the options on this tab to restore previous versions of files in a folder shared by a file server.

Understanding system protection

With System Restore enabled, a computer creates periodic snapshots of the system configuration. These snapshots are called *restore points*. System settings tracked include Windows settings and lists of programs that have been installed. If the computer has problems starting or isn't working properly because of a system configuration change, you can use a restore point to restore the system configuration to the point at which the snapshot was made. For example, suppose that your system is working fine, and then you install a new service pack release for Office. Afterward, the computer generates errors and Office applications won't run. You try to uninstall the update, but that doesn't work, so you decide to run System Restore. By using System Restore, you can restore the system by using a snapshot taken prior to the update.

NOTE System Restore can provide several different types of restore points. One type, System Checkpoint, is scheduled by the operating system and occurs at regular intervals. Another type of snapshot, Installation Restore Point, is created automatically based on events that are triggered by the operating system when you install applications. Other snapshots, known as Manual Restore Points, are created by users. You should recommend that users create Manual Restore Points prior to performing an operation that might cause problems on the system.

System Restore manages restore points on a per-drive basis. Each drive with critical applications and system files should be monitored for configuration changes. By default, System Restore is enabled only for the system drive. You can modify the System Restore configuration by turning on monitoring of other drives. If a drive isn't configured for System Restore monitoring, configuration changes are not tracked, and the disk cannot be recovered if problems occur.

NOTE Protection points are created daily for all drives being monitored by System Restore. Previous versions are not saved as part of a volume's automatically or manually created protection points. Use File History backups instead.

Configuring System Restore

You control how System Restore works by using the System Protection tab of the System Properties dialog box. The system process responsible for monitoring configuration and application changes is the System Restore Service. This service is configured for automatic startup and runs under the LocalSystem account. System Restore won't work properly if this service isn't running or configured appropriately.

System Restore saves system checkpoint information for all monitored drives and requires at least 300 MB of disk space on the system volume to save restore points. System Restore reserves additional space for restore points as necessary, up to 100 percent of the total disk capacity, but this additional space is always available for user and application storage. System Restore frees up additional space for you as necessary. If System Restore runs out of available space, the operating system over-writes previously created restore points.

You can configure the amount of disk space used by System Restore. By default, System Restore reserves at least 1 percent of the total disk capacity for saving restore points. For example, on a hard disk with a total capacity of 930 GB, System Restore would reserve 9.3 GB of disk space by default.

Complete the following steps to configure System Restore for each drive:

1. In Control Panel, tap or click System And Security, and then tap or click System.

2. In the System console, tap or click System Protection in the left pane.

3. To configure System Restore for a volume, select the volume in the Protection Settings list, and then tap or click Configure. This displays the System Protection For dialog box, shown in Figure 2-17.

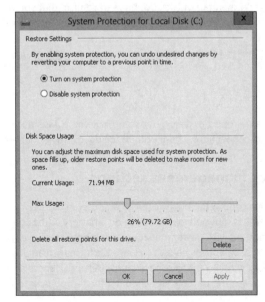

FIGURE 2-17 Configure System Restore on a per-drive basis.

4. Choose one of the following options:

- **Turn On System Protection** Choose this option to keep copies of system settings. This option is recommended for the system volume to ensure that you can restore the computer.

- **Disable System Protection** Choose this option to turn off System Restore. This option is not recommended for the system volume because you will not be able to restore the computer after configuration changes.

5. If you've enabled system protection, you can use the Disk Space Usage slider to adjust the maximum disk space that System Restore can use. If the maximum size is reached, System Restore deletes older restore points to make room for new ones.

6. Tap or click OK. (If you've turned off system protection, Windows removes all saved system settings, and you must confirm that you want to do this by tapping or clicking Yes. When Windows finishes removing all the restore point data, tap or click Close.)

If you are using System Restore to protect a computer and are absolutely certain that the system is in a stable state, you can remove all saved system settings to recover space on disks or to ensure that users don't apply a restore point that you don't want them to use. To do this, follow these steps:

1. In Control Panel, tap or click System And Security, and then tap or click System.

2. In the System console, tap or click System Protection in the left pane.

3. In the Protection Settings list, select the volume with which you want to work, and then tap or click Configure.

4. Tap or click Delete, and then tap or click Continue to confirm that you really want to delete all saved system settings. Repeat steps 3 and 4 for other volumes, as appropriate.

5. When Windows finishes removing all the restore point data, tap or click Close.

The Remote tab

The Remote tab in the System Properties dialog box controls Remote Assistance invitations and Remote Desktop connections. These options are discussed in Chapter 6.

Configuring power management settings

Power management settings control the behavior of a computer in different power use situations, such as when it is plugged in or running on a battery. Although all computers should be configured with power management settings to save energy, power management settings on laptops help to balance performance against energy usage. In some cases, you'll want to reduce laptop responsiveness and overall performance to increase the battery life, enabling the laptop user to run the laptop on battery for longer periods of time. In other cases, you might want to ensure moderate performance and a moderate battery life, or you might want to ensure maximum performance regardless of how this affects battery life.

The core aspects of power management are managed by using power plans, which are collections of power management settings that control power usage and consumption. A computer can have multiple power plans, but only one can be active at a time. In addition to power plans, most computers have preset behaviors for when the power button is pressed and for when the sleep button is pressed, and laptops have a default action for when you close the laptop's lid. Typically, closing a laptop's lid puts it into sleep mode, pressing and holding the power button shuts down a computer, and pressing the sleep button puts a computer into sleep mode. Through system-wide settings for power options, you can customize the power button and password-protection-on-wakeup behavior to meet the needs of individual users or groups of users.

Managing power options from the command line

Windows 8.1 includes the Power Configuration (Powercfg.exe) utility for managing power options from the command line. You can view a list of parameters for this utility by typing **powercfg /?** at a command prompt. The parameters you'll work with most often include the following:

- **-a** Lists the available sleep states on the computer and the reasons why a particular sleep state is not supported.
- **-d [guid]** Deletes the power plan specified by the GUID.
- **-devicequery all_devices_verbose** Lists detailed power support information for all devices on the computer. Be sure to redirect the output to a file, because this list is very long and detailed.
- **-energy** Checks the system for common configuration, device, and battery problems and then generates an HTML report in the current working directory.
- **-h** Switches the hibernate feature on or off.
- **-l** Lists the power plans configured on a computer by name and GUID.
- **-q [guid]** Lists the contents of the power plan specified by the GUID. If you don't provide a GUID, the contents of the active power plan are listed.
- **-requests** Displays all power requests made by device drivers. If there are pending requests for the display, these requests would prevent the computer from automatically powering off the displays. If there are pending requests for any device including the display, these requests would prevent the computer from automatically entering a low-power sleep state.
- **-s [guid]** Makes the power plan specified by the GUID the active power plan.
- **-x [setting] [value]** Sets the specified value for the specified setting in the active power plan.

NOTE By default, Windows 8.1 computers use hybrid sleep instead of hibernate. Hibernate should not be configured without first determining compatibility. Note also that the Power Configuration utility (Powercfg) accepts either a hyphen (-) or a slash (/) for commands. I prefer to use a hyphen because of its location on the keyboard.

The following is a sample listing returned by typing **powercfg -l** at a command prompt.

```
Existing Power Schemes (* Active)
-----------------------------------
Power Scheme GUID: 381b4222-f694-41f0-9685-ff5bb260df2e (Balanced)
Power Scheme GUID: 8c5e7fda-e8bf-4a96-9a85-a6e23a8c635c (High performance)
Power Scheme GUID: a1841308-3541-4fab-bc81-f71556f20b4a (Power saver)
Power Scheme GUID: c1d97820-3148-42a9-a587-75d618a9bb2b (Graphics Dept) *
```

The active plan is marked with an asterisk. From this listing, you can determine that this computer has four power plans and the active power plan is the Graphics Dept plan.

If you want to configure power plans or modify power settings by using Powercfg, you need to do so by using an elevated command prompt. When a parameter requires a GUID, the easiest way to obtain this value is to enter **powercfg -l** at an elevated command prompt, and then copy the value for the appropriate power plan. For example, if you want to make the Balanced plan the default plan for the computer in the previous example, you would enter the following at an elevated command prompt.

```
powercfg -s 381b4222-f694-41f0-9685-ff5bb260df2e
```

You determine the power modes that a computer supports by typing **powercfg -a** at a command prompt. Powercfg will list exactly what modes are and aren't supported, such as the following.

```
The following sleep states are available on this system:
Standby (S1 S3)
Hibernate
Hybrid Sleep
The following sleep states are not available on this system:
Standby (S2)
The system firmware does not support this standby state.
```

REAL WORLD Windows 8.1 supports a connected-standby mode in which the display is turned off but the device is powered on. In this power state, the device is technically on; however, the Desktop Activity Monitor suppresses desktop app execution, making the mode similar to the S3 sleep state. The Desktop Activity Monitor does this by suspending or throttling desktop software processes, which in turn minimizes resource usage and extends battery life. Software that doesn't support connected standby might cause the device to wake.

If a computer has problems entering sleep or hibernate mode, you can use powercfg -a to possibly determine what is causing the problem. If the firmware doesn't support a particular mode, you might in some (limited) cases be able to update the firmware to gain support for a particular mode. If a device that doesn't support a particular mode is causing a problem, you might be able to remove the device and replace it with a compliant device.

Any time you want to evaluate a computer's power configuration and device compatibility, you can generate a Power Efficiency Diagnostics report by typing **powercfg -energy** at a command prompt. When you run powercfg -energy, the report is generated as an HTML document called Energy-Report.html. In the report, you'll find the results of power management compliance for devices. Any device that doesn't support power management appropriately will be listed, along with the error details. For example, if a USB device doesn't properly enter the Suspend state, you'll get the detailed information about the errors encountered and the device configuration. If a power management capability has been disabled because of a compatibility issue, you'll find this in the report, too. For example, if the PCI Express Active-State Power Management feature isn't supported on the hardware and the feature has therefore been disabled, you'll find this listed in the report. Warnings and additional information about devices and compatibility are also provided, including details on supported sleep states and processor power management capabilities.

> **REAL WORLD** For laptops, important information is provided on battery charging and battery life. If a battery is nearing or at the end of its useful life, you'll be able to tell this because the battery life is limited and the battery details will show that the battery isn't holding a charge as it should. You'll then know that you need to replace the laptop's battery.

To dig even deeper into power management issues, you can get comprehensive power support details for every device on the computer by entering the following command.

```
powercfg -devicequery all_devices_verbose > power.txt
```

Power.txt is the name of the file in the current working directory in which the power information will be saved.

When you've configured Windows PowerShell for remote access, you can easily execute Powercfg on multiple remote computers. To do this, enter the name of each remote computer to check on a separate line in a file called Computers.txt, and then save this file. Next, open an elevated administrator Windows PowerShell prompt and enter the following commands.

```
$comp = get-content c:\computers.txt
$s = new-pssession -computername $comp
invoke-command -session $s { powercfg.exe -energy }
```

Here, C:\Computers.txt is the path to the Computers.txt file. Update this path as appropriate for the location in which you saved the file. On each computer, an Energy-Report.html file will be created in the default directory for the user account used to access the computer. If you would rather not have to retrieve the HTML document from each computer, you can write the report to a share and base the report name on the computer name, as shown in the following example.

```
$comp = get-content c:\computers.txt
$s = new-pssession -computername $comp
invoke-command -session $s { powercfg.exe -energy -output
"\\fileserver46\data\$env:computername.html"}
```

Here, you write the report to the \\fileserver46\data share and name the file by using the value of the *ComputerName* environment variable. Note that when you work with Windows PowerShell and are referencing commands with executable files, you must specify the .exe file extension with the program name.

Working with power plans

On mobile computing devices, the notification area of the taskbar includes a Power icon. Tapping or clicking this icon shows the battery state and the power plan that you are using. Tapping or clicking either of the links provided in the notification status dialog box opens the Power Options page in Control Panel. Out of the box, most configurations of Windows 8.1 have three preferred power plans:

- **Balanced**   A power usage plan that balances energy consumption and system performance. The processor speeds up when more resources are used and slows down when less are needed. This is the default power plan. Use this plan for users who work with a wide variety of applications, including those that are moderately graphics-intensive, such as Microsoft PowerPoint, and those that are not graphics-intensive, such as Microsoft Word and Outlook.

- **High Performance**   A high-power usage plan that optimizes the computer for performance at a direct cost to battery life. This plan ensures that you always have enough power for using graphics-intensive programs or playing multimedia games. Use this plan when performance is essential and users work primarily with graphics-intensive applications or applications that perform complex arithmetic calculations. Note that you might have to tap or click Show Additional Plans to view this power plan.

- **Power Saver**   A low-power usage plan designed to reduce power consumption. This plan slows down the processor to maximize the battery life. Use this plan for users who work primarily with non-graphics-intensive applications, such as Word and Outlook.

Power plan settings are divided into two general categories: basic and advanced. Basic power settings control when a computer dims or turns off its display, as well as when the computer enters sleep mode. It's important to note that mobile computing devices have On Battery and Plugged In settings that can be configured independent of each other. For example, you might want a computer's display to dim after 2 minutes of inactivity when on battery or after 5 minutes of inactivity when plugged in.

Advanced power settings determine precisely whether and when power management components on a computer are shut down and how those components are configured for performance. The advanced power settings available depend on the computer's configuration and include the following:

- **Battery\Critical Battery Action**   Specifies the action to take when the battery reaches a critical level. You can set this option to Sleep, Hibernate, or Shut Down.

- **Battery\Critical Battery Level**   Determines the percentage of battery remaining that initiates the critical battery action. Typically, the default value is 5 percent, meaning that the computer will enter critical power mode when there is 5 percent of battery power remaining. Although you can set any percentage, a critical level of 3 to 5 percent is often best.

- **Battery\Reserve Battery Level**   Determines the percentage of battery remaining that initiates reserve power mode. Typically, the default value is 7 percent, meaning that the computer will enter reserve power mode when 7 percent of battery power is remaining. Although you can set any percentage, a reserve level of 5 to 18 percent is often best.

- **Desktop Background Settings\Slide Show**   Determines whether the slide show feature for the desktop background is available or paused. The default setting is Available. If you set this option to Paused, background slide shows on the desktop will be disabled.

- **Display\Turn Off Display After**   Determines whether and when a computer's display is turned off to conserve power. Use a setting of Never to disable this feature. Use a specific value in minutes to specify how long the computer must be inactive before the display is turned off.

- **Display\Dim Display After**   Determines the length of time before the display dims when the computer is inactive. Use a specific value in minutes to determine how long the computer must be inactive before the display is dimmed.

- **Display\Dimmed Display Brightness**   Specifies the brightness level to use when the display is dimmed. Use a specific value as a percentage of maximum brightness.

- **Display\Enable Adaptive Brightness**   Monitors ambient light sensors to detect changes in ambient light and adjust the display brightness accordingly.

- **Hard Disk\Turn Off Hard Disk After**   Determines whether and when a computer's hard disk is turned off to conserve power. Use a setting of Never to disable turning off the hard disk. Use a specific value in minutes to determine how long the computer must be inactive before the hard disk is turned off. Windows 8.1 provides a combo box for setting numeric values. Tapping or clicking and holding the up or down arrow enables you to rapidly scroll through values. If you scroll down from 1, the next value is Never. You can also enter a value. If you enter a value of 0, this is interpreted as Never.

- **Multimedia Settings\When Playing Video**   Determines the power optimization mode used when playing video. If you set this option to Optimize Video Quality, the computer will use the best playback quality possible for video. If you set this option to Balanced, the computer will use a balanced approach, adjusting playback quality to some degree to save power. If you set this option to Optimize Power Savings, the computer will actively adjust the playback quality to save power.

- **Multimedia Settings\When Sharing Media**   Determines what the computer does when a device or another computer plays media from the computer. If you set this option to Allow The Computer To Enter Away Mode, the computer will not enter sleep mode when sharing media with other devices or computers. If you set this option to Allow The Computer To Sleep, the computer can enter sleep mode after an appropriate period of inactivity regardless of whether media is being shared with other computers or devices. If you set this option to Prevent Idling To Sleep, the computer will enter sleep mode when sharing media with other devices or computers only if a user puts the computer in sleep mode.

- **PCI Express\Link State Power Management**   Determines the power saving mode to use with PCI Express devices connected to the computer. You can set this option to Off, Moderate Power Savings, or Maximum Power Savings.

- **Power Buttons And Lid\Lid Closed Button Action**   Specifies the action to take when someone closes the lid on a mobile computer. You can set this option to Do Nothing, Sleep, Hibernate, or Shut Down.

- **Power Buttons And Lid\Power Button Action**   Specifies the action to take when someone pushes and holds the computer's power button. You can set this option to Do Nothing, Sleep, Hibernate, or Shut Down.

- **Power Buttons And Lid\Sleep Button Action**   Sets the default action for the sleep button. Use this setting to override the computer's default action. You can set this option to Do Nothing, Sleep, or Hibernate. You cannot, however, use an option that is not supported by the computer.

- **Processor Power Management\Maximum Processor State**   Sets a maximum or peak performance state for the computer's processor. To save power and reduce energy consumption, lower the permitted maximum performance state. But you lower the performance state at a direct cost to responsiveness and computational speed. Although reducing the maximum processing power to 50 percent or less can cause a significant reduction in performance and responsiveness, it can also provide a significant power savings.

- **Processor Power Management\Minimum Processor State**   Sets a minimum performance state for the computer's processor. To save power and reduce energy consumption, lower the permitted minimum performance state—but you lower the performance state at a direct cost to responsiveness and computational speed. For example, a value of 5 percent would lengthen the time required to respond to requests and process data while offering substantial power savings. A value of 50 percent helps to balance responsiveness and processing performance while offering a moderate power savings. A value of 100 percent would maximize responsiveness and processing performance while offering no power savings.

- **Processor Power Management\System Cooling Policy** Determines whether the operating system increases the fan speed before slowing the processor. If you set this option to Passive, this feature is limited, and the processor might run hotter than normal. If you set this option to Active, this feature is enabled to help cool the processor.

- *PlanName*\Require A Password On Wakeup Determines whether a password is required when a computer wakes from sleep. You can set this option to Yes or No. With domain computers, this option is set to Yes and can be controlled only through Group Policy.

- **Sleep\Allow Hybrid Sleep** Specifies whether the computer uses Windows 8.1 sleep mode rather than the sleep mode used in earlier versions of Windows. You can set this value to On or Off. Hybrid sleep mode puts the computer in a low-power consumption state until the user resumes using the computer. When running on battery, laptops and tablets continue to use battery power in the sleep state, but at a very low rate. If the battery runs low on power while the computer is in the sleep state, the current working environment is saved to the hard disk, and then the computer is shut down completely.

- **Sleep\Allow Wake Timers** Determines whether timed events should be allowed to wake the computer from a sleep state. If you set this option to Disable, timed events won't wake the computer. If you set this option to Enable, timed events can wake the computer.

- **Sleep\Hibernate After** Determines whether and when a computer hibernates to conserve power. When a computer goes into hibernation, a snapshot of the user workspace and the current operating environment is taken by writing the current memory to disk. When a user turns the computer back on, reading the memory from disk restores the user workspace and operating environment. In Windows 8.1, this setting isn't normally used because the standard configuration is to sleep after a period of inactivity. Use a setting of Never to disable this feature. Use a specific value in minutes to determine how long the computer must be inactive before the computer hibernates.

- **Sleep\Sleep After** Determines whether and when a computer enters a sleep state to conserve power. Use a setting of Never to disable this feature. Use a specific value in minutes to determine how long the computer must be inactive before the computer enters a sleep state.

- **USB Settings\USB Selective Suspend Setting** Determines whether the USB selective suspend feature is available. If you set this option to Disabled, selective suspend will not be used with USB devices. If you set this option to Enabled, selective suspend can be used with USB devices.
- **Wireless Adapter Settings\Power Saving Mode** Specifies the power saving mode to use with any wireless adapters connected to the computer. You can set this option to Maximum Performance, Low Power Saving, Medium Power Saving, or Maximum Power Saving.

As you can tell, the advanced power settings control every facet of power management. The differences in the advanced settings are what really set the power plans apart from each other. For example, whereas the High Performance plan ensures performance by allowing the computer's processor to always run at 100 percent power consumption, the Power Saver and the Balanced plans reduce energy consumption by configuring the processor to use a minimum power consumption rate of 5 percent and a maximum rate of 100 percent.

When configuring power plans, it's important to allow components to turn off after periods of inactivity. Turning off components separately enables a computer to progressively go into sleep mode. When a computer is fully in sleep mode, all power-manageable components are switched off so that the computer uses less power. When the computer is brought out of sleep mode, the components, such as the monitor and hard disks, are turned back on, restoring the user workspace. You should configure sleep mode so that when a laptop is running on batteries, it goes into power conservation mode when the user is away from the laptop for a relatively short period of time, such as 20 or 30 minutes.

Because a computer can have multiple power plans, each plan can be optimized for the way a laptop is used at a particular time. You can configure multiple power plans for different situations. At home or in the office, laptops might need different power management configurations than they do when users are giving presentations. In one case, you might want to configure the laptop to quickly conserve energy when running on batteries. In another case, you might want to ensure that the laptop never turns off its hard disk or wireless adapters.

Selecting and optimizing power plans

Although computers can have multiple power plans, only one plan can be active at a time. To select or optimize a power plan, follow these steps:

1. In Control Panel, tap or click System And Security, and then tap or click Power Options.

2. As shown in Figure 2-18, you can specify the power plan to use by selecting it in the plans list.

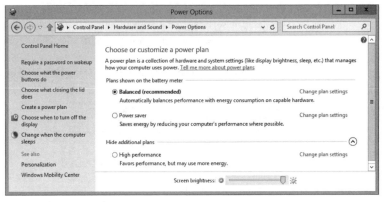

FIGURE 2-18 Choose a power plan.

3. Tap or click Change Plan Settings for the plan with which you want to work. This displays the Edit Plan Settings page, shown in Figure 2-19. Note that mobile computing devices have separate On Battery and Plugged In settings.

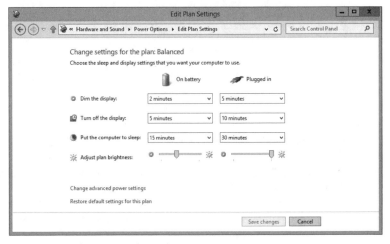

FIGURE 2-19 Configure power plan settings.

4. For a mobile computing device with a dimmable display, use the Dim The Display list to specify whether and when the computer's display is dimmed. Choose Never to disable this feature.

5. Use the Turn Off The Display list to specify whether or when the computer's display automatically turns off. Choose Never to disable this feature.

6. Use the Put The Computer To Sleep list to specify whether or when the computer automatically enters sleep mode. Choose Never to disable this feature.

7. If you want to configure advanced options, tap or click Change Advanced Power Settings. Use the settings in the Power Options dialog box, shown in Figure 2-20, to configure the advanced settings. Tap or click OK to save any changes you've made.

8. If you've made changes to Turn Off Display After or Sleep After, tap or click Apply to save these changes.

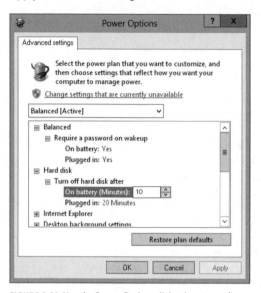

FIGURE 2-20 Use the Power Options dialog box to configure advanced power options.

In Group Policy, you can use a preference item to optimize power plans on computers throughout a domain by completing the following steps:

1. Open a Group Policy Object for editing in the Group Policy Management Editor. To configure preferences for computers, expand Computer Configuration\Preferences\Control Panel Settings, and then select Power Options. To configure preferences for users, expand User Configuration\Preferences \Control Panel Settings, and then select Power Options.

2. Press and hold or right-click the Power Options node, point to New, and then tap or click Power Plan (At Least Windows 7). This opens the New Power Plan (At Least Windows 7) Properties dialog box.

3. From the Action list, select Update to update the power plan's settings or select Replace to delete the power plan and then re-create it exactly as you specify.

4. From the selection list, choose the power plan with which you want to work, such as Balanced.

5. To set the plan as the active plan, select the Set As The Active Power Plan check box.

6. Use the options provided to configure the settings for the power plan.

7. Tap or click OK. The next time policy is refreshed, the preference item will be applied as appropriate for the Group Policy Object in which you defined the preference item.

Creating power plans

In addition to the preferred power plans included with Windows 8.1, you can create power plans as needed. To create a power plan, follow these steps:

1. In Control Panel, tap or click System And Security, and then tap or click Power Options.

2. In the left pane, tap or click Create A Power Plan. This displays the Create A Power Plan page, as shown in Figure 2-21.

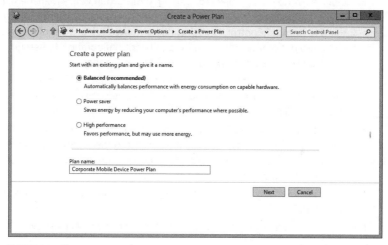

FIGURE 2-21 Create a power plan.

3. To prepopulate the power plan settings, select the preferred power plan that is closest to the type of plan you want to create.

4. In the Plan Name text box, enter a descriptive name for the plan, and then tap or click Next. This displays the Edit Plan Settings page.

5. For laptops and tablets, use the Dim The Display list to specify whether and when the computer's display is dimmed. Choose Never to disable this feature.

6. Use the Turn Off The Display list to specify whether or when the computer's display automatically turns off. Choose Never to disable this feature.

7. Use the Put The Computer To Sleep list to specify whether or when the computer automatically enters sleep mode. Choose Never to disable this feature.

8. Tap or click Create to create the plan. The Power Options page is displayed with updates to include the plan you created as a new preferred plan that replaces the plan you selected previously. You'll find the original preferred plan under Show Additional Plans. Tap or click the Expand button on the right to display the original plan.

9. The plan you created is selected by default. Tap or click Change Plan Settings for this plan to display the Edit Plan Settings page, and then tap or click Change Advanced Power Settings to display the Power Options dialog box.

10. After you configure the advanced power options as appropriate, tap or click OK to save any changes you've made.

You can access Group Policy and use a preference item to create power plans on computers throughout a domain by completing the following steps:

1. Open a Group Policy Object for editing in the Group Policy Management Editor. To configure preferences for computers, expand Computer Configuration\Preferences\Control Panel Settings, and then select Power Options. To configure preferences for users, expand User Configuration\Preferences \Control Panel Settings, and then select Power Options.

2. Press and hold or right-click the Power Options node, point to New, and then select Power Plan (At Least Windows 7). This opens the New Power Plan Properties dialog box.

3. From the Action list, select Create. To prepopulate the power plan settings, select the preferred power plan that is closest to the enter of plan you want to create. After you choose a plan, tap or click in the selection list and then enter the name of the new plan.

4. From the selection list, choose the power plan you want to work with, such as Balanced.

5. To set the plan as the active plan, select the Set As The Active Power Plan check box.

6. Use the options provided to configure the settings for the power plan.

7. Tap or click OK. The next time policy is refreshed, the preference item will be applied as appropriate for the Group Policy Object in which you defined the preference item.

Configuring systemwide power button and password protection on wakeup settings

fSystemwide settings for power options enable you to customize the way that the power button and password protection on wakeup works for all users who log on to the computer. You can configure the power button so that when it is pressed, the system shuts down, hibernates, or enters sleep mode. You can configure the computer so that when it wakes from sleep, a password is required to unlock the screen.

To set systemwide power settings, follow these steps:

1. In Control Panel, tap or click System And Security, and then tap or click Power Options.

2. In the left pane, tap or click Choose What The Power Buttons Do.

3. Use the When I Press The Power Button list to specify whether the computer should do nothing, shut down, sleep, or hibernate when the power button is pressed. You cannot, however, use an option that is not supported by the computer.

4. Use the When I Press The Sleep Button list to specify whether the computer should sleep, hibernate, or do nothing when the sleep button is pressed. Again, you cannot use an option that is not supported by the computer.

5. If available, use the When I Close The Lid list to specify whether the computer should sleep, hibernate, or do nothing when the computer lid is closed. Again, you cannot use an option that is not supported by the computer.

6. If the options for Password Protection On Wakeup and Shutdown Settings are not available, tap or click the Change Settings That Are Currently Unavailable link.

7. Use the Require A Password option to specify that the computer requires a password on wakeup. It is a good idea to prompt for a password to help ensure the security of the system.

8. Select Turn On Fast Startup to save system information to a file on the system disk when you shut down the computer. This file is then read during boot to enable faster startup. When you restart the computer, Fast Startup is not used.

9. Select the power options that you want displayed when you click the power button.

10. Tap or click Save Changes when you have finished making changes.

Managing power options in policy settings

In Group Policy, you'll find policy settings for managing power options in the Administrative Templates for Computer Configuration under System\Power Management. The following five subnodes are provided:

- **Button Settings** Includes policies for setting plugged-in and on-battery actions for the power button, the sleep button, and the laptop lid. This also controls the way the power button works on the Tasks screen, which is displayed by pressing Ctrl+Alt+Delete.

- **Hard Disk Settings** Includes policies for setting plugged-in and on-battery actions for turning off the hard disks.

- **Notification Settings** Includes policies for controlling notifications and actions for adverse battery conditions.

- **Sleep Settings** Includes policies for setting permitted device and application sleep states.

- **Video And Display Settings** Includes policies for setting plugged-in and on-battery actions for the display, the display brightness, and desktop background slide shows.

To apply a policy setting, enable the policy, and then select the appropriate action.

Through Group Policy, you can also specify an active power plan. How you work with Power Management policies depends on whether you want to use a default power plan, an updated preferred plan, or a custom power plan that you've created. If you want all computers that process a particular policy to use one of the Windows 8.1 default power plans, follow these steps:

1. After you open the Group Policy Object that you want to work with for editing, expand Administrative Templates policies for Computer Configuration under System\Power Management.

2. Double-tap or double-click Select An Active Power Plan.

3. Select Enabled, and then use the Active Power Plan list to select the plan to use. The options are High Performance, Power Saver, and Automatic. If you choose Automatic, Windows 8.1 uses the Balanced power plan in most cases.

4. Tap or click OK.

If you want all computers that process a particular policy to use an updated preferred plan or a custom power plan that you've created, follow these steps:

1. After you open the Group Policy Object that you want to edit, expand Computer Configuration\Administrative Templates\System\Power Management.

2. Double-tap or double-click Specify A Custom Active Power Plan.

3. Select Enabled. In the Custom Active Power Plan (GUID) text box, enter the GUID of the power plan to use.

4. Tap or click OK.

TIP To determine the GUID of a power plan, get a list of the power plans configured on a computer by typing **powercfg -l** at an elevated command prompt.

Using alarms and configuring alarm actions

Alarms determine whether a laptop sounds an alarm or displays a warning message when its battery reaches a certain level. You can configure three levels of alarms and notifications for laptops:

- **Low Battery Alarm** The Low Battery Alarm is meant to alert the user when the battery power level is nearly depleted. The low-power state is activated by default when the battery has 10 percent or less power remaining. On a battery with 8 hours of useful life, 10 percent is about 48 minutes of use.

- **Reserve Battery Alarm** The Reserve Battery Alarm is meant to alert the user when the battery is using reserve power. The reserve-power state is activated by default when the battery has 7 percent or less power remaining. On a battery with 8 hours of useful life, 7 percent is about 34 minutes of use.

- **Critical Battery Alarm** The Critical Battery Alarm is meant to alert the user when the battery is about to fail. The critical-power state is activated by default when the battery has 5 percent or less power remaining. On a battery with 8 hours of useful life, 5 percent is about 24 minutes of use.

An alarm action associated with low and critical alarms enables you to dictate what specific actions the operating system should take when the alarm level is reached.

Possible actions include shutting down the computer, entering sleep mode, or entering hibernate mode. Starting with Windows Vista, you could turn off low-battery notifications by enabling the Turn Off Low Battery User Notification policy. In Windows 7, the reserve battery alert was added to notify users that batteries were running on reserve power. Because there are different considerations for configuring the alert levels, I'll examine each separately in the sections that follow.

Configuring low-battery notification and actions

As stated previously, the low-battery notification is a warning that the system is getting low on power. When entering the low-power state, the system notifies the user with either a text prompt alone or a text prompt and an audible alarm. In some cases, you might want to configure the computer to go a step further and enter standby mode in addition to, or instead of, giving a warning.

To configure the low-battery notification and actions, follow these steps:

1. After you open the Group Policy Object that you want to edit, expand Administrative Templates policies for Computer Configuration under System\Power Management\Notification Settings.

2. To set the low-battery notification action, double-tap or double-click Low Battery Notification Action. Select Enabled, and then use the Low Battery Notification Action list to select the action, such as Sleep. Tap or click OK.

3. To specify when the low-battery alarm is triggered, double-tap or double-click Low Battery Notification Level. Select Enabled, and then use the Low Battery Notification Level combo box to set the appropriate alarm level. Tap or click OK.

   TIP The default low-battery alarm level is based on the total battery life and typically is 10 percent. On most systems, this is an appropriate value; however, I've found that on some systems, especially those with poor batteries, this isn't enough, and I increase the level to between 12 and 15 percent. In contrast, on energy-efficient systems or those with two batteries, the default value is often too much. Here, I adjust the level so that the user is notified when about 20 minutes of battery power remains. However, keep in mind that over time the efficiency level of batteries decreases and batteries will eventually fail unless they are replaced periodically. Create energy reports to help you identify failing batteries.

Configuring reserve-power mode

Reserve-power mode is designed to notify users that the battery is operating on reserve power. To configure reserve-battery notification, follow these steps:

1. After you open the Group Policy Object that you want to edit, expand Administrative Templates policies for Computer Configuration under System\Power Management\Notification Settings.

2. To specify when the reserve-battery alarm is triggered, double-tap or double-click Reserve Battery Notification Level. Select Enabled, and then use the Reserve Battery Notification Level combo box to set the appropriate alarm level. Tap or click OK.

Configuring critical-battery alarms

Critical-battery alarms are designed to ensure that systems enter an appropriate mode prior to running out of power. When entering a critical-power state, the system notifies the user and then enters sleep mode. In sleep mode, the computer's power-manageable components shut off to conserve power. I often configure the low-power alarm so that the computer enters sleep mode. I then configure the critical-battery alarm to have the computer enter hibernation mode or shut down. This takes power management to the next level and helps preserve the system before power is completely exhausted.

To configure the critical-battery actions, follow these steps:

1. After you open the Group Policy Object that you want to edit, expand Administrative Templates policies for Computer Configuration under System\Power Management\Notification Settings.

2. To set the critical-battery notification action, double-tap or double-click Critical Battery Notification Action. Select Enabled, and then use the Critical Battery Notification Action list to select the action, such as Hibernate or Shut Down. Tap or click OK.

3. To specify when the critical-battery alarm is triggered, double-tap or double-click Critical Battery Notification Level. Select Enabled, and then use the Critical Battery Notification Level combo box to set the appropriate alarm level. Tap or click OK.

TIP The default critical-alarm level is based on the total battery life and typically is 5 percent. In most cases, this value is appropriate. However, if you plan for the computer to go into hibernation or shut down, you might want to reduce this value. You might also want to take into account the battery life. If a computer has a long battery life, the default typically is too high, but if a computer has a short battery life, it might not be high enough. I usually set the critical-power alarm so that the alarm action is triggered when 6 to 8 minutes of power is remaining.

CHAPTER 3

Customizing the desktop and the interface

As an administrator, you'll often be asked to help users customize their desktops and user profile data. Windows 8.1 provides many desktop and screen customization options. Although these options are useful, they can cause problems that you might be asked to help resolve. You might also find users struggling to fix these issues on their own, so you might want to offer some help. This chapter focuses on the configuration and troubleshooting of the following areas:

- PC settings, the taskbar, and toolbars
- Desktop themes and backgrounds
- Custom desktop content
- Screen savers
- Display appearance and settings
- Logging on to the desktop instead of Start

Optimizing PC settings

The PC Settings screen and its related pages are designed to provide easy access to settings commonly used for customizing the user interface and the way that apps can be used. You can display the PC Settings screen by using one of the following techniques:

- With touch UI, slide in from the right, tap Settings, and then tap Change PC Settings.

- With the mouse and keyboard, press Windows key + I, and then click Change PC Settings.

You navigate between pages by tapping or clicking the name of the page. The top-level pages available include the following:

- **PC And Devices**   Provides quick access to commonly used configuration settings, including lock screen, display, power, and AutoPlay options. Note that when you are using a Remote Desktop connection to configure a computer, you won't be able to configure PC And Devices/Microsoft Display options. Display options can be configured only when you are logged on locally.

- **Accounts**   Provides options for managing basic account settings, including the account picture and sign-in options. Also provides options for managing local accounts and connecting the computer to a Microsoft account.

- **SkyDrive**   Provides options for connecting to a Microsoft account on the computer and accessing files saved to Microsoft SkyDrive. By connecting a Microsoft account, you can sync PC settings from the Microsoft account to the currently logged-on domain account.

- **Search And Apps**   Provides options for configuring online search and sharing settings. Also provides options for configuring app installation, default apps, and app notifications.

- **Privacy**   Provides options for controlling app access to account and location information. Also provides options for controlling whether apps can access the computer's webcam and microphone.

- **Network**   Provides options for managing networking and joining workplace networks. Under Network/Connections, you'll find current Ethernet, Wi-Fi, DirectAccess, and VPN connections. Select a connection to view, and optionally copy, its configuration settings, including the MAC address of the network card. With Wi-Fi connections, you can enable device discovery and data usage display. You also can specify whether the connection is metered.

- **Time And Language**   Provides options for- setting the computer date, time, region, and language. Prior to Windows 8, the input language context was managed per thread by default. As a result, the input language used in one program could be different from the input language in another program if you changed the input language in one program but not in others. Now Windows manages the input language on a per-user basis by default. If you change the input language in the currently active program and then open another program or switch to another open program, the input language in that program will also change because the current input language settings follow the focus by default.

- **Ease Of Access**   Provides quick access to accessibility options, including the Narrator, Magnifier, and High Contrast features. You'll also find handy keyboard and mouse options. Under Ease of Access\Keyboard, use the On-Screen Keyboard option to enable or disable the on-screen keyboard. Under Ease of Access\Mouse, use the Mouse Keys options to control whether the numeric keypad can be used to move the mouse pointer around on the screen.

- **Update And Recovery**   Provides quick access to options for working with the Windows Update, File History, and Recovery features of the operating system.

Figure 3-1 shows the PC And Devices page in PC Settings. Pages and options you have might be slightly different depending on your computing device.

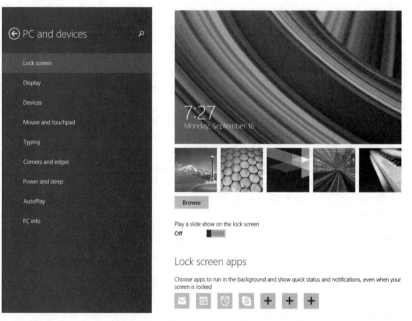

FIGURE 3-1 Use PC Settings pages and options to customize the user interface.

NOTE   Throughout this section, I use the term *apps* to refer to desktop apps, as opposed to traditional desktop programs. For more information about apps, see Chapter 7, "Installing and maintaining applications."

Each user who logs on to a computer has separate settings. The sections that follow examine key areas of the operating system that can be configured by using these pages and options.

Personalizing the lock screen

On the PC And Devices\Lock Screen page, you can choose a picture to display in the background by tapping or clicking the picture you want to use. If you want to use a picture from somewhere else on your computer, select Browse, and then use the options provided to navigate to and choose the picture you want to use. When you browse for pictures, the default folder is This PC\Pictures. You can also search in the following ways:

- To search another folder on the computer, tap or click Go Up. You'll then have quick access to the Desktop, Documents, Downloads, Music, and Videos folders as well as fixed and removable media volumes.

- To search for files on a network share, tap or click This PC, and then select Network. On the Network screen, you'll find and can access any currently mapped network locations. To map a new location, enter the network path, such as \\CorpServer23\Data.

Some apps, those referred to as *lock screen apps*, can run in the background and show quick status and notifications even when the screen is locked. Typically, the messaging, mail, and calendar apps are configured to display quick status information by default. Other apps installed on the computer might also be able to show quick status and notifications on the lock screen. Tap or click the Add option (which appears as a plus sign) to display a list of these apps and then tap or click an app to add it. To remove a lock screen app, tap or click the app and then tap or click Don't Show Quick Status Here.

Some apps, like Calendar and Weather, can display a detailed status on the lock screen, but normally only one app can actively display detailed status at a time, and that app is listed under Choose An App To Display Detailed Status. If no detailed status app has been added, tap or click the Add option (which appears as a plus sign), and then tap or click the app you want to add. To remove the detailed status app, tap or click the app, and then tap or click Don't Show Detailed Status On The Lock Screen.

> **REAL WORLD** The Force A Specific Default Lock Screen Image setting controls whether you can personalize the image on the lock screen. If you enable this setting on a domain-joined computer, you can specify the path to an image that must be displayed on the lock screen when no user is signed in. The path can be a local path on the computer, such as %WinDir%\web\screen\corp-ls.jpg, or a UNC path to a network share, such as \\FileServer18\Images\corp-ls.jpg. In Group Policy, you'll find this setting in the Administrative Templates policies for Computer Configuration, under Control Panel\Personalization.

Personalizing account settings

On the Accounts\Your Account page, you can choose an account picture to display. A silhouette graphic is used by default, but any picture can be added as an account picture. If you want to use a picture from somewhere else on your computer, tap or click Browse, and then use the options provided to navigate to and choose the picture you want to use.

If the computer has a camera, you can create an account picture by clicking Camera and following the prompts. You also use the Accounts\Your Account page to manage the logged-on account. If the logged-on account is using a Microsoft account, you can use the options provided to switch to a local account, and you can also use the options provided to switch from a local account to a Microsoft account.

The settings on the Accounts\Sign-In Options page allow you to create or change a picture password for the logged-on user (if allowed in Group Policy). You also can control whether a user must enter a password when waking the computer. For more information on working with user accounts, see Chapter 5, "Managing user access and security."

You can personalize colors on the account's Start screen by completing the following steps:

1. Display the Personalize options for Start by using one of the following techniques:

    ■ With the touch UI, slide in from the right, tap Settings, and then tap Personalization.

    ■ With the mouse and keyboard, point to the hidden button in the lower-right corner of the screen to display the Charms bar. On the Charms bar, click Settings, and then click Personalize.

2. Select one of the default background images provided. Next, select a color to display behind the background image. A default color palette is provided that is close in hue to the colors used in the image. To display a different color palette, use the color selector.

3. Select an accent color for the background image. A default color palette is provided that is close in hue to the colors used in the image. To display a different color palette, use the color selector.

REAL WORLD When working with backgrounds and colors for the Start screen, keep the following in mind:

■ Force A Specific Background And Accent Color in the Administrative Templates for Computer Configuration under Control Panel\Personalization controls whether you can personalize colors on the Start screen. If you enable this setting, you can specify background and accent colors for the Start screen in Group Policy and users will be unable to change these colors. You must specify the colors as hexadecimal RGB values, similar to the way you set background colors for webpages in HTML. The colors you use must have at least a 2:1 contrast ratio with white text or the setting will not be applied.

■ Force A Specific Start Background for Computer Configuration under Control Panel \Personalization controls whether you can personalize the background image on the Start screen. If you enable this setting, you can specify a numeric identifier for one of the available background images and users cannot change the background image. A value of 1 indicates the first default background; a value of 2, the second; and so on.

Personalizing search and apps settings

The Search page in the Search And Apps section allows you to personalize the way search works. Windows 8.1 tracks a history of your searches, and it can use this search history to show the apps that you search most often at the top of your search results and to save searches for future suggestions. Use the Search History options to modify the way this works or to delete the current search history.

Certain apps are configured for quick sharing, allowing you to quickly share photos, documents, or other items. The Share page allows you to personalize the way sharing works. Windows 8.1 tracks a history of the apps that you use for sharing and can display these apps in a prioritized list. Up to five apps are in the list by default. Tap or click the Items In List drop-down box to select a different number of apps. Tap or click Clear List to clear and reset the list.

Certain apps, such as Mail and People, are configured for sharing automatically. Options are provided to turn sharing on or off for each app individually. Simply tap or click the related button to switch sharing on or off.

Many apps can display notifications, which can be controlled from the Notifications page in the Search And Apps section. Top-level notification controls include:

- **Show App Notifications** Controls whether apps can display notifications on Start and the desktop
- **Show App Notifications On The Lock Screen** Controls whether apps can display notifications on the lock screen
- **Play Notification Sounds** Controls whether apps can play notification sounds

Tap or click the control to turn the related notifications on or off. In addition to being able to turn notifications on or off for individual apps, you can also set quiet hours to stop notifications during certain hours of the day.

> **TIP** On the PC And Devices\Corners And Edges page under App Switching, you can specify whether a user can switch between recent apps by tapping or clicking in the upper-left corner of the screen. A list of recently used apps can also be displayed by swiping in from the left edge. When app switching is allowed, Windows 8.1 tracks recently used apps in a history; you can clear this history by tapping or clicking Clear List.

Managing privacy settings

Apps can use your name and account picture by default. You configure these and related settings on the General page in the Privacy section. Simply tap or click the related button to specify whether you want this information to be available to apps.

Apps can use the computer's location to provide relevant content by default. On the Privacy\Location page, you can control the availability of location data to apps. You can disable app access to location data completely by setting Let Windows And Apps Use My Location to Off. Alternatively, you can enable access for specific apps by setting Let Windows And Apps Use My Location to On and then using the additional options provided to specify which apps can use the location data.

Apps can use the computer's webcam by default. On the Privacy\Webcam page, you can control the availability of the webcam to apps. You can disable app access to the webcam completely by setting Let Apps Use My Webcam to Off. Alternatively, you can enable webcam access for specific apps by setting Let Apps Use My Webcam to On, and then using the additional options provided to specify which apps can use the webcam.

Apps can use the computer's microphone by default. On the Privacy\Microphone page, you can control the availability of the microphone to apps. You can disable app access to the microphone completely by setting Let Apps Use My Microphone to Off. Alternatively, you can enable microphone access for specific apps by setting Let Apps Use My Microphone to On, and then using the additional options provided to specify which apps can use the microphone.

Configuring sync settings

When the currently logged-on user has a Microsoft account, you can control the way settings are synchronized between devices on the SkyDrive\Sync Settings page. Settings that can be synchronized include the following:

- The user's Start screen tiles and layout
- Appearance settings for colors, backgrounds, and account picture
- Desktop personalization settings for themes, the taskbar, and more
- Sign-in passwords for some apps, websites, networks, and HomeGroups
- Ease of Access options and language preferences
- Browser settings, browser history, and browser favorites
- Other Windows settings for File Explorer, the mouse, and more

The Sync Your Settings On This PC option is the top-level control. Turn this setting on or off depending on whether you want settings to be synchronized between devices.

When synchronization is allowed, use the additional options provided to control the type of settings that are synchronized. Because Windows 8.1 also can recognize when a computer is on a metered connection, such as a cellular network, you can turn syncing on or off over metered connections and specify whether syncing is ever allowed when the metered connection is roaming.

In the Administrative Templates for Computer Configuration, under Windows Components\Sync Your Settings, you'll find the following settings for controlling how settings can be synced:

- Do Not Sync Apps
- Do Not Sync Apps Settings
- Do Not Sync Desktop Personalization
- Do Not Sync On Metered Connections

- Do Not Sync Other Windows Settings
- Do Not Sync Passwords
- Do Not Sync Personalize
- Do Not Sync Start Settings
- Do Not Sync Browser Settings

Working with desktops and startup applications

In the Windows operating system, items on the desktop and startup applications are configured with shortcuts, and the location of the shortcut determines how the shortcut is used. For example, if you want to configure startup applications for all users, you can add shortcuts to the %SystemDrive%\ProgramData\Microsoft \Windows\Start Menu\Programs\Startup folder. These applications then automatically start when a user logs on to the system locally. If you want to configure startup applications for a particular user, you can add shortcuts to the %UserProfile% \AppData\Roaming\Microsoft\Windows\Start Menu\Programs\Startup folder.

Creating shortcuts for desktops, startup, and more

In File Explorer, you can create shortcuts for the desktop, folders, and startup applications by logging on to a user's computer and creating shortcuts in the appropriate locations. In Group Policy, you can create shortcuts for desktops, startup applications, and more by using Shortcuts preferences, and these preference items are applied automatically to all users and computers that process the related Group Policy Object.

To configure Shortcuts preferences, follow these steps:

1. Open a Group Policy Object for editing in the Group Policy Management Editor. To configure preferences for computers, expand Computer Configuration\Preferences\Windows Settings, and then select Shortcuts. To configure preferences for users, expand User Configuration\Preferences\Windows Settings, and then select Shortcuts.

2. Press and hold or right-click the Shortcuts node, point to New, and then select Shortcut. This opens the New Shortcut Properties dialog box, as shown in Figure 3-2.

3. In the Action list, select Create, Update, or Replace as appropriate. Then, complete the other options as discussed later in this section.

4. Use the options on the Common tab to control how the preference is applied. Often, you'll want to apply a shortcut only once. If so, select Apply Once And Do Not Reapply.

5. Tap or click OK. The next time policy is refreshed, the preference item will be applied as appropriate for the Group Policy Object in which you defined the preference item.

FIGURE 3-2 Create a shortcut by using a preference item.

In the Location list, you'll find a list of special folders that you can use with shortcuts. Table 3-1 provides a summary of these folders.

TABLE 3-1 Special folders for use with shortcuts

SPECIAL FOLDER	USAGE
All Users Desktop	Desktop shortcuts for all users
All Users Explorer Favorites	Explorer favorites for all users
All Users Programs	Programs menu options for all users
All Users Start Menu	Start menu options for all users
All Users Startup	Startup applications for all users
Desktop	Desktop shortcuts for a specific user
Explorer Favorites	Favorites for a specific user
Explorer Links	Favorite links for a specific user
My Network Places	Network shortcuts for a specific user
Programs	Programs menu options for a specific user
Quick Launch Toolbar	Toolbar folder with shortcuts for a specific user

SPECIAL FOLDER	USAGE
Recent	Recently used document shortcuts for a specific user
Send To	Send To menu shortcuts for a specific user
Start Menu	Start menu shortcuts for a specific user
StartUp	Startup applications for a specific user

Shortcuts can point to local and network files, as well as to remote Internet resources. Shortcuts for working with local or network files are referred to as *link shortcuts*. Shortcuts for working with remote Internet resources are referred to as *URL shortcuts*.

A link shortcut is usually used to start an application or open a document rather than access a URL in a browser. Because of this, link shortcuts have different properties than URL shortcuts. The properties are summarized in Table 3-2. If you set any property incorrectly or set a property that isn't supported by a linked application, the shortcut might not be created or might not work as expected. In this case, you need to correct the problem and try to create the shortcut again.

One of the most valuable options is the Arguments property. You can use this property to set arguments to pass in to an application that you are starting. By using this property, you can create a shortcut that starts Microsoft Word and opens a document by setting the target path for Word and the argument for the document to open.

When you add shortcuts to the desktop or menus, you can specify a sequence of keystrokes that activates the shortcut. The keyboard shortcut sequence must be specified with at least one modifier key and a key designator. The following modifier keys are available:

- Alt
- Ctrl
- Shift

TABLE 3-2 Link shortcut properties

PROPERTY	DESCRIPTION	SAMPLE VALUE
Arguments	Arguments to pass to an application started through the shortcut.	C:\Gettingstarted.doc
Comment	Sets a descriptive comment for the shortcut.	Opens the Getting Started Document
Icon File Path	Sets the location of an icon for the shortcut. If not set, a default icon is used.	C:\Program Files\Internet Explorer\Iexplore.exe

PROPERTY	DESCRIPTION	SAMPLE VALUE
Icon Index	Sets the index position of the icon for the shortcut. Few applications have multiple icons indexed, so the index is almost always 0.	0
Location	Specifies where the shortcut should be created.	Desktop
Name	Sets the name of the shortcut.	Getting Started
Run	Sets the window style of the application started by the shortcut. The available styles are Normal Window, Minimized, and Maximized.	Normal Window
Shortcut Key	Sets a keyboard shortcut sequence that activates the shortcut. This property can be used only with desktop shortcuts and Start menu options.	Alt+Shift+Z
Start In	Sets the working directory of the application started by the shortcut.	C:\Working
Target Path	Sets the path of the file to execute.	%WinDir%\Notepad.exe
Target Type	Specifies the type of shortcut you are creating. Choose File System Object for link shortcuts, URL for URL shortcuts, and Shell Object for Explorer shell shortcuts.	File System Object

Modifier keys can be combined in any combination, such as Alt+Ctrl or Shift+Ctrl, but the combination shouldn't duplicate key combinations used by other shortcuts. Key designators include the alphabetic characters (A–Z) and numeric characters (0–9), as well as End, Home, Page Up, and Page Down. For example, you could create a shortcut that uses the sequence Shift+Alt+G.

When you create shortcuts for applications, the applications normally have a default icon that is displayed with the shortcut. For example, if you create a shortcut for Windows Internet Explorer, the default icon is a large E. When you create shortcuts to document files, the Windows default icon is used in most cases.

If you want to use an icon other than the default icon, you can use the Icon Location property. Normally, the icon location equates to an application name, such as Iexplore.exe or Notepad.exe, and the icon index is set to 0. Windows has to be able to find the executable file in the path; otherwise, the icon can't be set. Because of this, be sure to enter the full path to the executable file.

The working directory sets the default directory for an application. This directory is used the first time that a user opens or saves files.

URL shortcuts open Internet documents in an appropriate application. For example, webpages are opened in the default browser, such as Internet Explorer. With URL shortcuts, you can't use the Arguments, Start In, Run, or Comment properties.

Adding and removing startup applications

Administrator-installed or user-installed applications that run in the background can be managed through the Startup folder. Startup programs that are made available only to the currently logged-on user are placed in the Startup folder that is located within the profile data for that user (%UserProfile%\AppData\Roaming\Microsoft \Windows\Start Menu\Programs), and startup programs that are available to any user that logs on to the computer are placed in the Startup folder for all users (%SystemDrive%\ProgramData\Microsoft\Windows\Start Menu\Programs).

To add or remove startup programs for all users, follow these steps:

1. In File Explorer, browse to the hidden %SystemDrive%\ProgramData \Microsoft\Windows\Start Menu folder. If hidden items aren't being displayed, tap or click View, and then select Hidden Items.

2. In the left pane, tap or click the Programs folder under Start Menu, and then tap or click Startup.

3. You can now add or remove startup programs for all users. To add a startup program, create a shortcut to the program that you want to run. To remove a startup program, delete its shortcut from the Startup folder.

To add or remove startup programs for a specific user, follow these steps:

1. Log on as the user whose startup applications you want to manage. In File Explorer, browse to the hidden %UserProfile%\AppData\Roaming\Microsoft \Windows\Start Menu folder.

2. In the left pane, tap or click the Programs folder under Start Menu, and then tap or click Startup.

3. You can now add or remove startup programs for this user. To add a startup program, create a shortcut to the program that you want to run. To remove a startup program, delete its shortcut from the Startup folder.

NOTE Technically, you don't need to log on as the user to manage that user's startup applications—it's just easier if you do. If you can't log on as the user, access the Users folder on the system drive and work your way down through the user profile data folders. These are listed by account name.

Using Group Policy preferences, you specify applications that should be started after a user logs on by creating shortcuts in the AllUsersStartup and Startup folders. The AllUsersStartup folder sets startup applications for all users that log on to a system. The Startup folder sets startup applications for the current user.

When you create a shortcut for a startup application, the only options you need to set in most cases are Name, Target Type, Location, and Target Path. Occasionally you might also want to set a working directory for an application or specify startup arguments.

If you later want to remove a startup application, you delete it by creating a preference with the action set to Delete.

Customizing the taskbar

The taskbar provides quick access to frequently needed information and active applications. You can change the taskbar's behavior and properties in many ways. This section explores key techniques you can use to modify the taskbar.

Understanding the taskbar

The taskbar is one of the least appreciated areas of the Windows desktop. Users and administrators tend to pay very little attention to its configuration, yet we use it day in and day out, relying on it for quick access to just about everything we do with the Windows operating system. If you find that users are having frequent problems accessing Windows features or running applications, you can help them by tailoring the taskbar to their needs. The Windows taskbar can contain several toolbars to assist users in different ways.

Sometimes you can provide tremendous productivity increases simply by adding a frequently used item to the taskbar. For example, most people spend a lot of time finding and reading documents. They browse the web or their corporate intranet to find the latest information. They open documents in Microsoft Word, Excel, PowerPoint, or other applications, finding documents individually or also starting applications to read those documents. By adding an Address bar to the taskbar, users can access documents directly and start the appropriate application automatically. They just need to enter the document path and press Enter. As time passes, the history feature of the Address bar tracks more and more of the user's previously accessed documents, making it easier to find the information the user needs.

Pinning shortcuts to the taskbar

Windows 8.1 allows you to pin commonly used programs directly to the taskbar. You can do this whenever you are working with the Start screen. Simply press and hold or right-click an item you want to add to the taskbar, and then tap or click Pin To Taskbar. After you pin an item to the taskbar, you can change the item's position on the taskbar by tapping or clicking and dragging the program's icon. To unpin an item, press and hold or right-click the item on the taskbar, and then tap or click Unpin This Program From Taskbar.

Changing the taskbar's size and position

By default, the taskbar appears at the bottom of the screen and is sized so that one row of options is visible. As long as the taskbar's position isn't locked, you can dock it at any edge of the Windows desktop and resize it as necessary. To move the taskbar, simply tap or click it and drag it to a different edge of the desktop. As you drag the taskbar, the taskbar will appear at the edge of the Windows desktop, and when you release the mouse button, the taskbar will remain in the new location. To resize the taskbar, point to the taskbar's edge, and then drag it up or down.

Auto-hiding, locking, and controlling taskbar visibility

When you want to control the visibility of the taskbar, you have several options. You can enable the Auto Hide feature to hide the taskbar from view when it's not in use. You can lock the taskbar so that it can't be resized or repositioned. You can also make the taskbar appear in a specific location and with a specific appearance. After the taskbar is positioned and sized the way a user wants it, you should lock it. In this way, the taskbar has a fixed location, and users don't have to hunt for it.

To configure the taskbar, follow these steps:

1. Press and hold or right-click the taskbar, and then tap or click Properties.

2. On the Taskbar tab, select the appropriate Taskbar appearance options. You can lock the taskbar, auto-hide the taskbar, and use small icons.

3. Use the Taskbar Location On Screen list to select the location for the taskbar on the desktop. You can select Bottom, Left, Right, or Top.

4. Use the Taskbar Buttons list to specify whether taskbar buttons are combined and labels are hidden. Choose Always Combine, Hide Labels to always combine buttons of the same type and hide their labels. Choose Combine When Taskbar Is Full to combine buttons only when the taskbar is full. Choose Never Combine to never combine buttons.

5. Tap or click OK.

> **TIP** Locking the taskbar is one of the most useful taskbar options. If you lock the taskbar when it is optimized, users will have fewer problems caused by accidentally altering taskbar options. Locking the taskbar doesn't prevent users from changing the taskbar on purpose. If users really want to change the taskbar, all they need to do is press and hold or right-click the taskbar and then clear Lock All Taskbars.

Controlling programs in the notification area

The notification area or system tray is the area on the far right of the taskbar that shows the system clock and notification icons from applications. The two standard notification icons are for Action Center and the Network console. When you point to icons in the notification area, a tooltip provides information about the state of the application. To control an application in this area, press and hold or right-click the application icon to display a menu of available options. Each application has a different menu of options, most of which provide quick access to routine tasks.

You can optimize the notification area by setting properties that control whether system icons—such as for the clock, speaker volume, and network—are displayed and whether application icons are displayed or hidden.

Controlling icon display in the notification area

The notification area can display both application and system icons. Icons for applications appear in the notification area for several reasons. Some programs, such as Action Center, are managed by Windows itself, and their icons appear periodically when notifications are pending. Other types of programs, such as antivirus programs, are configured to load at startup and then run in the background. You can often enable or disable the display of icons through setup options for the related applications, but Windows 8.1 provides a common interface for controlling icon display in the notification area. You can specify whether and how icons are displayed on a per-application basis.

To control the display of icons in the notification area, follow these steps:

1. Press and hold or right-click the taskbar, and then tap or click Properties.

2. On the Taskbar tab, for the Notification Area setting, tap or click Customize to display the Notification Area Icons page, as shown in Figure 3-3.

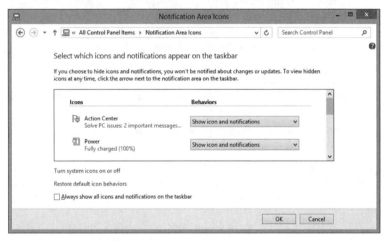

FIGURE 3-3 Configure notification icons.

3. If you want all icons to be displayed, select Always Show All Icons And Notifications On The Taskbar, and then tap or click OK. Skip the remaining steps.

4. If you want to customize the appearance of icons, clear Always Show All Icons And Notifications On The Taskbar. You can now optimize the notification behavior. Each entry in the left column has a selection menu in the right column with the following options:

   - **Hide Icon And Notifications** Never displays the icon and notifications

   - **Only Show Notifications** Displays only notifications

   - **Show Icon And Notifications** Always displays the icon and notifications

5. When you have finished updating the notification entries, tap or click OK twice.

Optimizing toolbars

Several toolbars are available for the taskbar. The toolbar that most users are familiar with is the Quick Launch toolbar—available in prior versions of Windows but not in Windows 8 or 8.1—that provided quick access to commonly used programs and the Windows desktop. The taskbar can display any of several toolbars that come with Windows 8.1, and users can create their own toolbars as well.

Displaying toolbars

Toolbars available for the taskbar include:

- **Address** Provides an Address box into which you can enter a URL or other address that you want to access, either on the web, on the local network, or on the local computer. When full file paths are specified, the default application for the file is started to display the specified file.

- **Links** Provides access to the Links folder on the Favorites menu for Internet Explorer. To add links to files, webpages, or other resources, drag shortcuts onto the Links toolbar. To remove links, press and hold or right-click the link and tap or click Delete. When prompted, confirm the action by tapping or clicking Yes.

- **Desktop** Provides access to all the shortcuts on the local desktop so that you don't have to minimize application windows or tap or click the Show Desktop button on the right end of the taskbar to access them.

- **Touch Keyboard** Provides quick access to the touch keyboard.

To display or hide individual toolbars, follow these steps:

1. Press and hold or right-click the taskbar to display the shortcut menu.
2. Point to Toolbars, and then select the toolbar name in the list provided. This switches the toolbar on and off.

> **TIP** By default, a name label is displayed for most toolbars. You can turn off the name label by pressing and holding or right-clicking the toolbar and then choosing Show Title to clear that command. If the taskbar is locked, you must first unlock it by clearing Lock The Taskbar on the shortcut menu.

Creating personal toolbars

You can create personal toolbars for users as well. Personal toolbars are based on existing folders, and their buttons are based on a folder's contents. The toolbars that you might create most often are ones that point to shared folders on the network. For example, if all users have access to CorpData, a shared folder in which corporate information is stored, and UserData, a folder in which personal information is stored, you can add toolbars to the taskbar that point to these resources. When users want to access one of these folders, they can simply tap or click the corresponding tool-bar button.

You can create personal toolbars by completing these steps:

1. Press and hold or right-click the taskbar to display the shortcut menu. Tap or click Toolbars, and then tap or click New Toolbar to display the New Toolbar—Choose A Folder dialog box, which is similar to the Open dialog box.

2. Use the options provided to navigate to and select the folder you want to use as a basis for a toolbar.

3. When you tap or click Select Folder, the folder is displayed as a new toolbar on the taskbar. If you add shortcuts to the toolbar view, the shortcuts are added to the folder. Similarly, if you delete items from the toolbar view, the items are removed from the folder.

NOTE When it comes to personal toolbars, there's good news and bad news. The good news is that most users find them valuable. The bad news is that if a user decides to close a toolbar, it must be re-created before it can be viewed on the taskbar again.

Working with desktop themes

Desktop themes are combinations of backgrounds plus sets of sounds, icons, and other elements that help personalize the desktop and the operating environment. Administrators tend to hate themes; users tend to love them. In this section, you'll learn how to apply themes, how to tailor individual theme options, and how to delete themes.

Applying and removing themes

Several types of themes are available, and some themes are installed with the oper-ating system. To apply a theme, follow these steps:

1. Press and hold or right-click an open area of the desktop, and then tap or click Personalize. This opens the Personalization console in Control Panel, shown in Figure 3-4.

2. Use the theme list to select the theme you want to use. If you want to use a theme from the Microsoft website, tap or click Get More Themes Online to open the Microsoft website in your default browser. To use an online theme, select it, and then tap or click Download Theme. When prompted, select a save location. When the download is complete, tap or click Open in the Download Complete dialog box. The theme is now available for use and is applied.

3. The lower portion of the Personalization console provides appearance options for the selected theme. To change one of these items, tap or click it.

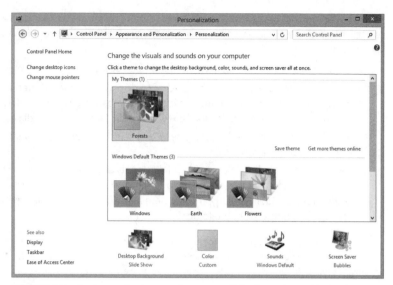

FIGURE 3-4 Use the Personalization console to access dialog boxes for configuring themes, display settings, and more.

To restore the original desktop theme, follow these steps:

1. Press and hold or right-click an open area of the desktop, and then tap or click Personalize.

2. Select Windows as the theme.

TIP   Because the display of themes is controlled by the Themes service, you can stop this service if you need to quickly turn off themes without changing their configuration, such as when you are troubleshooting or trying to resolve an issue. To stop the Themes service, enter the following command at an elevated command prompt: **net stop themes**. To restart the Themes service, enter the following command at an elevated command prompt: **net start themes**.

Tailoring and saving themes

When you apply a theme to the Windows desktop, many different system settings can be affected. Typically, users might like a theme but dislike a specific aspect of it, such as the sounds. To fix this, you can change the system setting that the user doesn't like and then save the updated theme so that he or she can restore it in the future.

You manage themes by using the Personalization console, which you open by pressing and holding or right-clicking an area of the desktop and then tapping or clicking Personalize.

In the Personalization console, the primary settings that themes affect are as follows:

- **Screen savers** To change the screen saver, tap or click Screen Saver. In the Screen Saver Settings dialog box, select a screen saver, or select None to remove the screen saver, and then tap or click OK.

- **Sounds** To change sounds, tap or click Sounds. In the Sound dialog box, use the Sound Scheme list box to select a different set of program event sounds. To restore the default, select Windows Default. To turn off program event sounds, select No Sounds. Tap or click OK. If you are turning off sounds, you might also want to clear the Play Windows Startup Sound check box.

- **Mouse pointers** To change mouse pointers, tap or click Change Mouse Pointers in the left pane. In the Mouse Properties dialog box, use the Scheme list box on the Pointers tab to select a different set of pointers. Tap or click OK.

- **Desktop background** To change the desktop background, tap or click Desktop Background. Use the Picture Location list to select the location of the pictures to use for a background. Tap or click Browse to display the Browse For Folder dialog box. You can also choose Windows wallpapers to use as backgrounds from the %SystemRoot%\Web\Wallpaper folder, which is where standard backgrounds included with Windows 8.1 are stored by default. Tap or click the background you want to use, set the picture position, and then tap or click Save Changes.

- **Color schemes** To change color schemes, tap or click Color. Tap or click the color you want to use, and then tap or click Save Changes.

Deleting custom themes

Themes that users install from other locations can take up a lot of space on the hard disk. To delete a theme and remove the theme-related files, follow these steps:

1. Press and hold or right-click an open area of the desktop, and then tap or click Personalize.

2. Under My Themes, press and hold or right-click the theme to be deleted, and then tap or click Delete Theme. Windows removes that theme's definition file and the theme-related media files.

IMPORTANT By default, definition files for themes installed by Windows are located in the %WinDir%\Resources\Themes folder, and themes created by users are stored in their user profiles. If you want to determine the total space used by themes, check the space used by these folders and their subdirectories. You shouldn't delete files from these folders manually. Instead, use the technique just described.

Optimizing the desktop environment

When you open programs or folders, they appear on the desktop. You can arrange open programs and folders on the desktop by pressing and holding or right-clicking an empty area of the taskbar and then selecting Cascade Windows, Show Windows Stacked, or Show Windows Side By Side. If you tap or click Show The Desktop, Windows minimizes all open windows and displays the desktop. Tapping or clicking Show Open Windows restores the minimized windows to their previous states.

You can put files, folders, and shortcuts on the desktop. Any file or folder that you save on the desktop appears on the desktop. Any file or folder that you drag from a File Explorer window to the desktop stays on the desktop. To add a shortcut to a file or folder to the desktop, press and hold or right-click the file or folder, point to Send To, and then tap or click Desktop (Create Shortcut).

Beyond these basic techniques, Windows 8.1 provides many additional ways to optimize the desktop environment. One technique is to add a background containing a corporate logo or other symbol to the standard desktop build. This is particularly useful with loaner laptops; for example, you can create a logo with a message such as "Technology Department Loaner." Another technique is to use Windows gadgets to add custom content directly to the desktop.

Setting the desktop background

Windows 8.1 provides multiple sets of background images and groups these images into named sets according to the folders in which the image files are stored. On the computer's hard disk, background images are stored in subfolders of the %WinDir% \Web\Wallpaper folder. Each folder represents a named set. For example, images in the Landscapes folder are displayed in the Landscapes set of background images.

Background images can be created as .bmp, .gif, .jpg, .jpeg, .dib, and .png files. If you add an image in one of these formats to any of the subfolders in the %WinDir% \Web\Wallpaper folder, the image will be available as part of that set. If you want to create a new set, simply create a folder under the %WinDir%\Web\Wallpaper folder and add the appropriate images to this folder.

To set the background for the desktop, follow these steps:

1. Press and hold or right-click an open area of the desktop, and then tap or click Personalize. In the Personalization console, tap or click Desktop Background. This displays the Desktop Background page, as shown in Figure 3-5.

2. When you select Windows Desktop Backgrounds as the Picture Location, Windows 8.1 organizes desktop backgrounds into sets of similar images. Use the scroll bar to navigate between sets, such as Nature or Windows.

3. Tap or click the image you want to use as the background. If you can't find a background that you want to use, tap or click Browse to search for a background on the file system or network.

FIGURE 3-5 Select which desktop background to use.

4. Use the Picture Position options to select a display option for the background. Picture Position options include:

- **Center** Centers the image on the desktop background. Any area that the image doesn't fill uses the current desktop color.

- **Fill** Fills the desktop background with the image. The sides of the image might be cropped.

- **Fit** Fits the image to the desktop background. Current proportions are maintained. This is a good option for photos and large images that you want to view without stretching or expanding.

- **Stretch** Stretches the image to fill the desktop background. The current proportions are maintained as much as possible, but the height is stretched to fill any remaining gaps.

- **Tile** Repeats the image so that it covers the entire screen. This is a good option for small images and icons.

5. When you are finished updating the background, tap or click Save Changes.

Working with the default desktop icons

By default, only the Recycle Bin is added to the desktop. Double-tapping or double-clicking the Recycle Bin icon opens a window where you can view files and folders that you've marked for deletion. By tapping or clicking Manage and then selecting Empty Recycle Bin, you permanently delete all the items in the Recycle Bin. By tapping or clicking Manage and then selecting Recycle Bin Properties, you can control how the Recycle Bin is used. Each volume on an internal disk has a Recycle Bin folder. If you tap or click the related folder, you can set the maximum size of the Recycle Bin on that volume or specify that files should be removed immediately when deleted.

Other common desktop icons you can add to the desktop are as follows:

- **Computer**   Adds the Computer console, which has been renamed This PC. Double-tapping or double-clicking the This PC icon opens a window from which you can access hard disk drives and devices with removable storage. Right-clicking the This PC icon and tapping or clicking Manage opens the This PC Management console. Pressing and holding or right-clicking the This PC icon and tapping or clicking Map Network Drive enables you to connect to shared network folders. Pressing and holding or right-clicking the This PC icon and tapping or clicking Disconnect Network Drive enables you to remove a connection to a shared network folder.

- **Control Panel**   Double-tapping or double-clicking the Control Panel icon opens Control Panel, which provides access to system configuration and management tools.

- **Network**   Double-tapping or double-clicking the Network icon opens a window from which you can access the computers and devices on your network. Pressing and holding or right-clicking the Network icon and tapping or clicking Map Network Drive allows you to connect to shared network folders. Pressing and holding or right-clicking the Network icon and tapping or clicking Disconnect Network Drive enables you to remove a connection to a shared network folder.

- **User's Files**   Double-tapping or double-clicking the User's Files icon opens your personal folder.

You can add or remove common desktop icons by following these steps:

1. Press and hold or right-click an open area of the desktop, and then tap or click Personalize. This displays the Personalization console.

2. In the left pane, tap or click Change Desktop Icons. This displays the Desktop Icon Settings dialog box, as shown in Figure 3-6.

3. The Desktop Icon Settings dialog box has check boxes for each of the default icons. Clear the corresponding check box to remove an icon. Select the check box to add an icon.

4. Tap or click OK.

You can hide all desktop icons by pressing and holding or right-clicking an open area of the desktop, pointing to View, and selecting Show Desktop Icons to clear the command. If you repeat this procedure and select Show Desktop Icons a second time, all the hidden desktop icons are restored.

If you no longer want an icon or a shortcut on the desktop, press and hold or right-click it, and then tap or click Delete. When prompted, confirm the action by tapping or clicking Yes. Note that if you remove an icon representing a file or folder from the desktop, the file or folder (and its contents) is deleted.

FIGURE 3-6 Use the Desktop Icon Settings dialog box to select the desktop icons to display and set their appearance.

Screen saver dos and don'ts

Screen savers are designed to turn on when a computer has been idle for a specified period of time. The original job of the screen saver was to prevent image burn-in on CRT monitors by displaying a continuously changing image. With today's monitors, burn-in is no longer a problem, but screen savers are still around. The primary benefit that they offer today is the ability to password-lock computers automatically when the screen saver turns on.

> **NOTE** The Desktop Windows Manager is used to compose the desktop. Unlike Windows 7, in which the Desktop Windows Manager could be disabled by end users and apps, the current Desktop Windows Manager is always on and cannot be disabled.

Configuring screen savers with password protection

Password-protecting a screen saver deters unauthorized users from accessing a computer, which can protect both the personal data of the user and the intellectual property of an organization. As an administrator, you should ensure that the computers you deploy have password-protected screen savers enabled.

You can password-protect a screen saver by performing the following steps:

1. Press and hold or right-click an open area of the desktop, and then tap or click Personalize.

2. Tap or click the Screen Saver link to display the Screen Saver Settings dialog box, as shown in Figure 3-7.

FIGURE 3-7 Set a screen saver with password protection for user and organization security.

3. Use the Screen Saver list box to select a screen saver. To disable the screen saver, select None and skip the remaining steps.

REAL WORLD Unfortunately, screen savers use a computer's resources, increasing both the energy usage of the computer (which otherwise would be idle) and its memory and processor usage. Some screen savers can also cause the processor to run at a higher utilization percentage. The reason for this is that some designs are very complex and the computer must make a lot of computations to maintain and update the screen saver image. For tips on reducing resource usage when screen savers turn on, see the following sections, "Reducing screen saver resource usage" and "Setting energy-saving settings for monitors."

4. Select On Resume, Display Logon Screen.

5. Use the Wait box to specify how long the computer must be idle before the screen saver is activated. A reasonable value is between 10 and 15 minutes.

6. Tap or click OK.

NOTE One of the best screen savers is the Photos screen saver, which displays a slide show of photos from the Pictures library by default, but you can select any other folder. By editing the settings, you can set the slide show speed and choose to shuffle the pictures rather than display them in sequence.

Reducing screen saver resource usage

A computer that is running Windows 8.1 and that performs background tasks or network duties such as print services should not be configured to use a complex screen saver, such as 3D Text. Instead, the computer should be configured with a basic screen saver, such as the Blank screen saver. You can also modify the settings for advanced screen savers to reduce resource usage. Typically, you do this by reducing the redraw and refresh rates of the advanced screen saver.

To reduce screen saver resource usage, follow these steps:

1. Press and hold or right-click an open area of the desktop, and then tap or click Personalize.

2. Tap or click the Screen Saver link to display the Screen Saver Settings dialog box.

3. If you want to use a screen saver that uses fewer resources without making configuration changes, use the Screen Saver list box to select a basic screen saver, such as Blank.

4. If you want to use 3D Text or another advanced screen saver but reduce its resource usage, select that screen saver and then tap or click Settings. Use the Settings dialog box to reduce the values for Resolution, Size, Rotational Speed, or similar settings that affect the drawing or refreshing of the screen saver.

5. Tap or click OK to close each of the open dialog boxes.

Setting energy-saving settings for monitors

Many newer monitors have energy-saving features that cause them to shut off after a certain period of inactivity. Enabling this feature can reduce the organization's electricity bill because monitors typically use a lot of electricity to stay powered up. On some systems, this feature might have been automatically enabled by the operating system during installation. This depends, however, on the operating system properly detecting the monitor and installing any necessary drivers.

On a portable laptop computer running on batteries, saving energy is especially important. By configuring the monitor to shut off when the computer is idle, you can save the battery life and extend the available battery time for when the laptop is unplugged.

To manage a monitor's energy settings, follow these steps:

1. Press and hold or right-click an open area of the desktop, and then tap or click Personalize.

2. Tap or click the Screen Saver link to display the Screen Saver Settings dialog box.

3. Tap or click Change Power Settings. The Power Options console in Control Panel is displayed.

4. In the left pane, tap or click Choose When To Turn Off The Display.

5. If the options on the Edit Plan Settings page are unavailable, select Change Settings That Are Currently Unavailable.

6. Use the selection list provided to specify when the monitor should be turned off to save energy. Mobile computer devices might have separate on-battery and plugged-in options.

7. Tap or click Save Changes.

NOTE If a computer is connected to a monitor that doesn't support energy-saving settings, some power options might be unavailable. If you are configuring the computer in a build area and are using a different monitor than the one the user will have, you might want to obtain the user's monitor or a similar monitor and repeat this process.

REAL WORLD Typically, you'll want to turn off the monitor after 10 to 15 minutes of idle time. On my office computer, I turn on the screen saver after 7 minutes and then turn off the monitor after 15 minutes of idle time. On my laptop, I use settings of 5 minutes and 10 minutes, respectively.

Modifying display appearance and video settings

The display appearance and video settings have a major impact on the look and feel of the Windows 8.1 desktop and its graphical elements. Appearance options control window, button, color, and font settings. Video settings control screen resolution, color quality, refresh frequency, hardware acceleration, and color management.

Configuring window color and appearance

Windows Aero is an enhanced interface that provides features such as the transparent taskbar background, live previews, smoother window dragging, animated window closing and opening, and more. As part of the setup process, Windows 8.1 runs a performance test and checks the computer to find out whether it meets the requirements to take advantage of optimized appearance features.

XDDM and VGA drivers cannot be used with Windows 8.1. The display hardware must support Windows Display Driver Model (WDDM) 1.2 or later. If the hardware doesn't, the computer will use the Microsoft Basic Display Driver.

Display drivers that support WDDM 1.2 will offer improved performance over earlier drivers while also reducing the overhead needed for temporary surfaces in local and system memory. WDDM 1.2 supports Direct3D implemented in a graphics processing unit (GPU) with at least 128 megabytes (MB) of graphics memory. Although individual nodes in a physical adapter can reset GPU timeout detection and recovery behavior, preemption of GPU direct memory access (DMA) packets cannot be disabled.

WDDM 1.3 adds support for wireless displays. WDDM 1.3 also supports improved resource sharing between integrated and discrete GPUs. These latter changes can provide a solid display performance boost for hybrid systems that have both integrated and discrete GPUs.

> **REAL WORLD** You can quickly determine how much graphics memory is available and whether a computer's display adapter supports WDDM by using System Information (Msinfo32.exe). You can access system information by tapping or clicking System Information on the Apps screen or by typing **msinfo32** into the Everywhere Search box, and then pressing Enter. In the Components list, select Display, and you'll find the display adapter type and the level of WDDM support (if applicable). The Adapter RAM value shows the amount of dedicated graphics memory.

On compliant systems, Windows 8.1 uses the Aero desktop by default to enable advanced display features and options, including Snap, which allows you to arrange windows side by side, and Shake, which allows you to temporarily hide all open windows except the one you are working with. To snap an active window to the side of the desktop by using the keyboard, press either the Windows key + Left Arrow or the Windows key + Right Arrow. To shake, drag the title bar of the window you want to keep open back and forth quickly. Then to restore the minimized windows, shake the open window again.

To configure color options for the display, follow these steps:

1. Press and hold or right-click an open area of the desktop, and then tap or click Personalize.

2. Tap or click the Color link to display the Color And Appearance page, as shown in Figure 3-8.

3. Change the color of windows by tapping or clicking one of the available colors. To make your own color, tap or click Show Color Mixer, and then use the Hue, Saturation, and Brightness sliders to create a custom color.

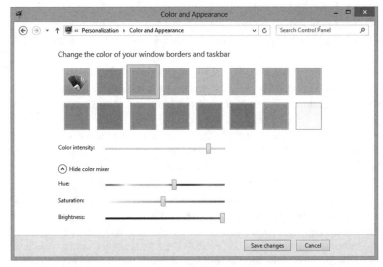

FIGURE 3-8 Configure the visual appearance of the display by using the options on the Color And Appearance page.

4. Use the Color Intensity slider to set the strength of the color and the level of transparency. Increase the intensity to make the color stronger and to reduce the transparency. Reduce the intensity to make the color dimmer and the transparency greater.

5. Tap or click Save Changes.

To better support the visually impaired, Windows 8.1 includes several Ease Of Access themes, including High Contrast #1, High Contrast #2, High Contrast White, and High Contrast Black. When you use these themes, the options of the Color And Appearance page change, and you can override the default color settings for individual graphical elements, such as the window background color, text color, and active window color. To do this, follow these steps:

1. Press and hold or right-click an open area of the desktop, and then tap or click Personalize.

2. Tap or click the Color link and then set the color to use for interface elements. For example, with active window titles, you can set foreground and background colors.

3. Tap or click OK, and then tap or click Save Changes.

Optimizing display readability

Regardless of whether users have 27-inch widescreens or 19-inch displays, you might find that users have difficulty reading text on the screen. Often, the readability of text on the screen decreases when you increase the display resolution, which results in the text on the screen becoming smaller. To understand why this happens, you need to understand how DPI works.

When you print documents on a printer, the number of dots per inch (DPI) determines the print quality. Generally, the higher the DPI, the better the quality of the printed document because images and text look crisper as you use more dots per inch. For example, a high-resolution picture printed at its normal size using 1,200 × 600 DPI generally looks much better than the same picture printed at 300 × 300 DPI. However, if you use scaling to print a 2 × 3–inch picture at 6 × 9 inches, you often get a poor result because the scaled image looks grainy.

For Windows-based computers, 96 DPI is the default for most monitors, and Windows 8.1 displays all UI elements, including text, at 96 DPI by default. When you change the display resolution, you change the scaling at which UI elements are displayed. For example, if a monitor has an optimal resolution of 1,920 × 1,200 and you use a display resolution of 800 × 600, the UI elements will seem large and grainy because you've caused the display to scale 800 × 600 pixels into a space optimized for 1,920 × 1,200 pixels.

Generally, you can determine the optimal resolution by multiplying a monitor's screen width by 96 and a monitor's screen height by 96. For example, a 24-inch widescreen monitor might have a screen that is 20 inches wide and 12.5 inches high. If so, the optimal display resolution is 1,920 × 1,200. However, at that size, text and UI elements on the screen might seem small, and you might need to make adjustments to improve readability. One way in which you can make adjustments is through an application. For example, in Word, users can use the Zoom combo box to scale text to a readable size.

Windows allows you to change the size of text for specific UI elements, including the text for title bars in dialog boxes, menus, message boxes, palettes, icons, and tooltips. When you increase or decrease the size of text in a specific part of the UI, you can improve readability. Each account on a computer has a separate setting for text size. You can specify text size for UI elements by completing the following steps:

1. In Control Panel, tap or click Appearance And Personalization. Under the Display heading, tap or click Make Text And Other Items Larger Or Smaller.

2. Tap or click the selection list under Change Only The Text Size, and choose the UI element you want to work with, such as Menus.

3. Use the Font Size list to set the desired size for the text on the previously selected UI element. Optionally, select Bold to display bold text.

4. Repeat steps 2 and 3 to set the text size of additional UI elements. When you are finished, tap or click Apply.

5. You need to log off and then log on as the user again for the changes to take effect.

Windows also allows you to use scaling to increase the size of text and other items on the screen. When you use scaling in this way, Windows magnifies the size of text and UI elements to the scale you choose. Each account on a computer has a separate setting for scaling. You can specify the scaling to use for text and UI elements by following these steps:

1. In Control Panel, tap or click Appearance And Personalization. Under the Display heading, tap or click Make Text And Other Items Larger Or Smaller.

2. The default scaling options allow you to choose a 100-percent scale (the default), a 125-percent scale, or a 150-percent scale. To use one of these scaling options, select Let Me Choose One Scaling Level For All My Displays, make a selection, and then select Apply.

3. To choose a custom setting of between 100 percent and 500 percent, tap or click Custom Sizing Options, and then use the Scale combo box to select or specify a scale.

4. You need to log off as the user and then log on as the user again for the changes to take effect.

IMPORTANT If you choose a setting higher than 200 percent, UI elements and text might be scaled so large that you cannot work with the computer. You might even be unable to get back into Control Panel to restore the original scaling. If you have a scaling issue, enter **dpiscaling** at a command prompt or in the Everywhere Search box. This will open the Display page directly, and you can then reset the scaling.

REAL WORLD If you've enabled scaling and the text in an application is blurred or unreadable, you might want to disable display scaling for that application. To do this, press and hold or right-click the application shortcut, and then tap or click Properties. On the Compatibility tab, select Disable Display Scaling On High DPI Settings, and then tap or click OK.

Configuring video settings

Video settings control screen resolution, color quality, refresh rate, hardware acceleration, and color management. This section focuses on making sure that Windows 8.1 has correctly identified the video card and monitor, and on optimizing various video settings.

IMPORTANT You cannot change display settings from a remote session. Display options can only be configured when you are logged on locally.

Checking the current video adapter and monitor

Every computer has a monitor driver and a video adapter driver. The monitor driver tells Windows about the capabilities of the monitor. The video adapter (or display) driver tells Windows about the capabilities of the graphics card.

Proper display is dependent on the computer using accurate information about the video adapter and the monitor. Different driver files are installed depending on which video adapter and monitor models Windows 8.1 detects on a system. These drivers are extremely important in determining which display resolutions, color depths, and refresh rates are available and appropriate for the system. If the adapter and monitor aren't detected and configured properly, Windows 8.1 won't be able to take advantage of their capabilities.

Current settings for the video adapter or monitor can be wrong for many reasons. Sometimes Plug and Play doesn't detect the device, and a generic device driver is used. Sometimes Windows Update installs an old driver. At other times, Windows 8.1 detects the wrong type of device, such as a different model. In this case, the device will probably work, but some features won't be available.

You can determine the current video adapter and monitor as configured for a computer in software settings by completing these steps:

1. Press and hold or right-click an open area of the desktop, and then tap or click Screen Resolution.

2. On the Screen Resolution page, shown in Figure 3-9, the currently identified monitors are listed in the Display list. The resolution and orientation are listed in the Resolution and Orientation lists. If the correct monitor isn't displayed or you want to examine the monitor settings further, see the "Changing the monitor driver" section later in this chapter.

3. Select a monitor in the Display list, and then tap or click the Advanced Settings link. The video adapter for the monitor is listed. If the correct video adapter isn't displayed or you want to examine the driver settings further, see the next section, "Changing the video driver."

4. Tap or click OK twice.

FIGURE 3-9 Check the monitor and video adapter configuration.

> **REAL WORLD** Another way to determine the current video adapter and monitor as configured for a computer in software is to run the DirectX Diagnostic Tool by typing **dxdiag** in the Everywhere Search box and pressing Enter.

Both of the techniques discussed in this section assume that the correct drivers are installed, however. Neither of these techniques will tell you whether the correct information is being displayed. See "Changing the video driver" for details on how you can confirm that the correct drivers are installed.

Changing the video driver

If you followed the previous instructions and the video driver shown does not match the make and model installed on the computer, you might want to try to install a different driver. For example, if the computer has a generic S3 video driver configured and you are sure the computer has an NVIDIA GeForce video adapter, you should change the video driver.

To determine whether the video card make and model are correct, you need to know how the system is configured. The system documentation can tell you which video adapter is installed. Other administrators are also useful resources. Typically, someone else on the technology team will know immediately what video adapter is installed on a particular type of computer. If you can't figure out the make and model of the video adapter, you have several options. If the current settings are working, you can leave the display settings alone.

You can also try the following techniques to determine the video adapter's make and model:

- Shut down the computer, and then turn it back on (but don't use the Restart option to do this, because some computers might not fully initialize when you select Restart). Watch the screen when the computer first turns on. The name of the video card might appear briefly before Windows 8.1 begins loading.

- Shut down the computer, and then remove the computer cover. Locate the name and model number on the video adapter itself. If the monitor is still attached to the rear of the computer, the video adapter is the card to which the monitor cable is connected.

- If the video adapter is built into the computer's motherboard (meaning that there isn't a separate card), check the motherboard to determine whether you can find a chip that lists the video information on it, or write down the motherboard model number and visit the manufacturer's website to determine whether the information is available.

- If you think the computer has an NVIDIA graphics card, you can use NVIDIA Smart Scan to identify the correct model and drivers. Currently, this program is located at *http://www.nvidia.com/Download/Scan.aspx*.

- If you think the computer has an AMD graphics card, you can use AMD Driver Autodetect to identify the correct model and drivers. Currently, this program is located at *http://support.amd.com/us/gpudownload/windows/Pages/auto_detect.aspx*.

After you determine the video adapter's make and model, find out whether you can locate the necessary drivers on the manufacturer's website. Some video adapters come with installation discs. On the disc, you might find a setup program. Run this program to install the video driver. If the installation disc contains the drivers but no setup program, you need to install the drivers manually.

IMPORTANT The drivers on the installation disc that came with a video adapter might not be the most current drivers. They will, however, be the correct drivers for the computer. After the correct drivers are installed, rather than generic or other drivers, you can update to the most current drivers by following the procedure I discuss in this section.

When you are ready to install the video adapter driver, follow these steps:

1. Press and hold or right-click an open area of the desktop, and then tap or click Screen Resolution.

2. On a system with multiple monitors or video cards, use the Display list to select the monitor with which you want to work.

3. Tap or click Advanced Settings. On the Adapter tab, shown in Figure 3-10, note the current information in the Adapter Type and Adapter Information panels. Tap or click Properties.

FIGURE 3-10 Note the current adapter information.

4. On the Driver tab, tap or click Update Driver. This starts the Update Driver Software Wizard.

5. Specify whether you want to search for the driver automatically or browse for the driver.

6. If you elect to search for the driver automatically, Windows 8.1 looks for a more recent version of the device driver and installs the driver if it is found. If a more recent version of the driver is not found, Windows 8.1 keeps the current driver. In either case, tap or click Close to complete the process, and then skip the remaining steps.

7. If you choose to browse for the driver, you can do so in either of the following ways:

   ■ **Search for the driver** If you want to search for the driver, tap or click Browse to select a search location. Use the Browse For Folder dialog box to select the start folder for the search, and then tap or click OK. Because all subfolders of the selected folder are searched automatically by default, you can select the drive root path, such as C, to search an entire drive. If you don't want to search all subfolders, clear the Search All Subfolders option.

   ■ **Choose the driver to install** If you want to choose the driver to install, tap or click Let Me Pick From A List Of Device Drivers On My Computer. The wizard then displays a list of compatible hardware. Tap or click the device that matches your video card. To view a wider array of choices, clear the Show Compatible Hardware check box. You'll then get a list of all video card manufacturers. Scroll through the list of manufacturers to find the manufacturer of the device, and then choose the appropriate device in the right pane.

8. After selecting a device driver, continue through the installation process by tapping or clicking Next. Tap or click Close when the driver installation is complete. If the wizard can't find an appropriate driver, you need to obtain one and then repeat this procedure. Keep in mind that in some cases, you need to restart the system to activate the newly installed or updated device driver.

IMPORTANT To use custom display drivers with Windows 8.1, the display hardware must support WDDM 1.2 or later. If the display hardware doesn't support WDDM 1.2 or later, the display driver is set as Microsoft Basic Display Driver and you won't be able to select another driver.

Changing the monitor driver

The overall display quality is controlled by the combined capabilities of a computer's monitor and video adapter. Most computers have at least one monitor connection available. The type of connections supported might include the following:

- High-Definition Multimedia Interface (HDMI) is the current digital standard for connecting video devices. HDMI can be used for computer displays, but it is better suited to other high-end video devices. Although HDMI can be adapted to a Digital Video Interface (DVI) connection, most computers that have an HDMI connector also have at least one DVI connector.

- Digital Video Interface (DVI) is the digital standard for computer-generated text and graphics. There are several formats for DVI. DVI-I and DVI-A can be adapted to Video Graphics Array (VGA); however, DVI-D cannot be adapted to VGA. Dual-Link DVI supports high-resolution monitors and is required on some very large displays for optimum picture quality. Because DVI cables can support one or more of these types at the same time, you should check your cables carefully to be sure you're using the correct ones.

- The 15-pin Video Graphics Array (VGA) is the analog standard for connecting monitors to computers. There are 9-pin VGA cables, and they are compatible with the 15-pin connector. It is still very common for monitors to have this connector, but newer connections such as DVI and HDMI are recommended if they are available.

NOTE A computer's monitor might have shipped with a VGA cable connected to it. If it is not the optimal connection type and the cable is designed to be removed, remove the VGA cable.

TIP Many computers have inputs for DisplayPort adapters. A DisplayPort adapter supports automatic adaptation to VGA, DVI, or HDMI depending on what type of display is connected to the port and what type of adapter is used between the display connector and the input connector on the back of the computer.

If a computer has a Plug and Play monitor, Windows 8.1 might have detected it and installed it properly, or it might have installed a similar driver, but not the one that matches the monitor's make and model. For the best quality, Windows 8.1 should use the driver designed for the applicable monitor. Otherwise, the display mode, color depth, refresh rate, and color-matching options might not be appropriate for the monitor.

To change the monitor setup, follow these steps:

1. Press and hold or right-click an open area of the desktop, and then tap or click Screen Resolution.

2. On a system with multiple monitors or video cards, use the Display list to select the monitor with which you want to work.

3. Tap or click Advanced Settings. On the Monitor tab, tap or click Properties.

4. On the Driver tab, tap or click Update Driver. This starts the Update Driver Software Wizard.

5. Continue with the driver update, as described in steps 5–8 of the previous procedure.

Configuring multiple monitor support

Most laptops and tablets designed for Windows 8 and later can use docking hubs that allow you to dock the laptop or tablet to a large display or set up your workspace with several monitors. Most modern desktop PCs come with a video adapter that supports multiple monitors. You'll know this because the adapter will have multiple monitor connection ports. On these computers, you can connect multiple monitors and then extend a user's desktop across those monitors so that the user can view more information at one time. If you've connected multiple monitors to a computer, the Screen Resolution page will show one box for each monitor. The first monitor is labeled 1, the second is labeled 2, and so on. If you tap or click the monitor box, you can work with the monitor in the same way you would if you had selected the monitor from the Display list.

If a monitor you've connected doesn't have its own box, check the monitor connection and then turn the monitor on. Then, when you tap or click Detect, Windows should automatically detect the monitor.

If you've connected multiple monitors and are unsure which monitor is which, you can tap or click Identify to display the numeric identifier of each monitor on the monitor's screen. The numeric identifier appears as a large white numeral. If you find that the screens are represented in a different position than they are configured, you can drag the monitor boxes on the Screen Resolution page so that their position matches the physical layout of the monitors.

After you configure the monitors, you might want to extend the display across their screens. To do this, tap or click the box representing the second monitor (or select the second monitor in the Display list), and then select Extend Desktop To This Display from the Multiple Displays list. Generally, you will want screen 1 to be marked This Is Currently Your Main Display.

After you've configured your monitors, you'll find that pressing the Windows key + P is a convenient way to change the monitor configuration quickly. After pressing the Windows key + P, you can use any of the following options:

- Select PC Screen Only to use only the main computer monitor or the built-in screen on a laptop.

- Select Duplicate to display the main computer monitor or the built-in screen on a laptop to a second monitor.

- Select Extend to extend the display across two monitors.

- Select Second Screen Only to display only on an external monitor or projector.

With touch UI, you can access similar options by sliding in from the right, tapping Devices, and then tapping Second Screen.

Customizing display appearance

Screen resolution, color quality, and refresh rate are key factors that affect display appearance. *Screen resolution* is the number of pixels that make up the display. *Color quality* is the number of colors that can be displayed simultaneously on the screen. *Refresh rate* is the rate at which the screen is repainted.

Windows 8.1 automatically optimizes display settings for each of your monitors by selecting a screen resolution, color quality, and refresh rate that seem most appropriate based on its testing. Normally, the settings that Windows selects work well, but they might not be the optimal settings for your computer.

The best resolution to use depends on the size of the monitor and what the user plans to do with the computer. Designers and developers who need a large screen area will appreciate a higher resolution, such as 1,920 × 1,200. They can then view more of what they're working with on the screen. Users who spend most of their time reading email or working with Word documents might prefer a lower resolution, such as 1,280 × 1,024. At that resolution, screen elements are easier to see, and users will have less eyestrain. On a widescreen monitor, be sure to select a resolution that is appropriate for widescreen viewing.

Color quality depends greatly on screen resolution settings. Even though most current video cards display 32-bit color at a variety of screen resolutions, some video cards might not be capable of displaying 32-bit color at their maximum screen resolution. Video cards might display fewer colors when you set the screen resolution higher. In most cases, the higher the color quality that you can set, the better. Keep in mind that the amount of video memory required to maintain the video display is determined by multiplying the number of pixels on the screen (based on screen resolution) by the number of bits per pixel (determined by color quality). Furthermore, the maximum combination of resolution and color quality allowed is a function of the video memory on the video adapter.

You can set the screen resolution and color quality by completing the following steps:

1. Press and hold or right-click an open area of the desktop, and then tap or click Screen Resolution.

2. On a system with multiple monitors or video cards, use the Display list to select the monitor with which you want to work.

3. Tap or click Resolution, and then use the Resolution slider to set the display size, such as 1,024 × 768 pixels. Note that if the Resolution option is unavailable, you cannot change the resolution.

4. To view the display modes available for 32-bit color, tap or click Advanced Settings. On the Adapter tab, tap or click List All Modes. Note the screen resolutions that support 32-bit color.

5. Tap or click OK twice.

Your eyes can't perceive the display refresh, but a low refresh rate (under 72 Hz) can sometimes make your eyes tired if you look at the display too long. To view or set the refresh rate for a video card, follow these steps:

1. Press and hold or right-click an open area of the desktop, and then tap or click Screen Resolution.

2. On a system with multiple monitors or video cards, use the Display list to select the monitor with which you want to work.

3. Tap or click Advanced Settings. On the Adapter tab, tap or click List All Modes. The resolution sizes and refresh rates supported by the monitor are listed.

4. On the Monitor tab, use the Screen Refresh Rate list box to set the refresh rate.

CAUTION In many cases, the Hide Modes That This Monitor Cannot Display check box is disabled so that it cannot be selected. If you are able to clear this check box, keep in mind that if the refresh rate exceeds the capabilities of the monitor or the video card, the screen can become distorted. Additionally, running the computer at a higher refresh rate than it supports can damage the monitor and video adapter.

Color profiles allow you to get truer colors for specific uses. For example, you might need to more accurately match on-screen colors to print colors, and a color profile designed for this purpose can help you do that. After you obtain the color profile, you must install it on each monitor separately by following these steps:

1. Press and hold or right-click an open area of the desktop, and then tap or click Screen Resolution. Display 1 is selected by default. Tap or click 2 to configure settings for the second monitor.

2. Tap or click Advanced Settings. On the Color Management tab, tap or click Color Management.

3. In the Color Management dialog box, select the All Profiles tab to get information about currently installed color profiles. Tap or click Add.

4. In the Install Profile dialog box, find the color profile that you want to use and then tap or click Add.

5. In the Color Management dialog box, select the Devices tab. Tap or click the new profile, and then tap or click Set As Default Profile.

If you don't have a color profile and still would like the benefits of one, use the Display Color Calibration tool to fine-tune display colors to your liking. You can access this tool by typing **Dccw.exe** in the Everywhere Search box and pressing Enter.

Troubleshooting display problems

As I stated previously, every computer has a monitor driver and a video adapter driver. The monitor driver tells Windows about the capabilities of the monitor. The video adapter (or display) driver tells Windows about the capabilities of the graphics card.

Clearly, the monitor driver and video adapter driver have important roles on a computer. When you are installing video components or updating a computer, you should be sure that the computer has drivers that have been tested in your environment and proven to be reliable. If you suspect a problem with the drivers, update the drivers if possible. If you suspect the problem is due to the configuration of the computer, start the computer in safe mode and then modify the default settings.

Before you start detailed diagnostics and troubleshooting, determine what programs the user has been running. Programs created for early versions of Windows might cause compatibility issues. Close all running programs and check questionable programs to find out what display mode they are using. If a program requires an alternative display mode and switching into and out of this display mode is causing problems, you might be able to configure compatibility settings to resolve the problem. Press and hold or right-click the application shortcut, and then tap or click Properties. In the Properties dialog box, select the Compatibility tab. On the Settings panel, choose the appropriate option, such as Run In 640 x 480 Screen Resolution. If you are unsure which compatibility settings to use, press and hold or right-click the application shortcut, tap or click Troubleshoot Compatibility, and then follow the prompts in the Program Compatibility Wizard.

Many problems with monitors have to do with the connection between the monitor and the computer. If the monitor displays blotches, color spots, diagonal lines, or horizontal bars, or has other similar display problems, you'll want to check the monitor connection first. After you are sure the connections are all right, turn the monitor off for at least 10 seconds, and then turn the monitor back on. If you still are experiencing a problem and think that the problem has to do with the monitor itself, you can try to resolve it through additional troubleshooting.

Monitor flicker or jitter or a shaky image can be caused by configuration issues in addition to positional issues. If the monitor refresh rate is causing the problem, you can resolve it by changing the refresh rate settings, as discussed in the "Customizing display appearance" section earlier in this chapter. If a positional issue is causing the problem, you can resolve the problem by moving the cables and devices that might be causing electromagnetic interference, including power cables for other devices, large speakers, or desk lamps. If the problem persists, make sure the monitor has a shielded cable and that it is positioned away from air-conditioning units, large fluorescent lights, and so on.

If the monitor has built-in controls, check for an auto-tuning setting. Often, this will be a separate button, and when you press this button, the monitor will automatically adjust itself.

If blotches of color, color spots, or lines are the problem and resetting the connections doesn't work, you might need to perform a monitor degauss. This operation removes the buildup of stray magnetic fields around the monitor, which can distort the video image. Some monitors autodegauss by turning the monitor off and then on, some have a manual control only, and some combine both of these features. You might find a control labeled Degauss, or there might be a menu option within the monitor's software controls. While the monitor is degaussing, the screen might become distorted temporarily. This is normal behavior during the degauss process. If you manually degauss, wait 15 to 20 minutes before attempting a second degauss.

If problems persist, connect the monitor directly to the computer. Remove any extension cables connected between the monitor and the video adapter. Also, remove any antiglare screens or other similar devices that cover the monitor's screen. Check the video data cable for bent, broken, or missing pins. Although some pins are missing as part of the design, other pins that are missing or bent will cause display problems. If there are bent pins and the pins are repairable, turn the monitor off, unplug the monitor from the power source, and use tweezers or pliers to straighten the pins.

Optimizing corner and Start navigation

Windows 8.1 allows you to customize the way you navigate corners and the way you navigate between the Start screen, apps, and the desktop. For example, you can display the desktop instead of Start when you log on. You can display apps instead of Start, and more. Most of the related corner and Start options are in the Taskbar And Navigation Properties dialog box shown in Figure 3-11.

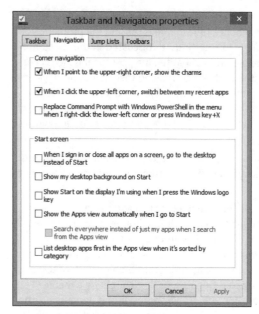

FIGURE 3-11 Configure navigation options.

You can configure corner navigation options by completing the following steps:

1. On the desktop, press and hold or right-click the taskbar and then select Properties.

2. In the Taskbar And Navigation Properties dialog box, on the Navigation tab, you can configure the following corner navigation options:

   - **When I Point To The Upper-Right Corner, Show The Charms**   Displays the Charms panel when you point to the upper-right corner of the screen. If you disable this option, the Charms panel is only displayed when you slide in from the right or when you point to the lower-right corner of the screen.

   - **When I Click The Upper-Left Corner, Switch Between My Recent Apps**   Allows you to switch between recent apps when you point to the upper-left corner of the screen. If you disable this option, the Recent Apps panel is only displayed when you slide in from the left.

   - **Replace Command Prompt With fWindows PowerShell...**   Displays options for Windows PowerShell rather than the command prompt on the shortcut menu that is displayed when you right-click in the lower left corner or press Windows key + X. If you disable this option, the shortcut menu has Command Prompt and command prompt (Admin) options instead of Windows PowerShell and Windows PowerShell (Admin) options.

3. Select Apply to apply any changes.

You can configure navigation options for the Start screen by completing the following steps:

1. On the desktop, press and hold or right-click the taskbar, and then select Properties.

2. In the Taskbar And Navigation Properties dialog box, on the Navigation tab, you can configure the following navigation options for Start:

   - **When I Sign In Or Close All Apps On A Screen, Go To The Desktop Instead Of Start**   Displays the desktop by default instead of Start whenever you log on or close all apps on a screen. If this option is disabled, Start is displayed by default when you log on, and you don't change screens when you close all apps.

   - **Show My Desktop Background On Start**   Displays the desktop background on start instead of the Start screen's background color. If this option is disabled, the default background color is displayed on the Start screen.

   - **Show Start On The Display I'm Using...**   When a computer has multiple displays, this option ensures that the Start screen is always displayed on the display with which you are actively working. If this option is disabled and a computer has multiple displays, Start normally is displayed only on the main display.

   - **Show The Apps View Automatically When I Go To Start**   Displays the Apps screen instead of the Start screen. If this option is enabled, you can use the Windows key to switch between the Apps screen and the desktop. To get to Start, you must then swipe down or click the Up arrow (in the lower-right portion of the display).

3. Select Apply to apply any changes.

Automating Windows 8.1 configuration

G roup Policy is a collection of preferences and settings that can be applied to user and computer configurations. Group Policy simplifies administration of common and repetitive tasks as well as tasks that are difficult to implement manually but can be automated. Group Policy is represented logically as an object called a Group Policy Object (GPO). Each GPO is a collection of policy settings and preferences.

Group Policy preferences, which are the focus of this chapter, enable you to automatically configure, deploy, and manage operating system and application settings, including settings for data sources, mapped drives, environment variables, network shares, folder options, and shortcuts. When you are deploying and setting up computers, you'll find that working with Group Policy preferences is easier than configuring the same settings manually on each computer, in Windows images, or through scripts used for startup, logon, shutdown, and logoff.

In this chapter, I introduce essential tasks for understanding and managing Group Policy preferences. In upcoming chapters, I'll show you how to put individual policy preferences to work to automate the configuration of your computers running Windows, whether you work in a small, medium, or large enterprise.

Understanding Group Policy preferences

You configure preferences in Active Directory–based Group Policy. Local Group Policy does not have preferences.

Accessing Group Policy in Active Directory

With Active Directory, each site, domain, and organizational unit (OU) can have one or more Group Policy Objects associated with it. You view and edit GPOs in the Group Policy Management Console (GPMC). On Windows-based servers, the GPMC is available as part of the standard installation. On Windows-based desktops, the GPMC is not available by default but is included in the Remote Server Administration Tools (RSAT), which can be installed on Windows-based desktops.

You can download the RSAT for Windows 8.1 by visiting the Microsoft Download Center (*http://download.microsoft.com/*). After you install the GPMC as part of the RSAT, you can run the GPMC from Server Manager. In Server Manager, select Tools, and then select Group Policy Management.

As shown in Figure 4-1, the left pane of the GPMC has two upper-level nodes by default: Group Policy Management (the console root) and Forest (a node representing the forest to which you are currently connected, which is named after the forest root domain for that forest). When you expand the Forest node, you find additional nodes, including:

- **Domains**   Provides access to the policy settings for domains in the forest being administered. You are connected to your logon domain by default; however, you can add connections to other domains. If you expand a domain, you can access the Default Domain Policy GPO, the Domain Controllers OU (and the related Default Domain Controllers Policy GPO), and GPOs defined in the domain.

- **Organizational Units**   Provides access to the policy settings for OUs in a related domain.

- **Sites**   Provides access to the policy settings for sites in the related forest. Sites are hidden by default.

GPOs found in domain, OU, and site containers in the GPMC are actually GPO links and not GPOs themselves. The actual GPOs are found in the Group Policy Objects container of the selected domain. Notice also that the icons for GPO links have a small arrow at the bottom left, similar to shortcut icons. You can open a GPO for editing by pressing and holding or right-clicking it, and then selecting Edit.

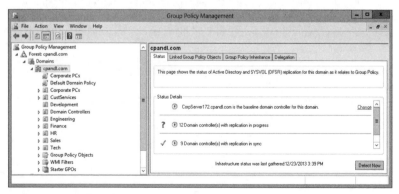

FIGURE 4-1 Access GPOs for domains, OUs, and sites.

After you've selected a policy for editing or created a new policy, use the Group Policy Management Editor to work with the GPOs. As Figure 4-2 shows, the Group Policy Management Editor has two main nodes:

- **Computer Configuration** Enables you to set policies that should be applied to computers, regardless of who logs on
- **User Configuration** Enables you to set policies that should be applied to users, regardless of which computer they log on to

NOTE Keep in mind that user configuration options set through local policy objects apply only to computers on which the options are configured. If you want the options to apply to all computers that the user might use, you must use domain, OU, or site policies.

FIGURE 4-2 When you're editing a GPO in the Group Policy Management Editor, you can view and manage policy settings and preferences.

You will find separate Policies and Preferences nodes under Computer Configuration and User Configuration. When you are working with policy preferences, you use the Preferences node. The options available under a Preferences node depend on whether you are working with Computer Configuration or User Configuration.

Essentials for working with preferences

Group Policy does not strictly enforce policy preferences, nor does Group Policy store preferences in the policy-related branches of the registry. Instead, Group Policy writes preferences to the same locations in the registry that an application or operating system feature uses to store the related setting. This approach allows you to use preferences with applications and operating system features that aren't Group Policy–aware.

Preferences do not disable application or operating system features in the user interface to prevent their use. Users can change settings that you've configured with policy preferences. However, preferences overwrite existing settings, and there is no way to recover the original settings.

As it does with policy settings, Group Policy refreshes preferences at a regular interval, which is every 90 to 120 minutes by default. This means that periodically the preferences you've configured will be reapplied to a user's computer. Rather than allowing a refresh, you can prevent Group Policy from refreshing individual preferences by choosing to apply preferences only once.

The way you use policy preferences depends on whether you want to enforce the item you are configuring. To configure an item without enforcing it, use policy preferences, and then disable automatic refreshes. To configure an item and enforce the specified configuration, use policy settings or configure preferences, and then enable automatic refreshes.

Because preferences apply to both computer configuration and user configuration settings, you will find a separate Preferences nodes under Computer Configuration and User Configuration. In both configuration areas, you'll find two top-level subnodes:

- **Windows Settings**   Used to manage general operating system and application preferences
- **Control Panel Settings**   Used to manage Control Panel preferences

Table 4-1 provides an overview of the available preferences and where they are located within the configuration areas and the top-level subnodes.

TABLE 4-1 Configurable preferences in Group Policy

PREFERENCE TYPE	LOCATION	POLICY CONFIGURATION AREA(S)
Applications | Application	Windows Settings	User
Data Sources | Data Source	Control Panel Settings	Computer and User
Data Sources | User Data Source	Control Panel Settings	User
Devices | Device	Control Panel Settings	Computer and User
Drive Maps | Mapped Drive	Windows Settings	User
Environment | Environment Variable	Windows Settings	Computer and User
Files | File	Windows Settings	Computer and User
Folder Options | Folder Options (at least Windows Vista)	Control Panel Settings	User
Folder Options | File Type	Control Panel Settings	Computer
Folder Options | Open With	Control Panel Settings	User
Folders | Folder	Windows Settings	Computer and User
Ini Files | Ini File	Windows Settings	Computer and User

PREFERENCE TYPE	LOCATION	POLICY CONFIGURATION AREA(S)
Internet Settings | Windows Internet Explorer 8 and 9	Control Panel Settings	User
Internet Settings | Windows Internet Explorer 10	Control Panel Settings	User
Local Users And Groups | Local User	Control Panel Settings	Computer and User
Local Users And Groups | Local Group	Control Panel Settings	Computer and User
Network Options | Dial-Up Connection	Control Panel Settings	Computer and User
Network Options | VPN Connection	Control Panel Settings	Computer and User
Network Shares | Network Share	Windows Settings	Computer
Power Options | Power Plan (at least Windows 7)	Control Panel Settings	Computer and User
Printers | Local Printer	Control Panel Settings	Computer and User
Printers | Shared Printer	Control Panel Settings	User
Printers | TCP/IP Printer	Control Panel Settings	Computer and User
Registry | Registry Item	Windows Settings	Computer and User
Registry | Collection Item	Windows Settings	Computer and User
Registry | Registry Wizard	Windows Settings	Computer and User
Regional Options	Control Panel Settings	User
Scheduled Tasks | Immediate Task (at least Windows 7)	Control Panel Settings	Computer and User
Scheduled Tasks | Scheduled Task (at least Windows 7)	Control Panel Settings	Computer and User
Services | Service	Control Panel Settings	Computer
Shortcuts | Shortcut	Windows Settings	Computer and User
Start Menu | Start Menu (at least Windows Vista)	Control Panel Settings	User

Configuring Group Policy preferences

Policy preferences are configured and managed differently from policy settings. You define preferences by specifying a management action, an editing state, or both.

Working with management actions

While you are viewing a particular preference area, you can use management actions to specify how the preference should be applied. Most preferences support the following management actions:

- **Create**   Creates a preference item on a user's computer. The preference item is created only if it does not already exist.

- **Replace**   Deletes an existing preference item and then re-creates it, or creates a preference item if it doesn't already exist. With most preferences, you have additional options that control exactly how the Replace operation works. Figure 4-3 shows an example.

FIGURE 4-3 Options available when configuring preferences depend on the management action that is selected.

- **Update**   Modifies designated settings in a preference item. This action differs from the Replace action in that it updates only settings defined within the preference item. All other settings remain the same. If a preference item does not exist, the Update action creates it.

- **Delete**   Deletes a preference item from a user's computer. With most preferences, you have additional options that control exactly how the Delete operation works. Often, the additional options will be the same as those available with the Replace operation.

The management action controls how the preference item is applied, or controls the removal of the item when it is no longer needed. Preferences that support management actions include those that configure the following:

- Applications
- Data sources
- Drive maps
- Environment
- Files
- Folders
- Ini files
- Local users and groups
- Network options
- Network shares
- Printers
- Registry items
- Scheduled tasks
- Shortcuts

Working with editing states

A small set of preferences support editing states, which present graphical user interfaces from Control Panel utilities. With this type of preference, the item is applied according to the editing state of each setting in the related interface. The editing state applied cannot be reversed, and no option is available to remove the editing state when it's no longer applied.

Preferences that support editing states include those that configure the following:

- Folder options
- Internet settings
- Power options
- Regional options
- Start menu settings

NOTE Only standard folder options support editing states.

Because each version of an application and the Windows operating system can have a different user interface, the related options are tied to a specific version. For example, folder option preference items for Internet Explorer 8 and 9 are configured separately from preference items for Internet Explorer 10.

By default, when you are working with preferences that support editing states, every setting in the interface is processed by the client and applied, even if you don't specifically set the related value. This effectively overwrites all existing settings applied through this interface.

The editing state of each related option is depicted graphically as follows:

- A solid green line indicates that the setting will be delivered and processed on the client.
- A dashed red line indicates that the setting will not be delivered or processed on the client.

When limited space on the interface prevents underlining, a green circle is displayed as the functional equivalent of the solid green line (meaning that the setting will be delivered and processed on the client), and a red circle is used as the functional equivalent of a dashed red line (meaning that the setting will not be delivered or processed on the client). Figures 4-4 and 4-5 show examples of preference items that use editing states.

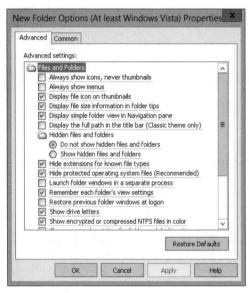

FIGURE 4-4 Note the editing state indicators.

You can use the following function keys to manage the editing state of options:

- **F5** Enables the processing of all settings on the selected tab. This is useful if you disabled processing of some settings and later decide that you want all settings on a tab to be processed.
- **F6** Enables the processing of the currently selected setting on the selected tab. This is useful if you disabled a setting and later decide you want the setting to be processed.
- **F7** Disables the processing of the currently selected setting on the selected tab. This is useful to prevent one setting from being processed on the client.
- **F8** Disables the processing of all settings on the selected tab. This is useful to prevent all settings on a tab from being processed on the client. It is also useful if you want only a few settings to be enabled.

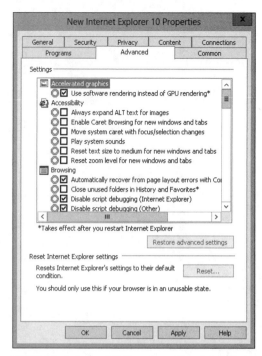

FIGURE 4-5 Circles provide alternative editing state indicators.

NOTE Keep in mind that the value associated with an option is separate from the editing state. Setting or clearing an option will not change the editing state.

Working with alternative actions and states

A few preferences support neither management actions nor editing states. Preferences of this type include those that configure devices, immediate tasks, and services.

With devices, as shown in Figure 4-6, you use the Action list to enable or disable a particular class and type of device. With immediate tasks, the related preference creates a task. The task runs and then is deleted automatically. With services, you use the related preference to configure an existing service.

FIGURE 4-6 Set the action to enable or disable the device.

Managing preference items

To view and work with preferences, you must open a Group Policy Object for editing in the Group Policy Management Editor, as discussed in "Accessing Group Policy in Active Directory" earlier in this chapter. Then you can manage preferences for either computers or users by using the following techniques:

- If you want to configure preferences that should be applied to computers, regardless of who logs on, double-tap or double-click the Computer Configuration node, double-tap or double-click the Preferences node, and then select the preference area with which you want to work.

- If you want to configure preferences that should be applied to users, regardless of which computer they log on to, double-tap or double-click the User Configuration node, double-tap or double-click the Preferences node, and then select the preference area with which you want to work.

Creating and managing a preference item

You manage preference items separately by selecting the preference area, and then working with the related preference items in the details pane. While you are viewing a particular preference area, you can create a related item by pressing and holding or right-clicking an open space in the details pane, pointing to New, and then selecting the type of item to create. Only items for the selected area are available. For example, if you are working with Printers under Computer Configuration, you have the option to create a TCP/IP Printer or Local Printer preference when you press and hold or right-click and point to New.

After you've created items for a preference area, you can press and hold or right-click an individual item to display a shortcut menu that allows you to manage the item, as shown in Figure 4-7.

Similar options are displayed on the toolbar when you select an item. In addition to pressing and holding or right-clicking an item and selecting Properties to display its Properties dialog box, you can double-tap or double-click a preference item to display its Properties dialog box. Then you can use the Properties dialog box to view or edit settings for the preference item.

On clients, the Group Policy client processes preference items according to their precedence order. The preference item with the lowest precedence (the one listed last) is processed first, followed by the preference item with the next lowest precedence, and so on until the preference item with the highest precedence (the one listed first) is processed.

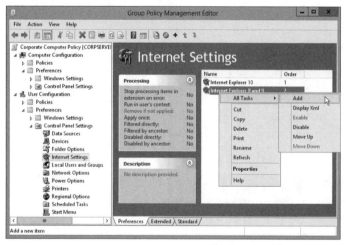

FIGURE 4-7 Manage preference items by using the Group Policy Management Editor and the shortcut menu.

Processing occurs in precedence order to ensure that preference items with higher precedence have priority over preference items with lower precedence. If there is any conflict between the settings applied in preference items, the settings written last win. To change the precedence order, select a preference area in the console tree, and then tap or click the preference item that you want to work with in the details pane. You'll then find additional options on the toolbar, which include:

- Move The Selected Item Up
- Move The Selected Item Down

To lower the precedence of the selected item, tap or click Move The Selected Item Down. To raise the precedence of the selected item, tap or click Move The Selected Item Up.

Setting Common tab options

All preference items have a Common tab, on which you'll find options that are common to preference items. Although the exact list of common options can differ from item to item, most preference items have the options shown in Figure 4-8.

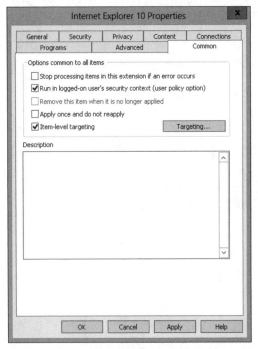

FIGURE 4-8 Set additional processing options on the Common tab.

These common options are used as follows:

- **Stop Processing Items In This Extension If An Error Occurs**   By default, if processing of one preference item fails, processing of other preference items will continue. To change this behavior, you can select Stop Processing Items In This Extension If An Error Occurs. With this option selected, a preference item that fails prevents the remaining preference items within the extension from being processed for a particular Group Policy Object. This setting doesn't affect processing in other Group Policy Objects.

- **Run In Logged-On User's Security Context**   By default, the Group Policy client running on a computer processes user preferences within the security context of either the Winlogon account (for computers running versions of Windows prior to Windows Vista) or the System account (for computers running Window Vista or later). In this context, a preference extension is limited to the environment variables and system resources available to the computer. Alternatively, the client can process user preferences in the security context of the logged-on user. This allows the preference extension to access resources as the user rather than as a system service, which might be required when using drive maps or other preferences for which the computer might not have permissions to access resources or might need to work with user environment variables.

- **Remove This Item When It Is No Longer Applied**   By default, when the policy settings in a Group Policy Object no longer apply to a user or computer, the policy settings are removed because they are no longer set in the Group Policy area of the registry. Default preference items are not removed automatically, however, when a Group Policy Object no longer applies to a user or computer. To change this behavior, you might be able to set this option for a preference item. When this option is selected, the preference extension determines whether a preference item that was in scope is now out of scope. If the preference item is out of scope, the preference extension removes the settings associated with the preference item.

  REAL WORLD   Generally, preferences that support management actions can be removed when they no longer apply, but preferences that support editing states cannot be removed when they no longer apply. If you select Remove This Item When It Is No Longer Applied, the management action is set as Replace. As a result, during Group Policy processing, the preference extension performs a Delete operation followed by a Create operation. Then, if the preference item goes out of scope (meaning that it no longer applies) for the user or computer, the results of the preference item are deleted (but not created). Item-level targeting can also cause a preference item to go out of scope.

- **Apply Once And Do Not Reapply**   Group Policy writes preferences to the same locations in the registry that an application or operating system feature uses to store the related setting. As a result, users can change settings that were configured by using policy preferences. However, by default, the results of preference items are rewritten each time Group Policy is refreshed to ensure that preference items are applied as administrators designated. You can change this behavior by setting this option. When this option is selected, the preference extension applies the results of the preference item one time and does not reapply the results.

- **Item-Level Targeting**   Item-level targeting allows you to filter the application of a preference item so that the preference item applies only to selected users or computers. When the Group Policy client evaluates a targeted preference, each targeting item results in a True or False value. If the result is True, the preference item applies and is processed. If the result is False, the preference item does not apply and is not processed. When this option is selected, tap or click the Targeting button to display the Targeting Editor, and then configure targeting as appropriate.

  REAL WORLD   A targeting item is evaluated as a logical expression. The logical expression can include environment variables as long as the environment variables are available in the current user context. After you create your logical expression, you'll need to ensure that the expression makes sense. In addition, if you hard-code a value when you meant to use an environment variable, the targeting will not work as expected.

CHAPTER 5

Managing user access and security

- Understanding user and group accounts **153**
- Managing User Account Control and elevation prompts **161**
- Managing local logon **168**
- Managing stored credentials **176**
- Managing local user accounts and groups **182**

Computers running Windows 8.1 can be configured to be members of a homegroup, a workgroup, a workplace, or a domain. When a workstation is configured as a member of a homegroup or a workgroup, user access and security are configured on the workstation itself. When a workstation is configured as a member of a workplace or a domain, user access and security are configured at two levels: the local system level and the domain level. User access can be configured at the local system level for a specific machine, at the workplace level for access to specific resources, and at the domain level for multiple systems or resources throughout the current Active Directory forest.

In this chapter, you'll learn how to manage local system access and local accounts. For further discussion of configuring domain access and permissions, see *Windows Server 2012 R2 Pocket Consultant: Essentials & Configuration* (Microsoft Press, 2013). Keep in mind that every task examined in this chapter and throughout this book can be performed through a local logon or a remote desktop connection.

Understanding user and group accounts

Windows 8.1 provides user accounts and group accounts. User accounts are designed for individuals, and group accounts, usually referred to as *groups*, are designed to simplify the administration of multiple users. You can log on with a user account, but you can't log on with a group account.

Two general types of user accounts are defined in Windows 8.1:

- **Local user accounts** User accounts defined on a local computer are called *local user accounts*. These accounts have access to the local computer only. You add or remove local user accounts with the User Accounts options in Control Panel or with the Local Users And Groups utility. Local Users And Groups is accessible in the System Tools node of Computer Management, a Microsoft Management Console (MMC) snap-in.

- **Domain user accounts** User accounts defined in Active Directory Domain Services are called *domain user accounts*. Through single sign-on, these accounts can access resources throughout a forest. When a computer is a member of an Active Directory domain, you can use the computer to create domain user accounts by using Active Directory Users And Computers. This MMC tool is available on the Tools menu in Server Manager when you install the Remote Server Administrator Tools on your computer running Windows 8.1.

TIP As with any locally installed administrative tool, Computer Management is available only when you've selected the Show Administrative Tools option. If this option isn't enabled, you can enable it from the Start screen. On Start, press Windows key + C to display the Charm bar, and then select Settings. On the Settings panel, select Tiles, and then select Show Administrative Tools.

Both local user accounts and domain user accounts can be configured as standard user accounts or administrator accounts. A standard user account on a local computer has limited privileges, and an administrator account on a local computer has extended privileges.

Windows 8.1 adds a special type of local account called a Microsoft account, which was not available until the release of Windows 8. Microsoft accounts can be thought of as synchronized accounts. When you connect a local or domain account to a Microsoft account, the account becomes a connected local or connected domain account. Here's how connected local accounts work:

- A user signs in to a computer by using an email address for his logon name and a password that is shared with his Microsoft account online.

- Because the user has connected to her Microsoft account, the user also is able to use the various connected features of that account.

Synchronizing the account allows the user to purchase apps and other content for their computer from Windows Store. It also allows synced content (files, photos, and more) and certain profile settings stored on SkyDrive to be available if the user logs on to another computer running Windows 8.1. Synced content between computers helps to give users a seamless experience regardless of which computer they log on to. Otherwise, connected local accounts work exactly like regular local accounts.

Connected domain accounts work in much the same way except that a domain user always logs on to a domain by using his domain logon name and password. A regular account can be converted into a connected account at any time. Similarly, a connected account can be converted to a regular account at any time.

REAL WORLD On corporate PCs, you might not want users to be able to create, connect, or log on with Microsoft accounts. In Group Policy, you can block Microsoft accounts by enabling the Accounts: Block Microsoft Accounts policy. This policy is found in the Security Options policies for Computer Configuration under Windows Settings\Security Settings\Local Policies. Use the Users Can't Add Microsoft Accounts setting to prevent users from creating Microsoft accounts. To prevent users from logging on with, connecting to, and creating Microsoft accounts, define the Accounts: Block Microsoft Accounts setting and select the Users Can't Add Or Log On With Microsoft Accounts option.

User account essentials

All user accounts are identified with a logon name. In Windows 8.1, the logon name for a regular account has the following two parts:

- **User name** The display text for the account
- **User computer or domain** The computer or domain in which the user account exists

For the user WilliamS, whose account is created for the computer ENGPC85, the full logon name for Windows 8.1 is ENGPC85\WilliamS. With a local computer account, WilliamS can log on to his local workstation and access local resources but is not able to access domain resources.

When you create a Microsoft account for a user, Windows 8.1 uses the name information you specify as the logon name. The user's first and last names are set as part of the display text. The full email address serves as the logon name because this is what's stored locally on the computer. When the user logs on and the computer is connected to the Internet, the user's settings and content can be synced and updated according to their preferences. If the computer isn't connected to the Internet, the user's settings and content come from their profile, as with regular user accounts.

When you are working with domains, the full logon name can be expressed in two different ways:

- The user account name and the full domain name separated by the at sign (@). For example, the full logon name for the user name Williams in the domain technology.microsoft.com would be *Williams@technology.microsoft.com.*
- The user account name and the domain separated by the backslash (\). For example, the full logon name for Williams in the technology domain would be technology\Williams.

Although Windows 8.1 displays user names when describing account privileges and permissions, the key identifiers for accounts are security identifiers (SIDs). SIDs are unique identifiers generated when security principals are created. Each SID combines a computer or domain security ID prefix with a unique relative ID for the user. Windows 8.1 uses these identifiers to track accounts and user names independently. SIDs serve many purposes, but the two most important are to enable you to easily change user names and to delete accounts without worrying that someone might gain access to resources simply by re-creating an account.

When you change a user name, you tell Windows 8.1 to map a particular SID to a new name. When you delete an account, you tell Windows 8.1 that a particular SID is no longer valid. Even if you create an account with the same user name later, the new account won't have the same privileges and permissions as the previous one because the new account will have a new SID.

User accounts can also have passwords, biometrics, and certificates associated with them. Passwords are authentication strings for an account. Passwords must conform to specific requirements. For examples, typical passwords must be at least eight characters.

Regarding biometrics, fingerprints are the only biometric factor supported by Windows at this time. By default, fingerprints are an authentication option for local logons whenever a computer has a fingerprint reader installed that supports the Windows Biometrics Framework. Additional configuration is required before fingerprints can be used for domain logons.

In Group Policy under Computer Configuration\Windows Components\Biometrics, you'll find several settings for managing how biometrics can be used. These settings include the following :

- **Allow Use Of Biometrics**   Controls whether the Windows Biometrics service is available to users. If you disable this policy setting, users will be prevented from using fingerprints for authentication. If this policy setting is enabled or not configured, the Windows Biometrics service is available to users.

- **Allow Users To Log On Using Biometrics**   Controls whether biometrics can be used for local logon or to elevate permissions during a local logon. If you disable this policy setting, users will be prevented from using fingerprints for local logon and privilege elevation. If this policy setting is enabled or not configured, users can use fingerprints for local logon and privilege elevation.

- **Allow Domain Users To Log On Using Biometrics**   Controls whether biometrics can be used for domain logon or to elevate permissions while logged on to a domain. If you disable this policy setting, users will be prevented from using fingerprints for domain logon and privilege elevation. If this policy setting is enabled or not configured, users can use fingerprints for domain logon and privilege elevation.

Windows 8.1 replaces the biometrics control panel previously available. Now fingerprint registration is a standard logon option when a compatible fingerprint reader is installed and fingerprints are permitted for authentication. To register fingerprints, navigate to PC Settings\Accounts\Sign-in Options. You'll then be prompted to add a fingerprint to the current account by swiping a finger on the fingerprint reader. Because several scans are necessary, you'll need to swipe the same finger several times. After registering a fingerprint, you'll be able to swipe a registered finger on the fingerprint reader and use this for logon and privilege elevation.

Certificates combine a public and private key to identify a user. You log on with a password or fingerprint interactively, whereas you log on with a certificate by using its private key, which is stored on a smart card. Although physical smart cards that users must carry with them require swiping the card in a smart card reader, Windows 8.1 also support virtual smart cards. With virtual smart cards, Windows 8.1 stores the smart card's certificate on the local computer and protects the smart card by using the computer's Trusted Platform Module (TPM) security chip. Virtual smart cards meet two-factor authentication requirements because the virtual smart card must be set up on the computer and any user who wants to use the virtual smart card must know the related PIN.

IMPORTANT Although credentials cannot be exported from a user's computer, virtual smart cards can be issued for the same user on multiple computers by using additional certificates. Multiple users can access network resources through the same computer by each being issued a virtual smart card on that computer. The Certificate Templates snap-in for the MMC now has a Smartcard Logon template that you can duplicate and use as the basis for certificates needed for virtual smart cards. After you create the required certificate, you can use the TPM VSC Manager (Tpmvscmgr.exe) to create a virtual smart card and then use the User Certificates Manager (certmgr.msc) to provision the virtual smart card with the certificate.

When you install Windows 8.1, the operating system installs default user accounts. You'll find several built-in accounts, which have purposes similar to those of accounts created in Windows domains. The key accounts are the following:

- **Administrator** Administrator is a predefined account that provides complete access to files, directories, services, and other facilities. You can't delete or disable this account. In Active Directory, the Administrator account has domainwide access and privileges. On a local workstation, the Administrator account has access only to the local system.

- **Guest** Guest is designed for users who need one-time or occasional access. Although guests have only limited system privileges, you should be very careful about using this account because it opens the system to potential security problems. The risk is so great that the account is initially disabled when you install Windows 8.1.

By default, these accounts are members of various groups. Before you modify any of the built-in accounts, you should note the property settings and group memberships for the account. Group membership grants or limits the account's access to specific system resources. For example, Administrator is a member of the Administrators group, and Guest is a member of the Guests group. Being a member of a group makes it possible for the account to use the privileges and rights of the group.

In addition to the built-in accounts, Windows 8.1 has several pseudo-accounts that are used to perform specific types of system actions. The pseudo-accounts are available only on the local system. You can't change the settings for these accounts with the user administration tools, and users can't log on to a computer with these accounts. The pseudo-accounts available include the following:

- **LocalSystem** LocalSystem is used for running system processes and handling system-level tasks. This account grants the logon right Log On As A Service. Most services run under the LocalSystem account. In some cases, these services have privileges to interact with the desktop. Services that need fewer privileges or logon rights run under the LocalService or NetworkService account. Services that run as LocalSystem include Background Intelligent Transfer Service, Computer Browser, Group Policy Client, Netlogon, Network Connections, Print Spooler, and User Profile Service.

- **LocalService** LocalService is used for running services that need fewer privileges and logon rights on a local system. By default, services that run under this account are granted the right Log On As A Service and the privileges Adjust Memory Quotas For A Process, Bypass Traverse Checking, Change The System Time, Change The Time Zone, Create Global Objects, Generate Security Audits, Impersonate A Client After Authentication, and Replace A Process Level Token. Services that run as LocalService include Application Layer Gateway Service, Remote Registry, Smart Card, SSDP Discovery Service, TCP/IP NetBIOS Helper, and WebClient.

- **NetworkService** NetworkService is used for running services that need fewer privileges and logon rights on a local system but must also access network resources. Like services that run under LocalService, services that run by default under the NetworkService account are granted the right Log On As A Service and the privileges Adjust Memory Quotas For A Process, Bypass Traverse Checking, Create Global Objects, Generate Security Audits, Impersonate A Client After Authentication, and Replace A Process Level Token. Services that run under NetworkService include BranchCache, Distributed Transaction Coordinator, DNS Client, Remote Desktop Services, and Remote Procedure Call (RPC). NetworkService can also authenticate to remote systems as the computer account.

Group account essentials

Windows 8.1 also provides groups, which you use to grant permissions to similar types of users and to simplify account administration. If a user is a member of a group that has access to a resource, that user has access to the same resource. You can give a user access to various work-related resources just by making the user a member of the correct group. Although you can log on to a computer with a user account, you can't log on to a computer with a group account. Because different Active Directory domains or local computers might have groups with the same name, groups are often referred to by *Domain\GroupName* or *Computer\GroupName* (for example, Technology\GMarketing for the GMarketing group in a domain or on a computer named Technology).

Windows 8.1 uses the following three types of groups:

- **Local groups** Defined on a local computer and used on the local computer only. You create local groups by using Local Users And Groups.
- **Security groups** Can have security descriptors associated with them. You use a server running Windows to define security groups in domains, by using Active Directory Users And Computers.
- **Distribution groups** Used as email distribution lists. These groups can't have security descriptors associated with them. You define distribution groups in domains by using Active Directory Users And Computers.

As with user accounts, group accounts are tracked by using unique SIDs. This means that you can't delete a group account and re-create it and then expect all the permissions and privileges to remain the same. The new group will have a new SID, and all the permissions and privileges of the old group will be lost.

When you assign user access levels, you have the opportunity to make the user a member of the built-in or predefined groups, including:

- **Access Control Assistance Operators** Members of this group can remotely query authorization attributes and permissions for resources on a computer.

    NOTE Windows has several operator groups. By default, no other group or user accounts are members of the operator groups. This is to ensure that you grant explicit access to the operator groups.

- **Administrators** Members of this group are local administrators and have complete access to the workstation. They can create accounts, modify group membership, install printers, manage shared resources, and more. Because this account has complete access, you should be very careful about which users you add to this group.
- **Backup Operators** Members of this group can back up and restore files and directories on the workstation. They can log on to the local computer, back up or restore files, and shut down the computer. Because of how this account is set up, its members can back up files regardless of whether the members have read/write access to the files. However, they can't change access permissions on the files or perform other administrative tasks.
- **Cryptographic Operators** Members can manage the configuration of encryption, Internet Protocol Security (IPSec), digital IDs, and certificates.
- **Event Log Readers** Members can view the event logs on the local computer.
- **Guests** Guests are users with very limited privileges. Members can access the system and its resources remotely, but they can't perform most other tasks.
- **Hyper-V Administrators** Members of this group can manage all features of Hyper-V. Virtualization technologies are built into Windows 8.1 and supported on 64-bit hardware with Second Level Address Translation (SLAT).

- **Network Configuration Operators** Members can manage network settings on the workstation. They can also configure TCP/IP settings and perform other general network configuration tasks.

- **Performance Log Users** Members can view and manage performance counters. They can also manage performance logging.

- **Performance Monitor Users** Members can view performance counters and performance logs.

- **Power Users** In earlier versions of Windows, this group is used to grant additional privileges, such as the capability to modify computer settings and install programs. In Windows 8.1, this group is maintained only for compatibility with legacy applications.

- **Remote Desktop Users** Members can log on to the workstation remotely by using Remote Desktop Services. After members are logged on, additional groups of which they are members determine their permissions on the workstation. A user who is a member of the Administrators group is granted this privilege automatically. (However, remote logons must be enabled before an administrator can remotely log on to a workstation.)

- **Remote Management Users** Members can access Windows Management Instrumentation (WMI) resources over management protocols.

- **Replicator** Members can manage the replication of files for the local machine. File replication is primarily used with Active Directory domains and servers running Windows.

- **Users** Users are people who do most of their work on a single workstation running Windows 8.1. Members of the Users group have more restrictions than privileges. They can log on to a workstation running Windows 8.1 locally, keep a local profile, lock the workstation, and shut down the workstation.

- **WindowsRMRemoteWMIUsers** Members can access WMI resources through the Windows Remote Management framework (Windows RM).

In most cases, you configure user access by using the Users or Administrators group. You can configure user and administrator access levels by setting the account type to Standard User or Administrator, respectively. Although these basic tasks can be performed by using the User Accounts options of Control Panel, you make a user a member of a group by using Local Users And Groups under Computer Management.

Domain vs. local logon

When computers are members of a domain, you typically use domain accounts to log on to computers and the domain. All administrators in a domain have access to resources on the local workstations that are members of the domain. Users, on the other hand, can access resources only on the local workstations they are permitted to log on to. In a domain, any user with a valid domain account can by default log on to any computer that is a member of the domain. When logged on to a computer, the user has access to any resource that his or her account or the groups to which the user's account belongs are granted access, either directly or indirectly with claims-based access policies. This includes resources on the local machine, in addition to resources in the domain.

You can restrict logons to specific domain workstations on a per-user basis by using Active Directory Users And Computers. In Active Directory Users And Computers, press and hold or right-click the user account, and then tap or click Properties. On the Account tab of the user's Properties dialog box, tap or click Log On To, and then use the options in the Logon Workstations dialog box to designate the workstations to which the user is permitted to log on.

> **REAL WORLD** Don't confuse logon workstation restrictions with Primary Computers. Primary computers are associated with the Redirect Folders On Primary Computers Only policy found in the Administrative Templates policies for Computer Configuration under the System\Folder Redirection path. This policy allows administrators to specify from which computer users can access roaming profiles and redirected folders. The goal of the policy is to protect personal and corporate data when users log on to computers other than the ones they use regularly for business. Data security is improved by not downloading and caching this data on computers a user doesn't normally use. In the context of the policy, a *Primary Computer* is a computer that has been specifically designated as permitted for use with redirected data by editing the advanced properties of a user or group in Active Directory and setting the msDS-PrimaryComputer property to the name of the permitted computers. The permitted computers must be running Windows 8, Windows Server 2012, or a later version of Windows.

When you work with Windows 8.1, however, you aren't always logging on to a domain. Computers configured in workgroups have only local accounts. You might also need to log on locally to a domain computer to administer it. Only users with a local user account can log on locally. When you log on locally, you have access to any resource on the computer that your account or the groups to which your account belongs are granted access.

Managing User Account Control and elevation prompts

User Account Control (UAC) affects which privileges standard users and administrator users have, how applications are installed and run, and much more. In this section, I'll extend the discussion in Chapter 1, "Introduction to Windows 8.1 administration," and provide a comprehensive look at how UAC affects user and administrator accounts. This is essential information to know when managing systems running Windows 8.1.

> **NOTE** Learning how UAC works will help you be a better administrator. To support UAC, many aspects of the Windows operating system had to be reworked. Some of the most extensive changes have to do with how applications are installed and run. In Chapter 7, "Installing and maintaining applications," you'll find a complete discussion of how the architectural changes affect programs running on Windows 8.1.

Redefining standard user and administrator user accounts

In early releases of Windows, malicious software programs could exploit the fact that most user accounts were configured as members of the local computer's Administrators group. Not only did this allow malicious software to install itself, but it also allowed malicious software to use these elevated privileges to wreak havoc on the computer, because programs installed by administrators could write to otherwise secure areas of the registry and the file system.

To combat malicious software, organizations have locked down computers, required users to log on using standard user accounts, and required administrators to use the Run As command to perform administrative tasks. Unfortunately, these procedural changes could have serious negative consequences on productivity. A person logged on as a standard user couldn't perform some of the most basic tasks, such as changing the system clock and calendar, changing the computer's time zone, or changing the computer's power management settings. Many software programs designed for early releases of Windows simply would not function properly without local administrator rights—these programs used local administrator rights to write to system locations during installation and during normal operations. Additionally, early releases of Windows didn't let you know beforehand when a task you were performing required administrator privileges.

User Account Control was introduced to improve usability while at the same time enhancing security by redefining how standard user and administrator user accounts are used. UAC represents a fundamental shift in computing by providing a framework that limits the scope of administrator-level access privileges and requires all applications to run in a specific user mode. In this way, UAC prevents users from making inadvertent changes to system settings and locks down the computer to prevent unauthorized applications from being installed or performing malicious actions.

Because of UAC, Windows 8.1 defines two levels of user accounts: standard and administrator. Windows 8.1 also defines two modes (run levels) for applications: standard user mode and administrator mode. Although standard user accounts can use most software and can change system settings that do not affect other users or the security of the computer, administrator user accounts have complete access to the computer and can make any changes that are needed. When an administrator user starts an application, her access token and its associated administrator privileges are applied to the application, giving her all the rights and privileges of a local computer administrator for that application. When a standard user starts an application, her access token and its associated privileges are applied to the application at run time, limiting her to the rights and privileges of a standard user for that application. Further, all applications are configured to run in a specific mode during installation. Any tasks run by standard-mode applications that require administrator privileges not only are identified during setup but require the user's approval to run.

In Windows 8.1, the set of privileges assigned to standard user accounts includes:

- Installing fonts, viewing the system clock and calendar, and changing the time zone.
- Changing the display settings and the power management settings.

- Adding printers and other devices (when the required drivers are installed on the computer or are provided by an IT administrator).

- Downloading and installing updates (when the updates use UAC-compatible installers).

- Creating and configuring virtual private network (VPN) connections. VPN connections are used to establish secure connections to private networks over the public Internet.

- Installing Wired Equivalent Privacy (WEP) to connect to secure wireless networks. The WEP security protocol provides wireless networks with improved security.

- Accessing the computer from the network and shutting down the computer.

Windows 8.1 also defines two run levels for applications: standard and administrator. Windows 8.1 determines whether a user needs elevated privileges to run a program by supplying most applications and processes with a security token. If an application has a standard token, or an application cannot be identified as an administrator application, elevated privileges are not required to run the application, and Windows 8.1 starts it as a standard application by default. If an application has an administrator token, elevated privileges are required to run the application, and Windows 8.1 prompts the user for permission or confirmation prior to running the application.

The process of getting approval prior to running an application in administrator mode and prior to performing tasks that change system configuration is known as *elevation*. Elevation enhances security and reduces the impact of malicious software by notifying users before they perform any action that could affect system settings and by preventing applications from using administrator privileges without first notifying users. Elevation also protects administrator applications from attacks by standard applications. For more information on elevation and how UAC works with applications, see Chapter 7.

By default, Windows 8.1 switches to the secure desktop prior to displaying the elevation prompt. The secure desktop restricts the programs and processes that have access to the desktop environment, and in this way reduces the possibility that a malicious program or user could gain access to the process being elevated. If you don't want Windows 8.1 to switch to the secure desktop prior to prompting for elevation, you can choose settings that use the standard desktop rather than the secure desktop. However, this makes the computer more susceptible to malware and attack.

Optimizing UAC and Admin Approval Mode

Every computer has a built-in local Administrator account. This built-in account is not protected by UAC, and using this account for administration can put your computer at risk. To safeguard computers in environments in which you use a local Administrator account for administration, you should create a new local Administrator account and use this account for administration.

UAC can be configured or disabled for any individual user account. If you disable UAC for a user account, you lose the additional security protections UAC offers and put the computer at risk. To completely disable UAC or to reenable UAC after disabling it, the computer must be restarted for the change to take effect.

Admin Approval Mode is the key component of UAC that determines whether and how administrators are prompted when running administrator applications. The default way that Admin Approval Mode works is as follows:

- All administrators, including the built-in local Administrator account, run in and are subject to Admin Approval Mode.

- Because they are running in and subject to Admin Approval Mode, all administrators, including the built-in local Administrator account, get the elevation prompt when they run administrator applications.

If you are logged on as an administrator, you can modify the way UAC works for all users by completing the following steps:

1. In Control Panel, tap or click System And Security. Under the Action Center heading, tap or click Change User Account Control Settings.

2. In the User Account Control Settings dialog box, as shown in Figure 5-1, use the slider to choose when to be notified about changes to the computer, and then tap or click OK. Table 5-1 summarizes the available options.

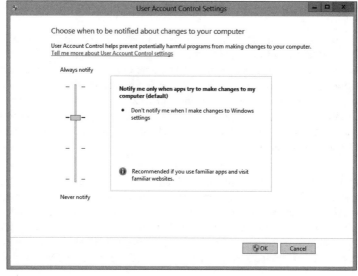

FIGURE 5-1 Set the notification level in the User Account Control Settings dialog box.

TABLE 5-1 User Account Control settings

OPTION	DESCRIPTION	WHEN TO USE	USES THE SECURE DESKTOP?
Always Notify	Always notifies the current user when programs try to install software or make changes to the computer, and when the user changes Windows settings	Choose this option when a computer requires the highest security possible and users frequently install software and visit unfamiliar websites.	Yes
Default	Notifies the current user only when programs try to make changes to the computer and not when the user changes Windows settings	Choose this option when a computer requires high security and you want to reduce the number of notification prompts that users receive.	Yes
Notify Me Only When ... (Do Not Dim My Desktop)	Same as Default but also prevents UAC from switching to the secure desktop	Choose this option when users work in a trusted environment with familiar applications and do not visit unfamiliar websites.	No
Never Notify	Turns off all UAC notification prompts	Choose this option when security is not a priority and users work in a trusted environment with programs that are not certified for Windows 8.1 because they do not support UAC.	No

In Group Policy, you can manage Admin Approval Mode and elevation prompting by using settings under Computer Configuration\Windows Settings\Security Settings\Local Policies\Security Options. These security settings are:

- **User Account Control: Admin Approval Mode For The Built-In Administrator Account** Determines whether users and processes running as the built-in local Administrator account are subject to Admin Approval Mode. By default, this feature is disabled, which means the built-in local Administrator account is not subject to Admin Approval Mode and is also not subject to the elevation prompt behavior stipulated for administrators in Admin Approval

Mode. If you disable this setting, users and processes running as the built-in local administrator are not subject to Admin Approval Mode and therefore not subject to the elevation prompt behavior stipulated for administrators in Admin Approval Mode.

- **User Account Control: Allow UIAccess Applications To Prompt For Elevation Without Using The Secure Desktop** Determines whether User Interface Accessibility (UIAccess) programs can automatically disable the secure desktop for elevation prompts used by a standard user. If you enable this setting, UIAccess programs, including Windows Remote Assistance, can disable the secure desktop for elevation prompts.

- **User Account Control: Behavior Of The Elevation Prompt For Administrators In Admin Approval Mode** Determines whether administrators subject to Admin Approval Mode get an elevation prompt when running administrator applications, and also determines how the elevation prompt works. By default, administrators are prompted for consent when running administrator applications on the secure desktop. You can configure this option so that administrators are prompted for consent without the secure desktop, prompted for credentials with or without the secure desktop (as is the case with standard users), or prompted for consent only for non-Windows binary files. You can also configure this option so that administrators are not prompted at all, in which case an administrator will be elevated automatically. No setting will prevent an administrator from pressing and holding or right-clicking an application shortcut and selecting Run As Administrator.

- **User Account Control: Behavior Of The Elevation Prompt For Standard Users** Determines whether users logged on with a standard user account get an elevation prompt when running administrator applications. By default, users logged on with a standard user account are prompted for the credentials of an administrator on the secure desktop when running administrator applications or performing administrator tasks. You can also configure this option so that users are prompted for credentials on the standard desktop rather than the secure desktop, or you can deny elevation requests automatically, in which case users will not be able to elevate their privileges by supplying administrator credentials. The latter option doesn't prevent users from pressing and holding or right-clicking an application shortcut and selecting Run As Administrator.

- **User Account Control: Only Elevate Executables That Are Signed And Validated** Determines whether applications must be signed and validated to elevate. If this option is enabled, only executables that pass signature checks and have certificates in the Trusted Publisher store will elevate. Use this option only when the highest security is required and you've verified that all applications in use are signed and valid.

- **User Account Control: Only Elevate UIAccess Applications That Are Installed in Secure Locations** Determines whether UIAccess programs must reside in a secure location on the file system to elevate. If this option is enabled, UIAccess programs must reside in a secure location under %SystemRoot%\Program Files, %SystemRoot%\Program Files (x86), or %SystemRoot%\Windows\System32.

- **User Account Control: Run All Administrators In Admin Approval Mode** Determines whether users logged on with an administrator account are subject to Admin Approval Mode. By default, this feature is enabled, which means administrators are subject to Admin Approval Mode and also subject to the elevation prompt behavior stipulated for administrators in Admin Approval Mode. If you disable this setting, users logged on with an administrator account are not subject to Admin Approval and therefore are not subject to the elevation prompt behavior stipulated for administrators in Admin Approval Mode.

REAL WORLD Related UAC settings for applications are discussed in Chapter 7. For more information, see the "Optimizing virtualization and installation prompting for elevation" section.

In a domain environment, you can use Active Directory–based Group Policy to apply the security configuration you want to a particular set of computers. You can also configure these settings on a per-computer basis using local security policy by following these steps:

1. Open Local Group Policy Editor. One way to do this is by pressing the Windows key, typing **gpedit.msc**, and then pressing Enter.

2. In the console tree, under Security Settings, expand Local Policies, and then select Security Options, as shown in Figure 5-2.

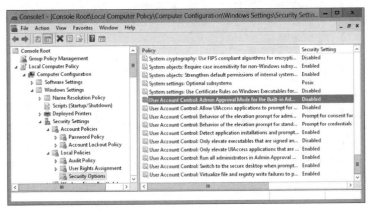

FIGURE 5-2 Select Security Options in the Local Security Policy console.

3. Double-tap or double-click the setting you want to work with, make any necessary changes, and then tap or click OK. Repeat this step to modify other security settings as necessary.

Managing local logon

All local computer accounts should have passwords. If an account is created without a password, anyone can log on to the account, and the account is not protected. However, a local account without a password cannot be used to remotely access a computer.

The sections that follow discuss how to create and work with local user accounts. Every workstation computer has local computer accounts, whether the computer is a member of a homegroup, a workgroup, or a domain.

Creating local user accounts in a homegroup or workgroup

Windows 8.1 supports two types of local user accounts: regular and connected. For a computer that is a member of a homegroup or a workgroup, you can create a regular local user account by following these steps:

1. In Control Panel, under the User Accounts And Family Security heading, tap or click Change Account Type. This displays the Manage Accounts page.

   As Figure 5-3 shows, the Manage Accounts page lists all configurable user accounts on the local computer by account type and with configuration details. If an account has a password, it is labeled Password Protected. If an account is disabled, it is listed as being off.

2. Select Add A New User In PC Settings. On the Other Accounts page in PC Settings, select Add An Account.

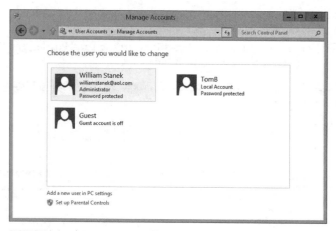

FIGURE 5-3 In a homegroup or workgroup, use the Manage Accounts page in Control Panel to view available accounts.

3. If you aren't connected to the Internet, you'll be prompted to create a regular local user account by default. Otherwise, you'll need to select the Sign In Without A Microsoft Account link.

4. Next, if the computer is connected to the Internet, tap or click Local Account. This is not necessary on a computer not connected to the Internet.

5. Enter the name of the local account. Optionally, set and confirm an account password and password hint.

6. Select Next, and then select Finish. The account is created as a standard user by default. To give the user full permissions on the local computer, you'll need to change to the administrator account type, as discussed in the section titled "Changing local user account types," later in this chapter.

A connected account is a Microsoft account. For a computer that is a member of a homegroup or a workgroup, you can create a Microsoft account by following these steps:

1. Open PC Settings. One way to do this is by pressing the Windows key + I, and then clicking Change PC Settings.

2. Under Accounts\Other Accounts, select Add An Account and follow the prompts to create the user account.

You must be connected to the Internet to create a Microsoft account. When you create a Microsoft account, Windows 8.1 connects to the Microsoft Store to determine whether an account has been set up for the email address you specified. If an account hasn't been set up, you are prompted to set up the account. To do this, you enter the email address and password to be associated with the account, as well as the user's first name, last name, and country/region.

Next, you are prompted to add security verification information, including the user's birth date, a phone number for sending a code to reset the account password as a text message or automated call, an alternate email address to use to send a message for resetting the account password, and a secret question and answer for verifying the user's identity if needed.

Finally, you must specify communication preferences and then enter verification text. When you click Finish, the Microsoft account is created online and on the local computer.

> **NOTE** If you aren't connected to the Internet when you try to create a Microsoft account, you'll only be able to create a local account. When you next have an Internet connection, you'll need to log on to the computer as that user, access the Accounts \Your Account page in PC Settings, and select Connect To A Microsoft Account. You'll then be prompted through the account creation process.

Synchronizing an account allows app settings, profile configuration options, and some profile content to be synced between the devices the account uses. Exactly what settings are and aren't synced is controlled with the options on the SkyDrive \Sync Settings page in PC Settings.

Granting access to an existing domain account to allow local logon

If a user needs to be able to log on locally to a computer and has an existing domain account, you can grant the user permission to log on locally by completing the following steps:

1. In Control Panel, under the User Accounts heading, tap or click the Change Account Type link to open the User Accounts dialog box, as shown in Figure 5-4. This dialog box lists all configurable user accounts on the local computer by domain and with group membership details.

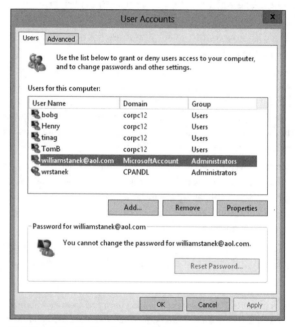

FIGURE 5-4 Use the User Accounts dialog box to manage local user accounts on a computer that is a member of a domain.

2. Tap or click Add. This starts the Add A User Wizard.

3. You are creating a local computer account for a user with an existing domain account. Enter the user's domain account name and domain in the text boxes provided, or click Browse to use the Select User option to choose a user account. Click Next.

4. Specify an account type:

- A standard user account is created as a member of the local Users group. To give the user the permissions of a normal user, select Standard.

- An administrator account is created as a member of the local Administrators group. To give the user full permissions on the local computer, select Administrator.

- An Other account is created as a member of a group you specify. To give the user the permissions of a specific group, select Other, and then select the group.

5. Tap or click Next, then tap or click Finish. If you need to set other permissions or add the user to other local groups, follow the steps specified in the section titled "Managing local user accounts and groups," later in this chapter.

Changing local user account types

The User Accounts utility provides an easy way to change account types for local users. You can quickly set the default account type as either standard user or administrator user. For more advanced control, however, you need to use Local Users And Groups to assign group membership to individual accounts. (See the "Adding and removing local group members" section later in this chapter.)

In a homegroup or workgroup, you can change the account type from standard local user to administrator local user and vice versa by completing the following steps:

1. In Control Panel, under the User Accounts heading, tap or click Change Account Type. This displays the Manage Accounts page.

2. Tap or click the account you want to change, and then tap or click Change The Account Type.

3. On the Change Account Type page, set the level of access for the user as either Standard User or Administrator, and then select Change The Account Type.

NOTE You won't be able to change the account type for the last administrator account on a computer. A computer must have at least one local administrator.

In a domain, you can change the account type for a local computer user by completing the following steps:

1. In Control Panel, under the User Accounts heading, tap or click the Change Account Type link. This displays the User Accounts dialog box.

2. On the Users tab, select the user account with which you want to work, and then select Properties.

3. On the Group Membership tab, set the type of account as Standard User or Administrator, or select Other and then select the group you want to use.

4. Tap or click OK twice.

Switching between connected and regular accounts

The PC Settings utility provides an easy way to switch between connected and regular accounts. In a homegroup or workgroup, you can change the account type from a regular local account to a Microsoft account and vice versa by completing the following steps:

1. Log on as the user and then open PC Settings. One way to do this is by pressing the Windows key + I, and then clicking Change PC Settings.
2. In PC Settings, select Accounts to display the Accounts\Your Account page.
3. Select Switch To A Local Account or Connect To A Microsoft Account, as appropriate, and then follow the prompts. You must be connected to the Internet to switch to a Microsoft account.

In a domain, you can change the account type from a regular domain account to a connected domain account and vice versa by completing the following steps:

1. Log on as the user and then open PC Settings. One way to do this is by pressing the Windows key + I, and then clicking Change PC Settings.
2. In PC Settings, select Accounts to display the Accounts\Your Account page.
3. Click Disconnect or Connect Your Microsoft Account, as appropriate, and then follow the prompts. You must be connected to the Internet to switch to a Microsoft account.

Creating passwords for local user accounts

In a homegroup or workgroup configuration, local user accounts can be created without passwords by default. This means that a user can log on simply by tapping or clicking his account name on the Welcome screen. To improve security, all local accounts should have passwords.

For the easiest management of local accounts, log on to each account that should have a password, and then assign a password by completing the following steps:

1. In PC Settings, select Accounts and then select Sign-In Options.
2. On the Sign-in Options page, under Password, select Add.
3. On the Create A Password panel, enter and then confirm the password to use. Optionally, add a password hint.
4. Select Next, and then select Finish. If you are logged on as the user when you create a password, you don't have to worry about losing encrypted data.

You can create a password without logging on as the user. However, if you create a password without logging on as the user, the user will lose access to her encrypted files, encrypted email, personal certificates, and stored passwords. This occurs because the user's master key, which is needed to access her personal encryption certificate and unlock this data, is encrypted with a hash that is based on an empty password. So when you create a password, the hash doesn't match, and there's no way to unlock the encrypted data. The only way to resolve this is to restore the original settings by removing the password from the account. The user should then be able to access her encrypted files. Again, this issue is related only to local user accounts for computers and not to domain user accounts. Administrators can change or reset passwords for domain user accounts without affecting access to encrypted data.

IMPORTANT When you create local accounts, you should add a password hint, which can be helpful in recovering a forgotten or lost password. Another technique for recovering a password is a password reset disk, which can be a floppy disk or a USB flash drive. It is important to note that these are the only techniques you should use to recover passwords for local user accounts unless you want to risk data loss.

You can create a password for a local user account by completing the following steps:

1. In Control Panel, under the User Accounts heading, tap or click Change Account Type. This displays the Manage Accounts page.

2. Tap or click the account with which you want to work. Any account that has a current password is listed as Password Protected. Any account without this label doesn't have a password.

3. Tap or click New Password. Enter a password, and then confirm it, as shown in Figure 5-5. Afterward, enter a unique password hint. The password hint is a word or phrase that can be used to obtain the password if it is lost or forgotten. This hint is visible to anyone who uses the computer.

4. Tap or click Create Password.

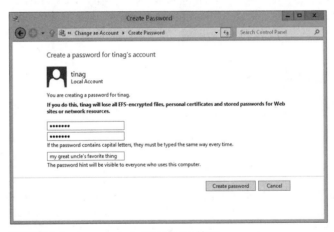

FIGURE 5-5 Create a password with a password hint.

Recovering local user account passwords

As discussed previously, in order to preserve access to any encrypted data and stored passwords that a user might have, it is preferable to try and recover a user password rather than change or remove the password.

Windows 8.1 provides two ways to recover user passwords:

- **Password hint**   A hint can be accessed on the Welcome screen. Ordinarily, the Welcome screen is displayed when the computer is started and no one is logged on. If someone is logged on to the workstation, ask him or her to log off. Tap or click the user's name to display the Password prompt, and then tap or click the blue Enter button to display the password hint. Hopefully, the password hint will help the user remember the password. If it doesn't, you need to use a password reset disk.

- **Password reset disk**   Password reset disks can be created for any local user account with a password. They enable anyone to change the password of the related local account without needing to know the old password. Because anyone with access to these disks can change account passwords, you should store password reset disks in a secure location. If users are allowed to create their own password reset disks, be sure they know how important the disks are.

NOTE Passwords for domain users and those for local users are managed differently. Administrators manage passwords for domain user accounts and can reset forgotten passwords by using the Active Directory Users And Computers console.

Passwords for local machine accounts can be stored in a secure, encrypted file on a password reset disk, which can be a floppy disk or a USB flash device. You can create a password reset disk for the current user as discussed in the "Creating and using a password reset disk" section in Chapter 1. You can reset a password for a local machine account as discussed in the "Resetting a user's password" section in Chapter 1.

Controlling logon

By default, Windows 8.1 displays a Lock screen and a Welcome screen whether a computer is part of a homegroup or workgroup or a domain. The difference between the Lock screen and the Welcome screen is an important one.

The Lock screen is displayed when no one is logged on. In PC Settings, you select PC And Devices, and then use the options on the Lock Screen page to set related settings. You can select a lock screen picture, choose apps to run in the background, and specify whether and how those apps display quick status and notifications. By default, the Messaging, Calendar, and Mail apps display quick status and notifications information. As an administrator, you can override these settings in Group Policy, by enabling Turn Off App Notifications On The Lock Screen in the Administrative Templates policies for Computer Configuration under the System\Logon path.

When you press and hold or click and then drag up on the Lock screen, the Welcome screen appears. When the Lock screen is displayed, pressing Enter on the keyboard also displays the Welcome screen. In a domain, the name of the last user to log on is displayed by default. You can log on with this account by entering the required password. You can log on as another user as well. On the Welcome screen, note the button to the left of the user picture. This is the Switch User button.

Tap or click Switch User, select one of the alternative accounts listed, and then provide the password for that account, or tap or click Other User to enter the user name and password for the account to use.

On the Welcome screen for computers that are part of a homegroup or workgroup, a list of accounts on the computer is displayed. To log on with one of these accounts, tap or click the account and enter a password, if required. Contrary to what many people think, the Welcome screen doesn't display all the accounts that have been created on the computer. Some accounts, such as Administrator, are hidden from view automatically.

The Welcome screen is convenient, but it also makes it easier for someone to try to gain access to the computer. Whether in a homegroup, workgroup, or domain, you can hide the accounts and require users to enter a logon name. Hiding the user name of the last user to log on can improve security by requiring users to know a valid account name for the computer. In Group Policy, you can hide the user name by enabling Interactive Logon: Do Not Display Last User Name. This Computer Configuration option is under Windows Settings\Security Settings\Local Policies \Security Options.

By default, domain users can't use PIN passwords but can use picture passwords. These Administrative Templates policies for Computer Configuration under the System\Logon path allow you to modify this behavior: Turn On PIN Sign In and Turn Off Picture Password Sign-In.

In a domain environment, you can use Active Directory–based Group Policy to apply your desired security configuration to a particular set of computers. You can also configure this setting on a per-computer basis by using local security policy. To configure local policy for a homegroup or workgroup computer, follow these steps:

1. Open Local Group Policy Editor. One way to do this is by pressing the Windows key, typing **gpedit.msc**, and then pressing Enter.

2. In the editor, under Computer Configuration, expand Windows Settings, Security Settings, Local Policies, and then select Security Options (see Figure 5-6).

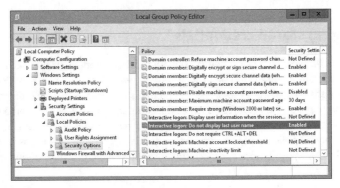

FIGURE 5-6 Disable account name display as a security best practice.

3. Double-tap or double-click Interactive Logon: Do Not Display Last User Name.

4. Select Enabled, and then tap or click OK.

5. Next, expand Computer Configuration, Administrative Templates, System, Logon, and then configure related policies as appropriate.

Removing accounts and denying local access to workstations

Domain administrators are automatically granted access to local resources on workstations. Other users aren't granted access to local resources on workstations other than to the computers to which they are permitted to log on. As workstations are moved around an organization, you might find that previous owners of a workstation still have access to its resources or that users who were granted temporary access to a workstation were never removed from the access list.

In a domain, you can control the workstations to which users can log on by using the account properties in Active Directory Users And Computers. Double-tap or double-click the account to display the Properties dialog box. On the Account tab, tap or click Log On To.

You can remove a user's local account and effectively deny logon by completing these steps:

1. Log on as a user with local administrator privileges. In Control Panel, under the User Accounts heading, tap or click Change Account Type. This displays the Manage Accounts page.

2. Select the account you want to remove, and then select Remove.

3. When prompted to confirm that you want to remove the account, select Yes.

The contents of the user's local profile, including the user's desktop and documents folders, are not removed along with the account. Anyone with administrator access to the local computer can access the user's profile folder in File Explorer. Profile folders are stored under %SystemRoot%\Users. Keep in mind that in a domain, unless further restrictions are in place with regard to logging on to a workstation, a user might still be able to gain access to the workstation by logging on with a domain account.

Managing stored credentials

In Windows 8.1, you can use Credential Manager to store credentials that can be used to try to automatically log on users to servers, websites, and programs. Credentials are stored in a user's profile. If you find that a user frequently has problems logging on to protected resources, such as the company intranet or an external Internet site, you can create a stored credential for each resource with which the user works. Applications that support credential management, such as web browsers and Microsoft Store apps, can then use the saved credentials during the logon process.

The following sections examine techniques for working with stored credentials.

REAL WORLD When you create a Microsoft account on a computer, a generic credential is created and stored for Windows Live. The Windows Live credential is what's used to access the Microsoft Store, SkyDrive, and other Microsoft services. Normally, you shouldn't edit or remove this credential. However, if the live credential and the stored credential somehow get out of sync, this is where you'd go to edit the email address and password used by the computer to access Microsoft services.

Using stored credentials

When a website, app, or another computer requests authentication through NTLM or the Kerberos protocol, you are prompted to save the credentials. This prompt has Save Password or Update Default Credentials options. If you choose the Save Password option, your credentials are saved and the next time you access the same website, app, or computer, Credential Manager can automatically provide the stored credentials. If you choose to update existing credentials, Credential Manager overwrites the previous credential with the new one and then stores the new credentials for future use.

Credential Manager supports four types of stored credentials:

- **Web credential** A credential for a website that includes a resource location, logon account name, and password

- **Windows credential** A credential that uses standard Windows authentication (NTLM or Kerberos) and includes a resource location, logon account name, and password

- **Certificate-based credential** A credential that includes a resource location and uses a certificate saved in the Personal store in Certificate Manager for authentication

- **Generic credential** A credential that uses basic or custom authentication techniques and includes a resource location, logon account name, and password

When you connect a local or domain account to a Microsoft account, credentials can be stored in SkyDrive to allow the same credentials to be used from any computer or device you use to access resources. Roaming with credentials in this way is enabled by default for non-domain–joined computers. However, credential roaming is blocked on domain-joined computers to prevent credentials that are stored on domain-joined computers from leaving the enterprise.

In domains, credentials in Microsoft accounts will not roam if you are using Credential Roaming. Additionally, because roaming user profiles use Credential Manager, there might be credentials conflicts between the credentials stored to support roaming and those credentials stored for general credential management. Because of this, Microsoft recommends that you use either stored credentials or roaming user profiles in domains, but not both.

In Group Policy, you can prevent Windows from storing credentials for domain authentication on a computer and in this way ensure that credentials used for roaming user profiles are not saved in Credential Manager. To do this, enable the Network Access: Do Not Allow Storage Of Passwords And Credentials For Network Authentication option, which is under Windows Settings\Security Settings\Local Policies\Security Options.

Adding Windows or generic credentials

Each user account has unique credentials. Individual credential entries are stored in the user's profile settings and contain information needed to log on to protected resources. If you are logged on to a domain account when you create a credential, and the account has a roaming profile (instead of a local or mandatory profile), the information stored in the credential is available when you log on to any computer in the domain. Otherwise, the information in the credential is available only on the computer on which you create the entry.

> **REAL WORLD** When your organization has computers that are in workgroups or homegroups rather than part of your domain, you'll find that stored credentials can save everyone a lot of time. For example, if Ted uses a computer that is a member of a workgroup for his daily activities but needs to access several different servers in several different locations or domains, you can make this process easier by creating a Windows credential for each resource. Now, no matter how Ted accesses the servers, he can be authenticated automatically and without having to provide alternate credentials. For example, if Ted maps a network drive to FileServer84 and you've set up a credential for this server, Ted doesn't have to select the Connect Using Different Credential option and then provide alternate credentials.

To add an entry to the currently logged-on user's credentials, follow these steps:

1. Log on as the user whose credentials you want to manage. In Control Panel, select User Accounts, and then select Manage Windows Credentials under Credential Manager.

   On the Credential Manager page, as shown in Figure 5-7, you'll find a list of current entries by credential type (if there are any credentials).

   > **NOTE** For simplicity, I often generalize and refer to the User Accounts heading in Control Panel. However, note that domain computers have a User Accounts heading in Control Panel, whereas computers in a workgroup or homegroup have a Users Accounts And Family Safety heading.

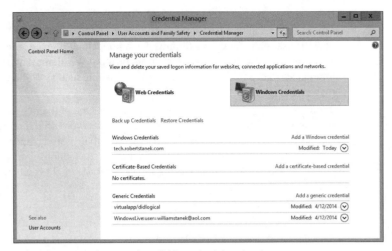

FIGURE 5-7 Review the currently available credentials and options.

2. Tap or click Add A Windows Credential or Add A Generic Credential, as appropriate for the type of credential you are creating. Then use the options provided to configure the credential (as shown in Figure 5-8). The available options are as follows:

- **Internet Or Network Address** The network or Internet resource for which you are configuring the credential entry. This can be a server name, such as Fileserver86; a fully qualified domain name for an Internet resource, such as www.microsoft.com; or an address containing a wildcard, such as *.microsoft.com. When you use a server name or fully qualified domain name, the entry is used for accessing a specific server or service. When you use a wildcard, the entry is used for any server in the specified domain. For example, the entry *.microsoft.com could be used to access *www.microsoft.com, ftp.microsoft.com, smtp.microsoft.com,* and *extranet. microsoft.com.*

FIGURE 5-8 Create the credential entry by setting the necessary logon information.

- **User Name** The user name required by the server, including any necessary domain qualifiers. To use the default domain for a resource, enter only the user name, such as **Williams**. For a nondefault domain, enter the full domain and account name, such as **technology\Williams**. For an Internet service, enter the full service account name, such as **Williams@ msn.com**.

- **Password** The password required by the server. One of the things most users forget is that whenever they change their password on the server or service, they must also change their password in their stored credential. If a user forgets to change the password in the stored credential, repeated attempts to log on or connect to the server or service might result in the account being locked.

   3. Tap or click OK to save the credential.

Adding certificate-based credentials

The Personal certificate store in the user's profile stores certificates that have been issued to authenticate the user. After you've added a certificate for the user, you can create a credential that uses the certificate to access a resource.

To add an entry for a certificate-based credential to the currently logged-on user's stored credentials, follow these steps:

1. Log on as the user whose credentials you want to manage. In Control Panel, tap or click User Accounts, and then tap or click Manage Windows Credentials under Credential Manager.

2. On the Credential Manager page, you'll find a list of current entries by credential type (if there are any credentials).

3. Tap or click Add A Certificate-Based Credential. In the Internet Or Network Address box, enter the name of the network or Internet resource for which you are configuring the credential entry. This can be a server name, a fully qualified domain name for an Internet resource, or an address containing a wildcard.

4. Tap or click Select Certificate. In the Select Certificate dialog box, tap or click the personal certificate that you want to use for the resource, and then tap or click OK.

5. Tap or click OK again to save the credential.

Editing credentials

You can edit credential entries at any time, but keep in mind that local entries are visible only on the computer on which they were created. This means that if you want to modify an entry, you must log on to the local workstation where the entry was created. The only exception is for users with roaming profiles. When a user has a roaming profile, credential entries can be edited from any computer to which the user is logged on.

Use the following steps to edit a user's credentials entries:

1. Log on as the user whose credentials entries you want to manage. In Control Panel, tap or click User Accounts, and then tap or click Manage Windows Credentials under Credential Manager.

   On the Credential Manager page, you'll find a list of current entries by credential type.

2. Tap or click the credential entry that you want to edit.

3. Tap or click Edit.

4. As necessary, specify new values for the user name and password or the certificate associated with the credential, and then tap or click Save.

REAL WORLD Windows 8.1 does not allow you to add or edit web passwords in Credential Manager. You must change web passwords through the website or app that requires them.

Backing up and restoring Windows credentials

You can back up a user's stored credentials separately from his computer data. After you back up credentials, you can restore the credentials or transfer them to a new computer simply by restoring the backup. In most cases, you should back up the credentials to removable media.

To back up a user's credentials, follow these steps:

1. Log on as the user whose credential entries you want to manage. In Control Panel, tap or click User Accounts, and then tap or click Manage Windows Credentials under Credential Manager.

   On the Credential Manager page, you'll find a list of current entries by credential type.

2. Tap or click Back Up Credentials.

3. On the Stored User Names And Passwords page, tap or click Browse. Use the Save Backup File As dialog box to select a save location and specify a name for the credential backup file. Credential backup files are saved with the .crd file extension. Tap or click Save.

4. Tap or click Next. Press Ctrl+Alt+Del to switch to the secure desktop. When prompted, enter and confirm a password for the credential backup file.

5. Tap or click Next, and then tap or click Finish.

To restore a user's credentials on the same or a different computer, follow these steps:

1. Log on as the user whose credential entries you want to manage. In Control Panel, tap or click User Accounts, and then tap or click Manage Windows Credentials under Credential Manager.

2. On the Credential Manager page, tap or click Restore Credentials.

3. On the Stored User Names And Passwords page, tap or click Browse. Use the Open Backup File dialog box to select the location and file to which you saved the credential backup files, and then tap or click Open.

4. Tap or click Next. Press Ctrl+Alt+Del to switch to the secure desktop. When prompted, enter the password for the credential backup file.

5. Tap or click Next, and then tap or click Finish.

Removing credential entries

When a user no longer needs a credential entry, you should remove it. To remove a user's credential entry, follow these steps:

1. Log on as the user whose credential entries you want to manage. In Control Panel, tap or click User Accounts, and then tap or click Manage Windows Credentials under Credential Manager.

   On the Credential Manager page, you'll find a list of current entries by credential type.

2. Tap or click the credential entry that you want to remove.

3. Tap or click Remove. When prompted to confirm the action, tap or click Yes.

As stated previously, local credential entries can be removed only on the computer on which they were created. When a user has a roaming profile, however, credential entries can be deleted from any computer to which the user is logged on.

Managing local user accounts and groups

Local user accounts and groups are managed much like domain accounts. You can create accounts, manage their properties, reset accounts when they are locked or disabled, and so on. In addition to being able to manage local user accounts with Control Panel, you can create local user accounts with Local Users And Groups or with policy preferences. You should:

- Use Local Users And Groups to manage local user accounts on one computer.
- Use policy preferences to manage local user accounts on multiple computers throughout a domain.

When working with policy preferences, you can manage users and groups through Computer Configuration entries or User Configuration entries. Use Computer Configuration if you want to configure preferences that should be applied to computers regardless of who logs on. Use User Configuration if you want to configure preferences that should be applied to users regardless of which computer they log on to.

TIP The procedures that follow use Computer Management to access the Local Users And Groups snap-in for MMC. You can also access this snap-in in a standalone console by typing **lusrmgr.msc** in the Everywhere Search box, and then pressing Enter.

Creating local user accounts

You can access Local Users And Groups and create a user account by completing the following steps:

1. Open Computer Management. Press and hold or right-click the Computer Management entry in the console tree, and then tap or click Connect To Another Computer on the shortcut menu. You can now select the work-station running Windows 8.1 whose local accounts you want to manage. (Domain controllers do not have local users or groups.)

2. Under the System Tools node, tap or click the Local Users And Groups node to expand it, and then select Users. In the details pane, you should find a list of the currently defined user accounts.

3. Press and hold or right-click Users, and then tap or click New User. This opens the New User dialog box, as shown in Figure 5-9.

FIGURE 5-9 Configure new workstation accounts by using the New User dialog box in Local Users And Groups.

The options in the dialog box are used as follows:

- **User Name**   The logon name for the user account. This name should follow the conventions for the local user name policy.

- **Full Name**   The full name of the user, such as **William R. Stanek**.

- **Description**   A description of the user. Normally, you would enter the user's job title, such as **Webmaster.** You could also enter the user's job title and department.

- **Password**   The password for the account. This password should follow the conventions of your password policy.

- **Confirm Password**   The password for the account. To ensure that you assign the account password correctly, simply retype the password to confirm it.

- **User Must Change Password At Next Logon**   If this check box is selected, the user must change the password upon logon.
- **User Cannot Change Password**   If this check box is selected, the user can't change the password.
- **Password Never Expires**   If this check box is selected, the password for this account never expires. This setting overrides the local account policy.
- **Account Is Disabled**   If this check box is selected, the account is disabled and can't be used. Use this option to temporarily prevent anyone from using an account.

4. Tap or click Create when you have finished configuring the new account.

You can access Group Policy and use a preference item to create a user account by completing the following steps:

1. Open a Group Policy Object for editing in the Group Policy Management Editor. To configure preferences for computers, expand Computer Configuration\Preferences\Control Panel Settings, and then select Local Users And Groups. To configure preferences for users, expand User Configuration \Preferences\Control Panel Settings, and then select Local Users And Groups.

2. Press and hold or right-click the Local Users And Groups node, point to New, and then select Local User. This opens the New Local User Properties dialog box, as shown in Figure 5-10.

3. In the Action list, select Create. The rest of the options in the dialog box are used as described in the previous procedure.

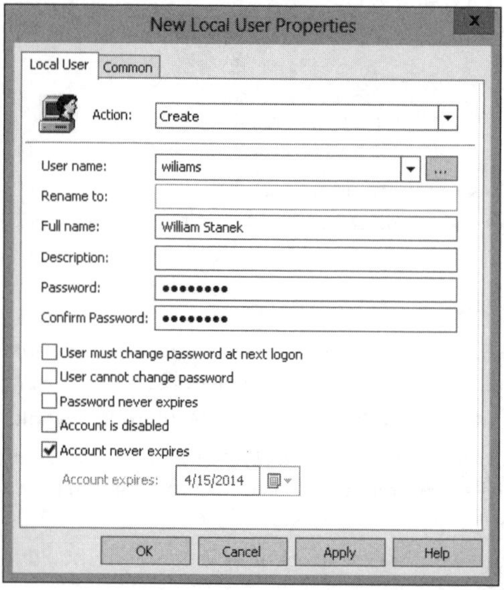

FIGURE 5-10 Configure new local user accounts in Group Policy.

4. Use the options on the Common tab to control how the preference is applied. In most cases, you'll want to create the new account only once. If so, select Apply Once And Do Not Reapply.

5. Tap or click OK. The next time Group Policy is refreshed, the preference item will be applied as appropriate for the Group Policy Object in which you defined the preference item.

Creating local groups for workstations

You create local groups with Local Users And Groups or with Group Policy. You can access Local Users And Groups and create a local group by completing the following steps:

1. Open Computer Management. Press and hold or right-click the Computer Management entry in the console tree, and then tap or click Connect To Another Computer on the shortcut menu. You can now select the workstation running Windows 8.1 whose local accounts you want to manage. (Domain controllers do not have local users or groups.)

2. Under the System Tools node, double-tap or double-click the Local Users And Groups node to expand it, and then select Groups. In the details pane, you should find a list of the currently defined group accounts.

3. Press and hold or right-click Groups, and then select New Group. This opens the New Group dialog box, as shown in Figure 5-11.

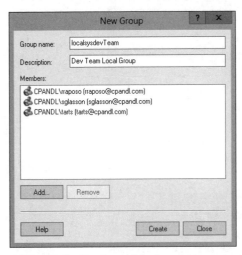

FIGURE 5-11 The New Group dialog box enables you to add a new local group to a workstation running Windows 8.1.

4. After you enter a name and description for the group, tap or click Add to open the Select Users dialog box and add names to the group.

5. In the Select Users dialog box, tap or click Locations to select the computer or domain in which the user accounts you want to work with are located.

6. Enter the name of a user you want to use in the Enter The Object Names To Select text box, and then tap or click Check Names. If matches are found, select the account you want to use, and then tap or click OK. If no matches are found, update the name you entered and try searching again. Repeat this step as necessary, and then tap or click OK when you have finished.

7. The New Group dialog box is updated to reflect your selections. If you made a mistake, select a name and remove it by tapping or clicking Remove.

8. Tap or click Create when you have finished adding or removing group members. Tap or click Close to close the New Group dialog box.

You can access Group Policy and use a preference item to create a local group by completing the following steps:

1. Open a Group Policy Object for editing in the Group Policy Management Editor. To configure preferences for computers, expand Computer Configuration\Preferences\Control Panel Settings, and then select Local Users And Groups. To configure preferences for users, expand User Configuration \Preferences\Control Panel Settings, and then select Local Users And Groups.

2. Press and hold or right-click the Local Users And Groups node, point to New, and then select Local Group. This opens the New Local Group Properties dialog box, as shown in Figure 5-12.

FIGURE 5-12 Configure new local group accounts in Group Policy.

3. In the Action list, select Create. Enter a name and description for the group.

4. To add members to the group, tap or click Add. In the Local Group Member dialog box, tap or click the browse button (the one with the three dots). Use the Select User, Computer, Or Group dialog box to select a user or group to add to the local group, and then tap or click OK twice. Repeat this step as necessary.

5. Use the options on the Common tab to control how the preference is applied. In most cases, you should create the new account only once. To do so, select Apply Once And Do Not Reapply.

6. Tap or click OK. The next time Group Policy is refreshed, the preference item will be applied as appropriate for the Group Policy Object in which you defined the preference item.

Adding and removing local group members

You can use Local Users And Groups to add or remove local group members by completing the following steps:

1. Expand Local Users And Groups in Computer Management, and then select the Groups folder in the left pane. Double-tap or double-click the group with which you want to work.

2. Tap or click Add to add user accounts to the group. This opens the Select Users dialog box. In the Select Users dialog box, enter the name of a user you want to use in the Enter The Object Names To Select text box, and then tap or click Check Names. If matches are found, select the account you want to use, and then tap or click OK. If no matches are found, update the name you entered and try searching again. Repeat this step as necessary, and then tap or click OK.

3. Use the Remove button to remove user accounts from the group. Simply select the user account you want to remove from the group, and then tap or click Remove.

4. Tap or click OK when you have finished.

You can access Group Policy and use a preference item to add or remove members from a local group by completing the following steps:

1. Open a Group Policy Object for editing in the Group Policy Management Editor. To configure preferences for computers, expand Computer Configuration\Preferences\Control Panel Settings, and then select Local Users And Groups. To configure preferences for users, expand User Configuration\Preferences\Control Panel Settings, and then select Local Users And Groups.

2. Press and hold or right-click the Local Users And Groups node, point to New, and then select Local Group. This opens the New Local Group Properties dialog box.

3. In the Action list, select Update to update the group's settings, or select Replace to delete the group and then re-create it exactly as you specify. If you update a group, you can enter a new name in the Rename To box.

4. Specify whether the current user should be added or removed as a member of the group, or select Do Not Configure For The Current User.

5. Specify whether all existing member users, all existing member groups, or both should be deleted.

6. To add or remove group members, tap or click Add. In the Local Group Member dialog box, in the Action list, select Add To This Group if you are adding a member, or select Remove From This Group if you are removing a member. Next, tap or click the browse button (the one with the three dots). Use the Select User, Computer, Or Group dialog box to select a user or group to add to or remove from the local group, and then tap or click OK twice. Repeat this step as necessary.

7. Use the options on the Common tab to control how the preference is applied, and then tap or click OK. The next time policy is refreshed, the preference item will be applied as appropriate for the Group Policy Object in which you defined the preference item.

Enabling or disabling local user accounts

Local user accounts can become disabled for several reasons. If a user forgets a password and tries to guess it, he might exceed the account policy for bad logon attempts. Another administrator could have disabled the account while a user was on vacation. When an account is disabled or locked out, you can enable it by using the methods described here.

When an account is disabled, you can enable it on a local computer by completing the following steps:

1. Expand Local Users And Groups in Computer Management, and then select the Users folder in the left pane.

2. In the right pane, double-tap or double-click the user's account name, and then clear the Account Is Disabled check box.

3. Tap or click OK.

When an account is locked out, you can enable it on a local computer by completing the following steps:

1. In Local Users And Groups, select the Users folder in the left pane.

2. In the right pane, double-tap or double-click the user's account name, and then clear the Account Is Locked Out check box.

3. Tap or click OK.

You can enable or disable accounts and set other account options through policy preferences by completing the following steps:

1. Open a Group Policy Object for editing in the Group Policy Management Editor. To configure preferences for computers, expand Computer Configuration\Preferences\Control Panel Settings, and then select Local Users And Groups. To configure preferences for users, expand User Configuration \Preferences\Control Panel Settings, and then select Local Users And Groups.

2. In the right pane, double-tap or double-click the user's account name to open the related Properties dialog box.

3. Select Update in the Action list. Make any necessary changes, and then tap or click OK. The next time policy is refreshed, the preference item will be applied as appropriate for the Group Policy Object in which you defined the preference item.

Creating a secure guest account

In some environments, you might need to set up a Guest account that can be used by visitors. Most of the time, you'll want to configure the Guest account on a specific computer or computers and carefully control how the account can be used. To create a secure Guest account, I recommend that you perform the following tasks:

- **Enable the Guest account for use** By default, the Guest account is disabled, so you must enable it to make it available. To do this, access Local Users And Groups in Computer Management, and then select the Users folder. Double-tap or double-click Guest, and then clear the Account Is Disabled check box. Tap or click OK.

- **Set a secure password for the Guest account** By default, the Guest account has a blank password. To improve security on the computer, you should set a password for the account. In Local Users And Groups\Select Users, press and hold or right-click Guest, and then select Set Password. Tap or click Proceed at the warning prompt. Enter the new password and then confirm it. Tap or click OK twice.

- **Ensure that the Guest account cannot be used over the network** The Guest account shouldn't be accessible from other computers. If it is, users at another computer could log on over the network as a guest. To prevent this, start the Local Security Policy tool from the Tools menu in Server Manager, or enter **secpol.msc** at a prompt. Then, under Local Policies\User Rights Assignment, ensure that the Deny Access To This Computer From The Network policy lists Guest as a restricted account (which is the default setting).

- **Prevent the Guest account from shutting down the computer** When a computer is shutting down or starting up, it's possible that a guest user (or anyone with local access) could gain unauthorized access to the computer. To help deter this, you should be sure that the Guest account doesn't have the Shut Down The System user right. In the Local Security Policy tool, expand Local Policies\User Rights Assignment, and ensure that the Shut Down The System policy doesn't list the Guest account (which is the default setting).

- **Prevent the Guest account from viewing event logs** To help maintain the security of the system, the Guest account shouldn't be allowed to view the event logs. To be sure this is the case, start Registry Editor by typing **regedit** at a command prompt, and then access the HKLM\SYSTEM\CurrentControlSet \Services\Eventlog key. Here, among other things, you'll find three important subkeys: Application, Security, and System. Make sure each of these subkeys has a DWORD value named RestrictGuestAccess, with a value of 1.

Renaming local user accounts and groups

When you rename an account, you give it a new label. Because the SID for the account remains the same, the permissions and properties associated with the account don't change. To rename an account while you are accessing a local computer, complete the following steps:

1. In Local Users And Groups, select the Users or Groups folder, as appropriate.

2. Press and hold or right-click the account name, and then tap or click Rename. Enter the new account name, and then tap or click a different entry.

To rename an account using Group Policy, complete the following steps:

1. Open a Group Policy Object for editing in the Group Policy Management Editor. To configure preferences for computers, expand Computer Configuration\Preferences\Control Panel Settings, and then select Local Users And Groups. To configure preferences for users, expand User Configuration \Preferences\Control Panel Settings, and then select Local Users And Groups.

2. Do one of the following:

   - If a preference item already exists for the user or group, double-tap or double-click the user or group name to open the related Properties dialog box. Select Update in the Action list. In the Rename To box, enter the new account name, and then tap or click OK.

   - If a preference item doesn't already exist for the user or group, you need to create one by using the techniques discussed previously. Because you want to rename the user or group, select Update in the Action list, and then enter the new account name in the Rename To box.

Deleting local user accounts and groups

Deleting an account permanently removes it. After you delete an account, if you create another account with the same name, you can't automatically get the same permissions because the SID for the new account won't match the SID for the account you deleted.

Because deleting built-in accounts can have far-reaching effects on the workstation, Windows 8.1 doesn't let you delete built-in user accounts or group accounts. In Local Users And Groups, you can remove other types of accounts by selecting them and pressing the Delete key or by pressing and holding or right-clicking and then tapping or clicking Delete. When prompted, tap or click Yes.

NOTE When you delete a user account by using Local Users And Groups, Windows 8.1 doesn't delete the user's profile, personal files, or home directory. If you want to delete these files and directories, you have to do it manually.

To delete an account by using Group Policy, complete the following steps:

1. Open a Group Policy Object for editing in the Group Policy Management Editor. To configure preferences for computers, expand Computer Configuration\Preferences\Control Panel Settings, and then select Local Users And Groups. To configure preferences for users, expand User Configuration\Preferences\Control Panel Settings, and then select Local Users And Groups.

2. Do one of the following:

   - If a preference item already exists for the user or group, double-tap or double-click the user or group name to open the related Properties dialog box. Select Delete in the Action list. On the Common tab, set the appropriate options, such as Apply Once And Do Not Reapply, and then tap or click OK.

   - If a preference item doesn't already exist for the user or group, you need to create one for the user or group by using the techniques discussed previously. Be sure to select Delete in the Action list, and then select the appropriate options on the Common tab.

Managing remote access to workstations

Windows 8.1 has several remote connectivity features. With Remote Assistance, users can send invitations to support technicians, enabling the technicians to service a computer remotely. With Remote Desktop, users can connect remotely to a computer and access its resources. In this chapter, you'll learn how to configure Remote Assistance and Remote Desktop. Typically, neither the Remote Assistance feature nor the Remote Desktop feature is enabled, so you must enable these features manually.

Remote Assistance and Remote Desktop can function through Network Address Translation (NAT) firewalls. Remote Assistance has built-in diagnostic tools. When troubleshooting requires restarting the computer, Remote Assistance sessions are reestablished automatically after the computer being diagnosed reboots.

Using the Steps Recorder prior to Remote Assistance

Prior to using Remote Assistance, you might want users to use the Steps Recorder to create a step-by-step record of the problem they are experiencing. The Steps Recorder is very easy to use. To start and use the Steps Recorder, complete the following steps:

1. Have the user start the Steps Recorder, as shown in Figure 6-1. One way to do this is by having the user press the Windows key, type **psr**, and then press Enter. Before the Steps Recorder is started, the user can prepare the environment by closing programs and dialog boxes that aren't related to the problem being diagnosed.

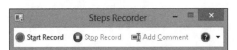

FIGURE 6-1 Begin recording to start tracking the steps leading to the issue to be diagnosed.

2. To turn on recording, the user taps or clicks Start Record. When recording has started, the user can perform the action that isn't working and tap or click Add Comment to add comments as she works.

3. When the user experiences the problem and the related errors have been displayed, she can stop recording by tapping or clicking Stop Record.

4. When the user stops recording, the Steps Recorder shows all the steps the user took while the problem was being recorded (see Figure 6-2). The user can then tap or click Save to display the Save As dialog box. The user selects a save location and name for the .zip file that contains the record of the problem in an embedded .mhtml file.

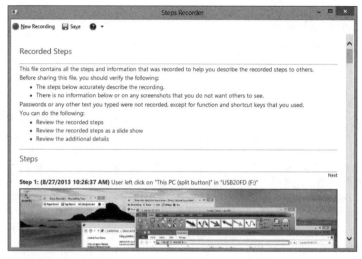

FIGURE 6-2 When the user stops recording, the Steps Recorder displays the recorded steps.

The user can send the .zip file to you in an email message or copy it to a file share. To review the recorded problem steps, you double-tap or double-click the .zip file to display its contents in File Explorer, and then double-tap or double-click the enclosed .mhtml file to open it in Internet Explorer.

You'll then find screen captures for all the steps the user took while the problem was being recorded. After the screen captures, you'll find automatically generated details for each step. You can use this information along with any user comments to help you troubleshoot the problem.

Using Remote Assistance to resolve problems

Remote Assistance enables support personnel to view a user's desktop and take control temporarily to resolve problems or walk the user through the execution of complex tasks. After Remote Assistance is configured locally or through Group Policy, as discussed in this section, you can work with this feature.

Understanding Remote Assistance

Only users running Windows desktop operating systems can initiate and respond to Remote Assistance invitations. In the enterprise, the easy way to work with Remote Assistance is as follows:

1. Be sure that Windows Firewall exceptions are created for the executable files Msra.exe and Raserver.exe, and open TCP port 135 for DCOM. Normally, these settings are configured by default through Group Policy.

2. Be sure that the user's computer is configured to allow Remote Assistance as discussed in "Configuring Remote Assistance" later in this chapter and that you can connect to the computer by its computer name or IP address.

Windows 8.1 can detect when configuration settings are blocking Remote Assistance connections. If this is the case, when a person needing help tries to invite help, she will get an alert in Windows Remote Assistance stating that this computer is not set up to send invitations (see Figure 6-3).

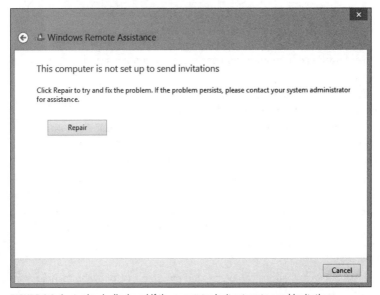

FIGURE 6-3 A warning is displayed if the computer isn't set up to send invitations.

The user will be able to tap or click Repair to have Windows Network Diagnostics look more closely at the problem. If the problem can be diagnosed, the user will then have the option to try implementing recommended repairs as an administrator (see Figure 6-4). If the user has Administrator permission on the computer, she can use this option to resolve the issue and can then close the troubleshooter.

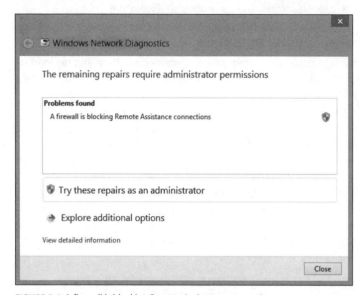

FIGURE 6-4 A firewall is blocking Remote Assistance connections.

With an enterprise configuration, you can provide remote assistance by following these steps:

1. Open Windows Remote Assistance. One way to do this is by pressing the Windows key, typing **msra.exe**, and then pressing Enter.

2. In the Windows Remote Assistance Wizard, tap or click Help Someone Who Has Invited You.

3. Tap or click Advanced Connection Option For Help Desk.

4. Enter the name or IP address of the computer you want to assist, and then tap or click Next to connect to the computer.

Users can initiate sessions by creating an invitation request. Support personnel initiate sessions by offering help to users. After a session is initiated, assistants can chat with users, observe their working screens, and, if permitted, control their computers.

Remote Assistance invitations can be created by using the following techniques:

- **Email invitation** Email invitations are sent as email messages to a named email address. An attachment provided in the message is used to initiate the Remote Assistance session. You might want to configure a standard email address, such as RemoteAssist@pocket-consultant.com, to allow users to send invitation requests easily to the support team. If this address is configured in Microsoft Exchange Server as a distribution list that delivers the invitations to support team members or as an additional mailbox for specific team members, support staff will be able to handle requests more efficiently and users will have a standard way of requesting help.

- **File invitation** File invitations are saved as Microsoft Remote Control Incident (MsRcIncident) files. Double-tapping or double-clicking the file name initiates the Remote Assistance session. You can use file invitations if you are using web-based email and need to attach the invitation separately. You might also want to configure a shared folder that is automatically mapped as a network drive for users and ensure that it's accessible by support personnel. Name the share something that easily identifies it as being used for assistance requests, such as HelpDeskRequests or AssistanceInvitations.

- **Easy Connect invitation** These use the Peer Name Resolution Protocol (PNRP) to send a Remote Assistance invitation over the Internet. Easy Connect requires access to a peer-to-peer network and an instant messaging program that supports Remote Assistance. Easy Connect generates an access password automatically, which allows the helper to connect directly to the computer. The helper's contact information is saved for quick reference in the future. (This technique works only when both the helper and the person being assisted are using Windows 7 or later.)

With Windows 8.1, invitations must be created with a control password. The control password provides an additional layer of security in the Remote Assistance configuration, ensuring that users are authorized to provide remote assistance and that they know the invitation password.

To work properly, Remote Assistance relies on the presence of a network connection between the user's computer and the assistant's computer. Remote Assistance uses UPnP, SSDP, PNRP, and Teredo for communications. Because most firewalls do not allow these communications by default, a firewall between the two computers might prevent the assistance session, and to ensure success, an exception must be created for outbound communications from the assistant's computer to the user's computer. To configure the required Windows Firewall exception for Remote Assistance, follow these steps:

1. In Control Panel, tap or click System And Security. Under the Windows Firewall heading, tap or click Allow An App Through Windows Firewall.

2. In the Allowed Apps window, scroll down until you find Remote Assistance. Ensure that the Remote Assistance check box is selected. Keep in mind that before you can make any changes, you must select the Change Settings button.

3. You'll find related check boxes for Domain, Private, and Public networks. Select or clear the check boxes to specify the network types for which Remote Assistance should be allowed. Tap or click OK.

Remote Assistance can work through NAT firewalls. When providing support through Remote Assistance, you'll find built-in diagnostic tools that you can run with a single tap or click. Finally, thanks to the automatic reconnect-after-restart feature, if you need to restart a computer that you are assisting remotely, you won't need to reconnect to the computer manually. The Remote Assistance session is reestablished automatically after the computer restarts.

Configuring Remote Assistance

Remote Assistance is a useful feature for help desks, whether in house or outsourced. A user can allow support personnel to view and take control of his desktop. This feature can be used to walk users through a complex process or to manage system settings while the user watches the progress of the changes. The key to Remote Assistance is in the access levels you grant.

When enabled, Remote Assistance is configured by default to let support person-nel view and control computers. Because users can send assistance invitations to internal and external resources, this could present a security concern for organiza-tions. To reduce potential security problems, you might want to allow support staff to view but not control computers. Computers running Windows Vista or later can be configured to allow connections only from computers running Windows Vista or later. This option is helpful to limit any possible compatibility issues and to ensure that any security enhancements in Windows Vista or later are available within Remote Assistance sessions.

Another key aspect of Remote Assistance you can control is the time limit for invitations. The default maximum time limit is 6 hours; the absolute maximum time limit you can assign is 30 days. Although the intent of a multiple-day invitation is to give support personnel a time window in which to respond to requests, it also means that they could use an invitation to access a computer over a period of 30 days. For instance, suppose you send an invitation with a 30-day time limit to a support per-son who resolves the problem the first day. That person would still have access to the computer for another 29 days, which wouldn't be desirable for security reasons. To reduce the risk to your systems, you'll usually want to reduce the default maxi-mum time limit considerably—say, to 1 hour. If the problem is not solved in the allotted time period, you can issue another invitation.

To configure Remote Assistance, follow these steps:

1. In Control Panel, tap or click System And Security. Under the System heading, tap or click Allow Remote Access. This opens the System Properties dialog box with the Remote tab displayed, as shown in Figure 6-5.

2. To disable Remote Assistance, clear the Allow Remote Assistance Connections To This Computer check box, and then tap or click OK. Skip the remaining steps.

3. To enable Remote Assistance, select Allow Remote Assistance Connections To This Computer.

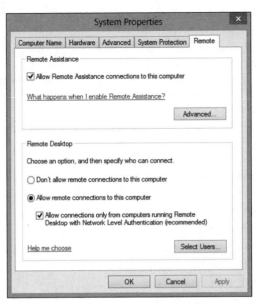

FIGURE 6-5 Use the Remote tab options to configure remote access to the computer.

4. Tap or click the Advanced button. This displays the Remote Assistance Settings dialog box, as shown in Figure 6-6.

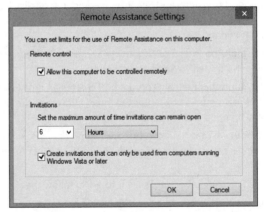

FIGURE 6-6 The Remote Assistance Settings dialog box is used to set limits for Remote Assistance.

5. The Allow This Computer To Be Controlled Remotely option sets limits for Remote Assistance. When selected, this setting allows assistants to view and control the computer. To provide view-only access to the computer, clear this check box.

6. The Invitations options control the maximum time window for invitations. You can set a value in minutes, hours, or days, up to a maximum of 30 days. (Though the dialog box allows you to select a value of up to 99 days, any value in excess of 30 is reset to 30 when you tap or click OK.) If you set a maximum limit value of 10 days, for example, a user can create an invitation with a time limit up to but not more than 10 days. The default maximum expiration limit is 6 hours.

7. Tap or click OK twice when you have finished configuring Remote Assistance options.

In Group Policy, you can manage Remote Assistance by using the following policy settings, which are found in the Administrative Templates policies for Computer Configuration under the \System\Remote Assistance path.

- Allow Only Windows Vista Or Later Connections
- Configure Offer Remote Assistance
- Configure Solicited Remote Assistance
- Customize Warning Messages
- Turn On Bandwidth Optimization
- Turn On Session Logging

Creating Remote Assistance invitations

To create a Remote Assistance invitation for email, follow these steps:

1. In Control Panel, under the System And Security heading, tap or click Find And Fix Problems. In the left pane of the Troubleshooting window, tap or click Get Help From A Friend.

2. On the Remote Assistance page, tap or click Invite Someone To Help You, and then tap or click Use E-Mail To Send An Invitation.

3. Windows 8.1 starts your default email program and creates an email message with the invitation. In the To box, enter the email address of the person you are inviting, and then tap or click Send.

4. In the Windows Remote Assistance dialog box, you'll find the connection password. This is the password the helper needs to use to connect to your computer.

To create a Remote Assistance invitation and save it to a file, follow these steps:

1. In Control Panel, under the System And Security heading, tap or click Find And Fix Problems. In the left pane of the Troubleshooting window, tap or click Get Help From A Friend.

2. On the Remote Assistance page, tap or click Invite Someone To Help You, and then tap or click Save This Invitation As A File.

3. Use the Save As dialog box to specify the path and file name for the invitation. If you specify the path to a network folder, the invitation can be accessed easily by an administrator with access to this network folder.

4. Give your helper the invitation file and the automatically generated password. This password is used by the person you are inviting and is valid only for the Remote Assistance session.

To create a Remote Assistance invitation for Easy Connect, follow these steps:

1. In Control Panel, under the System And Security heading, tap or click Find And Fix Problems. In the left pane of the Troubleshooting window, tap or click Get Help From A Friend.

2. On the Remote Assistance page, tap or click Invite Someone To Help You, and then tap or click Use Easy Connect.

3. Tell your helper the Easy Connect password. This password is generated automatically for this Remote Assistance session only.

By default, Remote Assistance invitations are valid for a maximum of 6 hours and enable support staff to remotely control a computer. You can change these settings by using the System Properties dialog box, as discussed in "Configuring Remote Assistance" earlier in this chapter. After you've sent the invitation by email or created the invitation file, the Windows Remote Assistance dialog box is displayed.

When you, as the helper, request shared control, the person you are helping gets a confirmation prompt asking if she would like to allow the helper to share control of the desktop (see Figure 6-7). The person being helped must tap or click Yes to permit shared control, but before that, you might want to have her allow you to respond to User Account Control (UAC) prompts. This permission is necessary to perform administrator tasks on the remote computer.

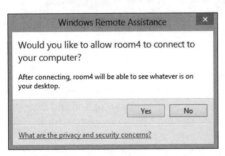

FIGURE 6-7 Before you can provide assistance, the user must confirm your access.

As shown in the upper-left corner of Figure 6-8, the Remote Assistance menu bar provides the following options to the helper:

- **Request Control/Stop Sharing**   Requests or stops sharing control of the computer.

- **Fit To Screen/Actual Size**   Resizes the other person's screen to fit your window or displays the screen at actual size.

- **Chat**   Opens a chat window for sending messages between the helper and the current user of the computer.

- **Settings**   Allows you to configure the session settings. By default, a log of the Remote Assistance session is saved in the %UserProfile%\Documents \Remote Assistance Logs folder on the helper's computer.

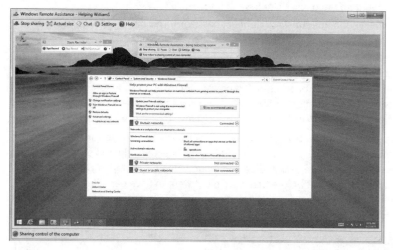

FIGURE 6-8 As a person providing assistance, you use the options on the menu bar to control the session.

You can use the Chat option to talk to the person you are assisting and pass instructions. For example, if you and the user are connected to a fast corporate network, you might want to instruct the user to use the Settings option and then increase the bandwidth allocated to the connection. Before you can perform management tasks on the user's computer, you must request control by tapping or clicking Request Control. When you request shared control, the person you are helping gets the confirmation prompt shown in Figure 6-9.

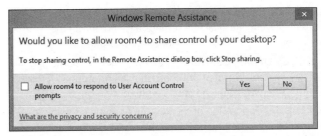

FIGURE 6-9 The user receiving assistance uses the options provided to control the session.

If you will need to perform any tasks on the user's computer that require administrator permissions, you should use Chat to instruct the user to select the Allow... option prior to selecting Yes. By selecting this option, the user allows you to elevate commands and perform administration tasks as might be needed. You, the helper, can end the session by closing the Remote Assistance window.

For the person being helped, a Remote Assistance dialog box appears on the desktop. As shown in Figure 6-10, this dialog box provides the following options:

- **Pause/Continue** Effectively pauses the Remote Assistance request by temporarily not allowing the helper to view the remote desktop. The person being helped must then tap or click Continue to resume the Remote Assistance session.

- **Stop Sharing** Stops sharing control of the computer and ends the Remote Assistance session.

- **Settings** Allows the person being assisted to configure the session settings.

    NOTE By default, the Remote Assistance log is created in the %UserProfile% \Documents\Remote Assistance Logs folder on the computer of the user requesting remote assistance and on the helper's computer.

- **Chat** Opens a chat window for sending messages between the helper and the current user of the computer.

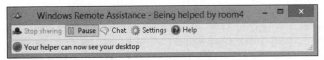

FIGURE 6-10 The user receiving assistance uses the options provided to control the session.

When you choose Settings, the Windows Remote Assistance Settings dialog box, shown in Figure 6-11, is displayed. The available settings depend on whether you are the helper or the person being helped and include the following:

- **Use ESC Key To Stop Sharing Control** When the person being helped presses the Esc key, shared control of the computer can be stopped if this option is selected. Otherwise, only the Stop Sharing option can be used.

- **Save A Log Of This Session** A log of the Remote Assistance session is saved automatically on the computer of the person being helped and the computer of the helper. The person being helped, the helper, or both can clear this option if a log of the session will not be needed.

- **Bandwidth Usage** By default, the bandwidth usage is configured so that the connection uses low resolution 16-bit color. Additionally, font smoothing, full-window drag, and desktop backgrounds are not enabled.

FIGURE 6-11 Remote Assistance settings are available to the person being helped.

TIP For faster connections, you might want to modify the bandwidth usage settings by using the Bandwidth Usage slider. With a medium setting, 32-bit color is allowed though desktop backgrounds and full-window drag are disabled. With a medium-high setting, only full-window drag is disabled. With a high setting, the connection has no bandwidth optimization.

When the person being helped presses the Esc key, shared control of the computer can be stopped if the related option is selected. Otherwise, the user can only use the Stop Sharing option. The person being helped also can use Pause and Resume to control the connection. When the connection is paused, the helper cannot view the desktop of the remote computer.

Offering remote assistance or answering a Remote Assistance invitation

If you know that a user is having problems with her computer, you can follow these steps to offer remote assistance rather than waiting for her to send you an invitation or Easy Connect password:

1. Start the Windows Remote Assistance Wizard. One way to do this is to type **msra** in the Everywhere Search box, and then press Enter.

2. In the Windows Remote Assistance Wizard, tap or click Help Someone Who Has Invited You.

3. Tap or click the Advanced Connection Option For Help Desk link.

4. Enter the name or IP address of the computer you want to assist, and then tap or click Next to connect to the computer.

5. If a problem occurs when attempting to make the connection, you'll find a warning prompt similar to the one shown in Figure 6-12. Select Troubleshoot to have Windows Network Diagnostics look more closely at the problem. If the problem can be diagnosed, you will then have the option to try implementing recommended repairs. Keep in mind, however, that the connection issue might be caused by a firewall running on the user's computer or another configuration issue on the user's computer.

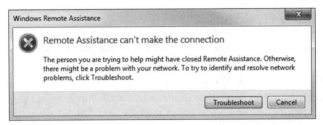

FIGURE 6-12 Remote Assistance displays a warning if the connection fails.

If someone has already created an invitation, you can answer the invitation by double-tapping or double-clicking the related email attachment or file. You can also answer an invitation saved to a file by following these steps:

1. Start the Windows Remote Assistance Wizard. One way to do this is to type **msra** in the Everywhere Search box and then press Enter.

2. In the Windows Remote Assistance Wizard, tap or click Help Someone Who Has Invited You.

3. Tap or click Use An Invitation File, and then use the Open dialog box to locate the invitation. Tap or click Open.

4. When prompted, provide the necessary password for the invitation.

5. Tap or click Finish. You are connected to the computer of the user needing assistance, provided that the user hasn't canceled the invitation, the invitation hasn't expired, and Remote Assistance is allowed. If a problem occurs when attempting to make the connection, you'll get a warning prompt similar to the one shown previously in Figure 6-12. Select Troubleshoot to try to identify and resolve the problem.

If someone is using Easy Connect and has sent you the password, you can answer the invitation by following these steps:

1. Start the Windows Remote Assistance Wizard. One way to do this is to type **msra** in the Everywhere Search box, and then press Enter.

2. In the Windows Remote Assistance Wizard, tap or click Help Someone Who Has Invited You.

3. Tap or click Use Easy Connect. When prompted, provide the password for the invitation.

4. Tap or click OK. You are connected to the computer of the user needing assistance. If a problem occurs when attempting to make the connection, you'll get a warning prompt similar to the one shown previously in Figure 6-12. Select Troubleshoot to try to identify and resolve the problem.

Using Remote Desktop

Unlike Remote Assistance, which provides only a controller view of the current user's desktop, Remote Desktop provides several levels of access:

- If a user is logged on to the desktop locally and then tries to log on remotely, the local desktop locks, and the user can access all of the running applications just as though he were sitting at the keyboard. This feature is useful for users who want to work from home or other locations outside the office, enabling them to continue to work with applications and documents that they were using prior to leaving the office.

- If a user is listed on the workstation's Remote Access list and is not otherwise logged on, she can initiate a new Windows session. The Windows session behaves as though the user were sitting at the keyboard. It can even be used when other users are also logged on to the computer. In this way, multiple users can share a single workstation and use its resources.

Configuring Remote Desktop access

Remote Desktop is not enabled by default. You must specifically enable it to allow remote access to a workstation. When it is enabled, any member of the Administrators group can connect to the workstation. Other users must be placed on a Remote

Access list to gain access to the workstation. To configure remote access, follow these steps:

1. In Control Panel, tap or click System And Security, and then tap or click System.

2. On the System page, tap or click Remote Settings in the left pane. This opens the System Properties dialog box to the Remote tab, as shown in Figure 6-13.

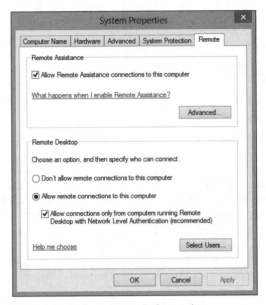

FIGURE 6-13 Configure Remote Desktop options.

3. To disable Remote Desktop, select Don't Allow Remote Connections To This Computer, and then tap or click OK. Skip the remaining steps.

4. To enable Remote Desktop, you can:

   - Select Allow Remote Connections To This Computer to allow connections from any version of Windows.

   - Also select Allow Connections Only From Computers Running Remote Desktop With Network Level Authentication to restrict the permitted connections to those from computers running Windows Vista or later (and computers with secure network authentication).

5. Tap or click Select Users. This displays the Remote Desktop Users dialog box, as shown in Figure 6-14.

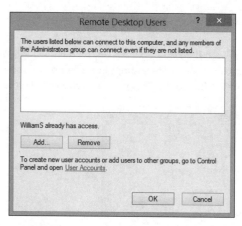

FIGURE 6-14 Specify the additional users allowed to make Remote Desktop connections.

6. To grant Remote Desktop access to a user, tap or click Add. This opens the Select Users Or Groups dialog box. In the Select Users Or Groups dialog box, tap or click Locations to select the computer or domain in which the users you want to work with are located. Enter the name of a user you want to work with in the Enter The Object Names To Select text box, and then tap or click Check Names. If matches are found, select the account you want to use and then tap or click OK. If no matches are found, update the name you entered and try searching again. Repeat this step as necessary, and then tap or click OK.

7. To revoke remote access permissions for a user account, select the account and then tap or click Remove.

8. Tap or click OK twice when you have finished.

Windows Firewall must be configured to allow inbound Remote Desktop exceptions. You can configure this on a per-computer basis in Windows Firewall for the domain profile and the standard profile. In Group Policy, you can configure this exception and manage Remote Desktop by using the policy settings shown in Table 6-1. These settings are found in the Administrative Templates policies for Computer Configuration under the paths shown.

TABLE 6-1 Policy settings for managing Remote Desktop

SETTING	COMPUTER CONFIGURATION PATH PATHS UNDER WINDOWS COMPONENTS \REMOTE DESKTOP SERVICES
Allow .Rdp Files From Unknown Publishers	\Remote Desktop Connection Client
Allow .Rdp Files From Valid Publishers And User's Default .Rdp Settings	\Remote Desktop Connection Client
Always Prompt For Password Upon Connection	\Remote Desktop Session Host \Security

SETTING	COMPUTER CONFIGURATION PATH
Automatic Reconnection	\Remote Desktop Session Host \Connections
Configure Server Authentication For Client	\Remote Desktop Connection Client
Deny Logoff Of An Administrator Logged In To The Console Session	\Remote Desktop Session Host \Connections
Do Not Allow Local Administrators To Customize Permissions	\Remote Desktop Session Host \Security
Do Not Allow Passwords To Be Saved	\Remote Desktop Connection Client
Limit Maximum Color Depth	\Remote Desktop Session Host \Remote Session Environment
Limit Maximum Display Resolution	\Remote Desktop Session Host \Remote Session Environment
Limit Number Of Monitors	\Remote Desktop Session Host \Remote Session Environment
Limit The Size Of The Entire Roaming User Profile Cache	\Remote Desktop Session Host \Profiles
Require Use Of Specific Security Layer For Remote (RDP) Connections	\Remote Desktop Session Host \Security
Set Client Connection Encryption Level	\Remote Desktop Session Host \Security
Select RDP Transport Protocols	\Remote Desktop Session Host \Connections
Select Network Detection On The Server	\Remote Desktop Session Host \Connections
Specify SHA1 Thumbprints Of Certificates Representing Trusted .Rdp Publishers	\Remote Desktop Connection Client
Turn Off Fair Share CPU Scheduling	\Remote Desktop Session Host \Connections
Turn Off UDP On Client	\Remote Desktop Connection Client
	OTHER PATHS
Disable Remote Desktop Sharing	\Windows Components\NetMeeting
Windows Firewall: Allow Inbound Remote Desktop Exceptions	\Network\Network Connections \Windows Firewall\Domain Profile
Windows Firewall: Allow Inbound Remote Desktop Exceptions	\Network\Network Connections \Windows Firewall\Standard Profile

Making Remote Desktop connections

As an administrator, you can make Remote Desktop connections to servers and workstations running Windows. Remote Desktop is installed automatically, but it is normally not enabled until you do so as discussed in the preceding section of this chapter. When remote access is enabled on a computer, all administrators have remote access to that computer. Other users can be granted remote access as well.

To make a Remote Desktop connection to a server or workstation, follow these steps:

1. At a command prompt, type **mstsc**, or press the Windows key, type **mstsc**, and then press Enter.

2. Tap or click Show Options. This displays the Remote Desktop Connection dialog box, shown in Figure 6-15.

FIGURE 6-15 In the Remote Desktop Connection dialog box, enter the name of the computer to which you want to connect, and then tap or click Connect.

3. In the Computer text box, enter the name of the computer to which you want to connect. If you don't know the name of the computer, use the drop-down list to choose an available computer, or select Browse For More in the drop-down list to display a list of domains and computers in those domains.

4. Specify additional options as necessary. If you've configured stored credentials for the computer, your saved credentials will be used automatically. You can edit or delete the credentials as necessary.

5. Tap or click Connect. If you haven't previously stored credentials for the computer, enter your credentials when prompted, and then tap or click OK. For domain logons, you can specify your user name in domain\username format if necessary, such as cpandl\williams for the WilliamS account in the Cpandl domain.

6. If the connection is successful, you'll see the Remote Desktop window on the selected computer, and you'll be able to work with resources on the computer. In the case of a failed connection, check the information you provided and then try to connect again. If you still can't connect, the connection issue might be due to a firewall or another configuration issue.

NOTE Tapping or clicking Show Options in the Remote Desktop Connection dialog box displays a series of tabs that provide additional options for creating and saving connections. These options enable you to change the display size for the Remote Desktop, manage connections to local resources (such as printers, serial ports, and disk drives), run programs automatically on connection, and enable or disable local caching and data compression.

CHAPTER 7

Installing and maintaining applications

- Managing desktop apps **214**
- Managing application virtualization and run levels **217**
- Installing programs: the essentials **224**
- Deploying applications through Group Policy **229**
- Configuring program compatibility **230**
- Managing installed and running programs **235**

Desktop programs are applications that you can install and configure. Most desktop programs use the Windows Installer to make application management tasks easier. Administrators and support staff often install and configure the programs that are used on desktop computers. You might need to install and configure programs before deploying new computers, install new programs on computers when the programs are requested, and update programs when new versions become available. Also, as users install additional programs, you might be called on to help troubleshoot installation problems or to help uninstall programs.

Most program installation problems are fairly easy to solve if you know what to look for. Other problems are fairly difficult to resolve and require more work than you might expect. In this chapter, you'll learn how User Account Control (UAC) affects the way you install and run programs. You'll also learn about techniques for installing, uninstalling, and maintaining programs and installing and configuring desktop apps. Although the terms *applications* and *software* generally refer to both desktop programs and desktop apps elsewhere in this book—and an app is a program in the most general sense—it is important now to distinguish between desktop programs and desktop apps.

The focus of this chapter is on programs. I will use the term *app* in this chapter strictly to refer to desktop apps, and I will discuss apps first to give a context for the rest of the chapter.

Managing desktop apps

Apps can be purchased in the Windows Store and installed over the Internet. They also can be developed in-house or by third-party developers and deployed by using Group Policy. Although apps can be managed by using techniques similar to those used for desktop programs, apps have many distinct characteristics.

Working with apps: the essentials

On Windows 8.1, the Start screen replaces the traditional Start menu. A desktop app is automatically added to Start when you install it and will have a Start tile. A Start tile makes it easy to start and manage the app. You can press and hold or right-click the tile to display management options. Management options for tiles depend on the type of tile. Live tiles can update their content, and these updates can be turned on or off. Some tiles can be displayed in several sizes, and you might be able to make a tile smaller or larger. If you no longer want a tile to be displayed on Start, you can choose the Unpin From Start option.

You can start and manage apps that you unpin in several ways, including through the Apps list. Apps is the Windows 8.1 equivalent to the Programs menu in earlier releases of Windows. From the Start screen, you can display Apps by selecting the down button on the Start screen.

NOTE Desktop programs might not be added to Start or Apps automatically. For more information, see the "Making programs available to all or selected users" section later in this chapter.

When working with apps and tiles, you should be aware of a few handy keyboard shortcuts, which work with desktop programs as well:

- **Windows key + Left Arrow or Right Arrow** Toggles the screen snap position of the app. Snap splits the screen, so if the app is being displayed normally, Windows key + Left Arrow snaps it to the left and Windows key + Right Arrow snaps it to the right.
- **Windows key + Up Arrow** Displays the app in Full Screen mode.
- **Windows key + Down Arrow** Exits Screen Mode and returns the app to its original window state.

Windows 8.1 has important improvements when it comes to working with apps. With Windows 8.1, apps can use four tile sizes: small (70 x 70 pixels), medium (150 x 150 pixels), wide (310 x 150 pixels), and large (310 x 310 pixels). Because more than two apps can share the screen at the same time, you can open one app and have it remain in the foreground when you open another app that also is in the foreground. Apps can open other apps and share the screen with them. A single app can also use multiple monitors.

Windows 8.1 apps with live tiles start updating immediately after installation. Previously, you needed to run the app after installation to start receiving updates.

In Windows 8.1, one of the lock screen slots is available for alarm apps. When you place an alarm app in this slot, it becomes the system alarm app and can generate alarm notifications. The default alarm app is Alarms, which has timer, stopwatch, and alarm features. Although other apps could issue alarm notifications, the notifications are handled as normal notifications rather than priority alarm notifications. In the Administrative Templates policies for User Configuration under Start Menu And Taskbar\Notification, you'll find options for managing times when notifications should be allowed or blocked.

Configuring trusted apps and Windows Store access

Generally, apps are installed and updated over a network or the Internet. By default, computers running Windows 8.1 can install only trusted app packages that come from the Windows Store. If you want to install trusted apps developed in-house or by third-party developers, you'll need to enable the Allow All Trusted Apps To Install policy in the Administrative Templates policies for Computer Configuration under Windows Components\App Package Deployment.

You can manage user access to the Windows Store in several ways, including the following:

- Control the use of Microsoft accounts on a computer by enabling the Accounts: Block Microsoft Accounts policy. This policy is found in the Security Options policies for Computer Configuration under Windows Settings\Security Settings\Local Policies. When you enable this policy, you have two options. You can use the Users Can't Add Microsoft Accounts setting to prevent users from creating Microsoft accounts, or you can use the User Can't Add Or Log On With Microsoft Accounts setting to block users from logging on with and creating Microsoft accounts.

- Prevent users from accessing the Windows Store by enabling Turn Off The Store Application in the Administrative Templates policies for Computer Configuration under Windows Components\Store.

- Prevent computers from automatically downloading app updates by enabling Turn Off Automatic Download Of Updates On Win8 Machines in the Administrative Templates policies for Computer Configuration under Windows Components\Store. Alternatively, you can use Turn Off Automatic Download And Install Of Updates to prevent computers from automatically downloading and installing updates.

Enhancing security for apps and overriding default settings

Apps run in a unique context and have a lower integrity level than desktop programs. The lower integrity level might allow apps to perform tasks that could compromise security because you'd otherwise need to provide consent to continue, and you don't need to provide consent in these instances with apps. For example, by default, apps can open a file in a desktop program. With an unhandled file type or protocol, users get an Open With dialog box and can select a local application to open the unknown file type or protocol or use the Store service to find an application to do the same.

You can use several policies to enhance security and prevent these behaviors, including the following:

- To prevent an app from opening a desktop program associated with a file type automatically, enable Block Launching Desktop Apps Associated With A File in the Administrative Templates policies for User Configuration or Computer Configuration under Windows Components\App Runtime.

- To prevent an app from opening a desktop program associated with URL protocols (except for HTTP, HTTPS, and mailto, which are hardened), enable Block Launching Desktop Apps Associated With A URI Scheme in the Administrative Templates policies for User Configuration or Computer Configuration under Windows Components\App Runtime.

- To remove the Windows Store option in the Open With dialog box, enable Turn Off Access To The Store in the Administrative Templates policies for Computer Configuration under System\Internet Communication Management\Internet Communication Settings.

It's also important to point out that some apps can display notifications on the lock screen and that a notification history is maintained by default. The notification history allows users to log off and then log back on later and see the tile just as they did prior to logging off. To block notifications on the lock screen, enable Turn Off App Notifications On the Lock Screen in the Administrative Templates policies for Computer Configuration under System\Logon. To clear the notification history when a user logs off, enable Clear History Of Tile Notifications On Exit in the Administrative Templates policies for User Configuration under Start Menu And Taskbar.

Apps receive notifications through the Windows Push Notification Service (WNS). Live apps use WNS to update the content on their tiles, to display notifications, and to receive notifications. By using Administrative Templates policies for User Configuration under Start Menu And Taskbar\Notifications, you can control the use of WNS in several ways, including the following:

- To block the display of alerts that pop up on the screen (known as *toast notifications*) in Windows, generally you can enable Turn Off Toast Notifications. This setting doesn't affect taskbar notification balloons.

- To block the display of alerts that pop up on the lock screen, you can enable Turn Off Toast Notifications On The Lock Screen.

- To block updating of tiles and tile badges on the Start screen, you can enable Turn Off Tile Notifications.

- To block apps from sending notifications for updates and alerts, you can enable Turn Off Notifications Network Usage. Enabling this setting turns off the connection to Windows and WNS.

REAL WORLD Microsoft tracks app usage in several ways. You can control the tracking of app usage by using the Administrative Templates policies for User Configuration under Windows Components\Edge UI.

Enhancing networking security for apps

Windows 8.1 supports several important networking features related to applications in general and apps specifically. Windows 8.1 uses a feature called Windows Network Isolation to automatically discover proxies and private network hosts when a computer is connected to a domain. By default, any proxy detected is considered authoritative and any network host can be discovered via the private subnets available to the computer.

Proxy discovery and private host discovery are separate features. You control the proxy discovery process by using policies in the Administrative Templates policies for Computer Configuration under Network\Network Isolation. Enable the Internet Proxy Servers For Apps policy, and then enter a comma-separated list of authorized proxies that apps running on domain-connected computers can use for accessing the Internet. By default, this list of proxies is merged with the list of automatically discovered proxies. If you want only your listed proxies to be authoritative, enable Proxy Definitions Are Authoritative.

You can use the Intranet Proxy Servers For Apps policy to define authorized private network proxies. Enable this policy and then enter a comma-separated list of proxies that provide access to intranet resources. If you want only your listed proxies to be authoritative, enable Proxy Definitions Are Authoritative.

Policies in the Administrative Templates policies for Computer Configuration under Network\Network Isolation are also used to control private host discovery. Hosts discovered in this way are designated as private. Normally, private host discovery will not go across subnet boundaries.

You can enhance the discovery process by enabling the Private Network Ranges For Apps policy and then entering a comma-separated list of your company's IPv4 and IPv6 subnets. This tells Windows about the available subnets so that they can be used for private host discovery. By default, this list of subnets is merged with the list of automatically discovered subnets. If you enable Subnet Definitions Are Authoritative, only network hosts within address ranges specific in Group Policy will be discovered and considered private.

Managing application virtualization and run levels

User Account Control (UAC) changes the way that applications are installed and run, where applications write data, and what permissions applications have. In this section, I'll look at how UAC affects application installation, from application security tokens to file and registry virtualization to run levels. This information is essential when you are installing and maintaining applications on Windows 8.1.

Application access tokens and location virtualization

All applications used with Windows 8.1 are divided into two general categories:

- **UAC-compliant** Any application written specifically for Windows Vista or later is considered a compliant application. Applications certified as complying with the Windows 8.1 architecture have the UAC-compliant logo.

- **Legacy** Any application written for earlier versions of Windows is considered a legacy application.

The distinction between UAC-compliant applications and legacy applications is important because of the architectural changes required to support UAC. UAC-compliant applications use UAC to reduce the attack surface of the operating system. They do this by preventing unauthorized applications from installing or running without the user's consent and by restricting the default privileges granted to applications. These measures make it harder for malicious software to take over a computer.

> **NOTE** The Windows 8.1 component responsible for UAC is the Application Information service. This service facilitates the running of interactive applications with an "administrator" access token. You can tell the difference between the administrator user and standard user access tokens by opening two Command Prompt windows, running one with elevation (press and hold or right-click, and then tap or click Run As Administrator), and the other as a standard user. In each window, enter **whoami /all** and compare the results. Both access tokens have the same security identifiers (SIDs), but the elevated administrator user access token has more privileges than the standard user access token.

All applications that run on Windows 8.1 derive their security context from the current user's access token. By default, UAC turns all users into standard users even if they are members of the Administrators group. If an administrator user consents to the use of her administrator privileges, a new access token is created for the user. It contains all the user's privileges, and this access token—rather than the user's standard access token—is used to start an application or process.

In Windows 8.1, most applications can run using a standard user access token. Whether applications need to run with standard or administrator privileges depends on the actions the application performs. Applications that require administrator privileges, referred to as *administrator user applications*, differ from applications that require standard user privileges, referred to as *standard user applications*, in the following ways:

- Administrator user applications require elevated privileges to run and perform core tasks. After it is started in elevated mode, an application with a user's administrator access token can perform tasks that require administrator privileges and can also write to system locations of the registry and the file system.

- Standard user applications do not require elevated privileges to run or to perform core tasks. After it is started in standard user mode, an application with a user's standard access token must request elevated privileges to perform administration tasks. For all other tasks, the application should not run by using elevated privileges. Further, the application should write data only to nonsystem locations of the registry and the file system.

Applications not written for Windows 8.1 run with a user's standard access token by default. To support the UAC architecture, these applications run in a special compatibility mode and use file system and registry virtualization to provide "virtualized" views of file and registry locations. When an application attempts to write to a system location, Windows 8.1 gives the application a private copy of the file or registry value. Any changes are then written to the private copy, and this private copy is then stored in the user's profile data. If the application attempts to read or write to this system location again, it is given the private copy from the user's profile with which to work. By default, if an error occurs when the application is working with virtualized data, the error notification and logging information show the virtualized location rather than the actual location where the application was trying to work.

Application integrity and run levels

The focus on standard user and administrator privileges also changes the general permissions required to install and run applications. In early versions of Windows, the Power Users group gave users specific administrator privileges to perform basic system tasks when installing and running applications. Applications written for Windows 8.1 do not require the use of the Power Users group. Windows 8.1 maintains it only for legacy application compatibility.

As part of UAC, Windows 8.1 by default detects application installations and prompts users for elevation to continue the installation. Installation packages for UAC-compliant applications use application manifests that contain run-level designations to help track required privileges. Application manifests define the application's privileges as one of the following:

- **RunAsInvoker** Run the application with the same privileges as the user. Any user can run the application. For a standard user or a user who is a member of the Administrators group, the application runs with a standard access token. The application runs with higher privileges only if the parent process from which it is started has an administrator access token. For example, if you open an elevated Command Prompt window and then start an application from this window, the application runs with an administrator access token.

- **RunAsHighest** Run the application with the highest privileges of the user. The application can be run by both administrator users and standard users. The tasks the application can perform depend on the user's privileges. For a standard user, the application runs with a standard access token. For a user who is a member of a group with additional privileges, such as the Backup Operators, Server Operators, or Account Operators group, the application runs with a partial administrator access token that contains only the privileges the user has been granted. For a user who is a member of the Administrators group, the application runs with a full administrator access token.

- **RunAsAdmin** Run the application with administrator privileges. Only administrators can run the application. For a standard user or a user who is a member of a group with additional privileges, the application runs only if the user can be prompted for credentials required to run in elevated mode or if the application is started from an elevated process, such as an elevated Command Prompt window. For a user who is a member of the Administrators group, the application runs with an administrator access token.

To protect application processes, Windows 8.1 labels them with integrity levels ranging from high to low. Applications that modify system data, such as Disk Management, are considered high integrity. Applications performing tasks that could compromise the operating system, such as Internet Explorer, are considered low integrity. Applications with lower integrity levels cannot modify data in applications with higher integrity levels.

Windows 8.1 identifies the publisher of any application that attempts to run with an administrator's full access token. Then, depending on that publisher, Windows 8.1 marks the application as belonging to one of the following three categories:

- Windows Vista or later
- Publisher verified (signed)
- Publisher not verified (unsigned)

To help you quickly identify the potential security risk of installing or running the application, a color-coded elevation prompt displays a different message depending on the category to which the application belongs:

- If the application is from a blocked publisher or is blocked by Group Policy, the elevation prompt has a red background and displays the message "The application is blocked from running."

- If the application is administrative (such as Computer Management), the elevation prompt has a blue-green background and displays the message "Windows needs your permission to continue."

- If the application has been signed by Authenticode and is trusted by the local computer, the elevation prompt has a gray background and displays the message "A program needs your permission to continue."

- If the application is unsigned (or is signed but not yet trusted), the elevation prompt has a yellow background and red shield icon and displays the message "An unidentified program wants access to your computer."

Prompting on the secure desktop can be used to further secure the elevation process. The secure desktop safeguards the elevation process by preventing spoofing of the elevation prompt. The secure desktop is enabled by default in Group Policy, as discussed in the section "Optimizing UAC and Admin Approval Mode" in Chapter 5, "Managing user access and security."

Setting run levels

By default, only applications running with a user's administrator access token run in elevated mode. Sometimes you'll want an application running with a user's standard access token to be in elevated mode. For example, you might want to open the Command Prompt window in elevated mode so that you can perform administration tasks.

In addition to application manifests (discussed in the previous section), Windows 8.1 provides two different ways to set the run level for applications:

- Run an application once as an administrator
- Always run an application as an administrator

To run an application once as an administrator, press and hold or right-click the application's shortcut or menu item, and then tap or click Run As Administrator. If you are using a standard account and prompting is enabled, you are prompted for consent before the application is started. If you are using a standard user account and prompting is disabled, the application will fail to run. If you are using an administrator account and prompting for consent is enabled, you are prompted for consent before the application is started.

Windows 8.1 also enables you to mark an application so that it always runs with administrator privileges. This approach is useful for resolving compatibility issues with legacy applications that require administrator privileges. It is also useful for UAC-compliant applications that normally run in standard mode but that you use to perform administration tasks. As examples, consider the following:

- A standard application written for Windows 8.1 is routinely run in elevated mode and used for administration tasks. To eliminate the need to press and hold or right-click the application shortcut and choose Run As Administrator before running the application, you can mark it to always run as an administrator.

- An application written for early versions of Windows requires administrator privileges. Because this application is configured to use standard mode by default under Windows 8.1, the application isn't running properly and is generating numerous errors. To resolve the compatibility problem, you could create an application compatibility shim by using the Windows Application Compatibility Toolkit (ACT) version 5.5 or later. As a temporary solution, you can mark the application to always run as an administrator.

NOTE You cannot mark system applications or processes to always run with administrator privileges. Only nonsystem applications and processes can be marked to always run at this level.

REAL WORLD The Windows Application Compatibility Toolkit (ACT) is a solution for administrators that requires no reprogramming of an application. ACT can help you resolve common compatibility problems. For example, some applications run only on a specific operating system or when the user is an administrator. By using ACT, you can create a shim that responds to the application inquiry about the operating system or user level with a True statement, which allows the application to run. ACT also can help you create more in-depth solutions for applications that try to write to protected areas of the operating system or use elevated privileges when they don't need to. ACT can be downloaded from the Microsoft Download Center (*http://download.microsoft.com*).

You can mark a program to always run as an administrator by following these steps:

1. On the desktop, or in File Explorer, locate the program that you want to always run as an administrator.

2. Press and hold or right-click the program's shortcut, and then tap or click Properties.

3. In the Properties dialog box, tap or click the Compatibility tab, shown in Figure 7-1.

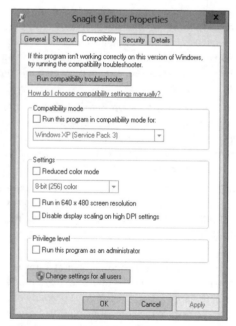

FIGURE 7-1 Access the Compatibility tab.

4. Do one of the following:

- To apply the setting to the currently logged-on user, select the Run This Program As An Administrator check box, and then tap or click OK.

- To apply the setting to all users on the computer and regardless of which shortcut is used to start the application, tap or click Change Settings For All Users to display the Properties dialog box for the application's .exe file, select the Run This Program As An Administrator check box, and then tap or click OK twice.

NOTE If the Run This Program As An Administrator option is unavailable, it means that the application is blocked from always running at an elevated level, the application does not require administrator credentials to run, or you are not logged on as an administrator.

The program will now always run by using an administrator access token. Keep in mind that if you are using a standard account and prompting is disabled, the program will fail to run.

Optimizing virtualization and installation prompting for elevation

With regard to applications, several areas of UAC can be customized, including:

- Automatic installation detection and prompting
- Virtualization of write failures

In Group Policy, you can configure these features by using settings for Computer Configuration under Windows Settings\Security Settings\Local Policies\Security Options. The security settings are as follows:

- **User Account Control: Detect Application Installations And Prompt For Elevation** Determines whether Windows 8.1 automatically detects application installation and prompts for elevation or consent. (This setting is enabled by default in Windows 8.1.) If you disable this setting, users are not prompted, so they will not be able to elevate permissions by supplying administrator credentials.

- **User Account Control: Virtualize File And Registry Write Failures To Per-User Locations** Determines whether file and registry virtualization is on or off. Because this setting is enabled by default, error notifications and error logging related to virtualized files and registry values are written to the virtualized location rather than the actual location to which the application was trying to write. If you disable this setting, the application will silently fail when trying to write to protected folders or protected areas of the registry.

NOTE Other related settings were discussed previously in Chapter 5, in the "Optimizing UAC and Admin Approval Mode" section.

In a domain environment, you can use Active Directory–based Group Policy to apply the security configuration you want to a particular set of computers. You can also configure these settings on a per-computer basis by using local security policy. To do this, follow these steps:

1. Open Local Security Policy. One way to do this is by pressing the Windows key, typing **secpol.msc**, and then pressing Enter. If you've enabled Show Administrative Tools as a Start setting, you'll also find a related tile on the Start screen.

2. In the console tree, under Security Settings, expand Local Policies, and then select Security Options.

3. Double-tap or double-click the setting with which you want to work, make any necessary changes, and then tap or click OK.

Installing programs: the essentials

Program installation is fairly straightforward. On the other hand, troubleshooting the many things that can go wrong and fixing problems are not so straightforward. To solve problems that might occur, you first need to understand the installation process. In many cases, the typical installation process starts when Autorun is triggered. Autorun in turn invokes a setup program. After the setup program starts, the installation process can begin. Part of the installation process involves checking the user's credentials to ensure that he or she has the appropriate privileges to install the program and prompting for consent if the user doesn't. As part of installing a program, you might also need to make the program available to all or only some users on a computer.

Occasionally, Windows might not be successful in detecting the required installation permissions. This can occur if the installation manifest for the program has an embedded RequestedExecutionLevel setting that has a value set as RequireAdministrator. Because the RequestedExecutionLevel setting overrides what the installer detects in Windows, the installation process fails any time you run the installer with standard user permissions. To solve this problem, back out of the failed installation by exiting, canceling the installation, or taking another appropriate action. Next, locate the executable file for the installer. Press and hold or right-click this file, and then tap or click Run As Administrator to restart the installation process with administrator privileges.

Application Control policies replace Software Restriction policies. Software Restriction policies control the applications that users can install and run on Windows Vista and earlier versions of Windows. Application Control policies control the applications that users can install and run on Windows 7 and later, as well as Windows Server 2008 Release 2 and later. Keep the following in mind:

- When you are editing a Group Policy Object, you can create and manage Software Restriction policies by using settings for computers under Computer Configuration\Policies\Windows Settings\Security Settings\Software

Restriction Policies, and settings for users under User Configuration\Policies \Windows Settings\Security Settings\Software Restriction Policies. Enforcement settings control how restrictions are applied. Designated file types determine what is and what is not considered an executable program.

- When you are editing a Group Policy Object, you can create and manage Application Control policies by using settings for computers under Computer Configuration\Policies\Windows Settings\Security Settings\Application Control Policies. You can now create separate rules for executable files, Windows installer files, and script files. Rules can be applied by publisher, file path, or file hash. A publisher rule gives you the most flexibility, enabling you to specify which products and versions to allow. For example, you could allow Microsoft Word 2010 or later.

Working with Autorun

When you insert an application disc, Windows 8.1 checks for a file named Autorun. inf. If present, Autorun.inf specifies the action that the operating system should take and might also define other installation parameters. Autorun.inf is a text-based file that can be opened in any standard text editor. If you were to examine the contents of an Autorun.inf file, you'd find something similar to the following code:

```
[autorun]
OPEN=SETUP.EXE AUTORUN=1
ICON=SETUP.EXE,4
SHELL=OPEN
DisplayName=Microsoft Digital Image Suite 9
ShortName=PIS
PISETUP=PIP\pisetup.exe
```

This Autorun.inf file opens a file named Setup.exe when a disc is inserted into a drive. Because Setup.exe is an actual program, this program is invoked. The Autorun. inf file also specifies an icon to use, the status of the shell, the program display name, the program's short name, and an additional parameter, which in this case is the location of another setup program to run.

The file that Autorun.inf specifies to open won't always be a program. Consider the following example:

```
[autorun]
OPEN=Autorun\ShelExec default.htm
```

This Autorun.inf file executes via the shell and opens a file named Default.htm in the computer's web browser. It's important to note that even in this case, the document opened in the web browser contains links that point to a setup program.

TIP With an application disc in a drive, you can restart the Autorun process at any time. Simply open and then close the drive bay.

Managing application setup and compatibility

Most applications have a setup program that uses InstallShield, Wise Install, or Windows Installer. When you start the setup program, the installer helps track the installation process and should also make it possible to easily uninstall the program when necessary. If you are installing an older application, the setup program might use an older version of one of these installers, and this might mean the uninstall process won't completely uninstall the program.

Even if you are absolutely certain that a program has a current installer, you should consider the possibility that you will need to recover the system if something goes wrong with the installation. To help ensure that you can recover your system, check that System Restore is enabled for the drive on which you are installing the program so that System Restore can create an automatic checkpoint before installing the program.

Although the installers for most current programs automatically trigger the creation of a restore point before making any changes to a computer, the installers for older programs might not. You can manually create a restore point, as discussed in Chapter 9, "Handling maintenance and support tasks." Then, if you run into problems, you can try to uninstall the program or use System Restore to recover the system to the state it was in prior to the program's installation.

Before installing any application, you should check to determine whether it is compatible with Windows 8.1. To determine compatibility, you can do the following:

- Check the software packaging, which should specify whether the program is compatible. Look for the Windows 8 logo.
- Check the software developer's website for a list of compatible operating systems.

NOTE As part of the compatibility check, look for updates or patches for the program. If any are available, install them after installing the program.

Windows 8.1 attempts to recognize potential compatibility problems before you install applications. If it detects one, you might get a Program Compatibility Assistant dialog box after you start a program's installer. Often, this dialog box contains information about the known compatibility issues with the program, and in many cases, it displays a possible solution. For example, you might be advised to install the latest service pack for the program before running the program on the computer. In some cases, the Program Compatibility Assistant might display the message "This program is blocked due to compatibility issues." Here, the program is blocked because it causes a known stability issue with Windows, and you can't create an immediate fix to work around the problem. Your only options are to tap or click the Check For Solutions Online button or tap or click Cancel. If you check for solutions online, the typical solution requires you to purchase an updated version of the program. If you cancel, you stop the installation process without checking for possible solutions.

If the installation continues but fails for any reason before it is fully complete (or fails to properly notify the operating system regarding completion), you'll also get a Program Compatibility Assistant dialog box. In this case, if the program installed correctly, tap or click This Program Installed Correctly. If the program didn't install correctly, tap or click Reinstall Using Recommended Settings to allow the Program Compatibility Assistant to apply one or more compatibility fixes, and then try again to run the installer.

When you start programs, Windows 8.1 uses the Program Compatibility Assistant to automatically make changes for known compatibility issues as well. If the Program Compatibility Assistant detects a known compatibility issue when you run an application, it notifies you about the problem and provides possible solutions for resolving the problem automatically. You can then allow the Program Compatibility Assistant to reconfigure the application for you, or you can manually configure compatibility as discussed in the section "Configuring program compatibility" later in this chapter.

Policies in the Administrative Templates policies for Computer Configuration under Windows Components\Application Compatibility are also used to control compatibility settings. The policies are as follows:

- **Prevent Access To 16-Bit Applications**   If enabled, this policy prevents the MS-DOS subsystem from running on computers. This also means any 32-bit program with 16-bit installers or other 16-bit components can't run.

- **Remove Program Compatibility Property Page**   If enabled, this policy makes the Compatibility tab unavailable on Properties dialog boxes for programs.

- **Turn Off Application Compatibility Engine**   If enabled, this policy prevents Windows from checking the compatibility database for known issues when programs are started. Although this might boost system performance when starting applications, it can result in a stop error on a blue screen if incompatible programs are run on the system and not configured properly.

- **Turn Off Inventory Collector**   If enabled, this policy prevents the Inventory Collector from collecting system inventories and sending this information to Microsoft as part of compatibility diagnostics. Collected information includes details on applications, files, devices, and drivers, and in secure environments you might not want this information to be sent to Microsoft.

- **Turn Off Program Compatibility Assistant**   If enabled, this policy allows legacy applications to run without Switchback protection. Switchback is a compatibility feature that works with legacy applications to address general compatibility issues that legacy applications are known to have when running on current Windows releases. Although this might boost application performance, applications with incompatibilities might become unresponsive or cause other problems on the system.

- **Turn Off Steps Recorder**   If enabled, this policy disables Steps Recorder, which might be required in some secure environments in which you wouldn't want user actions, including keyboard input, to be recorded at any time.

- **Turn Off Switchback Compatibility Engine**   If enabled, this policy prevents Windows from using the Switchback compatibility engine, which is otherwise enabled. The Switchback compatibility engine automatically provides legacy behavior to legacy applications while allowing current applications to use current application architecture. Typically you would only enable this policy setting if you must explicitly set the compatibility level for all your applications. You must restart the computer if you change this setting and want to apply the change.

Making programs available to all or selected users

After installation, most desktop programs should have related tiles on the Start screen and related options on the Apps list. This occurs because a program's shortcuts are placed in the appropriate subfolder of the Start Menu\Programs folder (%SystemDrive%\ProgramData\Microsoft\Windows\Start Menu\Programs) for all users so that any user who logs on to the system has access to that program. Some programs prompt you during installation to choose whether you want to install the program for all users or only for the currently logged-on user. Other programs simply install themselves only for the current user.

If setup installs a program so that it is available only to the currently logged-on user and you want other users to have access to the program, you need to take one of the following actions:

- Log on to the computer with each user account that should have access to the program, and then rerun Setup to make the program available to these users. You also need to run Setup again when a new user account is added to the computer and that user needs access to the program.

- For programs that don't require per-user settings to be added to the registry before running, you can in some cases make the program available to all users on a computer by adding the appropriate shortcuts to the Start Menu \Programs folder for all users. Copy or move the program shortcuts from the currently logged-on user's profile to the Start Menu\Programs folder for all users.

If you want to make a program available to all users on a computer, you can copy or move a program's shortcuts by completing the following steps:

1. In File Explorer, navigate to the currently logged-on user's Programs folder. This is a hidden folder under %UserProfile%\AppData\Roaming\Microsoft \Windows\Start Menu. In File Explorer, you view hidden items by selecting the Hidden Items check box on the View tab.

2. In the Programs folder, press and hold or right-click the folder for the program group or the shortcut with which you want to work, and then tap or click Copy or Cut on the shortcut menu.

3. Next, navigate to the Start Menu\Programs folder for all users. This hidden folder is under %SystemDrive%\ProgramData\Microsoft\Windows\.

4. In the Programs folder, press and hold or right-click an open space, and then tap or click Paste. The program group or shortcut should now be available to all users of the computer.

If you want to make a program available only to the currently logged-on user rather than all users on a computer, you can move a program's shortcuts by completing the following steps:

1. In File Explorer, navigate to the all-users Start Menu folder. This hidden folder is under %SystemDrive%\ProgramData\Microsoft\Windows\Start Menu.

2. In the Programs folder, press and hold or right-click the folder for a program group or the program shortcut that you want to work with, and then tap or click Cut.

3. In File Explorer, navigate to the currently logged-on user's Programs folder. This is a hidden folder under %UserProfile%\AppData\Roaming\Microsoft \Windows\Start Menu.

4. In the Programs folder, press and hold or right-click an open space, and then tap or click Paste. The program group or shortcut should now be available only to the currently logged-on user.

NOTE Moving a program group or shortcut hides the fact that the program is available on the computer—it doesn't prevent other users from running the program by using the Run dialog box or File Explorer.

Deploying applications through Group Policy

You can make applications available to users over the network through Group Policy. When you use Group Policy to deploy applications, you have the following two distribution options:

- Assign the application to users or computers. When an application is assigned to a computer, it is installed the next time the computer is started and is available to all users of that computer the next time users log on. When an application is assigned to a user, it is installed the next time the user logs on to the network. An assigned application can also be configured to be installed on first use. In this configuration, the application is made available through shortcuts on the user's desktop or Start screen. With install-on-first-use configured, the application is installed when the user clicks a shortcut to start the application.

- Publish the application and make it available for installation. When you publish an application, the application can be made available through extension activation. With extension activation configured, the program is installed when a user opens any file with an extension associated with the application. For example, if a user double-taps or double-clicks a file with a .doc or .docx extension, Microsoft Word could be installed automatically.

You deploy applications for computers by using a Windows Installer Package (.msi file) and policies under Computer Configuration\Policies\Software Settings \Software Installation. You deploy applications for users by using a Windows Installer Package (.msi file) and policies under User Configuration\Policies\Software Settings \Software Installation. The basic steps required to deploy applications through Group Policy are as follows:

1. For clients to access the Windows Installer Package, it must be located on a network share. As necessary, copy the Windows Installer Package (.msi file) to a network share that is accessible to the appropriate users.

2. In the Group Policy Management Editor, open the Group Policy Object from which you want to deploy the application. After it is deployed, the application is available to all clients to which the Group Policy Object applies. This means the application is available to computers and users in the related domain, site, or organizational unit (OU).

3. Expand Computer Configuration\Policies\Software Settings or User Configuration\Policies\Software Settings, press and hold or right-click Software Installation, point to New, and then tap or click Package.

4. Use the Open dialog box to locate the Windows Installer Package (.msi file) for the application, and then tap or click Open. You are then given the choice to select the deployment method: Published, Assigned, or Advanced.

5. To publish or assign the program, select Published or Assigned, and then tap or click OK. If you are configuring computer policy, the program is available the next time a computer affected by the Group Policy Object is started. If you are configuring user policy, the program is available to users in the domain, site, or OU the next time users log on. Currently logged-on users need to log off and then log on.

6. To configure additional deployment options for the program, select Advanced. You can then set additional deployment options as necessary.

Configuring program compatibility

If you want to install 16-bit or MS-DOS-based programs, you might need to make special considerations. Additionally, to get older programs to run, you might sometimes need to adjust compatibility options. Techniques for handling these situations are discussed in the following sections.

Special installation considerations for 16-bit and MS-DOS-based programs

The Prevent Access To 16-bit Applications setting under Computer Configuration \Windows Components\Application Compatibility controls whether 16-bit applications can run on Windows computers. If this setting is not configured, 16-bit applications might require elevated administrator privileges to run. If this setting is enabled, 16-bit applications are prevented from running; and if the setting is disabled, 16-bit applications can run and don't require elevated administrator privileges.

Many 16-bit and MS-DOS-based programs that don't require direct access to hardware can be installed and run on Windows 8.1 without any problems; however, most 16-bit and MS-DOS-based programs do not support long file names. To help ensure compatibility with these programs, Windows 8.1 maps long and short file names as necessary to ensure that long file names are protected when they are modified by a 16-bit or an MS-DOS-based program. Additionally, it's important to note that some 16-bit and MS-DOS-based programs require 16-bit drivers, which are not supported on Windows 8.1. As a result, these programs won't run.

Most existing 16-bit and MS-DOS-based programs were originally written for very early Windows operating systems. Windows 8.1 runs these older programs by using a virtual machine that mimics the 386-enhanced mode used by these very early Windows operating systems. Unlike on other recent releases of Windows, on Windows 8.1 each 16-bit and MS-DOS-based program runs as a thread within a single virtual machine. This means that if you run multiple 16-bit and MS-DOS-based programs, they all share a common memory space. Unfortunately, if one of these programs stops responding or "hangs," it usually means the others will also.

You can help prevent one 16-bit or MS-DOS-based program from causing others to hang or crash by running it in a separate memory space. To do this, follow these steps:

1. Press and hold or right-click the program's shortcut icon, and then tap or click Properties. If the program doesn't have a shortcut, create one, and then open the shortcut's Properties dialog box.

2. On the Shortcut tab, tap or click Advanced. This displays the Advanced Properties dialog box.

3. Select the Run In Separate Memory Space check box.

4. Tap or click OK twice to close all open dialog boxes and save the changes.

NOTE Running a program in a separate memory space uses additional memory; however, you'll usually find that the program is more responsive. Another added benefit is that you are able to run multiple instances of the program—so long as all the instances are running in separate memory spaces.

TIP The Windows command prompt (Cmd.exe) is a 32-bit command prompt. If you want to invoke a 16-bit MS-DOS command prompt, you can use Command.com. Enter **command** in the Run dialog box.

Forcing program compatibility

Some programs won't install or run on Windows 8.1 even if they work on previous versions of the Windows operating system. If you try to install a program that has known compatibility problems, Windows 8.1 should display a warning prompt telling you about the compatibility issue. In most cases, you should not continue installing or running a program with known compatibility problems, especially if the program is a system utility such as an antivirus program or a disk partitioning program, because running an incompatible system utility can cause serious problems. Running other types of incompatible programs can also cause problems, especially if they write to system locations on disk.

That said, if a program will not install or run on Windows 8.1, you might be able to run the program by adjusting its compatibility settings. Windows 8.1 provides two mechanisms for managing compatibility settings. You can use the Program Compatibility Troubleshooter Wizard, or you can edit the program's compatibility settings directly by using the program's Properties dialog box. Both techniques work the same way. However, the Program Compatibility Troubleshooter Wizard is the only way you can change compatibility settings for programs that are on shared network drives, CD or DVD drives, or other types of removable media drives. As a result, you can sometimes use the Program Compatibility Troubleshooter Wizard to install and run programs that would not otherwise install and run.

Using the Program Compatibility Troubleshooter Wizard

You can configure compatibility settings only for programs you've installed. You can't configure compatibility settings for programs included with the operating system. To try to automatically detect compatibility issues by using the Program Compatibility Troubleshooter Wizard, follow these steps:

1. Locate the program shortcut. Press and hold or right-click the program shortcut, and then tap or click Troubleshoot Compatibility. This starts the Program Compatibility Troubleshooter Wizard, as shown in Figure 7-2.

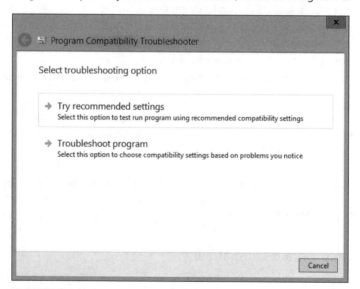

FIGURE 7-2 Troubleshoot program compatibility issues.

2. The wizard automatically tries to detect compatibility issues. To try to run the program you are troubleshooting with the recommended fixes, tap or click Try Recommended Settings. Next, review the settings that will be applied, and then tap or click Test The Program.

3. After running the program, tap or click Next, and then do one of the following:

■ Tap or click Yes, Save These Settings For This Program if the compatibility settings resolved the problem and you want to keep the settings.

■ Tap or click No, Try Again Using Different Settings if the compatibility settings didn't resolve the problem and you want to repeat this process from the beginning.

■ Tap or click No, Report The Problem To Microsoft And Check Online For A Solution if the compatibility settings didn't resolve the problem and you'd like to check for an online solution.

■ Tap or click Cancel if you want to discard the compatibility settings and exit the wizard.

To perform advanced troubleshooting and use the Program Compatibility Troubleshooter Wizard to specify the compatibility settings to use, follow these steps:

1. In File Explorer, locate the program shortcut by navigating the menus under %SystemDrive%\ProgramData\Microsoft\Windows\Start Menu\Programs. Press and hold or right-click the program shortcut, and then tap or click Troubleshoot Compatibility. This starts the Program Compatibility Troubleshooter Wizard.

2. Tap or click Troubleshoot Program. On the What Problems Do You Notice? page, you can specify information about problems you've found. The selections you make determine the wizard pages you get when you tap or click Next. They include the following:

■ **The Program Worked In Earlier Versions Of Windows But Won't Install Or Run Now** If you select this option, you are prompted on one of the subsequent wizard pages to specify which version. Because your choice sets the compatibility mode, choose the operating system for which the program was designed. When running the program, Windows 8.1 simulates the environment for the specified operating system.

■ **The Program Opens But Doesn't Display Correctly** If you are trying to run a game, an educational program, or any other program that requires specific display settings, such as a program designed for early versions of Windows, you can select this option and then choose the type of display problem you are having. Your selections restrict the video display: when you use 256 colors, 640 × 480 screen resolution, or both, Windows restricts the video display. This can help with programs that have problems running at higher screen resolutions and greater color depths. Your selections can also disable themes, desktop compositing (which prevents special visual effects on the desktop), and display scaling of high dots-per-inch (DPI) settings.

■ **The Program Requires Additional Permissions** If you choose this option, the program will be configured to run with administrator privileges.

- **I Don't See My Problem Listed** If you choose this option, the wizard displays optional pages for operating system and display issue selection. The wizard also sets the program to run as an administrator. Ultimately, choosing this option has the same effect as if you had selected all three of the previous options.

3. Review the compatibility settings that will be applied. If you don't want to apply these settings, tap or click Cancel and repeat this procedure to select different options. If you want to apply these settings, tap or click Test The Program, and the wizard runs the program with the compatibility settings you specified.

4. After running the program, tap or click Next to continue. When you continue, you are prompted to confirm whether the changes fixed the problem. Do one of the following:

   - If the compatibility settings resolved the problem and you want to keep the settings, tap or click Yes, Save These Settings For This Program.

   - If the compatibility settings didn't resolve the problem and you want to repeat this process from the beginning, tap or click No, Try Again Using Different Settings.

   - If the compatibility settings didn't resolve the problem and you'd like to check for an online solution, tap or click No, Report The Problem To Microsoft And Check Online For A Solution.

   - If you want to discard the compatibility settings and exit the wizard, tap or click Cancel.

NOTE If you've configured alternate display settings for a program, the program will run in the alternate display mode whenever you start it. To restore the original display settings, simply exit the program.

Setting compatibility options directly

If a program you have already installed won't run correctly, you might want to edit the compatibility settings directly rather than by using the wizard. To do this, follow these steps:

1. Press and hold or right-click the program's shortcut icon, and then tap or click Properties.

2. In the Properties dialog box, tap or click the Compatibility tab. Any option you select is applied to the currently logged-on user for the program shortcut. To apply the setting to all users on the computer and regardless of which shortcut is used to start the program, tap or click Change Setting For All Users to display the Properties dialog box for the program's .exe file, and then select the compatibility settings that you want to use for all users who log on to the computer.

NOTE Programs that are part of Windows 8.1 cannot be run in Compatibility mode. The options on the Compatibility tab are not available for built-in programs.

3. Select the Run This Program In Compatibility Mode For check box, and then use the selection menu to choose the operating system for which the program was designed.

4. If necessary, use the options in the Settings panel to restrict the video display settings for the program. Select Reduced Color Mode and then select either 8-bit (256) color or 16-bit (65536) color, as required. Select Run In 640 × 480 Screen Resolution, as required.

5. If necessary, you can also disable visual themes, desktop compositing, and display scaling of high DPI settings.

6. Tap or click OK. Double-tap or double-click the shortcut to run the program and test the compatibility settings. If you still have problems running the program, you might need to modify the compatibility settings again.

Managing installed and running programs

Windows 8.1 provides several management tools for working with programs. These tools include the following:

- **Task Manager** Provides options for viewing and managing running programs, as well as options for viewing resource usage and performance

- **Programs** Provides tasks for viewing installed programs, adding and removing programs, viewing installed updates, and more

- **Default Programs** Helps you track and configure global default programs for the computer, personal default programs for individual users, AutoPlay settings for multimedia, and file associations for programs

- **Windows Features** Helps you view and manage the Windows components installed on a computer

- **Assoc** Helps you view and manage file type associations

- **Ftype** Helps you view and manage file type definitions

These tools and related configuration options are discussed in the sections that follow.

Managing currently running programs

In Windows 8.1, you can view and work with a computer's currently running programs and processes by using Task Manager. You can open Task Manager by pressing Ctrl+Shift+Esc. Alternatively, press and hold or right-click the lower-left corner of the screen, and then tap or click Task Manager on the shortcut menu.

By default, Task Manager displays a summary list of running applications, as shown in Figure 7-3. You can manage an application by tapping or clicking it in the list. To exit an application (which might be necessary when it's not responding), tap or click the application in the Task list, and then tap or click End Task. To display other management options, press and hold or right-click the application in the Task list.

Task Manager
Diagnostics Troubleshooting Wizard
Microsoft Management Console
Microsoft Management Console
Microsoft Management Console
ServerManager
More details
End task

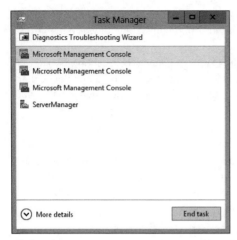

FIGURE 7-3 Use summary view to quickly manage running applications.

When working with the summary view, you can tap or click More Details to open the full Task Manager. You'll then find detailed information about running applications and processes, as shown in Figure 7-4. The Processes tab lists applications and processes running on the computer. Generally, items listed under the Apps heading are applications that you've started, processes being run in the background by Windows are listed under Background Processes, and all other processes running on the computer are listed under Windows Processes.

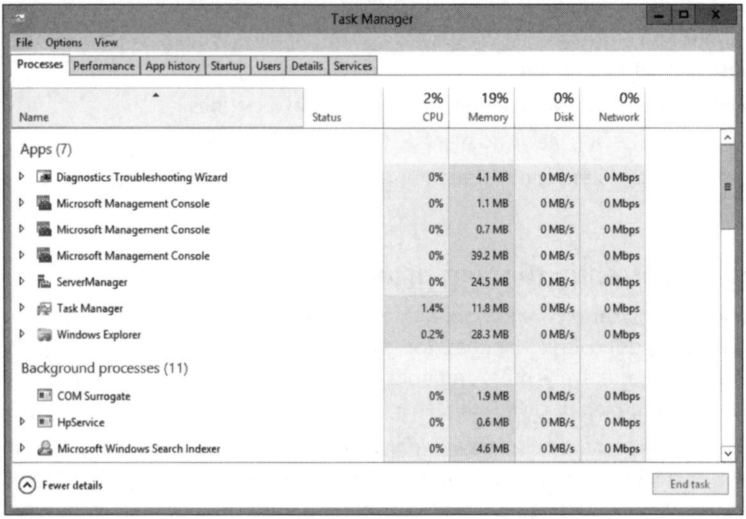

Task Manager
File Options View
Processes Performance App history Startup Users Details Services
Name Status 2% CPU 19% Memory 0% Disk 0% Network
Apps (7)
Diagnostics Troubleshooting Wizard 0% 4.1 MB 0 MB/s 0 Mbps
Microsoft Management Console 0% 1.1 MB 0 MB/s 0 Mbps
Microsoft Management Console 0% 0.7 MB 0 MB/s 0 Mbps
Microsoft Management Console 0% 39.2 MB 0 MB/s 0 Mbps
ServerManager 0% 24.5 MB 0 MB/s 0 Mbps
Task Manager 1.4% 11.8 MB 0 MB/s 0 Mbps
Windows Explorer 0.2% 28.3 MB 0 MB/s 0 Mbps
Background processes (11)
COM Surrogate 0% 1.9 MB 0 MB/s 0 Mbps
HpService 0% 0.6 MB 0 MB/s 0 Mbps
Microsoft Windows Search Indexer 0% 4.6 MB 0 MB/s 0 Mbps
Fewer details
End task

FIGURE 7-4 Use the full view of Task Manager to get an expanded view of running applications and processes.

Each application or process is listed by name, status, CPU usage, memory usage, disk usage, and network usage. A blank status means the application or process is in a normal state. As with the summary view, you can exit an application or stop a running process by tapping or clicking the application or process in the Task list, and then tapping or clicking End Task.

Double-tap or double-click the application or process to view related windows or processes. Display more management options by pressing and holding or right-clicking the application or process in the Task list. The options include Open File Location, which opens the folder containing the executable file for the application or process in File Explorer; Create Dump File, which creates a memory dump file for the selected process; Go To Details, which opens the Details tab with the process selected; and Properties, which opens the Properties dialog box for the executable file.

Managing, repairing, and uninstalling programs

Windows 8.1 considers any program you've installed on a computer or made available for a network installation to be an installed program. You use the setup program that comes with the program to install programs, and you use the Programs And Features page in Control Panel to manage programs.

You can use the Programs And Features page to view, add, remove, or repair installed programs by following these steps:

1. In Control Panel, tap or click Programs. Tap or click Programs And Features. You should get a list of installed programs.

2. In the Name list, press and hold or right-click the program with which you want to work. The options available depend on the program you are working with and include the following:

   - **Uninstall** Uninstalls the program
   - **Uninstall/Change** Uninstalls or modifies the program
   - **Change** Modifies the program's configuration
   - **Repair** Repairs the program's installation (if available)

When you are uninstalling programs, keep the following in mind:

- Windows warns you if you try to uninstall a program while other users are logged on. Generally, you should be sure that other users are logged off before uninstalling programs. Otherwise, you might cause other users to lose data or experience other problems.

- Windows will allow you to remove only those programs that were installed with a Windows-compatible setup program. Although most applications have a setup program that uses InstallShield, Wise Install, or Windows Installer, older programs might have a separate uninstall utility. Some older programs work by copying their data files to a program folder. In this case, you uninstall the program by deleting the related folder.

- Many uninstall programs leave behind data either inadvertently or by design. As a result, you often find folders for these applications within the Program Files folder. You could delete these folders, but they might contain important data files or custom user settings that could be used again if you reinstall the program.

- Sometimes, the uninstall process fails. Often, you can resolve any problem simply by rerunning the uninstaller for the program. Occasionally, you might need to clean up after the uninstall process. This might require removing program files and deleting remnants of the program in the Windows registry. A program called Microsoft Fix It Portable can help you clean up the registry. To learn more about this program and get the downloadable executable file, visit *http://support.microsoft.com/mats/Program_Install_and_Uninstall/*. At the Microsoft website, instead of choosing Run Now, click the Advanced options and then click the Download option to save the executable file. After downloading, run the executable file and follow the prompts to install it.

Designating default programs

Default programs determine which programs are used with which types of files and how Windows handles files on CDs, DVDs, and portable devices. You configure default programs based on the types of files those programs support, either globally for all users of a computer or only for the current user. Individual user defaults override global defaults. For example, you could select Windows Media Player as the global default for all types of files it supports, and then all users of the computer would use Windows Media Player to play the sound, audio, and video files it supports. If a specific user wanted to use Apple iTunes instead, for example, as the default player for sound and audio files, you could configure iTunes to be that user's default player for the types of media files it supports.

You can configure global default programs for all the users of a computer by following these steps:

1. In Control Panel, select Programs. Select Default Programs, and then select Set Program Access And Computer Defaults. You'll get the dialog box shown in Figure 7-5.

2. Choose a configuration from one of the following options:

   - **Microsoft Windows**   Sets the currently installed Windows programs as the default programs for browsing the web, sending email messages, playing media files, and so on

   - **Non-Microsoft**   Sets the currently installed programs as the default programs for browsing the web, sending email messages, playing media files, and so on

   - **Custom**   Enables you to choose programs as the defaults for browsing the web, sending email messages, playing media files, and so on

3. Select OK to save the settings.

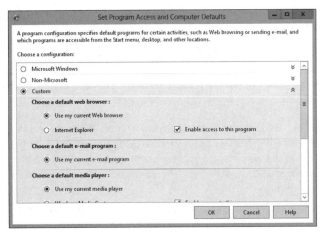

FIGURE 7-5 Choose a global default configuration.

To override global defaults, you can set default programs for individual users. You can configure default programs for the current user by following these steps:

1. In Control Panel, select Programs. Select Default Programs, and then select Set Your Default Programs.

2. Select a program in the Programs list with which you want to work.

3. If you want the program to be the default for all the file types and protocols it supports, select Set This Program As Default.

4. If you want the program to be the default for specific file types and protocols, select Choose Defaults For This Program. Select the extensions for which the program should be the default, and then select Save.

Managing the command path

Windows uses the command path to locate executable files. You can view the current command path for executable files by using the PATH command. In a command shell, type **path** on a line by itself, and then press Enter. In a Windows PowerShell console, type **$env:path** on a line by itself, and then press Enter. In the output from either technique, observe that Windows uses a semicolon (;) to separate individual paths, marking where one file path ends and another begins.

The command path is set during logon by using system and user environment variables. The path defined in the PATH system variable sets the base path. The path defined in the PATH user variable adds to the base path by using the following syntax:

%PATH%;*AdditionalPaths*

Here, %PATH% tells Windows to insert the current system paths, and *Additional-Paths* designates the additional user-specific paths to use.

CAUTION An improperly set path can cause severe problems. You should always test any command path change before using it in a live environment. The command path is set during logon. Therefore, you must log off and then log on again to view the effects of the revised path.

Don't forget about the search order that Windows uses. Paths are searched in order, with the last path in the PATH user variable being the last one searched. This can sometimes slow the execution of your programs and scripts. To help Windows find your programs and scripts faster, you should consider placing a required path earlier in the search order.

Be careful when setting the command path. It is easy to overwrite all path information accidentally. For example, if you don't specify %PATH% when setting the user path, you will delete all other path information. One way to ensure that you can easily re-create the command path is to keep a copy of the command path in a file:

- When you are working with the command prompt, you can write the current command path to a file by entering **path > orig_path.txt**. Keep in mind that if you are using a standard command prompt rather than an administrator command prompt, you won't be able to write to secure system locations. In this case, you can write to a subdirectory to which you have access or to your personal profile. To write the command path to the command-shell window, enter **path**.

- When you are working with the Windows PowerShell console, you can write the current command path to a file by entering **$env:path > orig_path.txt**. If you are using a standard console rather than an administrator console, you won't be able to write to secure system locations. In this case, you can write to a subdirectory to which you have access or to your personal profile. To write the command path to the Windows PowerShell window, enter **$env:path**.

At the command prompt or in the Windows PowerShell window, you can modify the command path by using the Setx.exe utility. You can also edit the command path by completing the following steps:

1. In Control Panel, tap or click System And Security, and then tap or click System.

2. In the System console, tap or click Change Settings, or tap or click Advanced System Settings in the left pane.

3. On the Advanced tab in the System Properties dialog box, tap or click Environment Variables.

4. Select the PATH variable in the System Variables list. Under System Variables, tap or click Edit.

5. By default, the path value is selected. Without pressing any other key, press the Right Arrow key. This should remove the selection highlight and place the insertion point at the end of the variable value.

6. Type a semicolon, and then enter a path to insert. Repeat this step as necessary, and then tap or click OK three times.

In Group Policy, you can use a preference item to modify the -command path by following these steps:

1. Open a Group Policy Object for editing in the Group Policy Management Editor. To configure preferences for computers, expand Computer Configuration\Preferences\Windows Settings, and then select Environment. To configure preferences for users, expand User Configuration\Preferences\Windows Settings, and then select Environment.

2. Press and hold or right-click the Environment node, point to New, and then tap or click Environment Variable. This opens the New Environment Properties dialog box.

3. In the Action list, select Update to update the path variable, or select Replace to delete and then re-create the path variable. Next, select User Variable to work with user variables.

4. In the Name box, enter **Path**. In the Value box, enter the variable value. Typically, you'll enter **%PATH%**; followed by the paths you want to add, using a semicolon to separate each path. If the affected computers have existing PATH user variable definitions, you must provide the related paths to ensure that these paths are retained.

5. Use the options on the Common tab to control how the preference is applied. In most cases, you'll want to create the PATH variable only once (rather than have Group Policy re-create the variable each time policy is refreshed). If so, select Apply Once And Do Not Reapply.

6. Tap or click OK. The next time policy is refreshed, the preference item will be applied as appropriate for the Group Policy Object in which you defined the preference item.

CAUTION Incorrectly setting the path can cause serious problems. Before deploying an updated path to multiple computers, you should test the configuration. One way to do this is to create a Group Policy Object in Active Directory that applies only to an isolated test computer. Next, create a preference item for this Group Policy Object, and then wait for a policy to refresh or apply policy using GPUpdate. If you are logged on to the computer, you need to log off and then log back on before you can confirm the results.

Managing file name extensions and file associations

File name extensions and file associations also are important for determining how applications run. The types of files that Windows considers to be executable files are determined by the extensions for executable files. File name extensions allow users to execute a command by using just the command name. File associations are what allow users to double-tap or double-click a file and open the file automatically in a related application. Two types of file name extensions are used:

- **Extensions for executable files** Executable files are defined with the *%PATHEXT%* environment variable and can be set by using the Environment Variables dialog box or with Group Policy preference items in much the same way as the PATH variable. You can view the current settings by typing **set pathext** at the command line or by typing **$env:pathext** at a Windows PowerShell prompt. The default setting is PATHEXT=.COM;.EXE;.BAT;.CMD;. VBS;.VBE;.JS;.JSE;.WSF;.WSH;.MSC. With this setting, the command line knows which files are executable and which files are not, so you don't have to specify the file name extension at the command line.

- **Extensions for applications** File name extensions for applications are referred to as *file associations*. File associations are what enable you to pass arguments to executable files and to open documents, worksheets, or other application files by double-tapping or double-clicking their file icons. Each known extension on a system has a file association that you can view at a command prompt by typing **assoc** followed by the extension, such as **assoc .doc** or **assoc .docx**. Each file association in turn specifies the file type for the file name extension. This can be viewed at a command prompt by typing . **ftype** followed by the file association, such as **ftype Word.Document.8** or **ftype Word.Document.12.**

NOTE Assoc and Ftype are internal commands for the command shell (Cmd.exe). To use the Assoc command in Windows PowerShell, enter **cmd /c assoc** followed by the extension, such as **cmd /c assoc .doc**. To use the Ftype command in Windows PowerShell, enter **cmd /c ftype** followed by the file association, such as **cmd /c ftype Word. Document.8.**

With executable files, the order of file name extensions in the *%PATHEXT%* variable sets the search order used by the command line on a per-directory basis. Thus, if a particular directory in the command path has multiple executable files that match the command name provided, a .com file would be executed before an .exe file, and so on.

Every known extension on a system has a corresponding file association and file type—even extensions for executable files. In some cases, the file type is the extension text without the period followed by the keyword file, such as cmdfile, exefile, or batfile, and the file association specifies that the first parameter passed is the command name and that other parameters should be passed on to the application. For example, if you enter **assoc .exe** to view the file associations for .exe executable files, you then enter **ftype exefile**. You'll find the file association is set to the following:

```
exefile="%1" %*
```

Thus, when you run an .exe file, Windows knows that the first value is the command that you want to run and anything else provided is a parameter to pass along.

File associations and types are maintained in the Windows registry and can be set by using the Assoc and Ftype commands, respectively. To create the file association at the command line, enter **assoc** followed by the extension setting, such as **assoc .pl=perlfile**. To create the file type at the command line, set the file-type mapping, including how to use parameters supplied with the command name, such as **ftype perlfile=C:\Perl\Bin\Perl.exe "%1" %***.

You can also associate a file type or protocol with a specific application by completing the following steps:

1. In Control Panel, tap or click Programs. Under Default Programs, tap or click Make A File Type Always Open In A Specific Program.

2. On the Set Associations page, current file associations are listed by file extension and the current default for that extension. To change the file association for an extension, tap or click the file extension, and then tap or click Change Program.

3. Do one of the following:

   - In the How Do You Want To Open This Type Of File? dialog box, programs registered in the operating system as supporting files with the selected extension are listed automatically. Simply tap or click a recommended program to set it as the default for the selected extension.

   - To view other available programs, click More Options to view other programs that might also support the selected extension. Tap or click a program to set it as the default for the selected extension. Alternatively, tap or click one of the Look For An App options to locate another program to use as the default.

In Group Policy, you can use a preference item to create new file types and file associations. To create a preference item for a new file type, follow these steps:

1. Open a Group Policy Object for editing in the Group Policy Management Editor. Expand Computer Configuration\Preferences\Control Panel Settings, and then select Folder Options.

2. Press and hold or right-click the Folder Options node, point to New, and then tap or click File Type. This opens the New File Type Properties dialog box.

3. In the Action list, select Create, Update, Replace, or Delete. Each action works as discussed in Chapter 4, "Automating Windows 8.1 configuration." You would use the Delete action to create a preference that removes an existing file type preference.

4. In the File Extension box, enter the extension of the file type without the period, such as **pl**.

5. In the Associated Class list, select a registered class to associate with the file type.

6. Use the options on the Common tab to control how the preference is applied. In most cases, you'll want to create the new variable only once. If so, select Apply Once And Do Not Reapply.

7. Tap or click OK. The next time policy is refreshed, the preference item will be applied as appropriate for the Group Policy Object in which you defined the preference item.

To create a preference item for a new file association, follow these steps:

1. Open a Group Policy Object for editing in the Group Policy Management Editor. Expand User Configuration\Preferences\Control Panel Settings, and then select Folder Options.

2. Press and hold or right-click the Folder Options node, point to New, and then tap or click Open With. This opens the New Open With Properties dialog box.

3. In the Action list, select Create, Update, Replace, or Delete.

4. In the File Extension box, enter the extension of the file type without the period, such as **pl**.

5. Tap or click the options button to the right of the Associated Program box, and then use the Open dialog box to select the program to associate with the file type.

6. Optionally, select Set As Default to make the associated program the default for files with the previously specified file extension.

7. Use the options on the Common tab to control how the preference is applied. In most cases, you'll want to create the new variable only once. If so, select Apply Once And Do Not Reapply.

8. Tap or click OK. The next time policy is refreshed, the preference item will be applied as appropriate for the Group Policy Object in which you defined the preference item.

Configuring AutoPlay options

In Windows 8.1, AutoPlay options determine how Windows handles files on CDs, DVDs, and portable devices. You can configure separate AutoPlay options for each type of CD, DVD, and other media your computer can handle by following these steps:

1. In Control Panel, tap or click Programs. Tap or click Default Programs, and then tap or click Change AutoPlay Settings. This displays the AutoPlay page in Control Panel.

2. As shown in Figure 7-6, use the media selection list to set the default Auto-Play option for each media type.

   For removable drives (such as USB memory sticks), you can specify an overall default or a default for each media type. To specify an overall default, clear the Choose What To Do check box and then select a preferred default. To specify individual defaults, select the Choose What To Do check box and then select a default action for each media type.

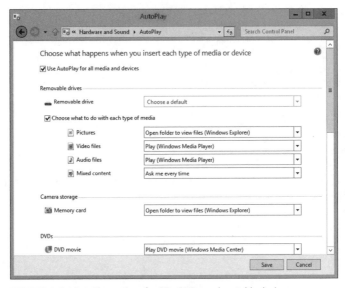

FIGURE 7-6 Set AutoPlay options for CDs, DVDs, and portable devices.

3. Tap or click Save to save your settings.

Adding and removing Windows features

Operating system components are considered Windows features that can be turned on or off rather than added or removed. You can turn on or off Windows features by following these steps:

1. In Control Panel, tap or click Programs. Under Programs And Features, tap or click Turn Windows Features On Or Off. This displays the Windows Features dialog box.

2. As shown in Figure 7-7, select the check boxes for features to turn them on, or clear the check boxes for features to turn them off.

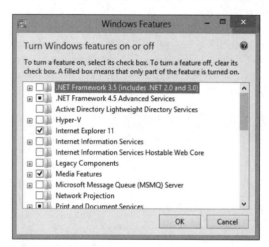

FIGURE 7-7 Add or remove operating system components.

3. Tap or click OK, and Windows 8.1 reconfigures components to reflect any changes you made.

Managing hardware devices and drivers

M anaging a computer's hardware configuration is largely about installing and maintaining operating system components, hardware devices, and device drivers. However, managing the hardware configuration of computers running Windows 7 and later is very different from managing the configuration of computers designed for earlier releases of Windows. Many aspects of Windows 8.1 are automatically monitored and updated and don't need to be configured or maintained in the same way as they were previously. Windows 8.1 uses the following features:

- Automatic maintenance that fixes problems identified by the operating system or reports them through Action Center
- Windows SmartScreen to warn users before running unrecognized apps from the Internet
- Built-in diagnostics to monitor hardware devices, physical memory, networking, and performance
- Problem reporting to try to automatically resolve configuration and performance issues
- Problem diagnosis to offer solutions to issues that cannot be automatically resolved
- Automatic updating of operating system components
- Driver updating to obtain necessary drivers and driver updates for detected hardware devices
- Improved automatic diagnostics for application and drive compatibility issues

From the moment you install Windows 8.1, these features start working to help you monitor and maintain computers. As an administrator, you can use these features to help guide your configuration and maintenance efforts. Separate tools are provided for managing the areas monitored by diagnostics, including hardware diagnostics, memory diagnostics, networking diagnostics, and performance diagnostics.

For configuring and maintaining hardware devices and drivers, you can also use Device Manager, Devices And Printers, and the Add Devices And Printers Wizard. You'll use these tools whenever you install, uninstall, or troubleshoot hardware devices and drivers. Other tools are available for managing specific types of hardware devices, such as keyboards, and video cards. To manage automatic updating and driver updating, you use Windows Update, which is provided as a Control Panel utility.

Working with the automated Help and support system

Automated Help and support fundamentally changes how the operating system works and how you support it. As an administrator, you should be sure to understand how the Help architecture works and how it can be configured.

Using automated Help and support

Windows 8.1 builds on the extensive diagnostics and problem resolution architecture that was developed for Windows 7 and extended for Windows 8. Although early releases of Windows included some Help and diagnostics features, those features were, for the most part, not self-correcting or self-diagnosing. The current framework, on the other hand, can detect many types of hardware, memory, and performance issues and resolve them automatically or help users through the process of resolving them.

Windows now includes more reliable and better-performing device drivers that prevent many common causes of hangs and crashes. Improved I/O cancellation for device drivers ensures that the operating system can recover gracefully from blocking calls and that fewer blocking disk I/O operations occur.

To reduce the downtime and restarts required for application installations and updates, Windows can use the update process to mark in-use files for update and then automatically replace the files the next time an application is started. In some cases, Windows can save the application's data, close the application, update the in-use files, and then restart the application. To improve overall system performance and responsiveness, Windows uses memory efficiently, provides ordered execution for groups of threads, and provides several process-scheduling mechanisms. By optimizing memory and process usage, Windows ensures that background processes have less impact on system performance.

By default, Windows uses SmartScreen, which displays a prompt asking for administrator approval before running an unrecognized app from the Internet. If you don't want to require administrator approval, you can configure this feature to display a warning instead, or you can turn SmartScreen off completely.

Windows provides improved guidance on the causes of unresponsive conditions. By including additional error-reporting details in the event logs, Windows makes it easier to identify and resolve issues. To automatically recover from service failures, Windows uses service-recovery policies more extensively than previous versions did. When recovering a failed service, Windows automatically handles both service and nonservice dependencies. Windows starts any dependent services and system components prior to starting the failed service.

In early releases of Windows, an application crash or hang is marked as Not Responding, and it is up to the user to exit and then restart the application. Windows now attempts to resolve the issue of unresponsive applications by using Program Compatibility Assistant (PCA) and Restart Manager. PCA can detect installation failures, run-time failures, and drivers blocked because of compatibility issues. To help resolve these issues, PCA provides options for running an application in compatibility mode or for getting help online through a Microsoft website. Restart Manager can shut down and restart unresponsive applications automatically. Thanks to Restart Manager, you might not have to intervene to try to resolve issues with frozen applications.

NOTE Diagnostic Policy Service and Program Compatibility Assistant Service must be running and properly configured for automated diagnostics and compatibility assistance to work properly. In the Computer Management console, you can configure these services by using the Services extension. One way to open Computer Management is by pressing the Windows key, entering **compmgmt.msc**, and then pressing Enter. This shortcut works so long as the Apps Search box is in focus.

REAL WORLD Technically, the top-level nodes in Computer Management are snap-in extensions. Each was added to a Microsoft Management Console (MMC) to create the console. Want to learn how? Enter **MMC** at a prompt. In the new console window, select Add Or Remove Snap-in on the File menu. While working with the Add Or Remove Snap-in dialog box, select Computer Management under Available Snap-ins, and then select Add. When prompted, select Local Computer and then select Finish. Next, in the Add Or Remove Snap-in dialog box, select Computer Management under Selected Snap-ins, and then click Edit Extensions. You can view each individual snap-in extension—and how the console was created by Microsoft.

Failed installations and nonresponsive conditions of applications and drivers are also tracked through Action Center. In these cases, the built-in diagnostics mechanisms can sometimes provide a problem response. You can view a list of current problems at any time by performing one of the following actions:

- Tap or click the Action Center icon in the notification area of the taskbar, and then tap or click Open Action Center.
- In Control Panel, tap or click Review Your Computer's Status under the System And Security heading.

In Action Center, shown in Figure 8-1, you get a list of problems organized into two broad areas: Security and Maintenance.

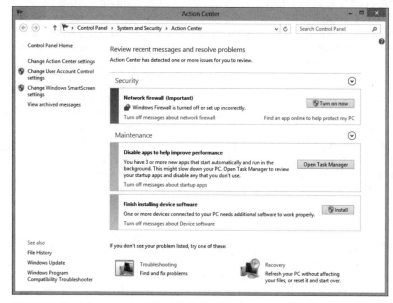

FIGURE 8-1 Check for known problems by using Action Center.

Problems are color-coded:

- Red is a warning about an important problem that requires your attention. For example, if the computer doesn't have virus protection software, this is a red warning.

- Orange is a caution about a problem that you might want to look at. For example, if a computer hasn't been scanned recently by Windows Defender, this is an orange warning.

You can tap or click the Security or Maintenance heading to expand the section and view more detailed information. Expanding the Security area displays the following information:

- The status of the network firewall, Windows Update, virus protection, and the computer's spyware and unwanted software protection

- The configuration of Internet security settings, User Account Control (UAC), Windows SmartScreen, and Network Access Protection

Expanding the Maintenance area displays information about the following:

- Links for managing the configuration of problem reports

- The status of File History and the computer's drives

- The status of Automatic Maintenance and links for managing maintenance

If you have just set up a computer and want to check for problems, or if you suspect a computer has problems that haven't been diagnosed, you can initiate automatic problem detection by following these steps:

1. In Action Center, tap or click the Maintenance heading, and then scroll down.

2. Below the list of current problems, you'll find an area labeled Check For Solutions To Problem Reports and a set of related links. Tap or click Check For Solutions to start the automated problem-reporting process. When this process is complete, Action Center is updated to include all newly discovered problems, and solutions are provided if known.

3. If automated diagnostics detects problems for which there are no solutions available, you can view additional information about the problems. In the Problem Reporting dialog box, tap or click View Problem Details to get more information about the problems detected, as shown in Figure 8-2. If you want to do your own troubleshooting, tap or click the links provided to extract data so that you can analyze the problems later. The data is extracted to the Temp folder in the logged-on user's profile. You need to make a copy of this data before you proceed.

4. In the Problem Reporting dialog box, tap or click Send Information to send this information to Microsoft, or tap or click Cancel to exit Problem Reporting without sending the information to Microsoft. If you send the information to Microsoft, the troubleshooting data is extracted to the Temp folder in the logged-on user's profile, sent to Microsoft, and then deleted from the Temp directory. The amount of data extracted and sent can be a significant amount.

FIGURE 8-2 Review detected problems for which there are no available solutions.

In Action Center, you can resolve detected problems that have known solutions by following these steps:

1. Each problem has a solution button or link. With Security problems, you can typically find programs online or scan the computer by using protection software. With Maintenance problems, you generally tap or click View Problem Response to display a page providing more information about the problem.

2. When you view the More Information page, keep the following in mind: When a driver or software issue is causing a problem, you'll find a link to download and install the latest driver or software update. When a configuration issue is causing a problem, you'll find a description of the problem and a step-by-step guide for modifying the configuration to resolve the problem.

3. When you have resolved a problem by installing a driver or software update, you can elect to archive the message for future reference by selecting the Archive This Message check box before you tap or click OK to close the More Information page.

When you are working with Action Center, you can get a reliability report for the computer to determine its past history of hardware and software problems. By reviewing this history, you can determine how stable the computer is and what devices or programs have caused problems. To access and work with Reliability Monitor, follow these steps:

1. In Action Center, tap or click the Maintenance heading, and then scroll down.

2. Below the list of current problems, you'll find an area labeled Check For Solutions To Problem Reports and a set of related links. Tap or click View Reliability History.

3. As shown in Figure 8-3, you then get a graphical depiction of the computer's stability. You can view the history by days or weeks. The default view is days. To view the history by weeks, tap or click the Weeks option for View By. The computer's stability is graphed with values ranging from 1, meaning poor reliability, to 10, meaning excellent reliability.

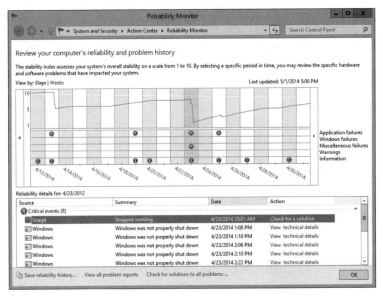

FIGURE 8-3 Review the graphical depiction of the computer's stability.

4. Events that could have affected stability are shown in the graph with information and/or warning icons. Tapping or clicking an icon displays details for the event in the Reliability Details list. As shown in Figure 8-3, events are listed by Source, Summary, and Date. Under Action, you'll find a link. If Windows was able to resolve the problem automatically, you'll get the View Problem Response link. Tapping or clicking this link displays information on how Windows resolved the problem. In other cases, you'll get the View Technical Details link. Tapping or clicking this link provides more information about the stability issue (as shown in Figure 8-4).

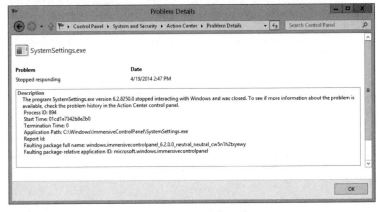

FIGURE 8-4 Review the report details to get more information.

5. At the bottom of the Reliability Monitor window you'll find these additional options:

- **Save Reliability History**   Enables you to save complete details about the computer's stability for future reference. The information is saved as a Reliability Monitor report and is formatted as XML. Tap or click Save Reliability History, and then use the dialog box provided to select a save location and file name for the report. You can view the report in Windows Internet Explorer by double-tapping or double-clicking the file.

- **View All Problem Reports**   Opens the Problem History window that shows a history of all problems that have been identified and their status. If you want to clear the history, tap or click Clear All Problem Reports.

- **Check For Solutions To All Problems**   Starts the automated problem reporting process. When this process is complete, Action Center is updated to include all newly discovered problems, and solutions will be provided if known.

Customizing automated Help and support

Windows 8.1 provides many controls that enable you to customize the way automated Help and support works. At a basic level, you can control which types of notification messages are displayed in Action Center. To fine-tune the feature, you can control the ways problem reporting and troubleshooting work.

Each user who logs on to a computer has separate notification settings. To specify the types of notifications that are displayed in Action Center, follow these steps:

1. In Action Center, tap or click Change Action Center Settings in the left pane.

2. On the Change Action Center Settings page, shown in Figure 8-5, select the check boxes for the types of notifications you want the user to get, and clear the check boxes for the types of notifications you don't need the user to get.

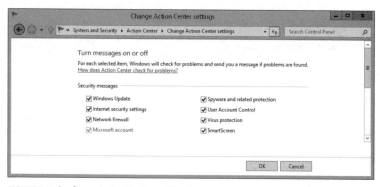

FIGURE 8-5 Configure Action Center notifications.

3. By default, usage information is sent to Microsoft as part of the Customer Experience Improvement Program. If you don't want to participate in this program, tap or click Customer Experience Improvement Program Settings, tap or click No, I Don't Want To Participate In The Program, and then tap or click Save Changes.

4. Tap or click OK.

In a standard configuration, each user who logs on to a computer has separate problem reporting settings. However, administrators also can specify that all users have the same reporting settings. To customize the way problem reporting works for the currently logged-on user or for all users, follow these steps:

1. In Action Center, tap or click Change Action Center Settings in the left pane.

2. On the Change Action Center Settings page, under Related Settings, tap or click Problem Reporting Settings.

3. You get the current configuration of problem reporting for the logged-on user. If you are able to modify the settings, the computer is configured so that each user can choose his or her problem report settings. If the settings are unavailable, the computer is configured so that all users have the same problem report settings.

4. If the computer has per-user problem report settings, select the problem report settings you want to use for the currently logged-on user, and then tap or click OK to save the settings. The options are:

   - Automatically Check For Solutions
   - Automatically Check For Solutions And Send Additional Report Data, If Needed
   - Each Time A Problem Occurs, Ask Me Before Checking For Solutions
   - Never Check For Solutions

5. If the computer has per-computer problem report settings, tap or click Change Report Settings For All Users. Next, select the problem report settings you want to use for all users, and then tap or click OK to save the settings. The options are as follows:

   - Automatically Check For Solutions
   - Automatically Check For Solutions And Send Additional Report Data, If Needed
   - Each Time A Problem Occurs, Ask Me Before Checking For Solutions
   - Never Check For Solutions
   - Allow Each User To Choose Settings

When problem reporting is enabled, you can exclude programs from problem reporting. To do this, follow these steps:

1. In Action Center, tap or click Change Action Center Settings in the left pane.

2. On the Change Action Center Settings page, under Related Settings, tap or click Problem Reporting Settings. Next, tap or click Select Programs To Exclude From Reporting.

3. On the Advanced Problem Reporting Settings page, you get a list of any programs that are currently excluded. You can now do the following:

- Add programs to exclude them from reporting. Tap or click Add, use the dialog box provided to navigate to and select the executable (.exe) file for the program, and then tap or click Open.

- Remove programs to stop excluding them from reporting. Tap or click the program in the list provided, and then tap or click Remove.

Each user who logs on to a computer has separate Windows SmartScreen settings. To configure how the SmarScreen works, follow these steps:

1. In Action Center, tap or click Change Windows SmartScreen Settings in the left pane.

2. In the Windows SmartScreen dialog box, specify how you want SmartScreen to work. By default, Windows displays a prompt asking for administrator approval before running an unrecognized app from the Internet. If you don't want to require administrator approval, you can display a warning instead or turn SmartScreen off completely.

3. Tap or click OK.

Each user who logs on to a computer has separate Automatic Maintenance settings. To configure how maintenance works, follow these steps:

1. In Action Center, tap or click the Maintenance heading, and then scroll down.

2. Below the list of current problems, you'll find an area labeled Automatic Maintenance. Tap or click Change Maintenance Settings.

3. On the Automatic Maintenance page, shown in Figure 8-6, you'll get the current settings for maintenance.

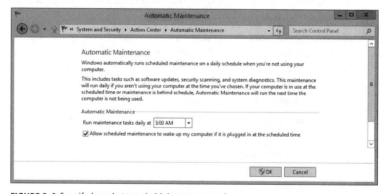

FIGURE 8-6 Specify how Automatic Maintenance works.

4. Use the Run Maintenance Tasks Daily At selection list to set the preferred start time for daily maintenance.

5. To enable Windows to wake the computer from sleep mode to run maintenance, select the check box provided.

6. Tap or click OK to save your settings.

Automatic Maintenance is built on the Windows Diagnostics framework. By default, Windows periodically performs routine maintenance at 3:00 A.M. if the computer is running on AC power and the operating system is idle. Otherwise, maintenance will start the next time the computer is running on AC power and the operating system is idle. Because maintenance runs only when the operating system is idle, maintenance can run in the background for up to three days. This enables Windows to complete complex maintenance tasks.

In Action Center, the Maintenance pane shows the status of Automatic Mainte-nance and provides management options as well. The status information shows the last run date and specifies whether any corrective action is needed. If maintenance is running, you'll get a status of maintenance in progress. If there's a problem with maintenance, you'll be notified of that as well. Tap or click Start Maintenance to start maintenance manually.

Automatic Maintenance operates as a scheduled task. In Task Scheduler, you'll find this task in the scheduler library under Microsoft\Windows\Diagnosis, and you can get detailed run details by reviewing the information provided on the task's History tab.

Each user who logs on to a computer has separate troubleshooting settings. To configure how troubleshooting works, follow these steps:

1. In Action Center, tap or click the Maintenance heading, and then scroll down.

2. Below the list of current problems, tap or click Troubleshooting. In the left pane of the Troubleshooting page, tap or click Change Settings.

3. On the Change Settings page, shown in Figure 8-7, you'll find the current settings for troubleshooting. By default, Windows periodically checks for routine maintenance issues and displays reminders when the System Mainte-nance troubleshooter can resolve problems. For example, the troubleshooter might notify the user that there are unused files and shortcuts that can be cleaned up.

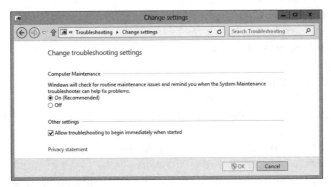

FIGURE 8-7 Specify how troubleshooting works.

4. By default, when the user starts a troubleshooter, troubleshooting begins automatically. If you'd rather have the user confirm that she wants to start troubleshooting, clear the Allow Troubleshooting To Begin Immediately When Started check box.

5. Tap or click OK to save your settings.

Troubleshooters help to automatically identify and resolve problems with the operating system. Automated troubleshooting relies on Windows PowerShell and related system services. So long as Windows PowerShell is installed, which is the case by default, and the required services are available, automated troubleshooting will work.

Standard troubleshooters include the following:

- **DirectAccess troubleshooter** Diagnoses and resolves problems that prevent the computer from using DirectAccess to connect to a workplace

- **Hardware And Devices troubleshooter** Diagnoses and resolves problems that prevent the computer from properly using a device

- **Homegroup troubleshooter** Diagnoses and resolves problems that prevent the computer from viewing computers or shared files in a homegroup

- **Incoming Connections troubleshooter** Diagnoses and resolves problems that block incoming connections

- **Internet Connections troubleshooter** Diagnoses and resolves problems that prevent the computer from connecting to the Internet and accessing the web

- **Internet Explorer Performance troubleshooter** Diagnoses and resolves problems that are affecting the overall performance of Internet Explorer

- **Internet Explorer Safety troubleshooter** Identifies issues with settings that could compromise the security of the computer and the safety of the user when browsing the web

- **Network Adapter troubleshooter** Diagnoses and resolves problems related to Ethernet, wireless, and other network adapters

- **Playing Audio troubleshooter** Diagnoses and resolves problems that prevent the computer from playing audio

- **Power troubleshooter** Diagnoses and resolves problems to fix a computer's power settings

- **Printer troubleshooter** Diagnoses and resolves problems that prevent the computer from using a printer

- **Program Compatibility troubleshooter** Diagnoses and resolves problems that prevent older programs from running on the computer

- **Recording Audio troubleshooter** Diagnoses and resolves problems that prevent the computer from recording audio

- **Search And Indexing troubleshooter** Diagnoses and resolves problems with the search and indexing features of Windows

- **Shared Folders troubleshooter** Diagnoses and resolves problems with accessing shared files and folders on other computers

- **System Maintenance troubleshooter**   Performs routine maintenance if the user does not

- **Windows Update troubleshooter**   Diagnoses and resolves problems that prevent the computer from using Windows Update

TIP   In Group Policy, administrators configure Access-Denied Assistance policies to help users determine who to contact if they have trouble accessing files and to display custom access-denied error messages. Use Enable Access-Denied Assistance On Client For All File Types to enable access-denied assistance for all file types. Configure how access-denied assistance works by using Customize Message For Access-Denied Errors. These policies are found in the Administrative Templates policies for Computer Configuration under System\Access-Denied Assistance.

In Action Center, you can access any of the available troubleshooters by scrolling down and then tapping or clicking Troubleshooting. As shown in Figure 8-8, troubleshooters are organized by category. These categories include the following:

- **Programs**   For troubleshooting compatibility issues with applications designed for earlier versions of Windows.

- **Hardware And Sound**   For troubleshooting issues with hardware devices, audio recording, and audio playback.

- **Network And Internet**   For troubleshooting issues with connecting to networks and accessing shared folders on other computers.

- **System And Security**   For troubleshooting issues with Windows Update, power usage, and performance. Tap or click Run Maintenance Tasks to clean up unused files and shortcuts and perform other routine maintenance tasks.

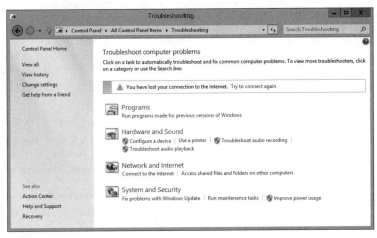

FIGURE 8-8 View and work with troubleshooters.

Table 8-1 lists Administrative Templates policies for managing Action Center and related features. In Group Policy, you can configure how automated troubleshooting and diagnostics work by using the Administrative Templates policies for Computer Configuration under System\Troubleshooting And Diagnostics.

TABLE 8-1 Policies for managing Action Center and related features

POLICY NAME	DESCRIPTION	ADMINISTRATIVE TEMPLATES LOCATION
Turn Off Windows Customer Experience Improvement Program	If this policy is enabled, users are opted out of the program. If this policy is disabled, users are opted into the program.	Computer Configuration under System\Internet Communication Management\Internet Communication Settings
Detect Application Failures Caused By Deprecated COM Objects	If you enable or do not configure this policy, Windows will detect programs trying to create deprecated COM objects and notify users.	Computer Configuration under System\Troubleshooting And Diagnostics\Application Compatibility Diagnostics
Detect Application Failures Caused By Deprecated Windows DLLs	If you enable or do not configure this policy, Windows will detect programs trying to use deprecated dynamic link libraries (DLLs) and notify users.	Computer Configuration under System\Troubleshooting And Diagnostics\Application Compatibility Diagnostics
Detect Compatibility Issues For Applications And Drivers	If you enable or do not configure this policy, Windows will detect installation failures, run-time failures, and drivers blocked because of compatibility issues and notify users.	Computer Configuration under System\Troubleshooting And Diagnostics\Application Compatibility Diagnostics
Notify Blocked Drivers	If this policy is enabled or not configured, Windows will notify users about drivers blocked because of compatibility problems.	Computer Configuration under System\Troubleshooting And Diagnostics\Application Compatibility Diagnostics
Troubleshooting: Allow Users To Access And Run Troubleshooting Wizards	If you enable or don't configure this policy, users can access and run the troubleshooting tools in Action Center.	Computer Configuration under System\Troubleshooting And Diagnostics \Scripted Diagnostics

POLICY NAME	DESCRIPTION	ADMINISTRATIVE TEMPLATES LOCATION
Troubleshooting: Allow Users To Access Online Troubleshooting Content On Microsoft Servers From The Troubleshooting Control Panel	If you enable or don't configure this policy, users who are connected to the Internet can access and search for troubleshooting content. Users can access this content by tapping or clicking Yes when prompted in Action Center to get the most up-to-date troubleshooting content.	Computer Configuration under System\Troubleshooting And Diagnostics \Scripted Diagnostics
Turn Off Application Compatibility Engine	If this policy is enabled, Windows does not check the compatibility database prior to starting applications.	Computer Configuration under Windows Components\Application Compatibility
Turn Off Program Compatibility Assistant	If this policy is enabled, Windows does not monitor user-initiated programs for known compatibility issues at run time.	User and Computer Configuration under Windows Components\Application Compatibility
Configure Report Queue	If this policy is enabled and configured, it allows an administrator to configure queuing and notification related to error reporting.	User and Computer Configuration under Windows Components\Windows Error Reporting\Advanced Error Reporting Settings
Disable Windows Error Reporting	If this policy is enabled, Windows Error Reporting will not send any information to Microsoft. Otherwise, Windows Error Reporting will send information.	User and Computer Configuration under Windows Components\Windows Error Reporting
Remove The Action Center Icon	If you enable this policy, the Action Center icon is not displayed in the notification area of the taskbar, although this doesn't prevent users from accessing Action Center through Control Panel. Otherwise, the Action Center icon is displayed.	User Configuration under Start Menu And Taskbar

Working with support services

To support automated diagnostics and problem resolution, Windows 8.1 provides separate components and tools for working with and managing diagnostics, problem reporting, and user assistance. These components all rely on the availability of the support services installed with the operating system. If you access the Services node under Services And Applications in the Computer Management administrative tool, you'll find a bundle of services dedicated to system support.

Table 8-2 provides an overview of key support services in Windows 8.1. Problem detection, troubleshooting, and resolution features are largely supported by the Diagnostic Policy Service and the Diagnostic System Host service. A third, related service, the Diagnostic Service Host service, starts only as needed.

TABLE 8-2 Support services in Windows 8.1

NAME	DESCRIPTION
Application Experience	Processes application compatibility cache requests for applications
Application Information	Enables users to run applications with additional administrative privileges
Application Management	Processes installation, removal, and enumeration requests for software deployed through Group Policy
Background Intelligent Transfer Service	Transfers files in the background by using idle network bandwidth
Diagnostic Policy Service	Enables problem detection, troubleshooting, and resolution for Windows components
Diagnostic Service Host	Enables diagnostics that need to run in a Local-Service context
Diagnostic System Host	Enables diagnostics that need to run in a Local-System context
Problem Reports and Solutions Control Panel Support	Provides support for system-level problem reports
Program Compatibility Assistant Service	Provides support for the Program Compatibility Assistant
Secondary Logon	Enables users to start processes under alternate credentials
Superfetch	Helps maintain and improve performance by prefetching component and application data based on usage patterns

NAME	DESCRIPTION
System Event Notification Service	Monitors system events and provides notification services
Task Scheduler	Enables a user to configure and schedule automated tasks
Themes	Enables the computer to use themes and provides the user experience for themes management
User Profile Service	Responsible for loading and unloading user profiles during logon and logoff
Windows Error Reporting Service	Enables errors to be reported when programs stop responding and enables solutions to be retrieved
Windows Event Log	Responsible for logging events
Windows Management Instrumentation	Provides system management information
Windows Modules Installer	Supports Windows updates of recommended and optional components
Windows Remote Management	Enables Windows PowerShell for remote use, and the WS-Management protocol for remote management
Windows Time	Used to synchronize system time with Coordinated Universal Time
Windows Update	Enables updating of Windows components and other programs

As is clear from the number of support services, the automated Help system built into Windows 8.1 is fairly complex. The system is designed to automatically monitor system health, perform preventative maintenance, and report problems so that they can be resolved. Related performance and reliability data can be tracked in Performance Monitor and in Reliability Monitor.

Support services provide the foundation for the enhanced support features in Windows 8.1. If critical services are not running or not configured properly, you might have problems using certain support features. You can view these and other services in Computer Management by completing the following steps:

1. In Control Panel, tap or click System And Security, tap or click Administrative Tools, and then double-tap or double-click Computer Management.

2. Press and hold or right-click the Computer Management entry in the console tree, and then tap or click Connect To Another Computer. You can now select the system whose services you want to view.

3. Expand the Services And Applications node by tapping or clicking it. Select Services, as shown in Figure 8-9. You should now get a complete list of services installed on the system. By default, this list is organized by service name. The key columns in this dialog box are as follows:

- **Name** The name of the service. Only services installed on the system are listed here. Double-tap or double-click an entry to configure its startup options.

- **Description** A short description of the service and its purpose.

- **Status** An indication of whether the status of the service is running, paused, or stopped. (Stopped is indicated by a blank entry.)

- **Startup Type** The startup setting for the service. Automatic services are started at startup. Users or other services start manual services. Disabled services are turned off and can't be started while they remain disabled.

- **Log On As** The account the service logs on as. The default in most cases is the LocalSystem account.

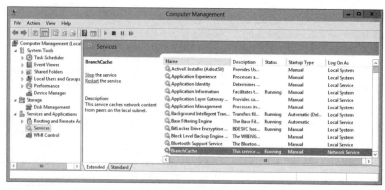

FIGURE 8-9 Use the Services view to manage services on Windows 8.1.

4. The Services pane has two views: Extended and Standard. To change the view, use the tabs at the bottom of the Services pane. In Extended view, quick links are provided for managing services. Tap or click Start to start a stopped service. Tap or click Restart to stop and then start a service. If you select a service in Extended view, you'll get a service description that details the service's purpose.

Starting, stopping, and pausing services

As an administrator, you'll often have to start, stop, or pause Windows 8.1 services. To start, stop, or pause a service, follow these steps:

1. In Computer Management, expand the Services And Applications node by tapping or clicking it, and then select the Services node.

2. Press and hold or right-click the service you want to manipulate, and then select Start, Stop, or Pause.

NOTE You can also choose Restart to have Windows stop and then start the service after a brief pause. Additionally, if you pause a service, you can use the Resume option to resume normal operation. When services that are set to start automatically fail, the status is blank, and you'll usually receive notification about this. Service failures can also be logged to the system's event logs. In Windows 8.1, you can configure actions to handle service failure automatically. For example, you can have Windows 8.1 attempt to restart the service for you.

Configuring service startup

You can set Windows 8.1 services to start manually or automatically. You can also turn them off permanently by disabling them. You configure service startup by following these steps:

1. In Computer Management, expand the Services And Applications node, and then select the Services node.
2. Press and hold or right-click the service you want to configure, and then tap or click Properties.
3. On the General tab, use the Startup Type drop-down list to choose a startup option from the following choices, and then tap or click OK:
   - **Automatic**   Starts the service at startup
   - **Automatic (Delayed Start)**   Delays the start of the service until all non-delayed automatic services have started
   - **Manual**   Enables the service to be started manually
   - **Disabled**   Turns off the service

Configuring service logon

You can configure Windows 8.1 services to log on as a system account or as a specific user by following these steps:

1. In Computer Management, expand the Services And Applications node, and then select the Services node.
2. Press and hold or right-click the service you want to configure, and then tap or click Properties.
3. Select the Log On tab. Do one of the following, and then tap or click OK.
   - Select Local System Account if you want the service to log on by using the system account (the default for most services). If the service provides a user interface that can be manipulated, select Allow Service To Interact With Desktop to enable users to control the service's interface.
   - Select This Account if you want the service to log on by using a specific user account. Be sure to enter an account name and password in the text boxes provided. Use the Browse button to search for a user account.

Configuring service recovery

Windows 8.1 automatically configures recovery for critical system services during installation. In most cases, you'll find that critical services are configured to restart automatically if the service fails. You cannot change these settings because they are not available.

To configure recovery options for any other service, follow these steps:

1. In Computer Management, expand the Services And Applications node, and then select the Services node.

2. Press and hold or right-click the service you want to configure, and then tap or click Properties.

3. Tap or click the Recovery tab.

4. You can now configure recovery options for the first, second, and subsequent recovery attempts. The following options are available:

   - **Take No Action**   The operating system won't attempt recovery for this failure but might still attempt recovery of previous or subsequent failures.

   - **Restart The Service**   Windows will stop and then start the service after a brief pause.

   - **Run A Program**   This enables you to run a program or a script in case of failure. The script can be a batch program or a Windows script. If you select this option, set the full file path to the program you want to run, and then set any necessary command-line parameters to pass in to the program when it starts.

   - **Restart The Computer**   This shuts down and then restarts the computer. Before you choose this option, double-check the computer's Startup and Recovery options. You want the system to select defaults quickly and automatically.

   TIP   When you configure recovery options for critical services, you can try to restart the service on the first and second attempts, and then reboot the computer on the third attempt.

5. Configure other options based on your previously selected recovery options, and then tap or click OK. If you elected to run a program as a recovery option, you need to set options in the Run Program panel. If you elected to restart the service, you need to specify the restart delay. After stopping the service, Windows 8.1 waits for the specified delay period before trying to start the service. In most cases, a delay of 1 to 2 minutes is sufficient.

Disabling unnecessary services

As an administrator, your job is to safeguard computer and network security, and unnecessary services are a potential source of security problems. For example, in many of the organizations that I've reviewed for security problems, I've found users' computers running Worldwide Web Publishing Service, Simple Mail Transfer Protocol (SMTP), and File Transfer Protocol (FTP) Publishing Service when these services weren't needed. Unfortunately, these services can enable anonymous users to access computers and can also open the computers to attack if not properly configured.

If you find unnecessary services, you have a couple of options. For services installed through features, you can remove the related feature to remove the unnecessary component and its related services. You can also simply disable the services that aren't being used.

To disable a service, follow these steps:

1. In Computer Management, expand the Services And Applications node, and then select the Services node.

2. Press and hold or right-click the service you want to configure, and then tap or click Properties.

3. On the General tab, select Disabled from the Startup Type drop-down list.

Disabling a service doesn't stop a running service; it prevents it from being started the next time the computer is started, which means that the security risk still exists. To address this, tap or click Stop on the General tab in the Properties dialog box, and then tap or click OK.

Managing services by using preferences

Rather than managing services on individual computers, you can use Group Policy preference items to configure services on any computer that processes a particular Group Policy Object (GPO). When you configure a service through preferences, the default value in most instances is No Change, meaning the setting is changed only if you specify a different value. As you can when you are configuring services manually, you can use Group Policy preferences to do the following:

- Start, stop, and restart services
- Set startup to manual, automatic, automatic (delayed start), or disabled
- Specify the logon account to use
- Set recovery options to handle service failure

To create a preference item to control a service, follow these steps:

1. Open a GPO for editing in the Group Policy Management Editor. Expand Computer Configuration\Preferences\Control Panel Settings.

2. Press and hold or right-click the Services node, point to New, and then tap or click Service. This opens the New Service Properties dialog box, shown in Figure 8-10.

3. In the Service Name box, enter the name of the service you want to configure. The service name is not the same as the display name. If you are unsure of the service name, tap or click the options button to the right of the text box, and then select the service from the list of available services on your management computer. Keep in mind that some services running on your management computer might not be available on users' computers, and vice versa.

FIGURE 8-10 Customize services for a GPO.

4. Use the options provided to configure the service as you want it to be configured on users' computers. Settings are processed only if you select a value other than No Change.

5. Use the options on the Common tab to control how the preference is applied. Often, you'll want to apply the service configuration only once. If so, select Apply Once And Do Not Reapply.

6. Tap or click OK. The next time policy is refreshed, the preference item will be applied as appropriate for the GPO in which you defined the preference item.

Installing and maintaining devices: the essentials

Many different types of devices can be installed in or connected to computers. The following are the key device types:

- **Cards/adapters** Circuit cards and adapters are plugged into expansion slots on the motherboard inside the computer case or, for a laptop, into expansion slots on the side of the system. Most cards and adapters have a connector into which you can plug other devices.

- **Internal drives** Many different types of drives can be installed, from DVD drives to hard disks. Internal drives usually have two cables. One cable attaches to the motherboard, to other drives, or to interface cards. The other cable attaches to the computer's power supply.

- **External drives and devices** External drives and devices plug into ports on the computer. The port can be standard, such as LPT1 or COM1; a port that you added with a circuit card; or a high-speed serial port, such as a USB port, eSATA, or an IEEE-1394 port (commonly called a FireWire port). Printers, scanners, USB flash drives, smartphones, and most digital cameras are attachable as external devices.

- **Memory** Memory chips are used to expand the total amount of physical memory on the computer. Memory can be added to the motherboard or to a particular device, such as a video card. The most commonly used type of memory is RAM.

Devices installed on the computer but not detected during an upgrade or installation of the operating system are configured differently from new devices that you install.

Installing preexisting devices

Windows 8.1 detects devices that were not automatically installed when the operating system was upgraded or installed. If a device wasn't installed because Windows 8.1 didn't include the driver, the built-in hardware diagnostics will, in many cases, detect the hardware and then use the automatic update framework to retrieve the required driver the next time Windows Update runs, provided that Windows Update is enabled and you've enabled driver updating as well as operating system updating.

Although driver updates can be downloaded automatically through Windows Update, they are not installed automatically. After upgrading or installing the operating system, you should check for driver updates and apply them as appropriate before trying other techniques to install device drivers. The basic steps to check for updates are as follows (a complete discussion of working with automatic updating is covered in Chapter 9, "Handling maintenance and support tasks"):

1. In Control Panel, tap or click System And Security, and then tap or click Windows Update.

2. In Windows Update, tap or click the Check For Updates link.

Typically, device driver updates are considered optional updates. The exceptions are for essential drivers, such as those for video, sound, and hard disk controllers. To address this, you should view all available updates on a computer, rather than only the important updates, to determine whether device driver updates are available. To install available device driver updates, follow these steps:

1. In Control Panel, tap or click System And Security, and then tap or click Windows Update.

2. In Windows Update, tap or click Check For Updates in the left pane. When Windows 8.1 finishes checking for updates, you might find that there are important updates as well as optional updates available, as shown in Figure 8-11. Tap or click Install Updates to install the important updates.

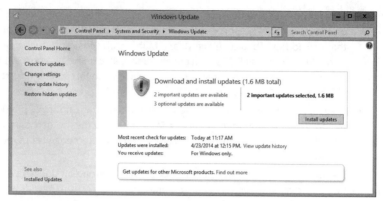

FIGURE 8-11 Check for updates on the Windows Update page.

3. Because driver updates are usually listed as optional, you should note whether any optional updates are available. If optional updates are available and you tap or click the related link, you might find that some or all of the optional updates are driver updates, as shown in Figure 8-12.

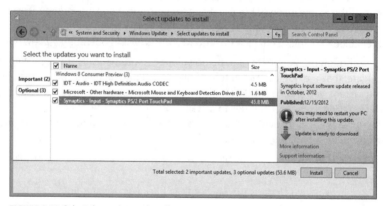

FIGURE 8-12 Select the update to install.

4. By default, optional updates are not selected for installation. To ensure that an update will be installed, select the related check box, and then tap or click Install to download and install the selected updates.

After you've installed the device driver, Windows 8.1 should detect the hardware within several minutes and install the device automatically. If Windows 8.1 detects the device but isn't able to install the device automatically, you might find a related solution in Action Center. You will then be able to view the problem response.

Installing internal, USB, FireWire, and eSATA devices

Most available new devices are Plug and Play compatible. This means that you should be able to install new devices easily by using one of the following techniques:

- For an internal device, review the hardware manufacturer's installation instructions because you might need to install device driver software prior to installing the device. Next, shut down the computer, insert the device into the appropriate slot or connect it to the computer, restart the computer, and then let Windows 8.1 automatically detect the new device.

- For a USB, FireWire, or eSATA device, simply insert the device into the appropriate slot or connect it to the computer, and then let Windows 8.1 automatically detect the new device.

NOTE Windows 8.1 expects USB, FireWire, and eSATA devices to be Plug and Play compatible. If a device isn't Plug and Play compatible, you might be able to install the device by using software from the manufacturer.

Depending on the device, Windows 8.1 should automatically detect the new device and then silently install a built-in driver to support it. Notifications are displayed only if there's a problem. Otherwise, the installation process just happens in the background.

The device should then run immediately without any problems. Well, that's the idea, but it doesn't always work that way. The success of automatic detection and installation depends on the device being Plug and Play compatible and a device driver being available.

Windows 8.1 includes many device drivers in a standard installation, and most of the time the device should be installed automatically. If driver updating is enabled through Windows Update, Windows 8.1 checks for new drivers automatically when you connect a new device or when Windows 8.1 first detects the device. Because Windows Update does not automatically install device drivers, you need to check for updates to determine if a driver is available for you to install.

NOTE For details on whether to use Windows Update to check for drivers automatically, see the section "The Hardware tab" in Chapter 2, "Configuring and optimizing Windows 8.1 computers." As discussed in Chapter 9, Windows Update must be enabled for this feature to work.

You'll know the device installed because it will be available for you to use. You also can confirm device availability in Devices And Printers. To open Devices And Printers, tap or click View Devices And Printers in Control Panel under the Hardware And Sound heading. For USB devices that do not have a custom driver, you often can use the generic Winusb.sys driver, which is the default USB driver included with Windows 8.1. When you connect a USB device that doesn't have a custom driver, Windows might use the generic Winusb.sys driver automatically. If this driver isn't used automatically, you can manually select it as discussed in "Installing a device by using the generic USB driver" later in this chapter.

However, the generic USB driver really isn't for USB devices with their own classifications. Devices with their own classifications include audio devices, audio/video devices, Human Interface Devices (HID), image devices, printers, mass storage devices, smart cards, and wireless host or hub controllers. These devices have their own generic drivers, which can be installed by using a process similar to that discussed in "Installing a device by using the generic USB driver" later in this chapter.

REAL WORLD Human Interface Devices are interactive input devices that are used to directly control computers, including:

- Sensory devices such as accelerometers and gyroscopes.

- Front-panel controls such as knobs, switches, buttons, and sliders on devices, such as the volume controls on speakers and headsets.

- Controls found on devices such as interactive displays, barcode readers, smartphones, and other consumer electronics.

- Controls, games, and simulation devices such as data gloves, throttles, steering wheels, and rudder pedals.

- Keyboards and pointing devices such as standard mouse devices, trackballs, and joysticks.

Human Interface Devices are a device class over USB and also a replacement for PS/2. Window 8.1 supports HID clients for mouse and mapper drivers, keyboard and keypad drivers, system control drivers (such as power buttons and laptop lid open/close sensors), consumer device controls, pen devices, touch screens, sensors, and UPS batteries. Windows 8.1 supports USB, Bluetooth, Bluetooth LE, and Inter-Integrated Circuit (I2C) as transports for HID. Windows 8.1 no longer supports legacy interactive input devices, such as HID minidrivers for game port devices and gameport bus drivers.

When a device has a custom driver, Windows 8.1 might automatically detect the new device, but the Driver Software Installation component might run into problems installing the device. If this happens, the installation silently fails. You'll know installation failed because the device will not be available for you to use. In Devices And Printers, you should get warning icons for both the computer and the device (as shown in Figure 8-13). In this case, if you touch or point to the computer device, you should get error status messages, such as the following:

Status: Driver is unavailable Status: Driver Error

Tap or click the computer device and the details pane should show the Needs Troubleshooting status.

You can perform the same procedures with the device you are trying to install. Touch or point to the computer device to get error status messages. Tap or click the device and the details pane to show the Needs Troubleshooting status. You might also get the following:

Status: Setup incomplete. Connect to the Internet.

To begin troubleshooting, tap or click Troubleshoot. This option is listed at the top of the Devices And Printers window when you select the computer or the device. The troubleshooter will walk you through solving the problem step by step. The most likely reason for device installation failure is that the device driver needed to be downloaded from the Internet. If so, the troubleshooter should rather quickly determine this and prompt you to install the driver, as shown in Figure 8-14.

FIGURE 8-13 Windows fails to install the device.

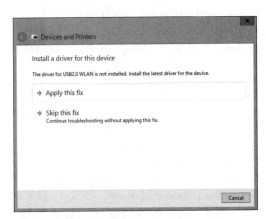

FIGURE 8-14 Windows displays a possible solution.

If Windows 8.1 doesn't detect and install the device, check the manufacturer's website for compatible installation software. After you have installation software for the device, run it, and then follow the prompts. The device should then be installed properly.

NOTE If Windows cannot install a device, there might be a problem with the device itself or the driver or a conflict with existing hardware. For additional details on troubleshooting, see the section "Troubleshooting hardware," later in this chapter.

After you've successfully installed a device, you might need to periodically perform maintenance tasks for the device and its drivers. When new drivers for a device are released, you might want to test them in a development or support environment to determine whether the drivers resolve problems that users have been experiencing. If the drivers install without problems and resolve outstanding issues, you might want to install the updated drivers on computers that use this device. The driver update procedure should be implemented as follows:

1. Check the device and driver information on each system prior to installing the new driver. Note the location, version, and file name of the existing driver.

2. Create a System Restore point, as discussed in Chapter 10, "Backing up and recovering a computer," in the section "Backing up and recovering system state by using System Restore."

3. Install the updated driver and optionally restart the computer. If the computer and the device function normally after the restart, the update can be considered a success.

4. If the computer or the device malfunctions after the driver installation, use the standard Device Manager features to roll back to the previously installed driver. If the computer cannot be restarted and the driver cannot be restored, recover the system by starting with the last known good configuration, and then restore the system to the System Restore point that you created in step 2.

Installing Bluetooth, wireless, and network devices

You can connect most Bluetooth, wireless, and network devices to a computer, including wireless network, storage, phone, keyboard, mouse, and media-extender devices. Often, these devices include installation software, but before you use the installation software, you should be sure it is compatible with Windows 8.1. If it isn't, you should check the device manufacturer's website for updated software.

Windows 8.1 supports Bluetooth, Bluetooth LE, and I2C transports. Before these devices can be used, they must be discovered and paired with Windows 8.1. To discover and pair a device with Windows 8.1, complete the following steps:

1. Display the PC Settings screen. With touch UI, slide in from the right, tap Settings, and then tap Change PC Settings. With the mouse and keyboard, press Windows key + I, and then click Change PC Settings.

2. In PC Settings, select Devices and then select Add A Device to have Windows search for available devices.

3. Select the device. Keep in mind that some devices require you to enable Bluetooth and then attempt to pair on the device.

Some devices connect directly to a computer. Others connect to a computer via a network. To connect a wireless device directly to a computer, do the following:

1. Most wireless and Bluetooth devices require you to connect a receiver to the computer. Some devices might share a receiver. For example, with a wireless keyboard and mouse desktop pack, you might need to plug a shared receiver into a USB slot on the computer.

2. Position the computer and receiver so that the receiver is within range of the device to which you want to connect. For example, a keyboard or mouse might need to be within 6 feet of the receiver, but the receiver for a wireless adapter might need to be within 100 feet of a wireless router.

3. Configure the device as necessary, and check that it is powered on. If you're trying to add a wireless network device, it must be configured for your wireless network before you can add it to a computer. Some wireless network devices need to be put into a discovery mode known as Wireless Protected Setup (WPS) before they can be detected.

4. The device should be detected and installed automatically. If the device isn't detected and installed, open Devices And Printers. In Devices And Printers, be sure that the device isn't already listed as available. If the device isn't available yet, tap or click Add Devices And Printers, and then follow the prompts.

5. If you have trouble connecting the device, try the following as part of troubleshooting:

   - Make sure the device isn't turned off, low on battery power, or in sleep mode. Some wireless devices have a button on them that you need to push to force a connection. Others, such as a Bluetooth phone, might have a setting in their software menu that you need to select to make them available. The receiver for a device might also have a button that you can press to force the receiver to scan for compatible wireless devices.

   - If wireless and Bluetooth capability is integrated into the computer, make sure that the wireless or Bluetooth transmitter is turned on. Many laptops have an external switch for turning the transmitter on or off.

   - If you suspect that the device is out of range, try moving it closer to the computer. If there's a wall between the device and the computer, try putting the device and the computer in the same room.

   - If a positional issue is causing the problem, you can resolve the problem by moving the cables and devices that could be causing electromagnetic interference, including power cables for other devices, large speakers, or desk lamps. If the problem persists, make sure the device is positioned away from air conditioning units, microwave ovens, and similar items.

To connect a wired or wireless device to a computer via a network, do the following:

1. Connect the device to the network and turn it on. Then configure its initial settings as appropriate for the network. For example, you might need to configure TCP/IP settings to use DHCP, or you might need to use a static IP address.

2. Wait up to 90 seconds for the device to be detected. The device should be detected and installed automatically. If the device isn't detected and installed, open Devices And Printers. In Devices And Printers, check whether the device is already listed as available. If the device isn't available yet, tap or click Add Devices And Printers, and then follow the prompts.

3. If you have trouble connecting the device, try the following as part of troubleshooting:

   - Make sure that a firewall isn't blocking connectivity to the device. You might need to open a firewall port to enable access between the computer and the device.

   - Make sure the device is turned on and connected to the same network as the computer. If your network consists of multiple subnets connected together, try to connect the device to the same network subnet. You can determine the subnet by looking at the computer's IP address.

   - Make sure the device is configured to broadcast its presence on the network. Most network devices automatically do this.

   - Make sure the network device has an IP address and proper network settings. With DHCP, network routers assign IP addresses automatically as devices connect to the network.

NOTE Not all detectable devices can be added to a computer. To find out if a device is able to be connected to your computer, check the information that came with the device or go to the manufacturer's website.

REAL WORLD Network discovery affects whether your computer can find other computers and devices on the network and whether other computers on the network can find your computer. By default, Windows Firewall blocks network discovery, but you can enable it by following these steps:

1. In Control Panel, tap or click Network And Internet.

2. Tap or click Network And Sharing Center.

3. In the left pane, tap or click Change Advanced Sharing Settings.

4. Under Network Discovery, tap or click Turn On Network Discovery for the Domain profile (and/or other profiles as appropriate), and then tap or click Save Changes.

Installing local and network printers

Windows 8.1 supports standard printers and three-dimensional (3-D) printers. 3-D printing involves creating 3-D content and passing it through the Windows spooler and driver filters to a 3-D manufacturing device, such as a 3-D printer. Most 3-D printing interfaces support submitting 3-D content in Open Packaging Conventions (OPC) format and submitting 2-D content in XML Paper Specification (XPS) format.

You can connect printers to computers in several different ways. Which option you choose depends on the printer. Some printers connect directly to a computer and are referred to as local printers. Others connect to a computer via a network and are referred to as network printers. Network printers include all printers on a network, such as Bluetooth and wireless printers, as well as printers that are connected to another computer and shared on the network.

Most printers have installation software that you use to initially configure the printer. For a printer that connects directly to a computer, you usually run this software once, and the software sets up the printer and configures a connection to the printer so that it can be used. For a network printer, you usually run this software once on your management computer to prepare the printer for use and then create connections to the printer on each computer that will use the printer.

Setting up a local printer

With a printer that has a USB connection, you connect the printer directly to the computer, and Windows should automatically detect and install it. If your printer connects by using a serial or parallel port, you might have to install the printer manually. To install a printer manually, follow these steps:

1. Turn on the printer. In Devices And Printers, check that the printer isn't already listed as available. If the printer isn't available yet, install it by following the remaining steps in this procedure.

2. In Devices And Printers, tap or click Add A Printer. The Add Printer Wizard attempts to detect the printer automatically. If the wizard finds the printer with which you want to work, tap or click it in the list provided, follow the prompts, and skip the rest of the steps in this procedure. If the wizard doesn't find the printer, tap or click The Printer That I Want Isn't Listed.

3. Tap or click Add A Local Printer Or Network Printer With Manual Settings, and then tap or click Next.

4. In the Use An Existing Port list, select the port to which the printer is connected, and then tap or click Next.

5. Do one of the following:

   ▪ Select the printer manufacturer and model, and then tap or click Next.

   ▪ If the printer isn't listed but you have the installation media, tap or click Have Disk, and then browse to the folder where the printer driver is stored. For help, consult the printer manual.

- If you don't have the installation media, tap or click Windows Update, and then wait while Windows checks for available drivers.

6. Complete the additional steps in the wizard, and then tap or click Finish. You can confirm that the printer is working by printing a test page.

You can manage local printers by using Group Policy preferences. I recommend this approach only for situations in which you can carefully target computers so that only computers that actually have local printers are configured.

To create a preference item to create, update, replace, or delete local printers, follow these steps:

1. Open a GPO for editing in the Group Policy Management Editor. To configure preferences for computers, expand Computer Configuration\Preferences \Control Panel Settings, and then select Printers. To configure preferences for users, expand User Configuration\Preferences\Control Panel Settings, and then select Printers.

2. Press and hold or right-click the Printers node, point to New, and then tap or click Local Printer. This opens the New Local Printer Properties dialog box.

3. In the New Local Printer Properties dialog box, select Create, Update, Replace, or Delete in the Action list.

4. In the Name box, enter the name of the printer. If you are creating a printer, this is the name that will be used for the new local printer. If you are updating, replacing, or deleting a printer, this name must match the targeted local printer.

5. In the Port list, select the port to which the local printer is connected.

6. In the Printer Path box, enter the Universal Naming Convention (UNC) path to a shared printer that is of the same type as the local printer you are configuring. The preference item will use this as an installation source for the printer driver.

7. Use the options on the Common tab to control how the preference is applied. Because you are enforcing a control, you will generally want to apply the setting every time Group Policy is refreshed. In this case, do not select Apply Once And Do Not Reapply.

8. Tap or click OK. The next time policy is refreshed, the preference item will be applied as appropriate for the GPO in which you defined the preference item.

To create a preference item to manage a shared local printer, follow these steps:

1. Open a GPO for editing in the Group Policy Management Editor. Expand User Configuration\Preferences\Control Panel Settings, and then select Printers.

2. Press and hold or right-click the Printers node, point to New, and then tap or click Shared Printer. This opens the New Shared Printer Properties dialog box.

3. In the New Shared Printer Properties dialog box, select Create, Update, Replace, or Delete in the Action list. If you are creating a Delete preference, you can specify that you want to delete all shared printer connections by setting the action to Delete and selecting Delete All Shared Printer Connections.

4. In the Share Path box, enter the UNC path of the shared printer. Optionally, choose a local port to which you want to map the shared connection. If you are using the Delete action, the shared printer associated with that local port is deleted. Alternatively, with the Delete action you can elect to unmap all local ports.

5. Optionally, set the printer as the default printer. If you are creating, updating, or replacing a shared printer connection and want the connection to be available each time the user logs on, choose the Reconnect option.

6. Use the options on the Common tab to control how the preference is applied. Because you are enforcing a control, you will generally want to apply the setting every time Group Policy is refreshed. In this case, do not select Apply Once And Do Not Reapply.

7. Tap or click OK. The next time policy is refreshed, the preference item will be applied as appropriate for the GPO in which you defined the preference item.

Setting up NFC, wireless, Bluetooth, or network printers

Tablets and other devices running Windows 8.1 can connect to NFC-enabled printers without having to install drivers. When a printer has a Near Field Communications (NFC) tag and this tag is enabled, users can connect to the printer simply by tapping their device against the printer.

If a printer uses a wireless or Bluetooth connection, you can prepare the computer and the printer as you would any similar device. Use the techniques discussed in the section "Installing Bluetooth, wireless, and network devices," earlier in this chapter, except connect to the printer in the same way that you connect to a network printer.

Make sure the printer is powered on and in a discoverable mode. You might need to manually turn on the printer's Bluetooth or wireless capabilities. If the printer has a wired connection, you might not be able to use its built-in dynamic addressing features. In this case, you might need to manually configure the printer's TCP/IP settings.

In Devices And Printers, be sure that the printer isn't already listed as available. If the printer isn't available yet, follow these steps to connect to it:

1. In Devices And Printers, tap or click Add A Printer. The Add Printer Wizard attempts to detect the printer automatically. If the wizard finds the printer with which you want to work, tap or click it in the list provided, follow the prompts, and skip the rest of the steps in this procedure. If the wizard doesn't find the printer, tap or click The Printer That I Want Isn't Listed.

2. In the Add Printer Wizard, tap or click Add Bluetooth, Wireless Or Network Discoverable Printer.

3. In the list of available printers, select the printer you want to use, and then tap or click Next.

4. If prompted, install the printer driver on your computer. Tablets and other devices running Windows 8.1 can connect to printers that support Wi-Fi Direct without having to install drivers. In these configurations, these devices try to form a peer-to-peer network with the printer, which is then used for printing.

5. Complete the additional steps in the wizard, and then tap or click Finish. You can confirm that the printer is working by printing a test page.

6. If you have trouble connecting to the printer, try the following as part of troubleshooting:

   - Be sure that a firewall isn't blocking connectivity to the printer. You might need to open a firewall port to enable access between the computer and the printer.

   - Be sure the printer is turned on and connected to the same network as the computer. If your network consists of multiple subnets connected together, try to connect the printer to the same network subnet. You can determine the subnet by looking at the computer's IP address.

   - Be sure the printer is configured to broadcast its presence on the network. Most network printers automatically do this.

   - Be sure the printer has an IP address and proper network settings. With DHCP, network routers assign IP addresses automatically as printers connect to the network.

You can manage network printers by using Group Policy preferences. To create, update, replace, or delete a connection to a network printer, follow these steps:

1. Open a GPO for editing in the Group Policy Management Editor. To configure preferences for computers, expand Computer Configuration\Preferences \Control Panel Settings, and then select Printers. To configure preferences for users, expand User Configuration\Preferences\Control Panel Settings, and then select Printers.

2. Press and hold or right-click the Printers node, point to New, and then tap or click TCP/IP Printer to open the New TCP/IP Printer Properties dialog box.

3. In the New TCP/IP Printer Properties dialog box, select Create, Update, Replace, or Delete in the Action list.

4. Do one of the following:

   - If you want to connect to the printer by IP address, enter the IP address in the IP Address box.

   - If you want to connect to the printer by its Domain Name System (DNS) name, select Use DNS Name, and then enter the fully qualified domain name of the printer.

5. In the Local Name box, enter the local name of the printer. If you are creating a printer connection, this is the name that will be displayed on users' computers. If you are updating, replacing, or deleting a printer connection, this name must match the targeted printer.

6. In the Printer Path box, enter the UNC path to a shared printer that is the same type of printer as the network printer you are configuring. The preference item will use this printer as an installation source for the printer driver.

7. Optionally, set the printer as the default printer.

8. Use the options on the Port Settings tab to specify the protocol, port number, and other options used by the printer.

9. Use the options on the Common tab to control how the preference is applied. Because you are enforcing a control, you will generally want to apply the setting every time Group Policy is refreshed. In this case, do not select Apply Once And Do Not Reapply.

10. Tap or click OK. The next time policy is refreshed, the preference item will be applied as appropriate for the GPO in which you defined the preference item.

Getting started with Device Manager

You use Device Manager to view and configure hardware devices. You'll spend a lot of time working with this tool, so you should get to know it before working with devices.

To access Device Manager and obtain a detailed list of all the hardware devices installed on a system, complete the following steps:

1. In Control Panel, tap or click System And Security, tap or click Administrative Tools, and then double-tap or double-click Computer Management.

    NOTE To work with a remote computer, press and hold or right-click the Computer Management entry in the console tree, and then tap or click Connect To Another Computer. Choose Another Computer, and then enter the fully qualified name of the computer with which you want to work, or tap or click Browse to search for the computer with which you want to work. Tap or click OK.

2. In the Computer Management console, expand the System Tools node and then select Device Manager. As shown in Figure 8-15, you should get a complete list of devices installed on the system. By default, this list is organized by device type, showing an alphabetical list sorted by device class. By using options on the View menu, you also can organize devices by connection, resources by type, or resources by connection.

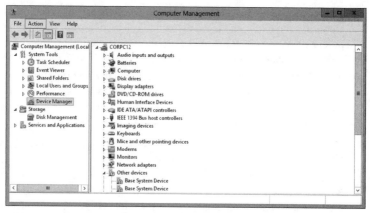

FIGURE 8-15 Use Device Manager to work with hardware devices.

3. Expand the device type to get a list of the specific instances of that device type. Select a device to work with it.

After you open Device Manager, you can work with any of the installed devices. If you press and hold or right-click a device entry, a shortcut menu is displayed. The options available depend on the device type, but they include the following:

- **Properties**   Displays the Properties dialog box for the device
- **Uninstall**   Uninstalls the device and its drivers
- **Disable**   Disables the device but doesn't uninstall it
- **Enable**   Enables a device if it's disabled
- **Update Driver Software**   Starts the Hardware Update Wizard, which you can use to update the device driver
- **Scan For Hardware Changes**   Tells Windows 8.1 to check the hardware configuration and determine whether there are any changes

TIP   The device list shows warning symbols if there are problems with a device. A yellow warning symbol with an exclamation point indicates a problem with a device. A red X indicates a device that was improperly installed. A white circle with a down arrow indicates a device disabled by the user or an administrator for some reason.

You can use the options on the View menu in the Computer Management console to change the default settings for which types of devices are displayed and how the devices are listed. The options are as follows:

- **Devices By Type**   Displays devices by the type of device installed, such as disk drive or printer. The device name is listed below the type. This is the default view.
- **Devices By Connection**   Displays devices by connection type, such as devices connected to a computer's Peripheral Component Interconnect (PCI) bus.

- **Resources By Type** Displays the status of allocated resources by the type of device using the resource. Resource types are direct memory access (DMA) channels, I/O ports, interrupt requests (IRQs), and memory addresses.

- **Resources By Connection** Displays the status of all allocated resources by connection type rather than device type. This view would enable you, for example, to trace resources according to their connection to the PCI bus, root ports, and so on.

- **Show Hidden Devices** Adds hidden devices to the standard views. This displays non–Plug and Play devices, as well as devices that have been physically removed from the computer but haven't had their drivers uninstalled.

Working with device drivers

For each hardware component installed on a computer, there is an associated device driver. The job of the device driver is to describe how the operating system uses the hardware abstraction layer (HAL) to work with a hardware component. The HAL handles the low-level communications tasks between the operating system and a hardware component. By installing a hardware component through the operating system, you are telling the operating system about the device driver it uses, and from then on, the device driver loads automatically and runs as part of the operating system.

Device driver essentials

Windows 8.1 includes an extensive library of device drivers. In the base installation of the operating system, these drivers maintained in the file repository of the driver store. Some service packs you install will include updates to the driver store. On 32-bit computers, you'll find the 32-bit driver store in the %SystemRoot% \System32\DriverStore folder. On 64-bit computers, you'll find the 64-bit driver store in the %SystemRoot%\System32\DriverStore folder and the 32-bit driver store in the %SystemRoot%\SysWOW64\DriverStore folder. The DriverStore folder also contains subfolders for localized driver information. You'll find a subfolder for each language component configured on the system. For example, for localized US English driver information, you'll find a subfolder called en-US.

Every device driver in the driver store is certified to be fully compatible with Windows 8.1 and is digitally signed by Microsoft to assure the operating system of its authenticity. When you install a new device that is Plug and Play–compatible, Windows 8.1 checks the driver store for a compatible device driver. If one is found, the operating system automatically installs the device.

Every device driver has an associated Setup Information file. This file ends with the .inf extension and is a text file containing detailed configuration information about the device being installed. The information file also identifies any source files used by the driver. Source files have the .sys extension. You might also find .pnf and .dll files for drivers, and some drivers have associated component manifest (.amx) files. The manifest file is written in XML, includes details about the driver's digital signature, and might also include Plug and Play information used by the device to automatically configure itself.

Every driver installed on a system has a source (.sys) file in the Drivers folder. When you install a new device driver, the driver is written to a subfolder of the Drivers folder, and configuration settings are stored in the registry. The driver's .inf file is used to control the installation and write the registry settings. If the driver doesn't already exist in the driver store, it does not already have an .inf file or other related files on the system. In this case, the driver's .inf file and other related files are written to a subfolder of DriverStore\FileRepository when you install the device.

Using signed and unsigned device drivers

Every device driver in the driver cache is digitally signed, which indicates that the driver has passed extensive testing by the Windows Hardware Quality Lab. A device driver with a digital signature from Microsoft should not cause your system to crash or become unstable. The presence of a digital signature from Microsoft also ensures that the device driver hasn't been tampered with. If a device driver doesn't have a digital signature from Microsoft, it hasn't been approved for use through testing, or its files might have been modified from the original installation by another program. This means that unsigned drivers are much more likely than any other program you've installed to cause the operating system to freeze or the computer to crash.

To prevent problems with unsigned drivers, Windows 8.1 warns you by default when you try to install an unsigned device driver. Windows can also be configured to prevent installation of certain types of devices. To manage device driver settings for computers throughout an organization, you can use Group Policy. When you do this, Group Policy specifies whether and how devices can be installed.

You can configure device installation settings on a per-computer basis by using the Administrative Templates policies for Computer Configuration under System \Device Installation.

> **TIP** If you're trying to install a device and find that you can't, device installation restrictions might be in place in Group Policy. You must override Group Policy to install the device.

Tracking driver information

Each driver being used on a system has a driver file associated with it. You can view the location of the driver file and related details by completing the following steps:

1. Start Computer Management. In the Computer Management console, expand the System Tools node.

2. Select Device Manager. You should now get a complete list of devices installed on the system. By default, this list is organized by device type.

3. Press and hold or right-click the device you want to manage, and then tap or click Properties. The Properties dialog box for that device opens.

4. On the Driver tab, tap or click Driver Details to display the Driver File Details dialog box. As shown in Figure 8-16, the following information is displayed:

- **Driver Files** The full file paths to locations where the driver files exist
- **Provider** The creator of the driver
- **File Version** The version of the file

Driver File Details

Intel(R) WiFi Link 5100 AGN

Driver files:

C:\Windows\system32\DRIVERS\NETwNs64.sys
C:\Windows\system32\drivers\vwifibus.sys

Provider:	Intel Corporation
File version:	14.2.1.2
Copyright:	Copyright © Intel Corporation 2009
Digital Signer:	Microsoft Windows

OK

FIGURE 8-16 The Driver File Details dialog box displays information on the driver file paths, the provider, and the file versions.

Installing and updating device drivers

To keep devices operating smoothly, it's essential that you keep the device drivers current. You install and update drivers by using the Found New Hardware, Add Hardware, and Update Driver Software Wizards. By default, these wizards can search for updated device drivers in the following locations:

- The local computer
- A hardware installation disc
- The Windows Update site or your organization's Windows Update server

In Group Policy, several policies control how information about devices is obtained and how Windows searches for drivers:

- **Turn Off Access To All Windows Update Features under Computer Configuration\Administrative Templates\System\Internet Communication Management\Internet Communication Settings** If this policy setting is enabled, all Windows Update features are blocked and not available to users. Users will also be unable to access the Windows Update website.

- **Turn Off Windows Update Device Driver Searching under Computer Configuration\Administrative Templates\System\Internet Communication Management\Internet Communication Settings** By default, Windows Update searching is optional when a device is being installed. If you enable this setting, Windows Update will not be searched when a new device is installed. If you disable this setting, Windows Update will always be searched when a new device is installed if no local drivers are present.

- **Specify Search Order For Device Driver Source Locations under Computer Configuration\Administrative Templates\System\Device Installation** If you disable or do not configure this policy setting, you can set the source location search order for device drivers on each computer. If you enable this policy, you can specify that Windows Update should be searched first, last, or not at all when driver software is being located during device installation.

- **Configure Device Installation Time-Out under Computer Configuration \Administrative Templates\System\Device Installation** If you disable or do not configure this policy, Windows 8.1 waits five minutes for a device installation task to complete before terminating the installation. If you enable this policy, you can specify the amount of time Windows 8.1 waits before terminating the installation.

- **Prevent Device Metadata Retrieval From The Internet under Computer Configuration\Administrative Templates\System\Device Installation** If you disable or do not configure this policy, Windows 8.1 retrieves device metadata for installed devices from the Internet and uses the information to help keep devices up to date. If you enable this policy setting, Windows 8.1 does not retrieve device metadata for installed devices from the Internet.

You can install and update device drivers by completing the following steps:

1. Start Computer Management. In the Computer Management console, expand the System Tools node.

2. Select Device Manager in the Computer Management console. You should get a complete list of devices installed on the system. By default, this list is organized by device type.

3. Press and hold or right-click the device you want to manage, and then tap or click Update Driver Software. This starts the Update Driver Software Wizard.

> **BEST PRACTICES** Updated drivers can add functionality to a device, improve performance, and resolve device problems. However, you should rarely install the latest drivers on a user's computer without testing them in a test environment. Test first, then install.

4. As shown in Figure 8-17, you can specify whether to install the drivers automatically or manually by selecting the driver from a list or specific location.

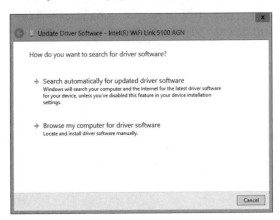

FIGURE 8-17 Choose whether to install a driver automatically or manually.

5. If you elect to install the driver automatically, Windows 8.1 looks for a more recent version of the device driver and installs the driver if it finds one. If a more recent version of the driver is not found, Windows 8.1 keeps the current driver. In either case, tap or click Close to complete the process, and then skip the remaining steps.

6. If you choose to install the driver manually, you can do the following:

   - **Search for the driver.** Tap or click Browse My Computer For Driver Software to select a search location. Use the Browse... dialog box to select the start folder for the search, and then tap or click OK. If you select Include Subfolders, you might have better results. With this option selected, all subfolders of the selected folder are searched automatically, and you could then select the drive root path, such as C, to search an entire drive.

   - **Choose the driver to install.** Tap or click Let Me Pick From A List Of Device Drivers On My Computer. The wizard then shows a list of compatible hardware. Tap or click the device that matches your hardware. To view a wider array of choices, clear the Show Compatible Hardware check box. You'll get a full list of manufacturers for the type of device with which you are working. As shown in Figure 8-18, you can scroll through the list of manufacturers to find the manufacturer of the device, and then select the appropriate device in the right pane.

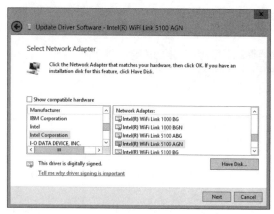

FIGURE 8-18 Select the appropriate device driver for the device you're adding.

NOTE If the manufacturer or device you want to use isn't listed, insert your device driver disc, and then tap or click Have Disk. Complete the process by following the prompts.

7. After selecting a device driver through a search or a manual selection, continue through the installation process by tapping or clicking Next. Tap or click Close when the driver installation is complete. If the wizard can't find an appropriate driver, you need to obtain one and then repeat this procedure. Keep in mind that in some cases, you need to restart the system to activate the newly installed or updated device driver.

Installing a device by using the generic USB driver

When you connect a USB device that doesn't have a custom driver, Windows might use the generic Winusb.sys driver to install the device automatically. If this driver isn't used automatically, you can manually select this driver by completing the following steps:

1. In Device Manager, press and hold or right-click the device you want to install, and then select Update Driver Software.

2. In the Update Driver Software Wizard, select Browse My Computer For Driver Software.

3. Select Let Me Pick From A List Of Device Drivers On My Computer.

4. In the Model list, select USB Input Device and then tap or click Next. Select Close when the driver installation is complete.

Enabling and disabling types of devices

By using Group Policy preferences, you can manage which hardware devices can be used on computers to which a GPO applies. You manage devices by enabling or disabling them according to the following specifications:

- **Device class**   A device class encompasses a broad range of similar devices, such as all DVD drives.

- **Device type**   A device type applies to specific devices within a device class, such as the NEC DVD-ROM RW ND-3530A ATA device.

NOTE If you want to manage devices by type, you need to configure a management computer with the devices you plan to work with and then create the preference items on that computer. A management computer is a computer with management options installed, including the Remote Server Administrator Tools (RSAT).

To create a preference item to enable or disable devices by class or type, follow these steps:

1. Open a GPO for editing in the Group Policy Management Editor. To configure preferences for computers, expand Computer Configuration\Preferences \Control Panel Settings, and then select Devices. To configure preferences for users, expand User Configuration\Preferences\Control Panel Settings, and then select Devices.

2. Press and hold or right-click the Devices node, point to New, and then tap or click Device. This opens the New Device Properties dialog box.

3. In the New Device Properties dialog box, select one of the following options in the Action list:

   - **Use This Device (Enable)**   Choose this option if you want to enable devices by class or type.

   - **Do Not Use This Device (Disable)**   Choose this option if you want to disable devices by class or type.

4. Tap or click the Options button to the right of Device Class, and then do one of the following:

   - Select a device class to manage devices by class.

   - Expand a device class node, and then select a device type to manage devices by type.

5. Use the options on the Common tab to control how the preference is applied. Because you are enforcing a control, you will generally want to apply the setting every time Group Policy is refreshed. In this case, do not select Apply Once And Do Not Reapply.

6. Tap or click OK. The next time policy is refreshed, the preference item will be applied as appropriate for the GPO in which you defined the preference item.

Restricting device installation by using Group Policy

In addition to enforcing code signing and search restrictions, Group Policy settings can be used to enable or prevent installation of devices based on device class. Devices that are set up and configured in the same way are grouped into a device setup class. Each device setup class has a globally unique identifier (GUID) associated with it. To restrict devices by using Group Policy, you need to know the GUID for the device setup class that you want to restrict.

The registry contains a key for each standard device setup class under HKEY_LOCAL_MACHINE\SYSTEM\CurrentControlSet\Control\Class. The registry keys are named according to the class GUID. When you select a class GUID registry key, the Class value specifies the device setup class that the GUID identifies. For example, if you select {4d36e965-e325-11ce-bfc1-08002be10318}, you'll find that the device setup class is for CD-ROM devices.

The policy settings for managing device installation are found under Computer Configuration\Administrative Templates\System\Device Installation\Device Installation Restrictions and include the following:

- Allow Administrators To Override Device Installation Restriction Policies
- Allow Installation Of Devices That Match Any Of These Device IDs
- Allow Installation Of Devices Using Drivers That Match These Device Setup Classes
- Prevent Installation Of Devices Not Described By Other Policy Settings
- Prevent Installation Of Devices That Match Any Of These Device IDs
- Prevent Installation Of Removable Devices
- Time (In Seconds) To Force Reboot When Required For Policy Changes To Take Effect

You can configure these policies by completing the following steps:

1. Open a GPO for editing in the Group Policy Management Editor.

2. Expand Computer Configuration\Administrative Templates\System\Device Installation\Device Installation Restrictions.

3. Double-tap or double-click the appropriate policy to view its Properties dialog box.

4. Set the state of the policy as Not Configured if you don't want the policy to be applied, Enabled if you want the policy to be applied, or Disabled if you want to block the policy from being used (all as permitted by the Group Policy configuration).

5. If you are enabling the policy and it has a Show option, tap or click Show to use the Show Contents dialog box to specify which device IDs should be matched to this policy, and then tap or click OK. In the Registry Editor, the

GUID for a device setup class is the entire key name, including the braces ({ and }). You can copy the key name and paste it into the Show Contents dialog box by following these steps:

   a. Open the Registry Editor. One way to do this is by pressing the Windows key, typing **regedit**, and then pressing Enter. This works so long as the Apps Search box is in focus.

   b. In the Registry Editor, press and hold or right-click the key name, and then select Copy Key Name.

   c. In the Show Contents dialog box, tap or click twice in the Value box so that the cursor changes to an insertion point. Press and hold or right-click, and then tap or click Paste.

   d. Delete the path that precedes the GUID value. The value you delete should be HKEY_LOCAL_MACHINE\SYSTEM\CurrentControlSet\Control \Class\.

   e. If you want to add the GUID for another device setup class, repeat steps b–d.

6. Tap or click OK.

Rolling back drivers

Sometimes you'll find that a device driver you installed causes device failure or other critical problems on a system. Don't worry: you can recover the system and use the previously installed device driver by following these steps:

1. If you are having problems starting the system, you need to start the system in safe mode as discussed in the section "Troubleshooting startup and shutdown" in Chapter 10.

2. Start Computer Management. In the Computer Management console, expand the System Tools node.

3. Select Device Manager in the Computer Management console. You should now get a complete list of devices installed on the system. By default, this list is organized by device type.

4. Press and hold or right-click the device you want to manage, and then tap or click Properties. This opens the Properties dialog box for the device.

5. Tap or click the Driver tab, and then tap or click Roll Back Driver. When prompted to confirm the action, tap or click Yes.

6. Tap or click OK to close the device's Properties dialog box.

NOTE If the driver file hasn't been updated, a backup driver file won't be available. In this case, the Roll Back Driver button will be inactive.

Removing device drivers for removed devices

Usually when you remove a device from a system, Windows 8.1 detects this action and automatically removes the drivers for that device. However, sometimes when you remove a device, Windows 8.1 doesn't detect the change, and you must remove the drivers manually. You can remove device drivers by completing the following steps:

1. Start Computer Management. In the Computer Management console, expand to the System Tools node.

2. Select Device Manager in the Computer Management console.

3. Press and hold or right-click the device you want to remove, and then tap or click Uninstall.

4. When prompted to confirm the action, tap or click OK.

Uninstalling, reinstalling, and disabling device drivers

Uninstalling a device driver uninstalls the related device. When a device isn't working properly, sometimes you can completely uninstall the device, restart the system, and then reinstall the device driver to restore normal operations. You can uninstall and then reinstall a device by completing the following steps:

1. Start Computer Management. In the Computer Management console, expand the System Tools node.

2. Select Device Manager in the Computer Management console. You should get a complete list of devices installed on the system. By default, this list is organized by device type.

3. Press and hold or right-click the device you want to manage, and then tap or click Uninstall.

4. When prompted to confirm the action, tap or click OK.

5. Restart the system. Windows 8.1 should detect the presence of the device and automatically reinstall the necessary device driver. If the device isn't automatically reinstalled, reinstall it manually, as discussed in the section "Installing and updating device drivers," earlier in the chapter.

To prevent a device from being reinstalled automatically, disable the device instead of uninstalling it. You disable a device by pressing and holding or right-clicking it in Device Manager, and then tapping or clicking Disable.

Enabling and disabling hardware devices

When a device isn't working properly, you might want to uninstall or disable it. Uninstalling a device removes the driver association for the device, so it temporarily appears that the device has been removed from the system. The next time you restart the system, Windows 8.1 might try to reinstall the device. Typically, Windows 8.1 reinstalls Plug and Play devices automatically, but it does not automatically reinstall non–Plug and Play devices.

Disabling a device turns it off and prevents Windows 8.1 from using it. Because a disabled device doesn't use system resources, you can be sure that it isn't causing a conflict on the system.

You can uninstall or disable a device by completing the following steps:

1. Start Computer Management. In the Computer Management console, expand the System Tools node.

2. Choose Device Manager in the Computer Management console. You should get a complete list of devices installed on the system. By default, this list is organized by device type.

3. Press and hold or right-click the device you want to manage, and then choose one of the following options:

   - Uninstall
   - Disable

4. If prompted to confirm the action, tap or click Yes or OK as appropriate.

Troubleshooting hardware

Built-in drivers diagnostics in Windows 8.1 can detect many types of problems with hardware devices. If a problem is detected, you might get a Problem Reporting balloon telling you there is a problem. Tapping or clicking this balloon opens Action Center. Action Center can also be accessed in Control Panel by tapping or clicking the System And Security link and then selecting Action Center.

Whenever a device is installed incorrectly or has another problem, Device Manager displays a warning icon indicating that the device has a problem. If you double-tap or double-click the device, an error code is displayed on the General tab of the device's Properties dialog box. As Table 8-3 shows, this error code can be helpful when trying to solve device problems. Most of the correction actions assume that you've selected the General tab in the device's Properties dialog box.

TABLE 8-3 Common device errors and techniques to resolve them

ERROR MESSAGE	CORRECTION ACTION
This device is not configured correctly. (Code 1)	Obtain a compatible driver for the device, and then tap or click the Update Driver button on the Driver tab to start the Update Driver Software Wizard.
The driver for this device might be corrupted, or your system might be running low on memory or other resources. (Code 3)	Tap or click the Update Driver button on the Driver tab to run the Update Driver Software Wizard. You might get an Out of Memory message at startup because of this error.
This device cannot start. (Code 10)	Tap or click the Update Driver button on the Driver tab to run the Update Driver Software Wizard. Don't try to automatically find a driver. Instead, choose the manual install option, and then select the device.
This device cannot find enough free resources that it can use. (Code 12)	Resources assigned to this device conflict with another device, or the firmware is incorrectly configured. Check the firmware, and check for resource conflicts on the Resources tab in the device's Properties dialog box.
This device cannot work properly until you restart your computer. (Code 14)	Typically, the driver is installed correctly, but it will not be started until you restart the computer.
Windows cannot identify all the resources this device uses. (Code 16)	Check whether a signed driver is available for the device. If one is available and you've already installed it, you might need to manage the resources for the device. Check the Resources tab in the device's Properties dialog box.
Reinstall the drivers for this device. (Code 18)	After an upgrade, you might need to log on as an administrator to complete device installation. If this is not the case, tap or click Update Driver on the Driver tab to reinstall the driver.
Your registry might be corrupted. (Code 19)	Remove and reinstall the device. This should clear out incorrect or conflicting registry settings.
Windows is removing this device. (Code 21)	The system will remove the device. The registry might be corrupted. If the device continues to display this message, restart the computer.
This device is disabled. (Code 22)	This device has been disabled by using Device Manager. To enable it, tap or click the Enable button on the Driver tab of the device's Properties dialog box.

ERROR MESSAGE	CORRECTION ACTION
This device is not present, is not working properly, or does not have all its drivers installed. (Code 24)	This might indicate a bad device or bad hardware. This error code can also occur with legacy devices; upgrade the driver to resolve.
The drivers for this device are not installed. (Code 28)	Obtain a compatible driver for the device, and then tap or click Update Driver to start the Update Driver Software Wizard.
This device is disabled because the firmware of the device did not give it the required resources. (Code 29)	Check the device documentation on how to assign resources. You might need to upgrade the firmware or enable the device in the system firmware.
This device is not working properly because Windows cannot load the drivers required for this device. (Code 31)	The device driver might be incompatible with Windows 8.1. Obtain a compatible driver for the device, and then tap or click Update Driver to start the Update Driver Software Wizard.
A driver for this device was not required and has been disabled. (Code 32)	A dependent service for this device has been set to Disabled. Check the event logs to determine which services should be enabled and started.
Windows cannot determine which resources are required for this device. (Code 33)	This might indicate a bad device or bad hardware. This error code can also occur with legacy devices; upgrade the driver and/or refer to the device documentation on how to set resource usage.
Windows cannot determine the settings for this device. (Code 34)	The legacy device must be manually configured. Verify the device jumpers or firmware settings, and then configure the device resource usage by using the Resources tab in the device's Properties dialog box.
Your computer's system firmware does not include enough information to properly configure and use this device. (Code 35)	This error occurs on multiprocessor systems. Update the firmware; check for a firmware option to use multiprocessor specification (MPS) 1.1 or MPS 1.4. Usually you want MPS 1.4.
This device is requesting a PCI interrupt but is configured for an ISA interrupt (or vice versa). (Code 36)	Legacy device interrupts are not shareable. If a device is in a PCI slot, but the slot is configured in firmware as reserved for a legacy device, this error might be displayed. Change the firmware settings.

ERROR MESSAGE	CORRECTION ACTION
Windows cannot initialize the device driver for this hardware. (Code 37)	Run the Update Driver Software Wizard by tapping or clicking the Update Driver button on the Driver tab.
Windows cannot load the device driver for this hardware because a previous instance of the device driver is still in memory. (Code 38)	A device driver in memory is causing a conflict. Restart the computer.
Windows cannot load the device driver for this hardware. The driver might be corrupted or missing. (Code 39)	Check to be sure that the hardware device is properly installed and connected and that it has power. If it is properly installed and connected, look for an updated driver or reinstall the current driver.
Windows cannot access this hardware because its service key information in the registry is missing or recorded incorrectly. (Code 40)	The registry entry for the device driver is invalid. Reinstall the driver.
Windows successfully loaded the device driver for this hardware but cannot find the hardware device. (Code 41)	If the device was removed, uninstall the driver, reinstall the device, and then, on the Action menu, tap or click Scan For Hardware Changes to reinstall the driver. If the device was not removed or doesn't support Plug and Play, obtain a new or updated driver for the device. To install non–Plug and Play devices, use the Add Hardware Wizard. In Device Manager, tap or click Action, and then tap or click Add Legacy Hardware.
Windows cannot load the device driver for this hardware because there is a duplicate device already running in the system. (Code 42)	A duplicate device was detected. This error occurs when a bus driver incorrectly creates two identically named devices, or when a device with a serial number is discovered in a new location before it is removed from the old location. Restart the computer to resolve this problem.
Windows has stopped this device because it has reported problems. (Code 43)	The device was stopped by the operating system. You might need to uninstall and then reinstall the device. The device might have problems with the no-execute processor feature. In this case, check for a new driver.

ERROR MESSAGE	CORRECTION ACTION
An application or service has shut down this hardware device. (Code 44)	The device was stopped by an application or service. Restart the computer. The device might have problems with the no-execute processor feature. In this case, check for a new driver.
Currently, this hardware device is not connected to the computer. (Code 45)	When you start Device Manager with the environment variable DEVMGR_SHOW_NONPRESENT_ DEVICES set to 1, any previously attached devices that are not present are displayed in the device list and assigned this error code. To clear the message, attach the device to the computer or start Device Manager without setting this environment variable.
Windows cannot gain access to this hardware device because the operating system is in the process of shutting down. (Code 46)	The device is not available because the computer is shutting down. When the computer restarts, the device should be available.
Windows cannot use this hardware device because it has been prepared for safe removal, but it has not been removed from the computer. (Code 47)	If you pressed a physical eject button, you'll get this error when the device is ready for removal. To use the device again, unplug it and then plug it in again, or restart the computer.
The software for this device has been blocked from starting because it is known to have problems with Windows. Contact the hardware vendor for a new driver. (Code 48)	The driver for this device is incompatible with Windows and has been prevented from loading. Obtain and install a new or updated driver from the hardware vendor.
Windows cannot start new hardware devices because the system hive is too large (exceeds the Registry Size Limit). (Code 49)	The system hive has exceeded its maximum size and new devices cannot work until the size is reduced. Devices that are no longer attached to the computer but are still listed in the system hive might cause this error. Try uninstalling any hardware devices that you are no longer using.

CHAPTER 9

Handling maintenance and support tasks

- Managing automatic updates **299**
- Detecting and resolving Windows 8.1 errors **311**
- Scheduling maintenance tasks **313**

Throughout this book, I've discussed support and troubleshooting techniques that you can use to administer Windows 8.1. In this chapter, you'll learn techniques for improving the support of computers regardless of their location and for recovering from specific types of problems. I'll start with a look at automatic updates, and then look at how you can detect and resolve Windows errors. Also, don't forget about the Steps Recorder (Psr.exe). As discussed in Chapter 6, "Managing remote access to workstations," you can use this tool to capture details related to the exact problem a user is having without needing access to the user's computer.

Managing automatic updates

The standard automatic updating feature in Windows 8.1 is called Windows Update. Not only is Windows Update used to update the operating system, it's also used to update programs that ship with the operating system and hardware device drivers. The sections that follow discuss how Windows Update works, and how it can be used to help keep a computer up to date.

Windows Update: the essentials

Windows Update is a client component that connects periodically to a designated server and checks for updates. After it determines that updates are available, it can be configured to download and install the updates automatically or to notify users and administrators that updates are available. The server component to which Windows Update connects is either the Windows Update website hosted by Microsoft or a designated Windows Update Services (WSUS) server hosted by your organization.

Windows Update supports distribution and installation of the following:

- **Critical updates** Updates that are determined to be critical for the stability and safeguarding of a computer
- **Security updates** Updates that are designed to make the system more secure
- **Update roll-ups** Updates that include other updates
- **Service packs** Comprehensive updates to the operating system and its components, which typically include critical updates, security updates, and update roll-ups
- **Optional updates** Updates that might be useful, including updates for drivers and firmware

NOTE By default, Windows Update gets updates for drivers from the Windows Update website. You can also specify that you want Windows Update to search the Windows Server Update Services managed server for driver updates, or to first search the Windows Server Update Services managed server, but if no update is found there, then search Windows Update. To do this, enable and configure the Specify The Search Server For Device Driver Updates policy in the Administrative Templates policies for Computer Configuration under System\Device Installation. Select Search Managed Server or Search Managed Server and then WU, as appropriate.

A key part of the extended functionality enables Windows Update to prioritize downloads so that updates can be applied in order of criticality; therefore, the most critical updates will be downloaded and installed before less critical updates. You can also control how a computer checks for and installs new updates. The default polling interval used to check for new updates is 22 hours. Through Group Policy, you can change this interval. By default, every day at 2:00 A.M. local time, computers install updates they've downloaded. You can modify the installation to require notification or change the install times.

Windows 8.1 reduces the number of restarts required after updates by allowing a new version of an updated file to be installed even if the old file is currently being used by an application or system component. To do this, Windows 8.1 marks the in-use file for update, and then automatically replaces the file the next time the application is started. With some applications and components, Windows 8.1 can save the application's data, close the application, update the file, and then restart the application. As a result, the update process has less impact on users.

REAL WORLD Automatic updating uses the Background Intelligent Transfer Service (BITS) to transfer files. BITS is a service that performs background transfers of files and enables interrupted transfers to be restarted. BITS version 4.0, which is included with Windows 8.1, improves the transfer mechanism so that bandwidth is used more efficiently, which in turn means that less data is transferred and the transfer is faster. Through Group Policy, BITS can be configured to download updates only during specific times and to limit the amount of bandwidth used. You configure these and other settings by using the Set Up A Work Schedule To Limit The Maximum Network Bandwidth Used For BITS Background Transfers policy. This policy is found in the Administrative Templates policies for Computer Configuration under Network\Background

Intelligent Transfer Service (BITS) in Group Policy. Additionally, by using BITS 4.0, Windows 8.1 can obtain updates from trusted peers across a local area network (LAN), as well as from an update server or from Microsoft directly. After a peer has a copy of an update, other computers on the local network can automatically detect this and download the update directly from the peer, meaning a required update might need to be transferred across the wide area network (WAN) only once rather than dozens or hundreds of times.

You can use automatic updating in several different ways. You can configure systems by using the following options:

- **Install Updates Automatically** With this option, the operating system retrieves all updates at a configurable interval (22 hours by default) and then installs the updates at a scheduled time, which by default is every day at 2:00 A.M. Users are not required to accept updates before they are installed. Updates are instead downloaded automatically and then installed according to a specific schedule, which can be once a day at a particular time or once a week on a particular day and time.

- **Download Updates But Let Me Choose Whether To Install Them** With this option (the default), the operating system retrieves all updates as they become available, and then prompts the user when the updates are ready to be installed. The user can then accept or reject each update. Accepted updates are installed. Rejected updates are not installed, but they remain on the system so that they can be installed later.

- **Check For Updates But Let Me Choose Whether To Download And Install Them** With this option, the operating system notifies the user before retrieving any updates. If the user elects to download the updates, she still has the opportunity to accept or reject them. Accepted updates are installed, whereas rejected updates are not installed; however, they remain on the system so that they can be installed later.

- **Never Check For Updates** When automatic updates are disabled, users are not notified about updates. Users can, however, download updates manually from the Windows Update website.

When Windows Update is configured for automatic download and installation, users are minimally notified of update availability or installation. You can get more information about an update by tapping or clicking a notification on the taskbar.

Restoring payloads and components via Windows Update

Windows can use Windows Update in several additional ways:

- Windows Update is used to restore removed payloads.
- Windows Update is used to reinstall corrupted components.

Binaries needed to install features of Windows are referred to as *payloads*. On servers running Windows Server 2012, not only can you uninstall an optional feature, but you can also uninstall and remove the payload for that optional feature by using the -Remove parameter of the Uninstall-WindowsFeature cmdlet.

You can install a feature and restore its payload by using the Install-WindowsFeature cmdlet. By default, payloads are restored via Windows Update. To specify alternate source file paths, you can enable and configure the Specify Settings For Optional Component Installation And Component Repair policy in the Administrative Templates policies for Computer Configuration under System. With this policy you can also specify that you never want to download payloads from Windows Update.

Alternate paths can be shared folders or Windows Imaging (WIM) files. Separate each alternate path with a semicolon. With WIM files, specify the Universal Naming Convention (UNC) path to the shared folder containing the WIM file and the index of the image to use with the following syntax.

```
wim:\\ServerName\ShareName\ImageFileName.wim:Index
```

Here, *ServerName* is the name of the server, *ShareName* is the name of the shared folder, *ImageFileName.wim* is the name of the WIM file, and *Index* is the index of the image to use, such as

```
wim:\\CorpServer62\Images\install.wim:2
```

If an operating system component is corrupted and Windows 8.1 detects this, the content required to repair the component can be downloaded from Windows Update. By default, the component update is done via Windows Server Update Services (WSUS), if available. By enabling and configuring the Specify Settings For Optional Component Installation And Component Repair policy, you can specify an alternate source file path. You can also specify that you want Windows Update to get the update directly from the Windows Update website, rather than going through WSUS.

Configuring automatic updating

Windows 8.1 organizes updates into the following broad categories:

- **Important updates**   Includes critical updates, security updates, update roll-ups, and service packs for the operating system and programs that ship with the operating system
- **Recommended updates**   Includes updates to drivers that are provided with the operating system and recommended optional updates
- **Microsoft product updates**   Includes updates for other Microsoft products that are installed on the computer, in addition to new optional Microsoft software
- **Point and print drivers**   Includes updates to drivers that provide client-side rendering capability
- **Firmware updates**   Includes updates to firmware for tablets and other devices (but generally does not apply to PCs)

NOTE   By default, Windows Update includes updates to web compatibility lists from Microsoft. Sites listed are displayed in Compatibility view automatically. You can configure this feature by using the Include Updated Website Lists From Microsoft policy setting. In Group Policy, this setting is located in the Administrative Templates policies for Computer Configuration under Windows Components\Internet Explorer\Compatibility View.

REAL WORLD When you are using a standard edition of Windows 8.1, Windows Update continues to search for compatible point and print drivers if it fails to find any on the computer itself or on the Windows Update site. If the computer does not find a match, it attempts to create a mismatch connection by using any available driver that supports the hardware. However, when you are using enterprise editions of Windows 8.1, you must explicitly enable the Extend Point And Print Connection To Search Windows Update policy to obtain the same behavior. This policy is found in Administrative Templates policies for Computer Configuration, under Printers.

Windows periodically checks to determine if updates are available whenever the computer has a connection to the Internet. Available updates are automatically downloaded in the background, provided the computer isn't on a metered Internet connection. By default, Windows 8.1 is configured to automatically install important updates during the maintenance window. Note that if installing updates is allowed and an update for Windows Update is present, Windows Update will update itself prior to checking for other updates.

You can configure automatic updates on a per-computer basis by completing the following steps:

1. In Control Panel, tap or click System And Security. Under Windows Update, tap or click Turn Automatic Updating On Or Off.

2. Use the selection list provided to specify whether and how updates should occur (as shown in Figure 9-1).

3. If you've enabled updates and also want to install drivers and optional updates, select the Give Me Recommended Updates The Same Way I Receive Important Updates check box.

4. Tap or click OK.

FIGURE 9-1 Configure Windows Update.

By using an extension component called Microsoft Update, you can extend Windows Update to include updates for other Microsoft products that are installed on the computer, in addition to new optional Microsoft software. When you install some Microsoft products, including Microsoft Office, Microsoft Update can be downloaded and installed automatically as part of the setup process.

You can determine whether a computer is using Microsoft Update by following these steps:

1. In Control Panel, tap or click System And Security, and then tap or click Windows Update.

2. If the computer is configured to use Microsoft Update, you'll get the following message in the lower portion of the page:

   ```
   You receive updates: For Windows and other products from Microsoft
   Update.
   ```

You can install Microsoft Update by completing the following steps:

1. In Control Panel, tap or click System And Security, and then tap or click Windows Update.

2. In the panel that says Get Updates For Other Products, click the related Find Out More link. This opens the Windows Update page at the Microsoft website in the default browser.

3. After you read about Microsoft Update, select I Agree To The Terms Of Use, and then click Install.

4. So long as automatic updates are enabled, the computer will get updates for Microsoft products as part of the automatic update process. From then on, when you are working with Windows Update, you can enable or disable Microsoft updates by selecting or clearing the Give Me Updates For Other Microsoft Products When I Update Windows check box.

By default, Windows Update runs daily at 2:00 A.M. as part of other automatic maintenance. Windows Update uses the computer's power management features to wake the computer from hibernation or sleep at the scheduled update time and then install updates. Generally, this wake-up-and-install process will occur whether the computer is on battery or AC power.

If a restart is required to finalize updates applied as part of automatic maintenance and there is an active user session, Windows caches the credentials of the user currently logged on to the console and then restarts the computer automatically. After the restart, Windows uses the cached credentials to sign in as this user. Next, Windows restarts applications that were running previously, and then locks the session by using the Secure Desktop. If BitLocker is enabled, the entire process is also protected by BitLocker encryption.

NOTE To be clear, the maintenance process normally runs whether a user is logged on or not. If no user is logged on when scheduled maintenance begins and a restart is required, Windows restarts the computer without caching credentials or storing information about running applications. When Windows restarts, Windows does not log on as any user.

IMPORTANT Because Windows automatically wakes computers to perform automatic maintenance and updates, you'll also want to carefully consider the power options that are applied. Unless a power plan is configured to turn off the display and put the computer to sleep, the computer might remain powered on for many hours after automatic maintenance and updates.

You can change the restart behavior in several ways. If you don't want updates to be installed automatically, you can select another update option, such as Download Updates But Let Me Choose When to Install Them. If you disable Sign-in Last Interactive User Automatically After A System-Initiated Restart, Windows will restart the computer but will not log in the last interactive user. In Group Policy, this setting is under Computer Configuration\Windows Components\Windows Logon Options.

To change when automatic maintenance occurs, follow these steps:

1. In Control Panel, tap or click System And Security. Under Windows Update, tap or click Turn Automatic Updating On Or Off.

2. Tap or click the Updates Will Be Automatically Installed During The Maintenance Window link. Use the selection list provided to choose the preferred maintenance time, such as 5:00 AM (as shown in Figure 9-2).

3. You can elect to wake the computer to perform scheduled maintenance by selecting the related check box. Unlike earlier releases of Windows that only wake the computer when it is on AC power, Windows 8.1 will wake the computer whether the computer is running on battery or AC power.

4. Tap or click OK.

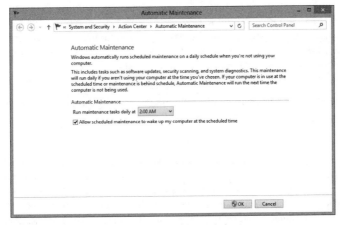

FIGURE 9-2 Manage the scheduled maintenance window.

If the computer is in use or powered off at the scheduled maintenance time, automatic maintenance normally will run the next time the computer is powered on and idle. Automatic maintenance also runs when the computer is powered on and idle if maintenance is behind schedule.

You'll find the following scheduled tasks related to automatic maintenance in the Task Scheduler Library, under Windows\TaskScheduler:

- **Regular Maintenance** Performs scheduled maintenance. When you change the maintenance schedule in Control Panel, Windows changes the run time for this task. This task runs whether a user is logged on or not and whether the computer is on AC or battery power. This task runs only when the computer is idle. If the computer isn't idle, the task runs as soon as possible after the scheduled start is missed.

- **Manual Maintenance** Manually triggers maintenance. In Action Center, you can manually start maintenance by selecting the Start Maintenance option on the Maintenance panel. Later, you can select the Stop Maintenance option to stop maintenance that you manually started. This task runs whether a user is logged on or not and whether the computer is on AC or battery power. Although this task runs only when the computer is idle, Windows 8.1 does not attempt to run the task as soon as possible after you start it.

- **Maintenance Configurator** Updates the configuration of the Regular Maintenance task when you change the maintenance schedule. This task runs whether a user is logged on or not and whether the computer is on AC or battery power. This task runs only when the computer is idle. If the computer isn't idle, the task runs as soon as possible after the scheduled start is missed.

- **Idle Maintenance** Triggers maintenance when the computer is idle. This task runs only when the computer is idle and running on AC power.

In an Active Directory domain, you can centrally configure and manage automatic updates by using the Administrative Templates policies for Computer Configuration under Windows Components\Windows Update. Table 9-1 summarizes the key policies and adds exceptions for a setting under User Configuration\Windows Components and a setting under Computer Configuration\Windows Components\Windows Logon Options. It's important to note that the following policy settings do not apply to Windows 8 or later:

- Enabling Windows Update Power Management To Automatically Wake Up The System To Install Scheduled Updates

- Re-Prompt For Restart With Scheduled Installations

TIP By using the Administrative Templates policies for Computer Configuration under Windows Components\Maintenance Scheduler, you can control the run schedule for automatic maintenance. The maintenance boundary is the daily scheduled time for starting automatic maintenance. For virtual machines running on a computer, Windows adds a random delay of up to 30 minutes. This delay is configurable as well.

TABLE 9-1 Policies for managing automatic updates

POLICY	FUNCTION
Allow Automatic Updates Immediate Installation	When enabled, this setting allows automatic updates to immediately install updates that do not interrupt Windows services or require the computer to be restarted. These updates are installed immediately after they are downloaded.
Allow Non-Administrators To Receive Update Notifications	When enabled, this setting allows any user logged on to a computer to receive update notifications as appropriate for the automatic updates configuration. If the setting is disabled or not configured, only administrators receive update notifications.
Always Automatically Restart At Scheduled Time	When the setting is enabled, Windows always restarts at the scheduled time even if a user is logged on to an active session.
Automatic Updates Detection Frequency	When enabled, this setting defines the interval to be used when checking for updates. By default, computers check approximately every 22 hours for updates. If you enable this policy and set a new interval, that interval will be used with a wildcard offset of up to 20 percent of the interval specified. This means that if you set an interval of 10 hours, the actual polling interval would depend on the computer and be between 8 and 10 hours.
Configure Automatic Updates	When you enable this setting, you can configure how automatic updates work by using similar options to those described earlier in this section. You can also include the installation as part of scheduled maintenance (if enabled). To do this, enable and configure the policies under Computer Configuration\Windows Components\Maintenance Scheduler.
Delay Restart For Scheduled Installations	By default, when a restart is required after an automatic update, the computer is restarted after a 15-minute delay. To use a different delay, enable this policy, and then set the delay time.

POLICY	FUNCTION
Enable Client-Side Targeting	When this setting is enabled and you've specified an intranet Microsoft update service location, an administrator can define a target group for the current Group Policy Object. With client-side targeting, administrators can control which updates are installed on specified groups of computers. Before an update is deployed, it must be authorized for a particular target group. The setting applies only when using an intranet Microsoft update service.
No Auto-Restart With Logged On Users For Scheduled Automatic Updates Installations	When enabled, this setting specifies that the computer will not automatically restart after installing updates that require a restart if a user is currently logged on. Instead, the user is notified that a restart is needed. Restarting the computer enforces the updates.
Remove Access To Use All Windows Update Features	When you enable this setting, all Windows Update features are removed. Users are blocked from accessing Windows Update, and automatic updating is completely disabled. (User Configuration policy)
Reschedule Automatic Updates Scheduled Installations	When enabled, this setting specifies the amount of time to wait after system startup before proceeding with a scheduled installation that was previously missed.
Sign-in Last Interactive User Automatically After A System-Initiated Restart	When this policy is disabled, Windows does not store the user's credentials for automatic sign-in after a Windows Update restart. (Windows Logon Options)
Specify Intranet Microsoft Update Service Location	When this setting is enabled, you can designate the fully qualified domain name of the Microsoft Update server hosted by your organization and of the related statistics server. Both services can be performed by one server.
Turn On Recommended Updates Via Automatic Updates	When this policy is enabled, recommended updates, including those for drivers and other optional updates, are installed along with important updates.

Checking for updates

The main Windows Update page provides details about the last time the computer or a user checked for updates, the last time updates were installed, and the current automatic update configuration. You can determine Windows Update usage or manually check for updates by following these steps:

1. In Control Panel, tap or click System And Security. Tap or click Windows Update. As shown in Figure 9-3, statistics are provided about the most recent check for updates, the last time updates were installed (even if not completely successful), and the current update configuration.

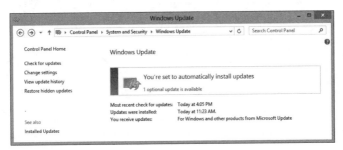

FIGURE 9-3 View update status.

2. If you want to manually check for updates, tap or click Check For Updates.

3. To install optional updates that might be available, tap or click the link that shows how many optional updates are available.

4. On the Select Updates To Install page, select the updates to install. When you select an update, as shown in Figure 9-4, you'll get additional information about the update, including the original release date, whether you'll need to restart the computer to complete the update, and whether the update is ready to be installed. Often, you'll also often have links to get additional information and support details.

5. Tap or click Install to install the selected updates. At any time, you can review the update history to determine which updates succeeded or failed. If a problem occurs and you want to uninstall an update, you can remove the update.

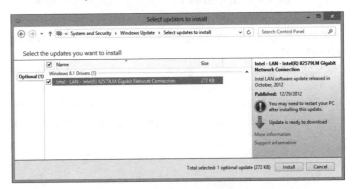

FIGURE 9-4 Select an update to get detailed information about the update.

Viewing update history and installed updates

The Windows Update download manager tracks both successful and failed updates by using an update history log. You can access this log by following these steps:

1. In Control Panel, tap or click System And Security. Tap or click Windows Update.

2. In the left panel, tap or click View Update History. This displays the View Update History page, shown in Figure 9-5.

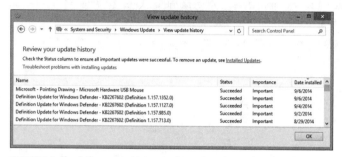

FIGURE 9-5 Check the update history to determine what updates have been installed.

On the View Update History page, updates listed with a Succeeded status were downloaded and installed. Updates listed with a Failed status were downloaded but failed to install. You also might get a status of Pending Restart or Canceled. Some updates can be completed only during startup of the operating system, and those updates will have a Pending Restart status. After the computer is restarted and the update is installed, the status will change as appropriate. The downloading of updates can be canceled for a variety of reasons. For example, users can cancel downloads of updates via Windows Update in Control Panel. Restarting the computer can cancel the download of an update as well.

To remove an update while accessing the View Update History page, tap or click Installed Updates. Then, on the Installed Updates page, press and hold or right-click the update that you do not want and tap or click Uninstall.

Removing automatic updates to recover from problems

If an automatic update causes a problem on a system, don't worry. You can remove an automatic update in the same way in which you uninstall any other program. Simply follow these steps:

1. In Control Panel, tap or click System And Security. Tap or click Windows Update.

2. Tap or click View Update History, and then tap or click Installed Updates.

3. To remove an update, select it in the list provided, and then tap or click Uninstall.

Hiding available updates

Over time, a user might accumulate a number of updates that were intentionally not installed but still appear on the list of updates available for installation. If you or the user has reviewed the update and you don't want to install it, you can hide the update by completing the following steps:

1. In Control Panel, tap or click System And Security. Tap or click Windows Update.
2. Tap or click the link telling you how many updates are available.
3. On the Select Updates To Install page, press and hold or right-click the update you do not want to install, and then tap or click Hide Update.

Restoring declined updates

If a user declines an update or has asked not to be notified about or install updates automatically, you can restore the updates so that they can be installed. To do this, complete the following steps:

1. In Control Panel, tap or click System And Security. Tap or click Windows Update.
2. Tap or click Restore Hidden Updates.
3. On the Restore Hidden Updates page, select an update you want to install, and then tap or click Restore.
4. Windows 8.1 will restore the update so that it can be selected and installed through the normal notification and installation process.

Detecting and resolving Windows 8.1 errors

Any particular computer can have dozens, and in some cases hundreds, of different components, services, and applications configured on it. Keeping all these components working properly is a big job, and the built-in diagnostics features discussed previously in this book do a good job of detecting common problems and finding solutions for them. As discussed in Chapter 8, "Managing hardware devices and drivers," known problems are tracked in the Problem Reports And Solutions console. Like the built-in diagnostic features, this console attempts to provide solutions to problems where possible. Not all problems can be automatically detected and resolved, and this is where the errors reported by Windows components, applications, services, and hardware devices become useful.

Using the event logs for error tracking and diagnosis

Windows 8.1 stores errors generated by processes, services, applications, and hardware devices in log files. Two general types of log files are used:

- **Windows logs** Logs used by the operating system to record general system events related to applications, security, setup, and system components
- **Applications and services logs** Logs used by specific applications or services to record application-specific or service-specific events

Entries in a log file are recorded according to the warning level of the activity. Entries can include errors in addition to general informational events. You'll get the following levels of entries:

- **Information**   An informational event, which is generally related to a successful action
- **Audit Success**   An event related to the successful execution of an action
- **Audit Failure**   An event related to the failed execution of an action
- **Warning**   A warning, details of which are often useful in preventing future system problems
- **Error**   An error, such as the failure of a service to start

In addition to level, date, and time, the summary and detailed event entries provide the following information:

- **Source**   The application, service, or component that logged the event.
- **Event ID**   An identifier for the specific event.
- **Task Category**   The category of the event, which is sometimes used to further describe the related action.
- **User**   The user account that was logged on when the event occurred. If a system process or service triggered the event, the user name is usually that of the special identity that caused the event, such as NetworkService, LocalService, or System.
- **Computer**   The name of the computer on which the event occurred.
- **Details**   In the detailed entries, this provides a text description of the event, followed by any related data or error output.

Viewing and managing the event logs

You can access event logs by using the Event Viewer node in Computer Management. To open Computer Management, from Control Panel, tap or click System And Security, Administrative Tools, and then Computer Management. Another way to open Computer Management is to press the Windows key, type **compmgmt.msc**, and then press Enter.

You can access the event logs by completing the following steps:

1. Open Computer Management. You are connected to the local computer by default. If you want to view logs on a remote computer, press and hold or right-click the Computer Management entry in the console tree (left pane), and then tap or click Connect To Another Computer. In the Select Computer dialog box, enter the name of the computer to which you want access, and then tap or click OK.

2. Expand the Event Viewer node, and then expand the Windows Logs node, the Application And Services Logs node, or both nodes to view the available logs.

3. Select the log that you want to view, as shown in Figure 9-6.

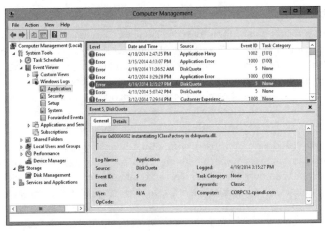

FIGURE 9-6 Event Viewer displays events for the selected log.

MORE INFO Pressing Windows key + X provides a shortcut menu for quickly accessing frequently used tools, including Computer Management and Event Viewer. After you open Event Viewer, you can connect to other computers by right-clicking the Event Viewer entry in the console tree (left pane), and then tapping or clicking Connect To Another Computer.

Warnings and errors are the two key types of events you'll want to examine. Whenever these types of events occur and you are unsure of the cause, double-tap or double-click the entry to view the detailed event description. Note the source of the error and attempt to resolve the problem by using the techniques discussed in this book. To learn more about the error and steps you can take to resolve it (if necessary), you can tap or click the Event Log Online link provided in the error description or search the Microsoft Knowledge Base for the event ID or part of the error description.

Scheduling maintenance tasks

When you manage desktop and laptop systems, you'll often want to perform routine maintenance tasks on a periodic or recurring basis. To do this, you can use the Task Scheduler service to schedule one-time or recurring tasks to run automatically. You automate tasks by running command-shell scripts, Windows Script Host (WSH) scripts, or applications that execute the necessary commands for you. Unlike earlier releases of Windows, Windows 8.1 includes an extensive library of preconfigured tasks. These tasks handle everything from uninstalling a Bluetooth device to defragmenting disks to performing Windows Defender scans.

Understanding task scheduling

Windows 8.1 provides several tools for scheduling tasks, including the Task Scheduler, the Schtasks command-line tool, and several Windows PowerShell cmdlets. You can use any of these tools for scheduling tasks on local and remote systems. The Task Scheduler includes several wizards for scheduling tasks that provide point-and-click interfaces for task assignment. Schtasks is the command-line counterpart. Windows PowerShell cmdlets available include New-ScheduledTask, New-ScheduledTaskAction, Set-ScheduledTask, Start-ScheduledTask, and Stop-ScheduledTask.

All of these scheduling tools use the Task Scheduler service to monitor the system clock and run tasks at specified times. The Task Scheduler service logs on as the LocalSystem account by default. This account usually doesn't have adequate permissions to perform administrative tasks. To overcome this problem, each task can be set to run as a specific user, and you set the user name and password to use when you create the task. Be sure to use an account that has adequate user privileges and access rights to run the tasks that you want to schedule.

NOTE The focus of this section is on the Task Scheduler. This is the primary tool you'll use to schedule tasks on Windows 8.1 systems. To learn more about Schtasks, enter **schtasks /?** at the command prompt.

Windows 8.1 has two general types of scheduled tasks:

- **Standard tasks** Used to automate routine tasks and perform housekeeping. These tasks are visible to users and can be modified if necessary.
- **Hidden tasks** Used to automate special system tasks. These tasks are hidden from users by default and should not be modified in most cases. Some hidden tasks are created and managed through a related program, such as Windows Defender.

In Windows 8.1, the creation and management of tasks is much more sophisticated than ever before. Every task can be configured to do the following:

- Run only when a user is logged on, or run regardless of whether a user is logged on
- Run with standard user privileges, or run with the highest privileges required (including administrator privileges)

Because tasks created on Windows 8 and later are not compatible with earlier releases of Windows, you cannot copy a Windows 8 or Windows 8.1 task to a computer running an earlier release of Windows and expect the task to run. However, when creating the task, you can specify that it should be created so that it is compatible with earlier releases of Windows so that you can use the task on computers running earlier releases of Windows.

Tasks can have many properties associated with them, including the following:

- **Triggers** Triggers specify the circumstances under which a task begins and ends. You can begin a task based on a schedule as well as on user logon, computer startup, or processor idling. You can also begin a task based on events, a user connecting or disconnecting from a Terminal Server session, or a user locking or unlocking a workstation. Tasks with event-based triggers can be the most powerful because they enable you to provide automated ways to handle errors and warnings.

- **Actions** Actions define the action a task performs when it is triggered. This allows a task to start programs, send email messages, or display messages.

- **Conditions** Conditions help qualify the conditions under which a task is started or stopped after it has been triggered. You can use conditions to wake the computer to run a task and to start the computer only if a specific network connection is available. You can use conditions to start, stop, and restart a task based on the processor idle time. For example, you might want to start a task only if the computer has been idle for at least 10 minutes, stop the task if the computer is no longer idle, and then restart the task again if the computer becomes idle once more. You can also use conditions to specify that a task should start only if the computer is on AC power and stop if the computer switches to battery power.

Windows 8.1 uses scheduled tasks to perform many routine maintenance tasks. Table 9-2 shows key tasks that are specific to Windows 8.1 PCs. Conditions and settings might be different for tablets and devices running Windows 8.1.

TABLE 9-2 Important tasks that are new for Windows 8.1

TASK NAME\TASK DESCRIPTION	RUNS ONLY WHEN IDLE	RUNS ONLY ON AC POWER	RUN AS SOON AS POSSIBLE IF MISSED	RUNS IF NO USER LOGGED ON
ApplicationData	Yes	Yes	Yes	Yes
When you start a program, Windows uses the Cleanup Temporary State task to clean up temporary files that were created the last time the program was used.				
AppxDeploymentClient	Yes	Yes	No	Yes
Windows uses the Pre-Staged App Cleanup task to clean up pre-staged apps whenever a user logs on or starts a pre-staged app.				

TASK NAME\TASK DESCRIPTION	RUNS ONLY WHEN IDLE	RUNS ONLY ON AC POWER	RUN AS SOON AS POSSIBLE IF MISSED	RUNS IF NO USER LOGGED ON
Data Integrity Scan When you use storage pools with Windows 8.1, Windows uses the related tasks to scan fault-tolerant volumes for latent corruptions and to perform fast crash recovery of fault-tolerant volumes.	No	Yes	Yes	Yes
FileHistory When the File History featured is configured, Windows uses this task to protect user files by copying them to a backup location.	No	Yes	No	Yes
SettingSync These tasks are used to sync Microsoft accounts. You'll find separate tasks for background uploads, backups, and tasking network state changes.	Yes	No	Varies by task	No
SkyDrive These tasks are used to sync Microsoft accounts. You'll find separate tasks for syncing general settings when idle and performing routine maintenance.	Yes	Yes	No	No
SpaceAgent SpaceAgentTask runs at startup and whenever you start SpaceAgent.exe. Windows uses this task to gather information about storage spaces being used.	Yes	No	No	Yes

TASK NAME\TASK DESCRIPTION	RUNS ONLY WHEN IDLE	RUNS ONLY ON AC POWER	RUN AS SOON AS POSSIBLE IF MISSED	RUNS IF NO USER LOGGED ON
Sysmain These tasks are used to maintain hybrid drives and to maintain the working set.	Yes	Varies by task	No	Yes
TPM These tasks are used to maintain a computer's TPM.	No	No	No	Yes
Work Folders These tasks are used to initiate synchronization of Work Folders when a user logs on and to perform related maintenance.	No	Varies by task	Varies by task	No

Viewing and managing tasks on local and remote systems

The current tasks configured on a system are accessible through the Task Scheduler node in Computer Management. Tasks are organized and grouped together by using a familiar folder structure, where base folders are named according to the operating system features, tools, and configuration areas to which they relate. Within a base folder, you'll find one or more related tasks.

You can view and manage the scheduled tasks configured on a computer by completing the following steps:

1. Open Computer Management. You are connected to the local computer by default. If you want to view tasks on a remote computer, press and hold or right-click the Computer Management entry in the console tree (left pane), and then tap or click Connect To Another Computer. In the Select Computer dialog box, enter the name of the computer that you want to access, and then tap or click OK.

2. Expand the Task Scheduler node, and then select the Task Scheduler Library node and view task status and active tasks as shown in Figure 9-7. The Task Status panel provides a summary of tasks running, stopped, and failed for a specified time period, which by default is the last 24 hours. The Active Tasks panel provides the name, next run time, run triggers, and location of all enabled tasks.

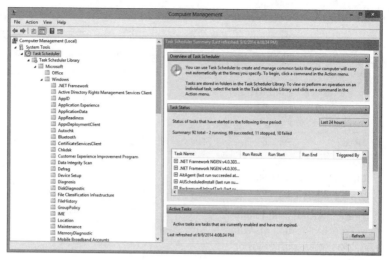

FIGURE 9-7 Select a task folder to view the related tasks.

3. When you select a task folder in the console tree, the first task in the folder is selected by default. If the folder has multiple tasks and you want to work with a different task, select that task instead.

4. When you've selected the task with which you want to work, you can view its properties by using the tabs shown in Figure 9-8. If you want to manage the task, press and hold or right-click the task in the main pane, and then do the following:

   - Tap or click Delete to delete a task.

   - Tap or click Disable to disable a task.

   - Tap or click Properties to edit the task's properties. Make the appropriate changes in the Properties dialog box, and then tap or click OK.

   - Tap or click Export to export a task to a file that can be imported on another computer. After you export the task, use Computer Management to connect to the other computer, press and hold or right-click the Task Scheduler Library node, and then tap or click Import Task. You can then use the Open dialog box to locate and open the task on the other computer.

   - Tap or click Run to run the task.

   - If the task is running, tap or click End to stop the task.

   NOTE Although you can modify and delete user-created tasks, most tasks created by the operating system cannot be configured or deleted. If operating system tasks are not shown, you can display these tasks by tapping or clicking View, and then selecting Show Hidden Tasks. Note also that when you are exporting tasks, the task's Configure For drop-down list setting determines the operating systems with which the task can be used.

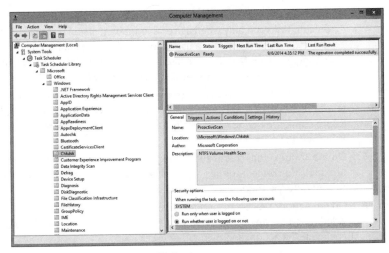

FIGURE 9-8 View and manage scheduled tasks.

You can view the scheduled tasks currently running on a computer by completing the following steps:

1. Open Computer Management. You are connected to the local computer by default. If you want to view tasks on a remote computer, press and hold or right-click the Computer Management entry in the console tree (left pane), and then tap or click Connect To Another Computer. In the Select Computer dialog box, enter the name of the computer that you want to access, and then tap or click OK.

2. Select the Task Scheduler node to read in its attributes. Press and hold or right-click the Task Scheduler node, and then select Display All Running Tasks.

Creating scheduled tasks

You can create a scheduled task by completing the following steps:

1. Open Computer Management. You are connected to the local computer by default. If you want to create tasks on a remote computer, press and hold or right-click the Computer Management entry in the console tree (left pane), and then tap or click Connect To Another Computer. In the Select Computer dialog box, enter the name of the computer that you want to access, and then tap or click OK.

2. Select and then press and hold or right-click the Task Scheduler node, and then tap or click Create Task. This starts the Create Task Wizard.

3. On the General tab, enter the name of the task, and then set security options for running the task:

   ■ If the task should run under a user account other than that of the current user, tap or click Change User Or Group. Use the Select User Or Group dialog box to select the user or group under which the task should run, and then provide the appropriate credentials when prompted later.

- Set other run options as necessary by using the options provided. By default, tasks run only when a user is logged on. If you want to run the task regardless of whether a user is logged on, select Run Whether User Is Logged On Or Not. You can also elect to run with highest privileges and configure the task for specified releases of Windows.

4. Use the Configure For list to choose the compatibility level. To configure the task for Windows 7 and later, choose **Windows 7, Windows Server 2008 R2**. To configure the task specifically for Windows 8.1 and later, choose **Windows 8.1**.

5. On the Triggers tab, create and manage triggers by using the options provided. To create a trigger, tap or click New, use the options provided to configure the trigger, and then tap or click OK.

6. On the Actions tab, create and manage actions by using the options provided. To create an action, tap or click New, use the options provided to configure the action, and then tap or click OK.

7. On the Conditions tab, specify any limiting conditions for starting or stopping the task.

8. On the Settings tab, choose any additional optional settings for the task.

9. Tap or click OK to create the task.

Troubleshooting scheduled tasks

When you configure tasks to run on a computer, you can encounter several types of problems. Some tasks won't run when they are supposed to. Others will start but won't stop. To determine the status of a task, select the task in the Task Scheduler and note the status, last run time, and last run result. If a task has a status of Queued, it is waiting to run at a scheduled time. If a task has a status of Ready, it is ready to run at its next run time. If a task should be running automatically but has a last run time of Never, you need to check the task's properties to determine why it isn't running. If the last run result is an error, you need to resolve the referenced problem so that the task can run normally.

Check a task's properties by tapping or clicking its entry in the Task Scheduler. The History tab provides detailed information on the task, from creation to its latest run time. Use the information to help you resolve problems with the task.

A task that is listed as Running might not, in fact, be running but instead might be a hung process. You can check for hung processes by using the Last Run Time column, which tells you when the task was started. If a task has been running for more than a day, there is usually a problem. A script might be waiting for input, the task might have problems reading or writing files, or the task might simply be a runaway task that needs to be stopped. To stop the task, press and hold or right-click it in the Task Scheduler, and then tap or click End.

Backing up and recovering a computer

Windows 8.1 provides File History as a central console for backing up and recovering personal files. You can access this console from Control Panel by tapping or clicking the Save Backup Copies Of Your Files With File History under the System And Security heading. Previous versions of files and folders might also be available for folders shared on the network by file servers. Other tools for backing up and recovering a computer's data include the Startup Repair tool, Windows Resume Loader, and System Restore. These tools are discussed in the sections that follow.

Backing up and recovering files and folders

File servers running Windows Server have a Previous Versions feature. Previous versions come from shadow copies and are created for folders that are shared on the network. Although Previous Versions is not a replacement for full system backups, it can be used to create automatic backups of changed files and folders on monitored drives. If a monitored file or folder was accidentally deleted or modified, you can recover the file or folder to the previous version.

In File Explorer, when you right-click a file or folder shared on the network by a file server and then select Properties, you get a Previous Versions tab. If you select this tab, available previous versions of the file or folder (if any) are listed. After you select a previous version, you can then use:

- The Open button to open any of the previous versions.
- The Copy button to create a copy of a previous version.
- The Restore button to revert the file or folder to a selected previous version.

There are several possible reasons why you might not get a previous version of a file on your computer, including the following:

- The file might be an offline file. Offline files are copies of network files. Client computers do not create previous versions of offline files; however, previous versions might be available on the server on which the file is stored.
- The file might be a system file. Previous Versions does not create copies of system files.
- The folder in which the file was stored has been deleted. In this case, you must open the properties for the folder that contained the folder that was deleted. Use this folder's Previous Versions tab to restore the folder, and then access the folder to recover the previous version of the file you want.
- No shadow copy has been created since the file was created and saved.

Recovering from a failed start

When a computer running Windows 8.1 starts and is not resuming from sleep mode or hibernate, Windows Boot Manager initializes the operating system by starting the Windows Boot Loader, which in turn starts the operating system by using information in the boot configuration data (BCD) store. If Windows 8.1 fails to start, the computer typically will go into recovery mode the next time you try to start the computer. After preparing automated recovery and attempting to diagnose the computer, you'll get an Automatic Repair screen. From this screen, you can select Restart to shut down and restart the computer or Advanced Options to display additional options that might help you repair the computer.

If you choose to restart the computer, Windows will do a full restart, which can sometimes resolve the problem.

If you choose Advanced Options, you'll have the following options:

- **Continue**   Exits the repair menu and continues to load the operating system
- **Use Another Operating System**   Exits the repair menu and enables you to select the operating system to load (if multiple operating systems are installed)
- **Turn Off Your PC**   Exits the repair menu and shuts down the computer
- **Troubleshoot**   Displays the Troubleshoot menu

REAL WORLD It's important to point out that whenever you are working with any of the recovery screens, you have full access to the mini-shell. Simply press Shift+F10 to open a command prompt in the mini-shell. The mini-shell gives you access to many of the same commands that you can access in the full command shell, including Diskpart, Mountvol, Netsh, Ping, Recover, Reg Query, Time, and Xcopy.

The Troubleshoot menu has three options:

- **Refresh Your PC** Reinstalls Windows 8.1 from the operating system image stored on the computer while maintaining personal files, accounts, and personalization settings. Although desktop apps and their related settings will be available after the refresh, any desktop programs that were previously installed will not be available.

- **Reset Your PC** Reinstalls Windows 8.1 from the operating system image stored on the computer and resets the installation to its original "factory" state. After a reset, no personal files, accounts, or personalization settings will be available, and you'll need to reinstall both desktop apps and desktop programs.

- **Advanced Options** Displays the Advanced Options menu.

The Troubleshoot\Advanced Options menu has five options:

- **System Restore** Enables you to use a restore point saved on the computer to restore Windows, as discussed later in this chapter in the section "Backing up and recovering system state by using System Restore."

- **System Image Recovery** Enables you to recover the computer by using a system image file. This is similar to a reset, except that you select the image file to use for recovery, and this image file can come from a remote computer. No personal files, accounts, or personalization settings will be available after recovery, and you'll need to reinstall both desktop apps and desktop programs (except for those that are already part of the system image).

- **Startup Repair** Enables you to start the Startup Repair tool, which can repair problems that prevent Windows from starting, including bad entries in the BCD store, corrupted system files, and damaged boot managers. Normally, this tool is started automatically if Windows detects a fixable problem.

- **Command Prompt** Enables you to access a command prompt and work with the commands and tools available in the recovery environment.

- **Startup Settings** Enables you to change the startup behavior for Windows 8.1. This allows you to restart the computer so that you can disable driver signature enforcement, early-launch anti-malware protection, and automatic restart on system failure. You can also enable low-resolution video mode, debugging mode, boot logging, and safe mode.

Recovering from a failed resume

When a computer running Windows 8.1 enters sleep mode or hibernates, a snapshot of the current state of the computer is created. For sleep mode, this snapshot is created in memory and then read from memory when a user wakes the computer. For hibernate mode, this snapshot is written to disk and then read from disk when a user wakes the computer. Both operations are handled by the Windows Resume Loader.

Problems with resuming a computer can occur for a variety of reasons, including errors in the snapshot, physical errors in memory, and physical disk errors. If there is a problem resuming after waking the computer from sleep, Windows Resume Loader proceeds to system-boot and the operating system starts without the sleep data. If there is a problem resuming after waking the computer from hibernate, Windows Resume Loader proceeds to system-boot and the operating system starts without the hibernate data.

In either instance, any work that wasn't saved before the computer entered sleep or hibernate mode is lost. However, most current applications are configured to save their working state automatically when the computer enters sleep mode. As a result, if you restart the applications that were running, recovery data might be available.

After a failed resume, Startup Repair can examine recent configuration changes that affected sleep or hibernate and reverse them. As an example, if you edited the active power plan so that the computer automatically hibernated after being in sleep mode for a set number of minutes, Startup Repair can remove that change.

Repairing a computer to enable startup

To start properly, computers running Windows 8.1 need access to specific system files. If a computer won't start because of a corrupted or missing system file, you can use the Startup Repair tool. Sometimes repairing a damaged or missing file won't fix all the computer's problems, and you might need to continue troubleshooting to diagnose and resolve the deeper problem.

Most other types of startup problems occur because something on the system has changed; for example, a device might have been incorrectly installed. The system configuration or registry might have been updated improperly, causing a conflict. Often you can resolve startup issues by using safe mode to recover or troubleshoot system problems. When you have finished using safe mode, be sure to restart the computer using a normal startup so that you can use the computer as you normally would.

In safe mode, Windows 8.1 loads only basic files, services, and drivers. The drivers loaded include those for the mouse, monitor, keyboard, mass storage, and base video. The monitor driver sets the basic settings and modes for the computer's monitor; and the base video driver sets the basic options for the computer's graphics card. No networking services or drivers are started unless you choose the Safe Mode With Networking option. Because safe mode loads a limited set of configuration information, it can help you troubleshoot problems.

Restart a system in safe mode by completing the following steps:

1. If the computer won't start normally, the Automatic Repair screen is displayed during startup. On the Automatic Repair screen, select Advanced Options, and then select Troubleshoot.

2. On the Troubleshoot screen, select Advanced Options, and then select Startup Settings.

3. On the Startup Settings screen, select Restart.

4. Select the safe mode option you want to use by pressing the function key corresponding to that option. The safe mode option you use depends on the type of problem you're experiencing.

If you don't want to use a safe mode option, press Enter to return to the operating system and resume normal startup. If you want to launch the computer's recovery environment instead, press F10 and then press F1.

The primary options are as follows:

- **Enable Debugging**   Enables debugging of the startup process.

- **Enable Safe Mode**   Loads only basic files, services, and drivers during the initialization sequence. The drivers loaded include those for the mouse, monitor, keyboard, mass storage, and base video. No networking services or drivers are started.

- **Enable Safe Mode With Networking**   Loads basic files, services, and drivers, in addition to services and drivers needed to start networking.

- **Enable Safe Mode With Command Prompt**   Loads basic files, services, and drivers, and then starts a command prompt instead of the Windows 8.1 graphical interface. No networking services or drivers are started.

TIP   In Safe Mode With Command Prompt, you can start the File Explorer shell from the command-line interface by pressing Ctrl+Shift+Esc to open Task Manager. On the File menu, tap or click New Task (Run) to open the Create New Task window. Enter **explorer.exe**, and then tap or click OK.

- **Enable Boot Logging**   Enables you to create a record of all startup events in a boot log.

- **Enable Low Resolution Video**   Enables you to start the system in low-resolution 640 × 480 display mode, which is useful if the system display is set to a mode that can't be used with the current monitor.

- **Disable Automatic Restart After Failure**   Prevents Windows from restarting after a crash, which, by default, would happen automatically. If Windows restarts repeatedly, you might have a firmware configuration problem.

- **Disable Driver Signature Enforcement**   Starts the computer in safe mode without enforcing digital signature policy settings for drivers. If a driver with an invalid or missing digital signature is causing startup failure, this will resolve the problem temporarily so that you can start the computer and resolve the problem by getting a new driver or changing the driver signature enforcement settings.

- **Disable Early Launch Anti-Malware Protection**   Starts the computer in safe mode without running the boot driver for the computer's anti-malware software. If the boot driver for the computer's anti-malware software is preventing startup, you'll need to check the software developer's website for an update that resolves the boot problem or configure the software without boot protection.

- **Start Windows Normally**   Starts the computer with its regular settings.

5. If a problem doesn't reappear when you start the computer in safe mode, you can eliminate the default settings and basic device drivers as possible causes. If a newly added device or updated driver is causing problems, you can use safe mode to remove the device, reverse the update, or install a different version of the driver software.

6. If you are still having a problem starting the system normally and suspect that problems with hardware, software, or settings are to blame, remain in safe mode and then try using System Restore to undo previous changes. See the "Backing up and recovering system state by using System Restore" section later in this chapter.

7. If System Restore doesn't work, start the computer in safe mode and try using the System Configuration utility to modify the boot options. You can start the System Configuration utility by pressing the Windows key, typing **msconfig.exe** (which normally is entered automatically into the Everywhere Search box), and then pressing Enter.

Recovering from a locked disk or invalid BCD settings

Computers with MBR disks require both a system and a boot partition to initialize and boot the operating system. Many modern computers with MBR disks have separate system and boot partitions. Typically, the system partition will not have a drive letter, whereas the boot partition will contain the operating system files and be set as the C: drive. In this configuration, the system partition must also be marked as the active partition.

If someone inadvertently marks another, non-system partition as the active partition, the computer will not be able to initialize and start the operation system. You also will not be able to use the standard repair tools to recover the computer. If you attempt to refresh the computer, you'll get an error on the Refresh Your PC screen stating:

Unable to access disk. The disk is locked.

If you attempt to reset the computer, you'll get a similar error on the Reset Your PC screen. To recover the computer from the Refresh Your Computer or Reset Your Computer screen, you'll need to do the following:

1. Press Shift+F10 to open a command prompt window in the mini-shell.

2. Start DiskPart by entering **diskpart** at the command prompt (as shown in Figure 10-1).

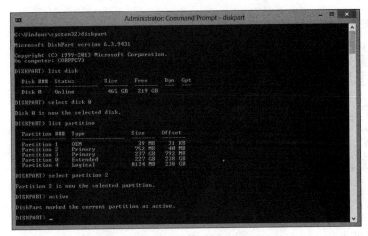

FIGURE 10-1 Use DiskPart to mark the appropriate partition as active.

3. In DiskPart, enter **list disk** to list the available disks.

4. Select the disk with which you want to work. For example, enter **select disk 0** to select the first disk.

5. Enter **list partition** to list the partitions on the selected disk.

6. Select the partition that should be marked as active. For example, enter **select partition 2** to select Partition 2.

   Typically, the system partition is a relatively small primary partition (as compared to a much larger primary partition that contains the actual operating system files and is used for boot).

7. After you select the partition, mark it as the active partition by entering **active**.

8. Close DiskPart by entering **exit,** and then close the command prompt by clicking the Close button.

9. On the Refresh Your Computer or Reset Your Computer screen, select Cancel.

10. On the Choose An Option screen, select Turn Off PC.

11. Start the computer. If you selected the correct system partition, the computer should now start normally.

Windows Boot Manager reports errors related to boot configuration data as shown in Figure 10-2. From any of the recovery screens, you can use a similar technique to modify a computer's boot configuration data. After you access the mini-shell, enter **bcdedit /?** to get help information, and then use the available commands to correct the boot configuration data.

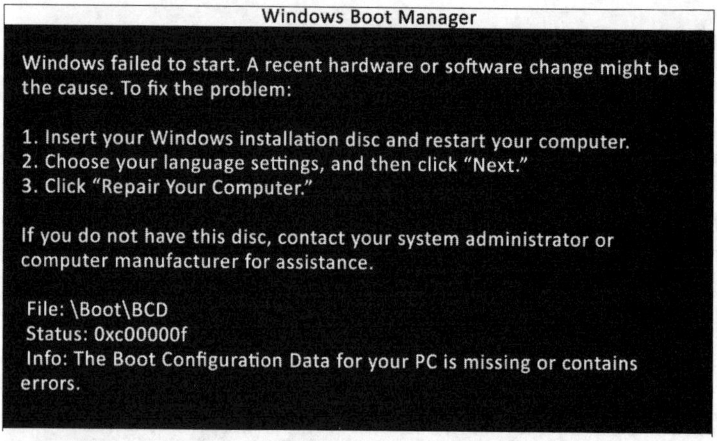

```
┌─────────────────────────────────────────────────────────────────┐
│                     Windows Boot Manager                          │
├─────────────────────────────────────────────────────────────────┤
│                                                                   │
│  Windows failed to start. A recent hardware or software change    │
│  might be the cause. To fix the problem:                          │
│                                                                   │
│  1. Insert your Windows installation disc and restart your        │
│     computer.                                                      │
│  2. Choose your language settings, and then click "Next."         │
│  3. Click "Repair Your Computer."                                 │
│                                                                   │
│  If you do not have this disc, contact your system administrator  │
│  or computer manufacturer for assistance.                         │
│                                                                   │
│  File: \Boot\BCD                                                  │
│  Status: 0xc00000f                                               │
│  Info: The Boot Configuration Data for your PC is missing or     │
│  contains errors.                                                 │
│                                                                   │
└─────────────────────────────────────────────────────────────────┘
```

FIGURE 10-2 This screen shows a failed start because of a Windows Boot Manager error.

However, don't confuse a locked disk problem with a boot configuration problem. To distinguish an active disk problem from a boot configuration problem, you need to access the Refresh Your PC or Reset Your PC screen in the recovery environment by completing the following steps:

1. Insert the Windows installation media, and then restart the computer.

2. When the computer starts, look for a message telling you what key to press to access the boot options. For example, you might need to press F12 to access the boot options.

3. Use the computer's Up Arrow and Down Arrow keys to select the appropriate boot option, such as CD/DVD Drive, and then press Enter.

4. When Windows Setup starts, choose the appropriate language settings, and then select Next.

5. On the next screen, don't select Install Now. Instead, select Repair Your Computer.

6. On the Choose An Option screen, select Troubleshoot.

7. On the Troubleshoot screen, select Refresh Your PC or Reset Your PC.

8. If you are unable to perform the refresh or reset because the disk is locked, you might need to ensure that the system partition is marked as the active partition. If you don't get this error or if you get another error, the problem is likely because of the boot configuration data.

Backing up and recovering system state by using System Restore

The section "The System Protection tab" in Chapter 2, "Configuring and optimizing Windows 8.1 computers" introduced System Restore and also discusses configuring this feature. Restore points can be used to recover systems that are experiencing problems after a system update, software installation, hardware installation, or other change. The following sections discuss how restore points can be created manually and how systems can be recovered by using restore points. Restore operations are reversible in most cases.

Understanding restore points

System Restore monitors the operating system for changes and creates restore points at regular daily intervals and before changes are introduced. The feature works by saving a snapshot of a computer's system configuration and writing the snapshot to disk so that it can be used to recover the system to a specific point in time if necessary. It's important to note that System Restore does not affect personal data. You can recover a system to a restore point without affecting a user's application data, cached files, or documents. System Restore doesn't write any information to the Documents folder either.

System Restore tracks and saves configuration information separately for each drive on a computer. This means that each drive has disk space made available to System Restore, and you can turn off monitoring of individual drives as needed. If a drive is configured for System Restore monitoring, you can recover from changes if a problem occurs. If a drive isn't configured for System Restore monitoring, configuration changes are not tracked, and changes cannot be recovered if a problem occurs. On most systems, you should configure System Restore for the system drive, which stores the operating system files, and for all drives containing critical applications.

Restore points can be restored in one of three ways: by checkpoint, by date, or by event. Individual snapshots scheduled by the operating system are called *system checkpoints*. Normal system checkpoints are made approximately every 24 hours. If a computer is turned off when a daily checkpoint is scheduled, System Restore creates the checkpoint the next time the computer is started.

NOTE Although earlier releases of Windows created an initial snapshot when you installed the operating system, an initial snapshot normally is not created when you install Windows 8.1. The reason for this is that PC Refresh and PC Reset are available as options to get the computer back to its original state. For more information on PC Refresh and PC Reset, see the "Recovering from a failed start" section earlier in this chapter.

When System Restore is enabled, some snapshots are created automatically based on events that the operating system triggers when you make changes or install applications. For simplicity, I call these snapshots *installation restore points*, and there's actually a group of them, each with a different purpose. The event-based snapshots are as follows:

- **Program name installation restore points**   Created prior to installing a program that uses a compatible installer. You can use installation restore points to track application installation and to restore a computer to the state it was in before the application was installed. Restoring the computer state means that all file and registry settings for the installed program are removed. It also means that programs and system files altered by the installation are restored to their previous state. After this is completed, the program won't work, and you'll need to reinstall it if the user wants to use it again.

CAUTION These are called *program name installation restore points* instead of *program uninstall restore points* for a very good reason. The restore process doesn't uninstall all the application files. It removes file and registry settings that might affect the operation of the computer. To completely uninstall a program, you need to use the Programs tool in Control Panel.

- **Automatic update restore points** Created prior to applying an automatic update. If a computer has problems after applying an automatic update, you can use the restore point to recover the computer to its previous state. (You can also use the Programs tool to remove automatic updates.)

- **Restore operation restore points** Created prior to restoring a computer. If you find that you used the wrong restore point or that the restore point doesn't work, you can use these restore points to undo the restore operation and recover the computer to the state it was in before you reversed the previous settings.

- **Unsigned device driver restore points** Created prior to the installation of an unsigned or uncertified driver on a computer. If a computer has problems after you install an unsigned or uncertified driver, you can use these restore points to restore the computer to its state before you installed the driver. For signed and certified drivers, the normal rollback procedure should enable you to go back to the previous driver being used.

- **Microsoft Backup tool recovery restore points** Created prior to recovering files or system data by using the Backup tool. If the recovery fails or if the computer doesn't work properly after the recovery, you can undo the changes and restore the computer to its previous state.

Users can also create snapshots manually. These snapshots are called *manual restore points*. You should recommend that users create snapshots prior to performing any operation that could cause problems on the system.

You can restore computers when they are running in normal mode or safe mode. In normal mode, a restore operation restore point is created prior to restoration of the computer. But in safe mode, the restore operation restore point is not created because changes you make in safe mode aren't tracked and you can't undo them by using restore points. However, you can use safe mode to restore any previously created restore point.

Creating manual restore points

You can create a manual restore point by following these steps:

1. In Control Panel, tap or click System And Security, and then tap or click System.
2. In the left pane, tap or click System Protection.
3. Select the disk for which you want to create the restore point, and then tap or click Create.

4. Enter a description for the restore point, such as **Prior To Display Monitor Driver Update And Changes**. Tap or click Create.

5. When the restore point is created, tap or click OK.

Recovering from restore points

To recover a computer from a restore point when the operating system is running, follow these steps:

1. In Control Panel, tap or click System And Security, and then tap or click System.

2. In the left pane, tap or click System Protection and then tap or click System Restore. System Restore examines the available restore points on the computer. This process can take several minutes. When it completes, System Restore recommends a restore point. If you want to determine what programs the restore operation will affect, tap or click Scan For Affected Programs.

3. If you want to determine what additional restore points are available, select Choose A Different Restore Point, and then tap or click Next. Recent restore points are listed by date, time, description, and type. To view additional restore points that are available, tap or click Show More Restore Points. To determine what programs the restore operation will affect when using a particular restore point, tap or click a restore point, and then tap or click Scan For Affected Programs.

4. After you've selected a restore point or accepted the recommended restore point, tap or click Next to continue.

5. Tap or click Finish. When prompted, tap or click Yes to confirm that you want to use the selected restore point to restore the computer's system files and settings.

To recover a computer from a restore point when the operating system won't run, follow these steps:

1. If the computer won't start normally, the Automatic Repair screen is displayed during startup. On the Automatic Repair screen, select Advanced Options, and then select Troubleshoot.

2. On the Troubleshoot screen, select Advanced Options, and then select System Restore.

3. System Restore examines the available restore points on the computer. You'll then be able to select a restore point to use and the procedure is similar to steps 3 to 5 in the previous procedure.

During the restoration, System Restore shuts down Windows 8.1. After restoration is complete, Windows 8.1 restarts by using the settings in effect at the date and time of the snapshot. After the system restarts, the System Restore dialog box is displayed again. Read the message provided, and then tap or click Close. If Windows 8.1 isn't working properly, you can apply a different restore point or reverse the restore operation by repeating this procedure and selecting the restore operation that was created prior to applying the current system state.

Troubleshooting System Restore

System Restore isn't always successful in its recovery attempts. If System Restore fails to recover the computer to the point in time you are targeting, you can repeat the restore procedure to try to recover the computer. This time, select a different restore point.

Using PC recovery options

Computers that are designed for Windows 8 and later normally have a dedicated recovery partition that contains a recovery image. The recovery image typically is about 3 gigabytes (GB) to 8 GB in size, depending on version and customizations.

You can use the recovery image to refresh or reset the computer. A PC refresh reinstalls Windows 8.1 from the operating system image stored on the computer while maintaining personal files, accounts, and personalization settings. Although desktop apps and their related settings will be available after the refresh, any desktop programs that were previously installed will not be available. Thus, you normally can refresh a PC without affecting your personal files and settings.

A PC reset reinstalls Windows 8.1 from the operating system image stored on the computer and resets the installation to its original "factory" state. After a reset, no personal files, accounts, or personalization settings will be available, and you'll need to reinstall both desktop apps and desktop programs. Thus, when you reset a PC, you are starting over completely and resetting the PC to its factory settings.

Determining whether a computer has a recovery partition

When you are inventorying computers, you can determine whether a computer has a recovery image by completing the following steps:

1. Open an elevated, administrator command prompt. One way to do this is to press Windows key + Q and then enter **cmd** in the Search box. In the search results, right-click Command Prompt, and then select Run As Administrator.

2. To display information about the computer's recovery image, enter **recimg /showcurrent** at the command prompt.

If the computer has a recovery environment, you'll get information about the recovery image; otherwise, you'll get an error similar to the following:

```
There is no active custom recovery image.
Error Code - 0x80070490
```

Initiating a PC recovery

If a computer has a recovery environment, one way to start a recovery is to complete the following steps:

1. On the Automatic Repair screen, select Advanced Options, and then select Troubleshoot.

2. On the Troubleshoot screen, select Advanced Options, and then select Startup Settings.

3. On the Startup Settings screen, select Restart.

4. Press F10 instead of selecting a safe mode option, and then select F1 to launch the recovery environment.

Creating a recovery partition

If a computer doesn't have a recovery environment, you can create a recovery partition and image by completing the following steps:

1. Open an elevated, administrator command prompt. One way to do this is to press Windows key + Q and then enter **cmd** in the Search box. In the search results, right-click Command Prompt and then select Run As Administrator.

2. Create a folder for the recovery partition by entering **mkdir c:\recimage** at the command prompt.

3. Create a recovery image and store it in the new folder by entering **recimg -createimage c:\recimage** at the command prompt.

The Recimg utility will create a system snapshot and then write the recovery image to the specified folder. Recimg finalizes the creation process by registering the recovery image in the BCD.

NOTE The recovery image creation process can take a long time. You can cancel the image creation by pressing the Esc key.

Step by step, a normal recovery creation process proceeds as shown in the following example and sample output:

```
recimg -createimage c:\recimage

Source OS location:  C:
Recovery image path: c:\recimage\CustomRefresh.wim
Creating recovery image. Press [ESC] to cancel.
Initializing
100%
Creating snapshot
100%
Writing image (this may take a while)
100%
Registering image
100%

Recovery image creation and registration completed successfully.
```

The output of the command tells you the source location of the currently installed operating system and the complete path to the recovery image. The output also tells you which phases of the process have been started, allowing you to track the process to completion.

If the image creation and registration does not complete successfully, try to resolve any issues before using RecImg to try to create the image again. The most common problem you might encounter is a lack of available disk space. If there is insufficient disk space, you'll need to free space on the volume where you created the recovery folder. Otherwise, if the process completes successfully, you can confirm that the recovery image was created by entering **recimg /showcurrent** at the command prompt. The output identifies the registered path of the recovery image as shown in this following example and sample output:

```
recimg /showcurrent

\\?\GLOBALROOT\device\harddisk0\partition3\recimage
RecImg: Operation completed successfully
```

Creating a USB recovery drive

As an alternative to a recovery image stored on a computer, you can delete a computer's recovery image and create a USB recovery drive to use instead. This approach saves space on the computer but requires you to create a USB drive and then make sure this drive is available should a refresh or reset be required.

The USB flash drive fyou use for recovery should be at least 8 GB in size. Because the recovery drive creation process reformats the flash drive, any data stored on the device will be erased.

You can create a USB recovery drive by completing the following steps:

1. In Control Panel, enter **Recovery Drive** in the Search box. Under System, select Create A Recovery Drive to open the Recovery Drive Wizard.

2. If the computer has a recovery partition created by the computer manufacturer, you can choose to copy this recovery partition to the recovery drive by selecting the related option.

3. Select Next, and then select Create. The Recovery Drive Wizard will create the recovery partition on the USB flash drive in much the same way as the RecImg tool creates a recovery partition on a computer.

4. When the process is complete, you can optionally elect to delete the recovery partition on the computer. This frees up the space that was previously used by the partition.

5. Select Finish, and then remove the USB flash drive. Be sure to store the recovery drive in a safe location. Don't use the recovery drive to store any other data or files.

Creating and using File History

You can use File History to automate backups of personal files from libraries, the desktop, contacts, and favorites. You must have appropriate permissions to back up and restore files on a computer.

Configuring File History backups

Windows 8.1 can automatically create personal data backups. Personal data backups are used to periodically back up pictures, music, videos, email, documents, and other types of important files so that you can restore or use them on another computer if necessary. Specifically, the Public Documents, Public Pictures, Public Music, and Public Videos subfolders of the Users\Public folder is copied as part of the backup data, as are the Contacts, Desktop, Documents, Favorites, Pictures, Music, and Videos subfolders of the user's profile.

As Figure 10-3 shows, File History is configured in Control Panel. When working with File History, keep the following in mind:

- Personal data backups can be created only on removable media or network locations. They can't be created on a computer's internal disk drives.

- Personal data backups are created automatically when you enable the File History feature. By default, File History saves copies of files every hour.

- By default, saved versions of personal data are kept indefinitely so long as they don't exceed 5 percent of the disk space at the assigned location.

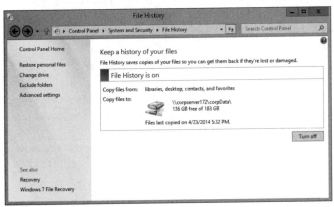

FIGURE 10-3 File History shows a summary of the current configuration, in addition to the available space in the selected save location.

With network locations, the personal data backup is created in a subfolder named in the following syntax: *UserName@DomainOrComputer,* such as WilliamS@Cpandl.com or WilliamS@CorpPC12. This folder has a subfolder set with the user's computer name, such as CORPC12, which in turn contains Configuration and Data subfolders. With removable media, a top-level folder called FileHistory is created first.

Enabling File History backups and configuring drives

With USB flash drives or other removable media, you can enable automated backups and create your first backup manually by following these steps:

1. Insert a USB flash drive or connect other removable media to the computer.
2. In Control Panel, tap or click Save Backup Copies Of Your Files With File History under the System And Security heading.
3. Tap or click Turn On. Windows 8.1 turns on File History and creates the initial backup.

With a network location, you can enable automated backups and create your first backup by following these steps:

1. In Control Panel, tap or click Save Backup Copies Of Your Files With File History under the System And Security heading.
2. Tap or click Select Drive, then tap or click Add Network Location. If network discovery and file sharing is disabled, tap or click the notification panel, and then tap or click Turn On Network Discovery And File Sharing.
3. In the Folder box, enter the UNC path to the folder in which the personal data should be stored, such as **\\CorpServer172\CorpData,** and then tap or click OK.
4. When you tap or click Turn On, Windows 8.1 turns on File History and creates the initial backup.

Using the options on the File History page, you can modify the default backup configuration in several ways. Each user can have only one File History drive at a time. You can change the File History drive to a new network location and Windows will allow you to move the data to a new network location automatically when you follow these steps:

1. On the File History page, tap or click Change Drive, and then tap or click Add Network Location.
2. In the Folder text box, enter the UNC path to the folder in which the personal data should be stored, such as **\\CorpServer96\UserData.** This location can't have existing File History data for the user.
3. Tap or click OK twice. When prompted, tap or click Yes if you'd like to move the user's personal data to the new location. If the location already has personal data for the user, the data won't be moved, and you'll need to tap or click OK when prompted to confirm that you understand this.

You can change the File History drive to removable media from a network location or to different removable media, follow these steps:

1. Insert a USB flash drive or connect other removable media to the computer.
2. On the File History page, tap or click Change Drive.
3. Tap or click the removable media to use, and then tap or click OK.
4. When prompted, tap or click Yes if you'd like to move the user's personal data to the new location. If the location already has personal data for the user, the data won't be moved, and you'll need to tap or click OK when prompted to confirm that you understand this.

Excluding folders from File History backups

By default, personal data backups created with the File History feature contain the Documents, Pictures, Music, and Videos subfolders of the Users\Public folder and the Contacts, Desktop, Documents, Favorites, Pictures, Music, and Videos subfolders of the user's profile. You can exclude folders from backups by following these steps:

1. In Control Panel, tap or click Save Backup Copies Of Your Files With File History under the System And Security heading.

2. Tap or click Exclude Folders. Any currently excluded folders are shown on the Exclude Folders page.

3. If you want to exclude a folder, tap or click Add. Use the Select Folder dialog box to select the folder to exclude and then tap or click Select Folder. As an example, if you wanted to exclude Public Documents, you'd expand Libraries and Documents, tap or click Public Documents, and then tap or click Select Folder.

4. If you want to include a folder that was previously excluded, select it in the Excluded list and then tap or click Remove.

Modifying default save settings

File History saves copies of files every hour by default and those saved versions are kept indefinitely as long as they don't exceed 5 percent of the disk space at the assigned location. You can modify the default save settings by following these steps:

1. In Control Panel, tap or click Save Backup Copies Of Your Files With File History under the System And Security heading.

2. Tap or click Advanced Settings. The current default values are listed on the Advanced Settings page, shown in Figure 10-4.

3. As necessary, use the Save Copies Of Files list to change when saved copies of files are created. This creates saved versions to which users can return, and they can also be used for recovery. You can reduce overhead related to File History by setting a longer save interval, such as Every 3 Hours or Every 6 Hours. Daily is the maximum duration.

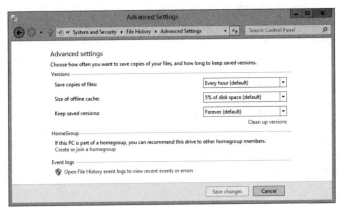

FIGURE 10-4 View and manage default settings for File History.

4. As necessary, use the Size Of Offline Cache list to control the maximum size of the file cache. Be sure to check the size of the related drive and increase or decrease this value as appropriate for the size of the drive and the available space. For example, if a drive has 2 terabytes (TB) of space, you might want to set the maximum size of the offline cache to 2 percent of disk space, whereas if the drive has only 100 GB of space, you might want to set the maximum size of the offline cache to 10 percent of disk space.

5. As necessary, use the Keep Saved Versions list to specify how long to keep saved versions. Choose a setting that makes sense for the way the user works. If you choose Forever, saved versions are kept indefinitely and will not be overwritten if the offline cache hits its size limit. If you choose Until Space Is Needed, saved versions are kept until the size of the offline cache grows to its limit, and then the oldest versions are overwritten as necessary to accommodate new versions. Any value in between these two settings keeps saved versions for a set amount of time before they are removed. However, if the size of the offline cache hits the limit, no new versions can be created until space is made available (by old versions reaching their time limit).

REAL WORLD On the Advanced Settings page, you can manually clean up file versions at any time. Tap or click Clean Up Versions. In the File History Clean Up dialog box, select which versions to delete, and then tap or click Clean Up. For example, you can specify that you want to clean up files older than six months or that you want to clean up all but the latest version.

Recovering personal data

You can recover personal data files you've backed up with File History by following these steps:

1. In Control Panel, tap or click Save Backup Copies Of Your Files With File History under the System And Security heading.

2. Tap or click Restore Personal Files. In the File History dialog box, use the Previous Version and Next Version buttons to navigate through the snapshots until you find the version with which you want to work. You can navigate folder structures within the snapshots just as you would folders on a hard drive.

3. Snapshots are listed with a date and time stamp and a version number (for example, Monday, May 6, 2013 5:11 PM | Version 5 of 12). When you find a folder or file to restore, tap or click it, and then tap or click Restore To Original Location. You can also select multiple items to restore.

TIP You can also restore files and folders to alternate locations. After you select the items you want to restore, tap or click the Options button in the upper-right corner of the File History dialog box, and then tap or click Restore To. You can then select an alternate restore location.

Troubleshooting startup and shutdown

As an administrator, you often need to troubleshoot problems with startup and shutdown. The sections that follow look at techniques for resolving common problems.

Resolving restart or shutdown issues

Normally, you can shut down or restart Windows 8.1 by using the Power options. When working with the Start screen or the desktop, this means to shut down or restart a server, you follow these steps:

1. Display options by sliding in from the right side of the screen or by moving the mouse pointer to the lower-right side of the screen.

2. Tap or click Settings, and then tap or click Power.

3. Tap or click Shut Down or Restart as appropriate.

In a standard configuration, you can also press the computer's physical power button to initiate an orderly shutdown by logging off and then shutting down. Although all of these approaches usually work, Windows 8.1 sometimes won't shut down or restart normally, and you must take additional actions. In those cases, follow these steps:

1. Press Ctrl+Alt+Del. The Windows screen should be displayed. Tap or click Task Manager. If the detailed view isn't shown, tap or click More Details.

2. On the Processes tab, look for an application or process that is not responding. If all applications appear to be running normally, skip to step 5.

3. Select the application that is not responding, and then tap or click End Task.

4. If the application fails to respond to the request, you'll get a prompt that enables you to end the application immediately or cancel the end-task request. Tap or click End Now.

5. Try shutting down or restarting the computer. Press Ctrl+Alt+Del to display the Windows screen again, tap or click the Power button in the lower-right corner of the screen, and then tap or click Restart or Shut Down as appropriate.

Windows 8.1 will also log off the current user and shut down the computer if you press the computer's power button. If any programs fail to respond, you'll have the option to force the logoff, or you can simply wait a few seconds for Windows to force the logoff.

REAL WORLD   As a last resort, you might be forced to perform a hard shutdown by pressing and holding down the computer's power button or by unplugging the computer. If you do this, Check Disk will probably run the next time you start the computer so that the computer can check for errors and problems that might have been caused by the hard shutdown. If Check Disk doesn't run automatically, you might want to run it manually.

Making sense of Stop errors

The "Setting recovery options" section in Chapter 2 details how to configure Windows 8.1 to write debugging information. If a major error occurs while Windows 8.1 is starting, installing a program, or performing another operation, you'll get a Stop error message across the entire screen. Read this information carefully and write down the following information:

- **Error name**   The error name should be on the third line of the error screen and is listed in all caps, such as KERNEL_STACK_INPAGE_ERROR.

- **Troubleshooting recommendations**   The error name is followed by the troubleshooting recommendations. These recommendations are based on the type of error that occurred and provide general guidelines on resolving the problem.

- **Error number**   The troubleshooting recommendations are followed by technical information. On the next line after the Technical Information heading, you'll find the word *STOP*, an error number, and a list of error parameters. The error number following Stop is what you should write down, such as STOP: 0X00000050.

- **Driver information**   Immediately following the line with the Stop error number is a line that lists the name of the driver associated with the error. This information is provided only if the error can be traced to a specific driver. Write down the driver name.

If the system is configured to write an event to the event logs if a Stop error occurs, and it was possible to write the event before the system crashed completely, the error number and error parameters will be written to an event in the System log with an event source of Save Dump. The event will also specify whether a dump file was created and where it was saved, if applicable.

REAL WORLD   Windows 8.1 includes an Online Crash Analysis feature that enables you to send the dump file to Microsoft Product Support Services. If error reporting is enabled, you will be prompted to send this debugging information to Microsoft when you restart the system. You have the option of sending the debugging information anonymously or using your Microsoft Connect account. If you send the debugging information with your name and contact information through Microsoft Connect, a technician might contact you for further information and might also be able to suggest an action to correct the problem.

After you have the Stop error information, you might need to start the system in safe mode, as discussed in the section "Repairing a computer to enable startup," earlier in this chapter. You can then look to resolve the problem by performing the following tasks:

- **Look up the Stop error on the Microsoft Knowledge Base**   Visit *support. microsoft.com* and perform a search of the Knowledge Base by using the error number as the keyword. If a known problem is related to the error code, you should find a related Knowledge Base article. As appropriate, follow the instructions given to resolve the issue.

- **Check the driver (if driver information was provided)** When you reboot the system, check the driver to be sure it is digitally signed. If the driver has been updated recently, you might consider rolling back to the previous driver version. Just because the driver is listed doesn't mean the driver is corrupt and needs replacing, however. The Stop error could have been caused by other factors.

- **Determine what has changed recently** Stop errors can be caused by both hardware and software. Closely review any programs or hardware that have been installed recently on the computer. If you added new hardware, check to be sure that the hardware is installed correctly; that the latest, signed drivers are installed; and that the hardware is properly configured. If you added new software, check to be sure that the installation completed successfully. You might also want to check for updates to the software.

- **Check system resources** Stop errors can occur if the system becomes critically low on RAM or disk space. After you get the system started, check the drives to determine the amount of free space available and, as necessary, free additional disk space by using Disk Cleanup or other tools. Also, open Task Manager by pressing Ctrl+Alt+Del and tapping or clicking Task Manager. Look at the Performance tab to check the amount of physical and virtual RAM available. If very little memory is available, determine which programs are using memory and whether there are problem programs, such as adware or spyware, running.

- **Repair system files** Stop errors can be caused by damaged or improper versions of system files. If you suspect a system file is the cause of the problem and the system won't start properly, you might need to repair the operating system or reinstall the operating system by using the repair options discussed in the "Repairing a computer to enable startup" section earlier in this chapter.

- **Check hardware and firmware** Stop errors can be caused by faulty hardware. If a computer frequently crashes, you might want to examine the hardware closely. Check the hardware drivers first; a driver might be causing the Stop errors. Check the physical hardware. Look specifically at the hard disks, RAM, CPU, and graphics card. A hard disk might be going bad, RAM might be defective, the CPU might have overheated, or the graphics card might be incompatible with Windows 8.1. Also, look at the firmware. Check the settings carefully. In addition, you might check whether an update is available from the motherboard's manufacturer.

Index

primary DNS suffix, name resolution and,
65
print drivers, 302, 303
printers
  3D, 277
  connecting, 277
  Group Policy preferences, 143
  local, 277–279
  network, 280, 281
  NFC-enabled, 279
  troubleshooting, 258
Print Spooler, LocalService accounts and,
158
Privacy page, 98
private host discovery, 217
private keys, 157
problem reporting, 251, 255, 256, 293
Problem Reports and Solutions Control
  Panel Support service, 262
processes, Task Manager and, 237
processor performance state, setting
  parameters for, 86
processor scheduling, 67
product keys, 29
Program Compatibility Assistant (PCA),
226, 227, 249, 261, 262
Program Compatibility Troubleshooter,
232, 233, 258
program name installation restore points,
329, 330
programs
  See applications
  compatibility, 230–235
  default, 238, 239
  installing, 224–229
  making available only to currently
    logged-on users, 229
  making available to all users, 228
  managing currently running, 235–237
  managing installed, 237
  modifying configuration of, 237
  performance settings, 67
  repairing, 237
  uninstalling, 237
Programs And Features page, 237, 246
program shortcuts, 228, 229
Programs tool, 235
protecting
  memory, 77
  systems, 77–79
proxy discovery, 217
pseudo-accounts, 157, 158
publisher identification, 220
publishing applications, 229

Q

quick sharing, 102
quick status, Lock Screen and, 100

R

RAM, virtual memory and, 68
Raserver.exe, 195
readability of text, 124
receivers, 275
Reclmg utility, 332, 333, 334
recommended updates, 302
reconnect-after-restart feature, Remote
  Assistance and, 198
Recording Audio troubleshooter, 258
recording steps that lead to an issue, 193,
194
recovering
  from failed starts, 322, 323
  from restore points, 331
  personal data, 338
recovering passwords, 174
recovering Windows 8.1
  Windows PE and, 9
  Windows Recovery Environment
    (Windows RE) and, 21
recovery
  data, from failed resume, 324
  drives, 334
  images, 332, 333, 334
  initiating, 333
  options, 74, 75
  partitions, 332, 333, 334
  services, 266
recovery mode, 322
Recycle Bin, 56, 117
redirected folders, 161
refresh rate
  defined, 132
  setting, 133
  troubleshooting, 135
Refresh Your PC option, 323, 326, 327, 328
regional options, 143
registry, 143
Registry Editor, 291
registry keys, for device setup classes, 290
Regular Maintenance task, 306
reinstalling
  devices, 293
  drivers, 292
Reliability Monitor, 252–254
remote access lists, 206
Remote Assistance
  described, 54

Setx.exe utility, 240
shadow copies, 321, 322
shaking windows, 123
Share charm, 4
Shared Folders, 46, 258
shared local printers, 278, 279
sharing
    configuring apps for, 102
    control of the desktop, 201, 202, 203, 204
    workstations with Remote Desktop, 206
shims, for compatibility, 221
shortcuts
    Group Policy preferences and, 104, 143
    icons for, 107
    link, 106
    location of, 105, 106
    menu, 45
    modifier keys, 107
    moving, 228, 229
    pinning to taskbar, 109
    URL, 106, 108
    working directory, 108
Show Administrative Tools, 5, 154
shutting down, 32, 339
SIDs. See security identifiers (SIDs)
signed applications, 166, 220
Sigverif.exe, 54, 57
single-instance storage, WIM format and, 38
sites, Group Policy and, 140
SkyDrive
    credential roaming, 177
    synchronizing devices, 98, 103, 170
    tasks, 316
Sleep\Allow Hybrid Sleep, 87
Sleep\Allow Wake Timers, 87
Sleep\Hibernate After, 87
sleep mode
    described, 35
    button actions, 86, 93
    configuring, 88
    snapshots and, 324
    when unsupported, 36
Sleep\Sleep After, 87
slide show for desktop background, power settings and, 85
smart cards, 157, 158
smartphones as external devices, 269
smart screening, 248, 256
SMB (Server Message Block), 53
snap-in extensions, 249

snapping windows, 123
snapshots
    manual, 330
    recovering personal data using, 338
    restore points and, 329
Software Restriction policies. See Application Control policies
solutions to computer problems
    See also troubleshooting
    Action Center responses, 252
    automatically checking for, 255
source (.sys) files, 284
SpaceAgent task, 316
SSDP Discovery Service, 158
stability of a computer
    viewing with Reliability Monitor, 252–254
standard tasks, 314
standard user accounts
    described, 30
    access tokens, 218, 220
    vs. administrator accounts, 162
    changing to administrator, 171
    elevated privileges and, 163, 166
standard user applications, 218, 219
standard user mode, 162, 163
Start charm, 4
starting services, 264
Start menu
    preferences for, 143
    vs. Start screen, 143
Start-ScheduledTask, 314
Start screen
    described, 214
    customizing navigation, 135
    navigation options, 137
    opening programs from, 4
    personalizing colors, 101
    vs. Start menu, 3
Start Settings pane, 5
Start tiles. See tiles
startup
    applications, configuring, 104–109
    failures, recovering from, 323
    folder, 108
    modes, 58
    options, 74, 75
    process, boot environment and, 38
    services, 265
    troubleshooting, 339
Startup And Recovery dialog box, 74
Startup Repair troubleshooter, 323, 324
Start Windows Normally option, 326

About the author

WILLIAM STANEK (*www.williamstanek.com*) is the award-winning author and series editor of the bestselling Pocket Consultant series. William is one of the world's leading technology experts and has more than 20 years of hands-on experience with advanced programming and development. Over the years, his practical advice has helped millions of programmers, developers, and network engineers all over the world. Dubbed "A Face Behind the Future" in 1996 by *The Olympian*, William has been helping to shape the future of the written word for more than two decades. William's 150th book was published in 2013. William's current books include *Exchange Server 2013: Configuration & Clients*, *Windows Server 2012 R2 Pocket Consultant: Essentials & Configuration*, and *Windows Server 2012 Inside Out*.

William has been involved in the commercial Internet community since 1991. His core business and technology experience comes from more than 11 years of military service. He has substantial experience in developing server technology, encryption, and Internet solutions. He has written many technical white papers and training courses on a wide variety of topics. He frequently serves as a subject matter expert and consultant.

William has an MS with distinction in information systems and a BS in computer science, magna cum laude. He is proud to have served in the Persian Gulf War as a combat crew member on an electronic warfare aircraft. He flew on numerous combat missions into Iraq and was awarded nine medals for his wartime service, including one of the United States of America's highest flying honors, the Air Force Distinguished Flying Cross. Currently, he resides in the Pacific Northwest with his wife and children.

William recently rediscovered his love of the great outdoors. When he's not writing, he can be found hiking, biking, backpacking, traveling, or trekking in search of adventure with his family!

Find William on Twitter at WilliamStanek and on Facebook at *www.facebook.com/William.Stanek.Author*. Please visit *www.Pocket-Consultant.com* to find links to stay in touch with William.

Now that you've read the book...

Tell us what you think!

Was it useful?
Did it teach you what you wanted to learn?
Was there room for improvement?

Let us know at http://aka.ms/tellpress

Your feedback goes directly to the staff at Microsoft Press,
and we read every one of your responses. Thanks in advance!